NELSON EDUCATION SERIES
IN HUMAN RESOURCE MANAGEMEI

SIXTH EDITION

Management of Occupational Health and Safety

NELSON EDUCATION SERIES
IN HUMAN RESOURCE MANAGEMENT

SIXTH EDITION

Management of Occupational Health and Safety

E. Kevin Kelloway
SAINT MARY'S UNIVERSITY

Lori Francis
SAINT MARY'S UNIVERSITY

Bernadette Gatien
SAINT MARY'S UNIVERSITY

Series Editor:
Monica Belcourt
YORK UNIVERSITY

NELSON EDUCATION

Management of Occupational Health and Safety, Sixth Edition

by E. Kevin Kelloway, Lori Francis, and Bernadette Gatien

Vice President, Editorial Higher Education:
Anne Williams

Acquisitions Editor:
Alwynn Pinard

Marketing Manager:
David Stratton

Developmental Editor:
Lisa Berland

Permissions Coordinator:
Melody Tolson

Senior Content Production Manager:
Imoinda Romain

Production Service:
Cenveo Publisher Services

Copy Editor:
Erin Moore

Proofreader:
Kavitha Ashok

Indexer:
BIM Publishing Services

Design Director:
Ken Phipps

Managing Designer:
Franca Amore

Interior Design:
Dianna Little

Cover Design:
Martyn Schmoll

Cover Images:
(background) urbancow/ iStockphoto; (foreground) Jill Wachter/Getty Images

Compositor:
Cenveo Publisher Services

Library and Archives Canada Cataloguing in Publication

Kelloway, E. Kevin (Edward Kevin), author

Management of occupational health and safety / E. Kevin Kelloway, Lori Francis, Bernadette Gatien. — Sixth edition.

(Nelson Education series in human resource management)

First edition: Occupational health and safety / James Montgomery ; second edition: Management of occupational health and safety / James Montgomery and Kevin Kelloway.

Includes bibliographical references and index.

ISBN 978-0-17-653216-1 (pbk.)

1. Industrial hygiene—Management—Textbooks. 2. Industrial safety—Management—Textbooks. 3. Industrial hygiene—Textbooks. 4. Industrial safety—Textbooks. I. Francis, Lori D. (Lori Denise), author II. Gatien, Bernadette, author III. Title. IV. Series: Nelson Education series in human resource management

HD7261.M65 2013
363.11   C2013-903325-4

ISBN-13: 978-0-17-653216-1
ISBN-10: 0-17-653216-1

For Debra
(EKK)

For Brian, Owen, and Sean
(LF)

For Mackenzie, Sid, Josh, and Bruce
(BG)

BRIEF CONTENTS

CONTENTS

ABOUT THE SERIES

The management of human resources has become an important source of innovation, competitive advantage, and productivity, more so than any other. More than ever, human resources management (HRM) professionals require the knowledge and skills to design HRM policies and practices that not only meet legal requirements but also are effective in supporting organizational strategy. Increasingly, these professionals turn to published research and books on best practices for assistance in developing effective HR strategies. The books in the *Nelson Series in Human Resources Management* are the best source in Canada for reliable, valid, and current knowledge about HRM practices.

The texts in this series include

- *Managing Performance through Training and Development*
- *Management of Occupational Health and Safety*
- *Recruitment and Selection in Canada*
- *Strategic Compensation in Canada*
- *Strategic Human Resources Planning*
- *An Introduction to the Canadian Labour Market*
- *Research, Measurement, and Evaluation of Human Resources*
- *Industrial Relations in Canada*
- *International Human Resource Management: A Canadian Perspective*

The *Nelson Series in Human Resources Management* represents a significant development in the field of HRM for many reasons. Each book in the series is the first and (now) best-selling text in the functional area. Furthermore, HR professionals in Canada must work with Canadian laws, statistics, policies, and values. This series serves their needs. It is the only opportunity that students and practitioners have to access a complete set of HRM books, standardized in presentation, which enables them to access information quickly across many HRM disciplines. The books are essential sources of information that meet the requirements for the CCHRA (Canadian Council of Human Resources Associations) National Knowledge exam for the academic portion of the HR certification process. This one-stop resource will prove useful to anyone looking for solutions for the effective management of people.

The publication of this series signals that the field of human resources management has advanced to the stage where theory and applied research guide practice. The books in the series present the best and most current research in the functional areas of HRM. Research is supplemented with examples of the best practices used by Canadian companies that are leaders in HRM. Each text begins with a general model of the discipline and then describes the implementation of effective strategies. Thus, the books serve as an introduction to the functional area for the new student of HR and as a validation source for the more experienced HRM practitioner. Cases, exercises, and notes provide opportunities for further discussion and analysis.

As you read and consult the books in this series, I hope you share my excitement in being involved in and knowledgeable about a profession that has such a significant impact on organizational goals—and on employees' lives.

Monica Belcourt, Ph.D., CHRP
Series Editor
September 2013

ABOUT THE AUTHORS

E. Kevin Kelloway

Dr. Kelloway is the Canada Research Chair in Occupational Health Psychology and a Professor of Psychology at Saint Mary's University, Halifax. He was the founding director of the CN Centre for Occupational Health and Safety and a founding principal of the Centre for Leadership Excellence.

Dr. Kelloway is a prolific researcher, having published more than 100 articles, book chapters, and technical reports. He is a Fellow of the Association for Psychological Science, the Canadian Psychological Association, and the Society for Industrial-Organizational Psychology. His research interests include occupational health psychology, leadership, the development and measurement of work attitudes and values, unionization, and innovation in organizations. He is co-author of *The Union and Its Members*: *A Psychological Approach* (Oxford University Press), *Using Flexible Work Arrangements to Combat Job Stress* (Wiley), and *Management of Occupational Health and Safety* (Nelson), and the author of *Using LISREL for Structural Equation Modeling*: *A Researcher's Guide* (Sage). With Dr. Julian Barling (Queen's University), he edited the book series *Advanced Topics in Organizational Psychology* (Sage) and has co-edited *Young Workers*: *Varieties of Experience* (APA). He also co-edited *Handbook of Work Stress* and *Handbook of Workplace Violence* (both Sage) as well as *Occupational Health and Safety for Small and Medium Sized Enterprises* (Elgar).

Dr. Kelloway frequently reviews for academic journals or conferences and serves on the editorial boards of the *Journal of Applied Psychology,* the *Journal of Leadership and Organizational Studies,* and *Canadian Psychology.* He is Associate Editor of *Work & Stress* and a section editor for *Stress & Health.* Dr. Kelloway also maintains an active practice consulting with private- and public-sector organizations on issues related to leadership, and occupational health psychology.

Lori Francis

Lori Francis holds a Ph.D. in industrial/organizational psychology from the University of Guelph. She is an Associate Professor in the Department of Psychology at Saint Mary's University in Halifax. Dr. Francis has broad research interests in occupational health psychology, including work stress, workplace aggression and violence, and health-related interventions in the workplace. Her Ph.D. dissertation on organizational injustice as a workplace stressor was awarded the International Alliance of Human Resources Researchers best doctoral dissertation award. She sits on the Board of Directors for the CN Centre for Occupational Health and Safety. Dr. Francis also has an extensive consulting record, having worked with government, military, and private industry.

Bernadette Gatien

Bernadette Gatien holds an M.Sc. and a Ph.D. in industrial organizational psychology from Saint Mary's University. Her research interests include safety culture and climate assessment, safety culture improvement, safety training and development, and the impact of leader behaviours on employee safety behaviours. Dr. Gatien has conducted applied research with various organizations in both the public sector and private industry. In addition to teaching in Saint Mary's departments of psychology and management, she continues to provide consulting services to organizations in need of safety-related organizational development.

PREFACE

Occupational health and safety (OH&S) has long been the preserve of safety engineers and technical experts. However, in most organizations health and safety is housed within the human resources management function for a number of reasons (see Chapter 1 of this text). The immediate implication is that human resources managers must have a solid understanding of health and safety issues, legislation, and programs. Like the previous five editions of this text, the sixth edition is intended to give the HR manager and the HR professional a basic understanding of the elements that combine to create an effective occupational health and safety program.

We think of the sixth edition as comprising three relatively distinct areas relevant to health and safety. In the first set of chapters, we set the stage by providing an overview of health and safety with specific reference to the human resource function (Chapter 1), the legislative context of health and safety in Canada (Chapter 2), and issues relating to workers' compensation (Chapter 3).

The next set of chapters focuses on the types of hazards in the workplace, with special reference to techniques for recognizing, assessing, and controlling those hazards (Chapter 4). Chapter 5 considers physical agents such as noise, vibration, temperature, and radiation. Chapter 6 focuses on chemical and biological agents in the workplace. Chapter 7 extends the focus on hazards to include psychosocial hazards in the workplace. Chapter 8 examines workplace violence as a particular hazard in the workplace. While these are arguably the most technical chapters in the book, we have tried to maintain a nontechnical focus and to present the information in a way that is most useful to human resources managers.

The last chapters in the book speak more directly to human resources managers and outline some of the major ways in which they become actively involved in health and safety. Chapter 9 focuses on training—one of the most popular, and arguably the most effective, health and safety interventions. Chapter 10 focuses on motivating safe working behaviour and considers the role of both safety culture and safety leadership in organizations. Chapter 11 presents an overview of emergency response planning, while Chapter 12 summarizes incident investigation techniques. Chapter 13 addresses the issues of disability management and return to work programs. Finally, Chapter 14 summarizes attempts to promote employee health and wellness in the workplace.

Throughout the text we have attempted to provide the reader with current examples, clear definitions of technical terms, and links to the vast amount of information found on the Web. The nature of OH&S legislation in Canada, and the existence of jurisdictional differences, mean that the information presented in this text will need to be supplemented with (for example) provincial or territorial standards and legislative requirements. We hope the student will find this book useful in and of itself and will also use it as a guide to other resources.

In addition to the new material and updating, the sixth edition retains several of the features that accompanied the previous edition of this book, including opening vignettes, Using the Internet, Exercises, and Weblinks. This book also maintains references to the professional capabilities that provincial and territorial human resources associations throughout Canada have agreed on for granting the designation of Certified Human Resources Professional (CHRP). Applicants for the CHRP designation must now pass two national exams based on required professional capabilities. We have linked sections of the text to relevant RPCs at the back of each chapter. These RPCs are listed at http://www.chrp.ca/rpc/body-of-knowledge. We hope that this linkage of our content to the RPCs will help students and practitioners prepare for the CHRP assessments.

NEW TO THIS EDITION

The most exciting change is the addition of Dr. Bernadette Gatien as co-author. Dr. Gatien has a great deal of experience in teaching undergrad OH&S classes using this text as well as in working with companies to improve their OH&S programs. Her research, practical, and teaching experiences in OH&S allow her to make a substantial contribution to the text and we are delighted to welcome her to the team.

The following list of specific chapter changes highlights some of the new key and updated topics and examples that have been included in the sixth edition.

Chapter 1: Introduction

- Updated and expanded coverage of the internal responsibility system

- New box on the healthy workplace

- Updated data and statistics

Chapter 2: Legislative Framework

- Updates on OH&S legislation

- New box on the right to refuse unsafe work

- Updates on the impact of Bill C-45, the "Westray legislation"

Chapter 3: Workers' Compensation

- New chapter-opening vignette on injured workers and prescription painkillers

- Legislative updates, including new "presumptive provisions"

- Appendix on calculating injury frequency and severity moved into the main content of the chapter

- Added section on prevention

Chapter 4: Hazard Recognition, Risk Assessment, and Control

- New opening vignette on the nuclear disaster in Japan

- Chapter re-ordered for a more logical flow

- Risk assessment revised and updated, with new tables
- Updated discussion of the contributing factors in the hazard identification process

Chapter 5: Physical Agents

- New opening vignette on risks associated with cellphones
- New information about the health effects and control of vibration
- New and expanded coverage of working in hot and cold environments
- New section on controlling radiation

Chapter 6: Chemical and Biological Agents

- New opening vignette on Lyme disease
- New box: Globally Harmonized System of Classification and Labelling Chemicals
- Added discussion of the three physical states of chemicals and associated health risks

Chapter 7: Psychosocial Hazards

- Expanded coverage of mental health issues at work
- Added coverage of CSA standards for psychological health and safety at work
- Updated and expanded box on prevalence and impact of mental health in the workplace

Chapter 8: Workplace Violence

- New section on guidelines and tools available to help recognize, assess, and control the risks of violence in the workplace

Chapter 9: Training

- Added discussion of when interventions besides training are appropriate
- New box on training delivery methods
- Updated coverage includes the addition of five new studies in the chapter

Chapter 10: Motivation

- Added coverage of self-determination theory, applied to OH&S
- New box on OH&S and social media

- Added discussion of active approaches to safety leadership
- New, updated section on OH&S management systems, including a detailed description of the CSA-Z1000-06 model

Chapter 11: Emergency Planning

- New opening vignette on the Deepwater Horizon oil spill
- Coverage of emergency planning expanded and high-rise tower evacuation added
- New exercise on the costs of emergency planning added

Chapter 12: Incident Investigation

- New opening vignette on the crash of the Sikorsky S-92 helicopter off the coast of Newfoundland
- The bow-tie model of risk assessment added

Chapter 13: Disability Management and Return to Work

- Updated and expanded overview of workplace injuries across Canada
- New box on the approach to disability management, featuring Vancouver Coastal Health
- Uses of databases for disability management added

Chapter 14: Workplace Wellness: Work–Family and Health Promotion Programs

- New illustrations of how concepts of preventive stress management, introduced in Chapter 7, are applied in work–family conflict interventions
- New discussion of CSA-Z1003-13, the recently introduced voluntary workplace standard for psychological health and safety
- Expanded discussion of a company's return on investment in health promotion programs

INSTRUCTOR ANCILLARIES

About the Nelson Education Teaching Advantage (NETA)

The **Nelson Education Teaching Advantage (NETA)** program delivers research-based instructor resources that promote student engagement and higher-order thinking to enable the success of Canadian students and educators.

Instructors today face many challenges. Resources are limited, time is scarce, and a new kind of student has emerged: one who is juggling school with work, has gaps in his or her basic knowledge, and is immersed in technology in a way that has led to a completely new style of learning. In response, Nelson Education has gathered a group of dedicated instructors to advise us on the creation of richer and more flexible ancillaries and online learning platforms that respond to the needs of today's teaching environments. Whether your course is offered in-class, online, or both, Nelson is pleased to provide pedagogically driven, research-based resources to support you.

The members of our editorial advisory board have experience across a variety of disciplines and are recognized for their commitment to teaching. They include:

Norman Althouse, Haskayne School of Business, University of Calgary

Brenda Chant-Smith, Department of Psychology, Trent University

David DiBattista, Department of Psychology, Brock University

Roger Fisher, PhD

Scott Follows, Manning School of Business Administration, Acadia University

Jon Houseman, Department of Biology, University of Ottawa

Glen Loppnow, Department of Chemistry, University of Alberta

Tanya Noel, Department of Biology, York University

Gary Poole, Senior Scholar, Centre for Health Education Scholarship, and Associate Director, School of Population and Public Health, University of British Columbia

Dan Pratt, Department of Educational Studies, University of British Columbia

Mercedes Rowinsky-Geurts, Department of Languages and Literatures, Wilfrid Laurier University

In consultation with the editorial advisory board, Nelson Education has completely rethought the structure, approaches, and formats of our key textbook ancillaries and online learning platforms. We've also increased our investment in editorial support for our ancillary and digital authors. The result is the Nelson Education Teaching Advantage and its key components: *NETA Engagement, NETA Assessment, NETA Presentation,* and *NETA Digital.* Each component includes one or more ancillaries prepared according to our best practices and may also be accompanied by documentation explaining the theory behind the practices.

NETA Engagement presents materials that help instructors deliver engaging content and activities to their classes. Instead of Instructor's Manuals that regurgitate chapter outlines and key terms from the text, NETA Enriched Instructor's Manuals (EIMs) provide genuine assistance to teachers. The EIMs answer questions like *What should students learn?, Why should students care?,* and *What are some common student misconceptions and stumbling blocks?* EIMs not only identify the topics that cause students the most difficulty, but also describe techniques and resources to help students master these concepts. Dr. Roger Fisher's *Instructor's Guide to Classroom Engagement (IGCE)* accompanies every Enriched Instructor's Manual. (Information about the NETA Enriched Instructor's Manual prepared for *Management of Occupational Health and Safety,* Sixth Edition, is included in the description of the IRCD below.)

NETA Assessment relates to testing materials. Under *NETA Assessment,* Nelson's authors create multiple-choice questions that reflect research-based best practices for constructing effective questions and testing not just recall but also higher-order thinking. Our guidelines were developed by David DiBattista, a 3M National Teaching Fellow whose recent research as a professor of psychology at Brock University has focused on multiple-choice testing. All Test Bank authors receive training at workshops conducted by Prof. DiBattista, as do the copyeditors assigned to each Test Bank. A copy of *Multiple Choice Tests: Getting Beyond Remembering,* Prof. DiBattista's guide to writing effective tests, is included with every Nelson Test Bank/Computerized Test Bank package. (Information about the NETA Test Bank prepared for *Management of Occupational Health and Safety,* Sixth Edition, is included in the description of the IRCD below.)

NETA Presentation has been developed to help instructors make the best use of PowerPoint® in their classrooms. With a clean and uncluttered design developed by Maureen Stone of StoneSoup Consulting, NETA Presentation features slides with improved readability, more multi-media and graphic materials, activities to use in class, and tips for instructors on the Notes page. A copy of *NETA Guidelines for Classroom Presentations* by Maureen Stone is included with each set of PowerPoint slides. (Information about the NETA PowerPoint® prepared for *Management of Occupational Health and Safety,* Sixth Edition, is included in the description of the IRCD below.)

NETA Digital is a framework based on Arthur Chickering and Zelda Gamson's seminal work "Seven Principles of Good Practice in Undergraduate Education" (AAHE Bulletin, 1987) and the follow-up work by Chickering and Stephen C. Ehrmann, "Implementing the Seven Principles: Technology as Lever" (AAHE Bulletin, 1996). This aspect of the NETA program guides the writing and development of our digital products to ensure that they appropriately reflect the core goals of contact, collaboration, multimodal learning, time on task, prompt feedback, active learning, and high expectations. The resulting focus on pedagogical utility, rather than technological wizardry, ensures that all of our technology supports better outcomes for students.

Be sure to visit Nelson Education's **Inspired Instruction** website at http://www.nelson.com/inspired to find out more about NETA. Don't miss the testimonials of instructors who have used NETA supplements and seen student engagement increase!

IRCD

Key instructor ancillaries are provided on the *Instructor's Resource CD* (ISBN 0-17-656167-6), giving instructors the ultimate tool for customizing lectures and presentations. (Downloadable Web versions are also available at http://www.nelson.com/site/kelloway.) The IRCD includes:

- **NETA Engagement:** The Enriched Instructor's Manual was written by Steven Robinson, of Georgian College. It is organized according to the textbook chapters and addresses eight key educational concerns, such as typical stumbling blocks student face and how to address them. Other features include suggested answers to exercises and cases.

- **NETA Assessment:** The Test Bank was written by Frances Tuer, of McMaster University. It includes over 350 multiple-choice questions written according to NETA guidelines for effective construction and development of higher-order questions. Also included are true/false and short answer questions, and Test Bank files are provided in Word format for easy editing and in PDF format for convenient printing whatever your system.

The Computerized Test Bank by ExamView® includes all the questions from the Test Bank. The easy-to-use ExamView software is compatible with Microsoft Windows and Mac OS. You can create tests by selecting questions from the question bank, modifying these questions as desired, and adding new questions you write yourself. You can administer quizzes online and export tests to WebCT, Blackboard, and other formats.

- **NETA Presentation:** Microsoft® PowerPoint® lecture slides for every chapter have been created by Greg Cole, of St. Mary's University. There is an average of 25 slides per chapter, many featuring key figures and tables from *Management of Occupational Health and Safety,* Sixth Edition. NETA principles of clear design and engaging content have been incorporated throughout.

- **Image Library:** This resource consists of digital copies of figures and short tables used in the book. Instructors may use these jpegs to create their own PowerPoint® presentations.

- **DayOne:** Day One—Prof InClass is a PowerPoint® presentation that you can customize to orient your students to the class and their text at the beginning of the course.

CourseMate

CourseMate brings course concepts to life with interactive learning and exam preparation tools that integrate with the printed textbook. Students activate their knowledge through quizzes, games, and flashcards, among many other tools. CourseMate provides immediate feedback that enables students to connect results to the work they have just produced, increasing their learning efficiency. It encourages contact between students and faculty: you can select to monitor your students' level of engagement with CourseMate, correlating their efforts to their outcomes. You can even use CourseMate's quizzes to practise "Just in Time" teaching by tracking results in the Engagement Tracker and customizing your lesson plans to address their learning needs.

STUDENT ANCILLARY

CourseMate

The more you study, the better the results. Make the most of your study time by accessing everything you need to succeed in one place. **CourseMate** includes:

- An interactive eBook with highlighting, note-taking, and an interactive glossary

- Interactive learning tools, including:
  - quizzes
  - flashcards
  - games
  - ...and more!

ACKNOWLEDGMENTS

For taking the time to review, we thank the following instructors: Anna Blake at York University, Bob Barnetson at Athabasca University, Wenlu Feng at Centennial College, Lisa Guglielmi at Seneca College, Karen Hamberg at Kwantlen Polytechnic University, Suzanne Kavanagh at George Brown College, Richard McFadden at Georgian College, Jody Merritt at St. Clair College, Colleen Morrison at College of the North Atlantic, David A. Morrison at Durham College, Bill Reid at Fanshawe College, Aaron Schat at McMaster University, Julie Aitken Schermer at University of Western Ontario, Kate Windsor at University of Waterloo, and Deborah M. Zinni at Brock University. Your insights are reflected in the current edition of the book, and we are appreciative of your efforts.

We would especially like to thank Catherine Fitzgerald of Okanagan University College for her comments and suggestions for exercises to include in the book. We would like to thank our colleagues at the CN Centre for Occupational Health and Safety (Vic Catano, Arla Day, Danielle Durepos, Mark Fleming, Debra Gilin-Oore, Camilla Holmvall, Catherine Loughlin, Jennifer Martinell, Margaret McKee, Steve Smith, Veronica Stinson, and Anthony Yue) and Valerie Wadman here at Saint Mary's for their support, and we acknowledge our network of colleagues across the country who are making significant contributions to the human resources side of occupational health and safety. These include Julian Barling (Queen's University), Kate Dupré (Memorial University), Gail Hepburn (University of Lethbridge), Aaron Schat (McMaster University), Mike Teed (Bishop's University), and Nick Turner (University of Manitoba). The late Rick Iverson (Simon Fraser University) was a colleague, a friend, and a scholar who made major contributions to understanding issues of worker safety. His death is a loss to the safety community and to us all.

We are also grateful for the support and guidance of Monica Belcourt (York University), and Alwynn Pinard (Acquisitions Editor) and Lisa Berland (Developmental Editor) at Nelson as well as those who worked on the book manuscript with us—Imoinda Romain (Senior Content Production Manager at Nelson), Erin Moore (Copy Editor), and Rajachitra S. (Project Manager).

We also wish to thank James Montgomery, who made important contributions as an author on previous editions.

E. Kevin Kelloway, Ph.D.
Canada Research Chair in Occupational Health Psychology
Director, CN Centre for Occupational Health and Safety
Saint Mary's University

Lori Francis, Ph.D.
Associate Professor of Psychology
Saint Mary's University

Bernadette Gatien, Ph.D.
Saint Mary's University

PART 1

Jill Wachter/Getty Images

Introduction and Overview

CHAPTER
1

Introduction

CHAPTER LEARNING OBJECTIVES

After reading this chapter, you should be able to:

- define occupational health and safety, occupational injury, and occupational illness
- describe the financial and social costs associated with occupational injuries and illnesses
- trace the development of modern models of health and safety management
- list and describe the role of the major stakeholders in occupational health and safety
- explain the connection between human resource management and occupational health and safety
- describe the links between human resource practices and health and safety

TAINTED MEAT IN A TAINTED WORKPLACE?

One of the largest meat recalls in Canadian history resulted from *E. coli* contaminated meat that sickened numerous consumers. XL Foods in Brooks, Alberta—one of the largest beef packing plants in the country—was shut down for a month and thousands of workers were laid off as a result of the recall. Although the focus of publicity was on the consumers of meat products, what about the workers who are also exposed to tainted products?

As an industry, meat packing can be both dirty and dangerous work. Workers may be exposed to pathogens and work in sometimes terrible conditions. As you might imagine, carcasses may be in contact with blood, bodily fluids, and feces. These may accumulate on work services leading to odours and the dangers of slipping. Plants can be both hot and humid making it uncomfortable to wear personal protective gear such as safety glasses or gloves. In the case of XL Foods, a large percentage of the 2,200 employees were temporary foreign workers. Temporary workers may not receive safety training or be aware of their rights under Canada's occupational health and safety laws. The volume of work means that production lines have to keep moving—to the extent that workers may not follow safe work procedures in order to keep up with the line. On top of the physical dangers, workers may be exposed to psychological trauma because of the need to kill other living things as part of their job.

These issues raise numerous questions about responsibility and accountability. How are safety considerations balanced with the need for private sector companies to produce products profitably? How much responsibility for protecting workers is borne by management? By the workers themselves? What is the role of government in establishing and enforcing safety standards?

Answering these questions is the focus of this chapter—and more broadly, this book. As you will see, questions about workplace safety can often be complex but there are clear roles for managers, employees, and government in establishing safe working conditions in all industries.

Source: Jean Lian, "Silence on the Floor," *Daily News* (Jan. 10, 2013). Found at: http://www.ohscanada.com/news/silence-on-the-floor/1001981474/.

Most of us go to work each day expecting to return home in more or less the same condition as when we left. For a distressingly high number of workers, this is not the case. Workplace accidents continue to occur, with consequences ranging from minor property damage to death. Human resource departments bear the greatest burden for monitoring an organization's occupational health and safety. If an HR department fails to meet that responsibility, the costs can be immense.

As shown in Figure 1.1, the number of workplace fatalities in Canada continues to increase. The most recent figures suggest that between 900 and 1,000 workers each year die as a result of workplace accidents and that almost 250,000 suffer an injury serious enough to warrant missing time from work (often called a **lost-time injury**). As one might expect, workplace fatalities and injuries are concentrated by industry. In Canada, construction, manufacturing, and transportation are the most dangerous industries in terms of workplace fatalities.

lost-time injury
a workplace injury that results in the employee missing time from work

Perhaps not surprisingly, occupational health and safety statistics vary widely by province and one needs to adjust for the size of the population in order to compare occupational health and safety statistics across jurisdictions. A common way of doing this is to calculate rates (e.g., fatality or injury rates) for a given

FIGURE  1.1

Workplace Fatalities in Canada: A Ten-Year History

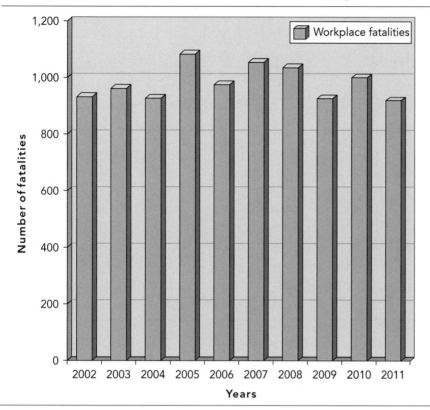

Source: Association of Workers' Compensation Boards of Canada, National Work Injuries Statistics Program, Table 22: Number of Fatalities, by Jurisdiction, 1993–2011. Found at: http://www.awcbc.org/common/assets/nwisptables/all_tables.pdf.

number of workers. A 2005 study showed that Prince Edward Island experienced 1.5 workplace fatalities for every 100,000 workers. In the territories (Northwest Territory, Nunavut, and Yukon), the comparable figure is 27.4 fatalities for each 100,000 workers. More than half of workplace fatalities are attributable to occupational diseases; the effects of asbestos account for most of these deaths.[1]

Occupational health and safety (OH&S) is the recognition, assessment, and control of hazards associated with the work environment. These hazards range from chemical, biological, and physical agents to psychosocial disorders such as stress. The goal of an organization's health and safety program is to reduce occupational injuries and illnesses. An **occupational injury** is any cut, fracture, sprain, or amputation resulting from a workplace accident. An **occupational illness** is any abnormal condition or disorder caused by exposure to environmental factors associated with employment.

OH&S issues affect a wide range of players, from employers, employees, and their families to all those who contribute to the insurance and compensation systems that have been developed to assist and rehabilitate workers. Moreover, health and safety concerns are no longer limited to industrial workers, who

occupational health and safety (OH&S)
the identification, evaluation, and control of hazards associated with the work environment

occupational injury
any cut, fracture, sprain, or amputation resulting from a workplace accident

occupational illness
any abnormal condition or disorder caused by exposure to environmental factors associated with employment

FIGURE (1.2)

Number of Lost-Time Injuries, 2011

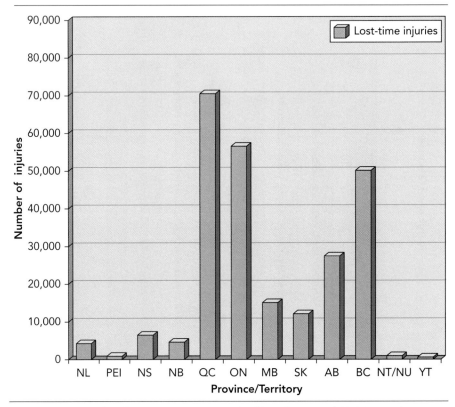

Source: Association of Workers' Compensation Boards of Canada, National Work Injuries Statistics Program, Table 1: Number of Accepted Time-Loss Injuries, by Jurisdiction, 1982–2011. Found at: http://www.awcbc.org/common/assets/nwisptables/all_tables.pdf.

face such hazards as mine explosions and transportation accidents; employees in white-collar environments are worrying more and more—rightly so—about repetitive strain injury and sick building syndrome. The rising costs associated with work-related injuries and illnesses and, more important, the public's decreasing tolerance for work-related hazards underlie the need to understand and implement effective OH&S policies and programs.

HISTORICAL DEVELOPMENT OF MODERN OCCUPATIONAL HEALTH AND SAFETY

Occupational injuries and illnesses have been with us throughout history. Documented cases of work-related illnesses go back as far as ancient Egypt, when stonemasons and potters experienced respiratory problems. As societies became more technologically advanced, cases of vomiting, copper-induced dermatoses (skin diseases), and hepatic (liver) degeneration began to occur. Labourers who worked with iron and in various alloying operations risked symptoms such as high fever, coughing, and headache, as well as diseases like lung cancer.[2]

With the advent of the Industrial Revolution, machinists and others working in the new industries were exposed to oils used for lubrication during the cutting and removing of metal. These oils, in conjunction with poor personal hygiene practices, resulted in serious dermatoses, such as acne and skin melanomas. When the spinning and weaving industries were mechanized, the resultant dust from hemp and flax caused *byssinosis* (**brown lung**).

In Canada, concern for occupational health and safety was first evident in the late nineteenth century, when Ontario passed legislation that established safety standards—for example, by mandating guards on machines. Quebec soon followed suit, and by the early twentieth century every jurisdiction in Canada had passed factory laws to regulate heating, lighting, ventilation, hygiene, fire safety, and accident reporting. Factory inspectors were appointed in each province and territory to enforce these standards and to conduct regular inspections of workplaces.

brown lung
a disease of the lungs caused by excessive inhalation of dust; the disease is in the pneumoconiosis family and often afflicts textile workers

The Royal Commission on the Relations of Capital and Labour in Canada (1889) had an important influence on the development of health and safety regulations. First, the commissioners made several recommendations for improving health and safety by establishing standards and mandating regular inspections. Second, the commissioners were the first to recommend a system for compensating victims of industrial accidents, regardless of who was at fault. Finally, the commissioners recommended that a labour bureau be created to oversee these activities.

The 1960s and 1970s were an important time for health and safety in Canada. Those decades saw the implementation of the Canada Labour (Standards) Code and the Canada Labour (Safety) Code. In 1974 the Ontario government formed the Royal Commission on the Health and Safety of Workers in Mines. Chaired by Dr. James Ham, this commission was the first to articulate the three principal rights of workers: the right to refuse dangerous work without penalty; the right to participate in identifying and correcting health and safety problems; and the right to know about hazards in the workplace. These three rights are still enshrined in current legislation and are the basis for many of Canada's health and safety programs. In 1988, for example, legislation was passed that established the Workplace Hazardous Materials Information System (WHMIS). Through federal and provincial cooperation, WHMIS has been established in every jurisdiction in Canada. In every jurisdiction, it is based on the fundamental right of workers to know about potential hazards in the workplace.

CHANGING PERSPECTIVES ON RISK AND LIABILITY

Until the early twentieth century, the dominant model of dealing with hazards in the workplace was the legal doctrine of **assumption of risk**. In essence, the assumption of risk stated that when a worker accepted employment, he or she also accepted all the normal risks associated with that occupation. Under this doctrine, employers bore little or no responsibility for worker health and safety. Indeed, employers were not responsible for providing compensation to injured workers unless the accident was *solely* the fault of the employer. Given that workplace accidents rarely have only one cause, it is not surprising that cases in which workers were compensated were few.

assumption of risk
the belief that a worker accepted the risks of employment when he or she accepted a job

OH&S Notebook 1.1

PREVENTING COMPUTER VISION SYNDROME

Work-related health concerns are not just of historical interest. New technologies have generated new health and safety concerns. One of these is computer vision syndrome, which results from the glare caused by the combination of bright office lights and computer monitors. It is estimated that 70% of adults experience computer vision syndrome. To reduce the health concerns associated with glare, organizations can do several things:

- Reduce ambient lighting levels (most offices are more than twice as bright as they need to be).
- Place monitors so that they are 90 degrees from any light source.
- Use task lighting (e.g., adjustable desk lamps).
- Ensure that monitors are functioning properly with minimal flicker and are adjusted for the comfort of the user.

Sources: Home Vision Therapy System, "Frequently Asked Questions." Found at: http://www.homevisiontherapy.com/faqs.html (Accessed Feb. 7, 2007); Alberta Association of Optometrists, "Are Your Kids at Risk for Computer Vision Syndrome?" Found at: http://www.optometrists.ab.ca/press/releases.htm?Step=2&PRK=4 (Accessed Feb. 7, 2007); CCOHS, "Eye Discomfort in the Office." Found at: http://www.ccohs.ca/oshanswers/ergonomics/office/eye_discomfort.html (Accessed Feb. 7, 2007).

---

accident proneness

the notion that some individuals are inherently more likely than others to be involved in accidents, as a result of individual characteristics

Associated with the assumption-of-risk doctrine was the belief that occupational injuries were caused by worker carelessness. In its most extreme form, this notion was expressed as a belief in the accident-prone personality. The concept of **accident proneness** was a focus of research for most of the twentieth century; it was based on the assumption that some individuals are inherently more likely to be involved in accidents than are others and that therefore most workplace accidents are caused by a small proportion of workers. Because workers in dangerous occupations or workplaces do tend to have more accidents than others, the belief in accident proneness appears to be supported. But this is like saying that Ontario drivers are the worst in Canada because of the high number of accidents on Highway 401. When we consider that the volume of traffic on the 401 exceeds that of all other highways in Canada, the higher number of accidents can be seen in perspective. It is now recognized that the concept of accident proneness has little empirical support. Modern health and safety programs have moved beyond these early beliefs, having recognized that enhancing occupational health and safety requires cooperation among multiple stakeholders. Government, employers, and employees all have a role to play in enhancing health and safety outcomes.

THE IMPORTANCE OF HEALTH AND SAFETY

Effective OH&S programs have important and far-reaching benefits for both employers and employees. Employers, employees, and the public should care about occupational health and safety for economic, legal, and moral reasons.

Economic Considerations

The economic costs associated with work-related injury are both direct and indirect. The example given in **OH&S Today 1.1** shows some of the direct and indirect

OH&S Today 1.1

Direct and Indirect Costs of Injury

A construction worker falls 3 metres off an unguarded scaffold and lands on the main floor, breaking his ankle and forearm. The direct costs of the injury include that worker's lost time, the time spent in investigating the incident, and the finding/training of a replacement worker, and are estimated at $1,810. This does not include the indirect costs (including the potential increase in Workers' Compensation Board assessment and the potential fines and legal costs associated with allowing an unsafe condition in the workplace). These indirect costs can be more than 10 times the direct costs of the incident. Note well that these costs come right from the bottom line—every dollar in cost is a dollar lost in profit. It is estimated that this one incident (direct costs only) will take 18 days' profit from the firm.

There are other costs to consider. The average cost of a Workers' Compensation claim is about $19,000, and these costs are paid by all employers through the assessment. There are also the costs experienced by the individual in the form of pain and suffering and the possible long-term effects of the injury. The claim's cost was derived by inserting fictional facts and data into the WorkSafeBC Safety Calculator. That calculator can be found at http://www2.worksafebc.com/sc/tours/default. htm. The actual cost of a claim may differ owing to variables such as time involved and the hourly rates used in the calculator.

Source: For this and other cost scenarios, see the incident cost calculator at http://www.hre.gov.ab.ca/whs/smallbus/calculator/tours/default.htm, February 7, 2007.

costs that can result from a work-related injury. Note that the costs illustrated in this one example are repeated hourly across the country. Cost calculations for specific injuries and workplaces can be estimated using an online calculator provided by WorkSafeBC.

It is estimated that the costs of workplace injuries exceed $12 billion a year.[3] The lost time attributable to injuries exceeds that of labour disruptions such as strikes or lockouts.[4] And those costs are unequally distributed—in Ontario, for example, it is estimated that 2% of all workplaces are responsible for 10% of all injuries and 21% of all costs.[5]

For at least two reasons, direct and indirect estimates must be considered underestimates of the true costs of workplace illness and injury. First, there is considerable evidence that workplace injuries are not accurately reported. Indeed, studies have suggested that the number of reported injuries may represent only one-tenth of actual injuries.[6] Second, occupational injury statistics do not adequately capture the extent of illnesses that are caused or exacerbated by exposure to workplace conditions. Deaths that *might* be attributable to occupational illnesses are not typically accounted for in statistical analyses of occupational fatalities.

It is clear that safety problems cost every man, woman, and child in Canada hundreds of dollars annually based on the direct and indirect costs of occupational injuries. But these figures only represent costs associated with an injury once it has occurred. Other costs to the employer include work stoppages and strikes due to unsafe working conditions. For example, in 1987, 1,000 employees at McDonnell Douglas Canada refused to work after the Ontario Ministry of Labour cited the company for hundreds of infractions of the province's Occupational Health and Safety Act. Labour disputes involving such safety issues as pollutant levels, safety equipment, and first aid facilities result in thousands of lost days of worker production. Incalculable costs include those associated with employees who quit or refuse to work in companies because of safety or health concerns.

Another indirect cost to companies is that of negative publicity when a death, accident, or serious health problem becomes public. The Occidental Chemical Company in California had a public relations nightmare to cope with when the media learned that one of its chemicals caused sterility in the workers who were handling the compound. However, managers who are committed to safety can turn adverse publicity into a marketing and recruitment advantage by advertising their concerns about employee safety.

Employers that are not concerned about the health and safety of their employees affect other employers and taxpaying citizens. Workers' Compensation rates are determined by industry sector. A negligent employer forces others in the sector to pay higher rates, and these costs are significant. The 12 Workers' Compensation Boards across Canada pay out $3 billion annually. The Alberta board estimates that a totally disabled young worker with children will have received $7 million in payments by age 72. Unsafe working conditions cause insurance premiums to escalate and health expenditures to increase.

Conversely, industry estimates indicate that up to 90% of safety-related changes made can result in positive paybacks through associated reductions in Workers' Compensation premiums. Programs such as the New Experimental Experience Rating (NEER) reward employers for implementing safe work practices by reducing Workers' Compensation costs based on the company's actual experience. Clearly, organizations have an economic interest in lowering the number of accidents and providing a safe working environment.

Legal Considerations

Every worker has the legal right to safe working conditions under OH&S acts. The Occupational Health and Safety Act of Ontario, section 25(2)(h), requires an employer to "take every precaution reasonable in the circumstances for the protection of a worker." The legal term for this requirement is **due diligence**.

due diligence
an expected standard of conduct that requires employers to take every reasonable precaution to ensure safety

From a legal perspective, due diligence is defined as the measure of prudence to be expected from, and ordinarily exercised by, a reasonable and prudent person under the particular circumstances depending on the relative facts of the special case. In other words, due diligence is a standard of conduct measured by what could be expected of a reasonable person in the same circumstances. Due diligence requires a business to foresee all unsafe conditions or acts and requires it to take precautions to prevent accidents that can reasonably be anticipated.[7] Similarly, a worker is required to work in compliance with health and safety legislation. This legislation is discussed at length in Chapter 2.

Moral Considerations

Aside from legal and economic considerations, employers have a moral obligation to employees and their families to provide the safest working environment possible. Two decades of research have provided consistent evidence that management commitment to health and safety results in higher levels of employee

OH&S Today 1.2

The Costs of Unhealthy Behaviour

Though there is no doubt that substantial human and economic costs are associated with unsafe workplaces, employers also incur substantial costs attributable to individual lifestyle choices. In their efforts to promote "wellness" (see Chapter 14), many employers have implemented smoking-cessation programs (often in conjunction with provincial or territorial laws that prohibit smoking in the workplace). Substantial economic gains may be associated with such initiatives. Based on a review of research from around the world, Kelloway and Barling concluded that smokers were absent from work 43% more often than nonsmokers. Though such estimates do not show up in the lost-time injury figures, absenteeism associated with smoking is a real and substantial cost for employers.

Sources: E.K. Kelloway and J. Barling, "Smoking and Absence from Work," in M. Krausz and M. Koslowsky, eds., *Voluntary Employee Withdrawal and Inattendance* (New York: Plenum, 2003), Pg. 167–78; J.E. Henningfield, L.M. Ramstrom, C. Husten, G. Giovino, J. Barling, C. Weber, E.K. Kelloway, V.J. Strecher, and M.J. Jarvis, "Smoking and the Workplace: Realities and Solutions," *Journal of Smoking-Related Diseases, Vol.* 5 (1994) Pg. 261–70.

motivation to work safely and better organizational safety records. Similarly, workers have a moral responsibility to learn about safety and health, to follow recommended workplace practices, and to be alert and responsible. In at least one study, the perception that managers, supervisors, and coworkers were committed to health and safety was the single biggest predictor of an employee's willingness to participate in health and safety programs.[8] Clearly, the economic, human, and social costs associated with workplace injury and illness are intolerable, and both employers and employees must work together to enhance occupational health and safety.

THE STAKEHOLDERS

Government

In Canada, Ontario was the first province to enact compensation legislation with the passage of the Workmen's Compensation Act in 1914. This legislation provided lost-time wages to almost every injured worker, thereby removing the right of workers to sue their employers. After the First World War, the federal and other provincial and territorial governments began to enact legislation to protect workers. The two main goals of this legislation were (1) to ensure that injured workers received compensation and that employers accepted liability, and (2) to prevent accidents and illness by establishing safe work environments.

As a result of continued improvement to health and safety legislation, the number of workplace accidents declined. For example, despite the addition of two million workers to the Canadian workforce between 1985 and 1993, the number of accidents dropped from 554,793 to 423,184.[9]

Besides passing laws, governments solicit or conduct research on health and safety issues and disseminate information. Ontario, Nova Scotia, and British

Columbia are world leaders in the development of chemical-exposure standards that are as strict as reasonably attainable based on hard scientific evidence. The federal government has created the Canadian Centre for Occupational Health and Safety (CCOHS) as a vital health and safety research and resource organization. CCOHS accesses a number of databases from around the world besides creating and maintaining its own comprehensive database. This organization's goal is to provide health and safety information to any worker who requests it.

CCOHS has developed an online information service called CCINFOWEB (http://ccinfoweb.ccohs.ca/). This program's vast database contains information on the toxicological effects of chemicals and biological agents, as well as material safety data sheets (MSDS) and the health and safety laws for all of Canada's jurisdictions. CCOHS also produces a wide variety of safety infograms and other publications.

Employers

Though every player has a role in occupational health and safety, that of a company's management team is the most pivotal. Managers have the means and the authority to monitor the workplace and to ensure compliance with safe practices. Moreover, organizations have the resources to hire health and safety professionals.

The employer is responsible for preparing a written OH&S policy and for ensuring that it is prominently displayed in the workplace. Employers are also required to

- provide and maintain equipment, materials, and protective devices;
- ensure that the manner in which the work is performed is safe and that the environment is free from hazards and serious risks;
- monitor their workplace and report minor, critical, disabling, and fatal injuries, as well as occupational illnesses and toxic substances (and to maintain the records of these occurrences for many years);
- establish health and safety committees with strong employee representation; alert employees to any known or perceived risks and hazards in the workplace; *and*
- provide employees with health and safety training.

Managers must be trained to recognize and control unsafe work environments; they cannot monitor and control what they do not recognize as unsafe. Supervisors who participated in a study of 70 construction sites failed to recognize 44% of the workplace hazards and felt that another 64% did not fall within their jurisdiction. Furthermore, these supervisors stated that 20% of the hazards were inevitable.[10] Clearly, in order to fulfill their responsibilities, managers must receive health and safety training.

Employees

Employees of an organization have a role to play in occupational health and safety both as individuals and as members of organized labour groups. As individuals, employees are required to perform their duties and tasks in a safe and responsible

OH&S Notebook 1.2

THE INTERNAL RESPONSIBILITY SYSTEM

The basis for most health and safety legislation in Canada is the **internal responsibility system (IRS)**. That system ensures that each "actor" (employees, employers, supervisors, etc.) takes personal responsibility for safety. The idea here is that individuals in the workplace are in the best position to ensure health and safety. Though government has a regulatory and legislative role to play, the primary responsibility for health and safety resides in the workplace.

Strahlendorf suggests that each term in "internal responsibility system" has a specific meaning. It is "internal" in that responsibility for health and safety is internal to the workplace and not dependent on external regulation. Safety is also internal in the sense that it is the way we do our work—safety is not an add-on, it is an intrinsic feature of the way we work. As Strahlendorf notes, we do not talk about "safety" versus "production" we talk about "safe production."

Responsibility in the context of the IRS means that each person in the organization—from the CEO on down—has specific and personal responsibilities for safety that vary according to the nature of

their role in the organization. Finally, Strahlendorf notes that the IRS is a "system" that is both (a) based on people in the system interacting and (b) self-correcting. Self-correcting mechanisms that are frequently enshrined in legislation would include procedures for work refusals or work stoppages and the institution of joint occupational health and safety committees.

Although virtually all Canadian health and safety legislation incorporates some elements of the IRS, Nova Scotia was the first province to define the internal responsibility system in its health and safety legislation. Under the act, employers must provide a safe workplace (this is sometimes known as the "general duty clause" in OH&S legislation). Employees are granted three specific rights that enable them to participate in ensuring a safe workplace:

(a) the right to refuse unsafe work;

(b) the right to be made aware of workplace hazards (i.e., the right to know); *and*

(c) the right to participate in OH&S decisions—typically through an OH&S committee.

Source: P. Strahlendorf, "Is Your Committee Effective?" *OHS Canada*, Vol. 23 (2007) Pg. 24–31.

manner and to wear protective equipment in compliance with company and legislative regulations. They are also required to report defective equipment and other workplace hazards to the safety professional, the Joint Health and Safety Committee, or the manager. Any employees who feel that a particular activity will endanger them or others have the right to refuse to carry out the activity.

internal responsibility system (IRS)

the system of shared responsibility for health and safety that is the basis for most Canadian OH&S legislation

Organized Labour

Organized labour also has a role to play in ensuring the proper management of safety at work.[11] One role of organized labour is to bring emerging problems and issues in health and safety to the attention of government and employers and to pressure other stakeholders to take corrective action. Organized labour and professional associations have also used the collective bargaining process to incorporate health and safety provisions in many contracts. These labour contracts attempt to formalize voluntary measures and extend legislative programs. For example, some contracts state that a union must have a full-time safety representative in all plants. Others bargain for more training on safety measures or more information on exposure to known toxic chemicals.

PARTNERSHIPS

Though all stakeholders support the concept of safe working conditions, not everyone is committed to implementing OH&S programs. There may be several reasons for stakeholders' lack of action in this area. Employers may be more concerned with production quotas than with safety records, because the costs of production are more visible. Employers may clean up their locations just before an announced safety inspection, thus ensuring a pass. Sometimes managers do not even recognize unsafe conditions, or they feel unable to do anything about those they do identify. Similarly, employers may be unaware of the methods and instruments by which rigorous monitoring of the workplace can be achieved. This situation is compounded by the fact that health and safety is rarely mentioned in management research, composing less than 1% of such research.[12] As a result, managers and prospective managers receive little or no training in health and safety issues. Also, those issues may be addressed in an industrial relations climate that emphasizes conflict between management and the union. In such an environment, health and safety issues may be seen as another bargaining chip.[13]

Another barrier to the implementation of OH&S programs is that the general medical establishment is neither well versed nor well trained in OH&S issues and occupational medicine. For instance, the effects of some industrial diseases are not apparent for years and are complicated by factors such as the worker's lifestyle and failure to follow safety regulations such as wearing protective equipment.

OH&S Today 1.3

A Predictable Path to Disaster at Westray

On May 9, 1992, at 5:20 a.m., the Westray coal mine in Plymouth, Nova Scotia, exploded. Despite extensive rescue efforts involving more than 170 mine rescue workers, 26 miners died in the mine. Charged with investigating the cause of the disaster, Justice Peter Richard titled his final report *The Westray Story: A Predictable Path to Disaster*, emphasizing that the disaster that rocked the community had been entirely preventable.

Justice Richard documented many causes of the disaster, but he focused in particular on a management style that emphasized production over safety and that showed disdain for safety concerns: workers were not provided training in safe mining procedures; supervisors did not have the authority to correct unsafe conditions;

and dangerous shortcuts were taken in the performance of mine tasks. Work procedures (e.g., the use of 12-hour shifts for miners) were also in violation of safety regulations. Despite excessive levels of gas and coal dust in the mine, unsafe procedures (e.g., the use of torches) were condoned if not encouraged. No meaningful dialogue existed on safety matters at the Westray mine— the Joint Health and Safety Committee did not function effectively. As Justice Richard noted, the operation of the mine defied every principle of safe mining.

The explosion at Westray provides a cautionary tale for human resource managers—it illustrates what happens when management does not make safety a priority and does not promote a culture of safety.

Source: Government of Nova Scotia, "The Westray Story: A Predictable Path to Disaster." Found at: http://www.gov.ns.ca/lwd/pubs/westray (Accessed Feb. 7, 2007).

OH&S Today 1.4

Young Workers at Risk

On November 18, 1994, Sean Kells, a husky young football player, was at work—it was his third day on the job. He was pouring a chemical from a large unmarked vat into a smaller container. A spark triggered by static electricity set off an explosion in which Sean suffered burns to 95% of his body, resulting in his death.

The Industrial Accident Prevention Association (IAPA) reports that workers between 15 and 24 accounted for 2,593 lost-time injuries in Ontario in 2007. This translated into more than 43,000 lost days and costs over $5 million.

Young people are at particular risk in the workplace for several reasons. First, a lack of experience and training means they may not recognize hazards in the workplace. Second, they may not be aware of their right to a safe working environment and their right to refuse unsafe work; they may not want to "rock the boat." Finally, as part-time or short-term employees, they may not be offered the same level of safety training as full-time employees.

Increasing recognition of the hazards faced by young people in the workplace has resulted in efforts to make sure they know their rights and responsibilities. Programs such as the Young Worker Awareness Program are designed to integrate this training in high-school curricula.

Sources: Safe Communities Foundation, "The Story of Sean Kells." Found at: http://www.safecommunities.ca/seankells.php (Accessed May 25, 2010); IAPA, "Lost Time Injury Illness Analysis for Young Workers Age 15–24, 2007." Found at: http://www.iapa.ca/main/documents/2005_IA_young_workers.pdf (Accessed May 25, 2010).

One way to overcome the barriers to the implementation of OH&S programs is to form alliances among the stakeholders. The three parties—employers, employees, and unions—have the same goal: the reduction of injuries and illnesses. It is a win–win situation in bargaining. The employer, by investing in health and safety programs, gains economically through a reduction in direct and indirect costs; it also gains through an improved public image that may strengthen employee loyalty and increase marketing opportunities. Employees gain through reduced risk of work-related injuries and illnesses. Unions gain through their ability to successfully champion the health and safety interests of their clients.

The federal and most provincial and territorial governments require every organization with 20 or more employees to establish a Joint Health and Safety Committee (i.e., one that includes employers *and* workers). Ontario has no requirement regarding the minimum number of employees if a designated substance—such as asbestos—is present. These committees respond to accidents; monitor the workplace; notify authorities about serious hazards, critical injuries, or deaths; hear complaints; and make recommendations.

HEALTH AND SAFETY PROFESSIONALS

One way to develop an effective OH&S program is to employ health and safety professionals. Doing so can produce returns equal to factors of two or more times the salaries paid. When the Oshawa Group employed safety professionals, its accident rate declined by 30% over five years.[14]

Managers and human resource experts cannot be expected to develop, manage, and evaluate an OH&S program, particularly when the issues cover the

OH&S Notebook 1.3

SAFETY PROFESSIONALS

Canadian registered safety professionals (CRSPs) are trained to (1) identify and appraise workplace hazards and evaluate the severity of an accident or loss, (2) develop and communicate hazard control policies, methods, and programs, (3) devise motivational programs to integrate safety procedures into operations, and (4) measure and evaluate the effectiveness of these programs and revise them as necessary. To achieve certification, safety professionals must meet specified academic, experience, and examination requirements.

Registered occupational hygienists (ROHs) are educated in a variety of fields (with degrees in chemistry, engineering, physics, biology, or medicine) and are trained to evaluate and control workplace hazards that may lead to sickness, impaired health, significant discomfort, and inefficiency.

Registered occupational hygienist technologists (ROHTs) perform similar functions as ROHs but typically have a college diploma rather than a university degree.

Physicians who enter the field of occupational medicine must do postgraduate work in such subjects as industrial toxicology, work physiology, industrial hygiene, respiratory diseases, and biostatistics.

Occupational health nurses are concerned with the prevention, recognition, and treatment of worker illness and injury and the application of nursing principles to individuals in the workplace.

spectrum from chemical hazards to workplace violence. To help managers operate an OH&S program, various types of safety and health experts may be hired or consulted. These people can be found through their associations, the Yellow Pages, or safety associations and provincial departments. Be advised, however, there are no legal requirements for the practice of occupational health and safety.

THE ROLE OF HUMAN RESOURCES

the three Es

a traditional approach to occupational health and safety that emphasized engineering, education, and enforcement

Traditional views of safety have emphasized **the three Es**. In the past, the goal was to develop *engineering* solutions to ensure safe work environments, equipment, and personal protective devices. To that end, health and safety professionals were tasked with *educating* supervisors and employers in the use of the equipment. Finally, health and safety programs focused on *enforcing* existing regulations and practices. To a great extent, these approaches have succeeded in creating safer workplaces. However, we now recognize that the three Es do not provide a total solution and that focusing on the people side of the workplace is likely to result in a safer workplace.

Not surprisingly, you will find that occupational health and safety is almost exclusively "managed" under the human resource function. There are several reasons why.

Safety Is a People Issue

Though great advances have been made through engineering solutions, it is increasingly apparent that effective safety programs depend on developing individual skills and abilities and on motivating individuals. These are the traditional concerns of human resource departments. Through orientation and other training programs, human resource professionals develop employee knowledge and skills. Through a variety of strategies including compensation and awareness programs, human resource professionals motivate safe working.

Perhaps most important, research has increasingly identified variables such as safety leadership[15] and safety climate[16,17] as predictors of safety outcomes (e.g., incidents, accidents, injuries). These issues are discussed in Chapter 10. Traditional areas of human resource practice such as job design have also been linked to safety outcomes.[18] More broadly, management programs such as the implementation of high-performance work systems[19] or lean manufacturing[20] have implications for occupational safety. Finally, safety concerns have direct implications for outcomes such as stress and turnover,[21] traditional areas of HR concern.

These research findings suggest that human resource decisions may affect safety even if safety was not considered at the time of the decision. For example, research on job insecurity suggests that when individuals fear losing their jobs they are more likely to "cut corners," ignore safety rules, and work unsafely. Thus, a rumour of corporate restructuring or plans for a layoff may have an impact on safety even though the two are not obviously connected.

Work scheduling (e.g., the number of hours worked) and work overload also have direct implications for safety. Individuals who are tired, under time pressure, or overworked may not be as attentive to safety issues. Again, the adoption of manufacturing systems such as lean manufacturing may result in individuals cutting corners or working unsafely in order to keep up with the pace of work. These observations suggest that human resources professionals need to monitor changes in the organization with an eye to their impact on occupational health and safety.

Safety Requires Legislative Compliance

As we have already seen, and will discuss in detail in Chapter 2, occupational health and safety is a very well developed area of labour law. Numerous standards and requirements are imposed on employers to maintain workplace safety. Administering compliance is a natural outgrowth of the human resource function. Human resource professionals already ensure compliance with other areas of labour law (e.g., employment equity, human rights legislation) and thus are well versed in dealing with such concerns.

Safety Decreases Costs

Workers' Compensation premiums, long-term disability coverage, sick-time provisions, and health plans all add to the costs of doing business. It is the responsibility of human resources to see that such costs are minimized. This duty has assumed increasing importance in an era in which double-digit increases in benefit premiums are not uncommon. Aside from minimizing costs, human resources has a role to play in ensuring that the benefits an organization pays for are used most effectively to help injured workers and ensure a prompt return to health (and to work).

Safety Relates to Other Human Resource Functions

Safety is linked to other human resource functions and must be considered in all areas of human resource management. Indeed, occupational health and safety is one of the outcomes of adopting a particular strategic orientation to health and safety.[22]

OH&S Today 1.5

The Healthy Workplace Movement

Occupational health and safety is increasingly seen in a broader context of establishing a healthy workplace. For example, in Canada the National Quality Institute describes a healthy workplace as comprising three elements: (a) health and safety, (b) health promotion, and (c) the psychosocial environment. Similarly, the World Health Organization defines a healthy workplace in terms of four elements: (a) health and safety, (b) the psychosocial environment, (c) personal health resources, and (d) enterprise community involvement.

The healthy workplace movement recognizes that workplaces have wide-reaching effects on worker health. Moreover, the healthy workplace movement is based on the belief that organizations must go beyond simply not harming individuals, to the active promotion of workers' health and well-being. While this sounds like a laudable and idealistic goal, the available data increasingly suggest that there is a very real "business case" for this belief. Organizations that implement healthy workplace programs can derive substantial economic benefits from their investment.

Source: J. Burton, *WHO Healthy Workplace Framework and Model: Background and Supporting Literature and Practice*, (Geneva: WHO, 2010). Found at: http://www.who.int/occupational_health/healthy_workplace_framework.pdf.

Safety programming in organizations often hinges on training initiatives, a traditional human resource function. Training, which is one of the most popular—and arguably one of the most effective—health and safety initiatives available,[23] is discussed in detail in Chapter 9. Research has established links between job insecurity and safety,[24] such that individuals who experience job insecurity are more likely to commit safety violations. Performance-based pay systems have been associated with increased injury rates; the implementation of teams in organizations

OH&S Notebook 1.4

DOES COST MOTIVATE?

Reduction in cost is generally seen as a powerful motivator among organizational decision makers. When an organization increases revenue (e.g., sales) by $1.00, their actual profit may be substantially smaller (e.g., $.05 to $.20). In this regard, every dollar in cost reduction goes straight to the bottom line—that is, every dollar saved is another dollar in profit (assuming that the cost savings do not require additional investment). Thus, there seem to be powerful economic reasons for businesses to improve occupational health and safety—by reducing the costs associated with injuries and incidents, they increase profitability.

Despite the logic of this argument, there is an increasing concern that organizations may see health and safety related costs as "fixed" or uncontrollable. In this view, organizations simply accept the increased costs of injuries and incidents; they incorporate them into their price structures (e.g., they pass the costs along to consumers) and do not attempt to improve safety to reduce costs. Moreover, companies may attempt to reduce costs in other areas in order to compensate for rising costs related to health and safety.

There is no clear resolution to this issue. The way an organization responds to increased costs may depend on the particulars of its situation. The point here is that the premise that all companies will concern themselves about health and safety in order to reduce costs is not necessarily always accurate.

may be associated with reduced injuries.[25] Clearly, the way we manage human resources has direct implications for occupational health and safety.

These links are illustrated at the end of each chapter in this text with the presentation of the required professional competencies (RPC's), the required professional competencies for certification as a human resources practitioner. Occupational health and safety is one of the eight major content areas defining the practice of human resource management. Throughout this text we highlight information that is closely tied to the professional standards for certification in human resources.

SUMMARY

This chapter has established the importance of occupational health and safety. We began by defining terms such as occupational health and safety, occupational injury, and occupational illness and by pointing out the unacceptably high rates of workplace injuries and fatalities. Second, we described the financial and social costs associated with occupational injuries and illnesses, showing that direct *and* indirect costs can be substantial. Third, we traced the development of modern models of health and safety management and described the role of the major stakeholders in modern occupational health and safety. We emphasized the role of the internal responsibility system and the notion that all parties have a stake in improving occupational health and safety. We ended the chapter by explaining the connection between human resource management and occupational health and safety and describing the links between human resource practices and health and safety. The management of occupational health and safety is a core area of practice for human resources practitioners.

Key Terms

accident proneness 8
assumption of risk 7
brown lung 7
due diligence 10
internal responsibility system (IRS) 13

lost-time injury 4
occupational health and safety (OH&S) 5
occupational illness 5
occupational injury 5
the three Es 16

Weblinks

Business News Network, "Health and Safety News"
http://www.esourcecanada.com/bnn/healthandsafety.asp

Canadian Centre for Occupational Health and Safety
http://www.ccohs.ca

Civilization.ca, "Beginnings: Craft Unions"
http://www.civilization.ca/cmc/exhibitions/hist/labour/labh08e.shtml

Parachute
http://www.parachutecanada.org/corporate

Workers' Health & Safety Centre, Ontario
http://www.whsc.on.ca

Workplace Safety and Insurance Board of Ontario, "New Experimental Experience Rating Program (NEER) Program Overview"
http://www.wsib.on.ca/en/community/WSIB/ArticleDetail?vgnextoid=ef00e35c8 19d7210VgnVCM100000449c710aRCRD

WorkSafeBC, "Safety Calculator"
http://www.healthandsafetycentre.org/sc/calculator/default.htm

Required Professional Capabilities (RPCs)

The following RPCs, listed by their CCHRA number, are relevant to the material covered in this chapter. All RPCs can be found at http://www.chrp.ca/rpc/body-of-knowledge.

RPC:170 Develops, implements, and ensures the application of policies, regulations, and standards relating to occupational health and safety.

RPC:171 Ensures compliance with legislated reporting requirements.

RPC:172 Ensures due diligence and liability requirements are met.*

RPC:173 Ensures that policies for required medical testing fall within the limits of statute & contract.

RPC:174 Develops and implements policies on the workplace environment.

RPC:175 Ensures adequate accommodation, modified work and graduated return to work programs are in place.

RPC:176 Ensures that modifications to the work environment are consistent with worker limitations.

RPC:177 Develops or provides for wellness and employee assistance programs to support organizational effectiveness.

RPC:178 Provides information to employees and managers on available programs.

RPC:179 Ensures that mechanisms are in place for responding to crises in the workplace, including critical incident stress management.

RPC:180 Establishes a joint Health & Safety Committee as required by law.*

RPC:181 Responds to any refusals to perform work believed to be unsafe.

RPC:182 Responds to serious injury or fatality in the workplace.

RPC:183 Analyzes risks to employee health & safety and develops preventive programs.

RPC:184 Establishes an investigation process for incidents and accidents in the workplace.

RPC:185 Ensures that security programs and policies minimize risks while considering the obligation of the employer and the rights of employees, union, and third parties.*

RPC:186 Establishes and implements strategies to minimize workers' compensation costs.

RPC:187 Prepares Organizational Health & Safety files for investigation and/or for litigation.

---

*Canadian Council of Human Resources Associations, Human Resources Professionals in Canada: Revised Body of Knowledge and Required Professional Capabilities (RPCs ®), 2007.

Discussion Questions

1. Why have people historically been more concerned about work-related injuries than work-related illnesses?
2. How has our understanding of personal liability for accidents changed over the years?
3. For what reasons, beside humanitarian ones, should workplace hazards be controlled?
4. Who are the stakeholders in health and safety? What roles do they play?

Using the Internet

1. How do organizations treat occupational health and safety? Find the websites for some major corporations in your area. Search them for information on health and safety. Who in the organization administers health and safety programs? What kinds of programs are in place?

Exercises

1. For one week, read the local newspapers and listen to the news. Make a note of the main topic of every article or item relating to occupational health and safety. What roles are the media playing? What OH&S issues are most likely to gain attention? Give reasons for your answers.
2. Interview a human resources manager about occupational health and safety. What is HR's role in the effective management of health and safety at work? What HR functions are involved in meeting the health and safety requirements?

Case 1 PRODUCTION OR SAFETY?

Atlantic Radiators Inc. manufactures automotive radiators. Demand for its products has resulted in an empty warehouse, and there is an urgent need to increase production to satisfy current customers. John Roberts is an employee of Atlantic Radiators. His job is to spray each radiator core with a dilute solution of hydrochloric acid and to bake the radiators in an oven. The acid acts as a flux on the solder-coated tubes. The baking process solders the radiator together.

John's supervisor has spoken to him several times about the need to speed up and not be the bottleneck in the production process. As a result, John has been taking some shortcuts, including neglecting to wear the proper eye protection. Today, he splashed some of the acid mixture in his eye and will now be off work for several days. As plant manager, you are responsible for reviewing this incident. Who is at fault here? What can be done to ensure that similar incidents will not occur in the future?

Case 2 DO WE NEED HEALTH AND SAFETY?

As the newly appointed manager of Global Insurance Company, Anuradha Das was trying to learn as much as possible about her new workplace. She was surprised to note the absence of the traditional health and safety bulletin board, and she asked her manager how health and safety information was being communicated to employees. "Are you kidding?" he replied. "This is an office. Our employees are mostly data-entry clerks. We don't have machines or equipment—what do we need with health and safety programs?" If you were Anuradha, how would you reply?

NOTES

1. A. Sharpe and J. Hardte, *Five Deaths a Day: Workplace Fatalities in Canada 1993 2005*, CSLS Research Report 2006–04 (Ottawa: Centre for the Study of Living Standards, 2006).
2. H.W. Janson, *History of Art*, 2nd ed. (Englewood Cliffs: Prentice Hall, 1985).
3. T. Moro, "Ontario Hiring 200 Workplace Inspectors," London Free Press, July 9, 2004.
4. J. Barling, E.K. Kelloway, and A. Zacharatos, "Occupational Health and Safety," in P.B. Warr, ed., *Psychology and Work*, 6th ed. (London: Penguin, 2002).
5. Moro, "Ontario Hiring 200 Workplace Inspectors."
6. Barling, Kelloway, and Zacharatos, "Occupational Health and Safety."
7. P. Strahlendorf, *Occupational Health and Safety Law Study Guide* (Toronto: Ryerson Polytechnic University Press, 2000).
8. T. Cree and E.K. Kelloway (1997), "Responses to Occupational Hazards: Exit and Participation," *Journal of Occupational Health Psychology* 2 (1997): 304–11.
9. Statistics Canada, *Work Injuries, 1991–1993* (Ottawa: Ministry of Supply and Services, 1994).
10. P.K. Abeytunga and H.R. Hale, "Supervisor's Perception of Hazards on Construction Sites," paper presented at the 20th Congress of the International Association of Applied Psychology, Edinburgh, July 1982.
11. E.K. Kelloway, "Labor Unions and Safety," in J. Barling and M. Frone, eds., *Psychology of Occupational Safety* (Washington: APA, 2003).
12. Barling, Kelloway, and Zacharatos, "Occupational Health and Safety."
13. Kelloway, "Labor Unions and Safety."
14. S. Boyes, "Doubles Strategy: When Human Resources and Occupational Health and Safety Work in Synchrony, Everybody Wins," *Human Resources Professional* 10, no. 7 (July–August 1993): 17–19.
15. J. Barling, C. Loughlin, and E.K. Kelloway, "Development and Test of a Model Linking Safety-Specific Transformational Leadership and Occupational Safety," *Journal of Applied Psychology* 87 (2002): 488–96.
16. D. Zohar, "A Group-Level Model of Safety Climate: Testing the Effect of Group Climate on Microaccidents in Manufacturing Jobs," *Journal of Applied Psychology* 85 (2000): 587–96.
17. Idem, "The Effects of Leadership Dimensions, Safety Climate, and Assigned Priorities on Minor Injuries in Work Groups," *Journal of Organizational Behavior* 23 (2002): 75–92.
18. J. Barling, E.K. Kelloway, and R. Iverson, "High-Quality Work, Job Satisfaction, and Occupational Injuries," *Journal of Applied Psychology* 88 (2003): 276–83.

19. A. Zacharatos, J. Barling, and R. Iverson, "High-Performance Work Systems and Occupational Safety," *Journal of Applied Psychology* 90 (2005): 77.

20. D. Mehri, "The Darker Side of Lean: An Insider's Perspective on the Realities of the Toyota Production System," *Academy of Management Perspectives* 20 (2006): 21.

21. J. Barling, E.K. Kelloway, and R. Iverson, "Accidental Outcomes: Attitudinal Consequences of Workplace Injuries," *Journal of Occupational Health Psychology* 8 (2003): 74–85.

22. J.D. Shaw and J.E. Delery, "Strategic HRM and Organizational Health Interventions," in D.A. Hoffman and L.E. Tetrick, eds., *Health and Safety in Organizations: A Multilevel Perspective* (San Francisco: Jossey-Bass, 2003).

23. M.J. Burke and S.A. Sarpy, "Improving Worker Safety and Health Through Interventions," in D.A. Hoffman and L.E. Tetrick, eds., *Health and Safety in Organizations: A Multilevel Perspective* (San Francisco: Jossey-Bass, 2003).

24. T. Probst, "Layoffs and Tradeoffs: Production, Quality, and Safety Demands Under the Threat of Job Loss," *Journal of Occupational Health Psychology* 7, no. 3 (2002): 211–20.

25. M. Kaminksi, "Unintended Consequences: Organizational Practices and Their Impact on Workplace Safety and Productivity," *Journal of Occupational Health Psychology* 6, no. 2 (2001): 127–38.

Legislative Framework

CHAPTER LEARNING OBJECTIVES

After reading this chapter, you should be able to:

- describe the regulatory framework surrounding occupational health and safety
- outline the duties of the major stakeholders under occupational health and safety legislation
- describe the structure and role of joint health and safety committees
- list and describe the three central elements of a WHMIS program
- describe the purpose and basic provisions of the transportation of dangerous goods acts

THE RIGHT TO KNOW

A "simple" workplace incident resulted in the imposition of 18 work orders for a blueberry farm in British Columbia. On April 19, 2012, 10 workers were spraying the blueberry fields with herbicide when the spray applicator tipped over and injured a worker. The injured worker was transported to the processing plant to receive first aid and subsequently an ambulance was called.

The work orders were issued for a variety of problems including the inability of the employer to show that workers had been trained, the employer's failure to conduct an immediate investigation into the incident, the employer's failure to report the incident as required, the failure to have up-to-date first aid procedures, and the failure to issue and train workers in the use of proper respiratory protection. Consideration of these issues shows the wide range of duties imposed by occupational health and safety legislation.

Source: Jean Lian, "Blueberry farm neglected to report worker injury," *OHS Canada*, Sept. 4, 2012. Found at: http://www.ohscanada.com/news/blueberry-farm-neglected-to-report-worker-injury/1001666221/.

Occupational health and safety is regulated under a variety of mechanisms, including acts, regulations, guidelines, standards, and codes. Moreover, each province and territory publishes its own regulations, which augment the federal ones (see **OH&S Notebook 2.1** for a complete list of regulations). Though this may seem confusing, the vast majority of workers and workplaces are regulated by provincial or territorial legislation. Thus employers and employees who operate in one area typically must be familiar with, and comply with, only one set of safety standards. This section provides an overview of the regulatory framework for occupational health and safety.

An **act** is a federal, provincial, or territorial law that constitutes the basic regulatory mechanism for occupational health and safety. Each jurisdiction publishes an act that sets out the basic intent and the general rights and duties of individuals affected by the law. **Regulations** explain how the general intent of the act will be applied in specific circumstances. Typically developed by Ministry of Labour officials, regulations have the same force of law as the act. **Guidelines and policies** are more specific rules but are not legally enforceable unless referred to in a regulation or act. Finally, **standards and codes** are design-related guides. Standards are established by the Canadian Standards Association (CSA), the American National Standards Institute (ANSI), the International Labour Organization (ILO), the International Organization for Standardization (ISO), the National Institute for Occupational Safety and Health (NIOSH), or the American Conference of Governmental Industrial Hygienists (ACGIH). OH&S regulations often refer to standards set by these last two agencies.

act
a federal, provincial, or territorial law that constitutes the basic regulatory mechanism for occupational health and safety

regulations
explain how the general intent of the act will be applied in specific circumstances

guidelines and policies
more specific rules that are not legally enforceable unless referred to in a regulation or act

standards and codes
design-related guides established by agencies such as the CSA or the ANSI

THE SCOPE OF OH&S LEGISLATION

The scope of the OH&S legislation differs from jurisdiction to jurisdiction. The statutes and regulations that have been enacted to protect the rights of workers have also established duties, which require compliance. The statutes provide the legal foundation, while the regulations enacted under the statute establish the

OH&S Notebook 2.1

OCCUPATIONAL HEALTH AND SAFETY LEGISLATION IN CANADA

Jurisdiction	Legislation Enforcement
Canada	Canada Labour Code, Regulations, Labour Canada
Alberta	Occupational Health and Safety Act, Department of Labour
British Columbia	Regulations under Workers' Compensation Board Compensation Act
Manitoba	Workplace Safety and Health Act, Department of Environment and Workplace Health and Safety
New Brunswick	Occupational Health and Safety Act, Occupational Health and Safety Commission
Newfoundland and Labrador	Occupational Health and Safety Act, Department of Labour
Northwest Territories and Nunavut	Northwest Safety Act, Commissioner of the Northwest Territories/Nunavut
Nova Scotia	Occupational Health and Safety Act, Department of Labour
Ontario	Occupational Health and Safety Act, Ministry of Labour
Prince Edward Island	Occupational Health and Safety Act, Department of Fisheries and Labour
Quebec	Act Respecting Occupational Health and Safety, Commission de la santé et de la sécurité du travail
Saskatchewan	Occupational Health and Safety Act, Department of Labour
Yukon	Occupational Health and Safety Act, Commissioner of Yukon, administered by the Workers' Compensation Board

framework within which the employer will conduct business in order to comply with the law. All Canadian OH&S legislation includes the following elements:

- an act
- powers of enforcement
- the right of workers to refuse to do unsafe work
- protection of workers from reprisals
- duties and responsibilities assigned to employers and others

Other elements, which vary among jurisdictions, include mandatory establishment of joint labour/management health and safety committees, health and safety policies, accident-prevention programs, and advisory councils on occupational health and safety.

Those responsible for managing health and safety and Workers' Compensation should be familiar with the administrative structure as it relates to enforcement, education, and compensation in their particular jurisdiction. Multinational and transportation companies may fall under two or more jurisdictions, which increases the administrative complexities.

The general duty provision requiring employers to take every reasonable precaution to ensure employee safety is Canada-wide. In the federal jurisdiction, the duty is sufficiently broad in scope that an employer could be held liable for failing to ensure the health and safety of an employee even if there was an absence of a specific violation to a regulatory provision. The term "ensure" is applied across Canada and is accepted to mean the strongest responsibility possible short of a guarantee.

OH&S Notebook 2.2

NEW STANDARDS FOR SAFETY

In 2006 the Canadian Standards Association published CSA Z1000-06: Occupational Health and Safety Management. This standard is based on wide consultation and has been described as "Canada's first consensus-based approach to occupational heath and safety." The purpose of the standard is to provide organizations with a model for implementing a health and safety program. While standards do not have the force of legislation, they do provide organizations with "best practices," and may provide the basis for a due diligence defence in the case of legal action. The Canadian Standards Association issues a wide variety of such standards dealing with issues ranging from workplace electrical safety (CSA Z462) to dealing with mental health issues in the workplace (CAN/CSA Z1003-13).

Sources: CCOHS, "Canada's first consensus-based occupational health and safety management standard." Found at: http://www.ccohs.ca/headlines/text190.html (Accessed Feb. 7, 2007); CCOHS "CSA announces new standard to help prevent Canadian workplace injuries and fatalities." Found at: http://www.ccohs.ca/ headlines/text190.html (Accessed Feb. 7, 2007).

OH&S Notebook 2.3

CANADIAN GOVERNMENT DEPARTMENTS RESPONSIBLE FOR OH&S

Below are the websites for agencies across Canada that are responsible for occupational health and safety in federal, provincial, and territorial jurisdictions.

Federal	http://www.hrsdc.gc.ca/en/home.shtml
Alberta	http://www.gov.ab.ca/hre/whs
British Columbia	http://www.worksafebc.com
Manitoba	http://www.gov.mb.ca/labour/safety
New Brunswick	http://www.whscc.nb.ca
Newfoundland and Labrador	http://www.gov.nl.ca/gs/ohs
Northwest Territories and Nunavut	http://www.gov.nt.ca
Nova Scotia	http://www.gov.ns.ca/enla/ohs
Ontario	http://www.labour.gov.on.ca/english/hs
Prince Edward Island	http://www.wcb.pe.ca
Quebec	http://www.csst.qc.ca
Saskatchewan	http://www.labour.gov.sk.ca
Yukon	http://www.wcb.yk.ca

It is important to note that labour legislation and standards relating to occupational health and safety are not static. Rather, they are continually being updated. Changes may be limited and specific, such as the enactment of a regulation dealing with workplace violence in Nova Scotia in 2005. Or the changes can be more general, amounting to a complete overhaul of relevant legislation. For example, Yukon published new and substantially updated OH&S legislation in 2006. Based on an extensive review, Ontario enacted new Occupational Health and Safety Standards in 2012 that contain substantially enhanced duties of employees and employers around issues of health and safety. Human resource practitioners and safety professionals need to maintain current awareness of standards, regulations, and legislation.

DUTIES AND RESPONSIBILITIES OF THE MAJOR STAKEHOLDERS

As mentioned in Chapter 1, occupational health and safety legislation in Canada is largely based on the notion of an internal responsibility system in which the major stakeholders in health and safety are assigned specific responsibilities. These stakeholders include employers, owners, contractors, supervisors, and workers. Some provinces and territories also impose duties on joint health and safety committees or representatives, but most jurisdictions are silent on this subject. The human resource practitioner should be well versed in labour laws and OH&S laws in order to make informed decisions about the corporation's health and safety program. The OH&S components attached to the various jurisdictions are listed in **OH&S Notebook 2.4.**

Duties of Employers, Owners, and Contractors

Employers have a primary duty to provide a safe work environment. Other duties include providing supervision, education, training, and written instructions where applicable, as well as assisting the Joint Health and Safety Committee or representative and complying with statutes and regulations. In Ontario the employer's responsibilities are extensive and include the following:

- ensuring that equipment is provided and properly maintained
- appointing a competent supervisor
- providing information (including confidential information) in a medical emergency
- informing supervisors and workers of possible hazards
- posting the OH&S Act in the workplace
- preparing and maintaining a health and safety policy and reviewing it annually (see **OH&S Today 2.1**)

All federal and provincial or territorial OH&S acts include **prescribed** duties that may come into effect by regulation at some time. These prescribed duties may include an employer's responsibility to establish occupational health services, or a description of the written procedures that may be required.

prescribed
under Ontario OH&S legislation, something to be undertaken because of legal or employer requirement, such as a rule or direction

OH&S Notebook 2.4

JURISDICTIONS AND OH&S COMPONENTS

Jurisdictions	Committees	Duties	Advisory Councils	Safety Policies	Accident-Prevention Programs
Canada	✓	✓		✓	✓
Alberta	Minister may order	✓	Report to minister, may hear appeals, other duties as assigned		✓
British Columbia	✓	✓		✓	✓
Manitoba	✓	✓	✓	✓	
New Brunswick	✓	✓		✓	
Newfoundland and Labrador	✓	✓		✓	
Northwest Territories/ Nunavut	✓	✓		✓	✓
Nova Scotia	✓	✓	✓	Director may order a code of practice	
Ontario	Minister may order	✓	Sector-based advisory councils/ associations		
	✓				
Prince Edward Island	Minister may order		✓	✓	✓
Quebec	Established by request of certified asso- ciation, or commission may order		✓	Sector-based advisory councils/ associations	Supply personal protective equipment free of charge
Saskatchewan	✓	✓	✓	✓	
Yukon	✓			✓	

constructor

in health and safety legislation, a person or company that oversees the construction of a project and that is ultimately responsible for the health and safety of all workers

Constructors/primary contractors have responsibilities similar to those outlined for employers. In some jurisdictions, when a construction project is scheduled to commence, a constructor/primary contractor has a duty to notify the authority within a specified time. Some jurisdictions require a written "Notice of Project" to be filed outlining the approximate cost, scope, commencement date, and duration of the project.

OH&S Today (2.1

Nelson Education Ltd.'s Safety Philosophy

Nelson Education's Health and Safety Committee is vitally interested in the health and safety of its employees. Protection from injury or occupational disease is a major continuing objective of Nelson, and we will make every effort to provide a safe, healthy working environment.

Nelson will meet and, where possible, exceed the letter and intent of all applicable legislation. Health and safety will be managed as a priority area in Nelson with adequate resources and employee involvement in the development of programs. Objectives and standards will be established for health and safety programs, and performance will be measured. Hazards in the workplace will be identified and eliminated or controlled. Where hazards cannot be eliminated, programs will be put into place to safeguard the health and safety of the employees. Information necessary for the protection of our employees will be maintained and communicated to those affected.

Every employee must recognize and accept their own responsibility to work safely, maintain a safe workplace, and to report any and all unsafe conditions and practices immediately.

Duties of Supervisors

The duties assigned to supervisors are similar across Canada. "Supervisor" is broadly interpreted to refer to a person (with or without a title) who has charge of a workplace and authority over a worker. Supervisors can be union members, association members covered under a collective agreement, plant managers, general managers, lead hands, forepersons, school principals, or self-employed individuals. The criteria used in Ontario to determine whether a person would be held to be a supervisor include having the authority to promote or recommend promotion, to discipline workers, or to schedule or assign work. Besides these criteria, in Ontario a competent supervisor is familiar with the OH&S Act and regulations and has knowledge of potential hazards, and so on, in the workplace (OH&S Act, ss. 1(1), 25(2)(c)). A supervisor's duties include the following:

- ensuring that workers comply with the OH&S Act and regulations
- ensuring that workers use or wear safety equipment, devices, or clothing
- advising workers of possible hazards
- providing written instructions if applicable
- taking every reasonable precaution to ensure the protection of workers

Duties of Workers

Duties of workers are included in the majority of statutes. In some jurisdictions the responsibilities are laid out by regulation. The inclusion of workers' responsibilities and duties is relatively new in health and safety legislation. Before the late 1970s, all responsibility for workplace health and safety rested with the employer. Now, though the employer is totally responsible for paying for health and safety activities, everyone is responsible for making them work.

A worker's duties include the following:

- complying with the OH&S Act and regulations
- properly using the safety equipment and clothes provided
- reporting hazards, such as defective equipment, to the supervisor
- reporting any contraventions of the act or regulations

Workers are prohibited from making any safety device ineffective, using any hazardous equipment or machine in unsafe conditions, or engaging in rough or boisterous conduct.

JOINT HEALTH AND SAFETY COMMITTEES

Joint health and safety committees in the workplace are required by law in nine jurisdictions; the minister responsible has the discretionary power to require the formation of committees in the remaining four jurisdictions (see **OH&S Notebook 2.4**).

The primary function of the joint health and safety committee is to provide a nonadversarial atmosphere in which labour and management can work together to create a safer and healthier workplace. Joint committees are structured in such a way that equal or better representation is required from workers who do not exercise managerial responsibilities. Each workplace requiring a committee must train and certify at least one management member and one worker member. Subjects taught during the training (which may run from one to three weeks) include law, general safety, hygiene, routes of entry (into the body), indoor air quality, chemical safety, certified workers' rights and duties, and joint committees. Certified members may be involved in inspections, work refusals, and bilateral work stoppages when there is an imminent hazard to a worker. They may also investigate critical accidents, attend at the beginning of hygiene testing, and respond to worker concerns (see **OH&S Notebook 2.5**).

The existence of joint health and safety committees grows out of the idea of an internal responsibility system (IRS)—the suggestion that work and safety are inexorably linked and that all parties in the workplace have a responsibility to improve health and safety.[1] A review of the literature generally supports the effectiveness of joint committees in managing health and safety.[2] In particular, the existence of joint health and safety committees leads to a reduction in the number of workplace injuries.[3] As Weil points out, the existence of a Joint Health and Safety Committee does not mean that the committee is effective.[4]

Indeed, like any other workplace group, committees may take some time before they become effective. Joint committees can improve health and safety through prevention, education, and training and by providing an ongoing forum for problem resolution.[5]

WORK REFUSALS

The right to refuse unsafe work without fear of reprisal is now available to workers in every jurisdiction in Canada. Exceptions or limitations to the right to refuse unsafe work vary across the country. In essence, a worker does

OH&S Notebook 2.5

LEGISLATIVE REQUIREMENTS FOR JOINT HEALTH AND SAFETY COMMITTEES

Committees are mandatory in

Federal	workplaces with 20 or more employees
Alberta	workplaces that are required to establish a committee by the ministry
British Columbia	workplaces with 20 or more employees
Manitoba	workplaces with 20 or more employees
New Brunswick	workplaces with 20 or more employees
Newfoundland and Labrador	workplaces with 10 or more employees
Northwest Territories and Nunavut	workplaces as determined by the chief safety officer
Nova Scotia	workplaces with 20 or more employees
Ontario	workplaces with 20 or more employees
Prince Edward Island	workplaces with 20 or more employees
Quebec	workplaces where the union (or 10% of the workforce) requests that the employer establish a committee
Saskatchewan	workplaces with 10 or more employees
Yukon	workplaces with 20 or more employees

OH&S Notebook 2.6

JOINT HEALTH AND SAFETY COMMITTEES AT A GLANCE

Joint health and safety committees are made up of representatives from both management and unions or workers. They are charged with the responsibility of enhancing health and safety in the workplace.

Most health and safety legislation mandates the establishment of joint committees. For example, in Ontario the legislation requires a committee in workplaces with more than 20 employees, unless designated substances (such as asbestos) are present. The size of the committee varies with the number of employees, but the intent is to represent all areas of the workplace. The committee has four principal functions:

- identify potential hazards
- evaluate these potential hazards
- recommend corrective action
- follow up implemented recommendations

To meet these responsibilities, the committee is required to meet regularly (at least every three months) and to regularly inspect the workplace. At least two members of the committee (one management and one labour) receive specialized training that meets standards established by the Workplace Safety and Insurance Board (in Ontario); these members play more specialized roles as certified health and safety committee members.

Source: Ontario Ministry of Labour, "A Guide for Joint Health and Safety Committees (JHSCs) and Representatives in the Workplace." Found at: http://www.labour.gov.on.ca/english/hs/pubs/jhsc/index.php (Accessed Feb. 7, 2007).

not have the right to refuse unsafe work if such work is a normal condition of employment, or if the worker, by his or her refusal, places another life in jeopardy.

In Ontario, police, firefighters, teachers, and health care workers are among those professionals who have been granted what is known as a limited right of refusal. For example, a firefighter has the right to refuse to use unsafe equipment during an exercise. A nurse has the right to refuse to use equipment suspected to be defective until his or her concern has been investigated and resolved; however, a nurse does not have the right to refuse unsafe work if the lives of patients are placed in jeopardy as a result of the refusal. The Ontario Provincial Police had their old revolvers replaced by modern pistols after a refusal based on the defectiveness of the old units; other police services followed.

The procedure for reporting a refusal to perform unsafe work is, for the most part, consistent across jurisdictions. Once the worker has apprised the supervisor of the suspected work hazard, an investigation is conducted by the supervisor and a worker representative (union, JHSC member, or coworker).

The investigation results in either a return to work or a continued refusal. In the latter situation, a ministry inspector/officer conducts an investigation and provides a written decision. In the meantime, a replacement worker may not be assigned the work that has been refused unless he or she has been informed about the circumstances surrounding the refusal. The refusing worker who continues to receive the regular remuneration for the job may be assigned alternative work but not sent home.

In New Brunswick and Prince Edward Island, the supervisor and JHSC can make a judgment that the refusal is not based on reasonable grounds. The employee may then refer the matter to an OH&S officer, who will make the final determination. As "reasonable grounds" is not defined, it appears to leave the door open for a subjective rather than an objective decision.

STOP-WORK PROVISIONS (ONTARIO)

In 1990 an Act to Amend the Ontario Occupational Health and Safety Act was given Royal Assent. The amendments are far reaching and promise profound changes in how employers will do business in Ontario. Among the most significant provisions are expanded powers for certified members of the JHSC.

The provisions for stopping work take two forms, one bilateral and the other unilateral. A certified member of a JHSC may, in the course of an inspection or investigation, have reason to believe that a dangerous circumstance exists. The certified member will ask a supervisor (and possibly a second certified member of the JHSC) to investigate. Following the investigation and possible remedial actions taken by the supervisor, if the certified members, representing both management and labour, find that the dangerous circumstance still exists, they may direct the employer to stop work. The legislation defines "dangerous circumstance" as follows:

- a provision of the act or the regulation is being contravened
- the contravention presents a danger or a hazard to a worker
- the danger or hazard is such that any delay in controlling it may seriously endanger a worker

OH&S Today 2.2

The Right to Refuse Unsafe Work

Although the right to refuse unsafe work is well-enshrined in occupational health and safety legislation, enactment of that right can be problematic. On August 13, 2012, correctional workers at a jail in Hamilton, Ontario, were tasked with conducting a search of the cells for a missing piece of metal. Fearing that inmates could have made a knife out of the metal, workers refused to conduct the search unless they were allowed to wear protective vests while searching. The employer initially refused—arguing that wearing the vests would likely intimidate inmates. A Ministry of Labour investigation also concluded that there was no enhanced risk and vests were not needed. Nonetheless, management eventually allowed the guards to don vests to conduct the search.

Although the initial issue was resolved, there remains a dispute about whether or not management can discipline the workers for refusing the work. The union argues that this is a safety issue and the refusal was warranted under the Occupational Health and Safety Act. However, the employer argues that there was no safety issue and, thus, the refusal was unwarranted.

Source: Sabrina Nanji, "Jail guards locked out after bulletproof vest brouhaha," *OHS Canada*, Sept. 10, 2012. Found at: http://www.ohscanada.com/news/jail-guards-locked-out-after-bulletproof-vest-brouhaha/1001682264/.

The unilateral provision will apply in the case of an employer who has, in the opinion of a government-appointed adjudicator, taken insufficient steps to protect workers from serious risk to their health and safety. The action will be taken by a certified worker member. A second circumstance may allow the unilateral provision to apply. An employer may advise the JHSC in writing of a willingness to adopt the unilateral power of the certified worker member to stop work in dangerous circumstances; this advisory is required in Ontario.

WORKPLACE HAZARDOUS MATERIALS INFORMATION SYSTEM

The Workplace Hazardous Materials Information System (WHMIS) began in the United States in the early 1980s in the form of the Hazard Communication Standard. WHMIS reflects the belief that workers have the right to know about hazards that may be associated with certain chemicals used in the workplace, and, by extension, the community. In Ontario this right to know extends to citizens.

WHMIS is the brainchild of industry, labour, and government representatives committed to developing regulations that meet the right-to-know standard. In Canada, all jurisdictions were involved in creating the first Canada-wide health and safety legislation. To ensure the desired consistency in regulations, the federal government created a model OH&S regulation, which was then used by the provincial and territorial governments. The Hazardous Products Act defines a hazardous product and controls its use by requiring disclosure of the substance and its concentration in a manufactured product. Other federal statutes and regulations governing controlled products include the Controlled Products Regulations, the Ingredient Disclosure List, and the Hazardous Materials Review Act and related regulation.

The federal legislation, which was limited in application to federally regulated workplaces, required the provinces and territories to create enabling legislation to empower the jurisdictions. The WHMIS legislation came into force across Canada between 1988 and 1990. Workers now have a right to information about any potentially hazardous chemical in the work environment, including its handling, storage, use, and emergency instructions.

The WHMIS legislation is based on three elements:

- labels designed to alert the worker that the container contains a potentially hazardous product
- material safety data sheets (MSDSs) outlining a product's potentially hazardous ingredient(s) and procedures for safe handling of the product
- employee training

Ontario has added three further elements:

- hazardous materials inventory requirement
- physical agents (such as noise)
- the public's right to know

Labels

That controlled substances need labelling is the most widely understood element of the WHMIS program. There are two types of WHMIS labels: workplace labels and supplier labels. Workplace labels identify the WHMIS class of the material. There are six WHMIS classes (some of which have subclasses), as follows:

Class A—Compressed Gas
Class B—Flammable and combustible material
    Division 1: Flammable gas
    Division 2: Flammable liquid
    Division 3: Combustible liquid
    Division 4: Flammable solid
    Division 5: Flammable aerosol
    Division 6: Reactive flammable material
Class C—Oxidizing material
Class D—Poisonous and infectious material
    Division 1: Materials causing immediate and serious toxic effects
        Subdivision A: Very toxic material
        Subdivision B: Toxic material
    Division 2: Materials causing other toxic effects
        Subdivision A: Very toxic material
        Subdivision B: Toxic material
    Division 3: Biohazardous infection material
Class E—Corrosive material
Class F—Dangerously reactive material
(See Figure 2.1 for WHMIS class symbols and subclass designations.)

The supplier label, the more comprehensive of the two, must be attached to the container when it is delivered to the workplace. (See Figure 2.2 for an example

FIGURE 2.1

WHMIS Class Symbols and Subclass Designations

What the symbol represents

 Class A— Compressed gas

 Class D, Division 2— Poisonous and infectional material: Other toxic effects

 Class B— Combustible and flammable material

 Class D, Division 3— Poisonous and infectional material: Biohazardous infectious material

 Class C—Oxidizing material

 Class E— Corrosive material

 Class D, Division 1— Poisonous and infectious material: Immediate and serious toxic effects

 Class F— Dangerously reactive material

Source: CCHOS, WHMIS - Classification. Found at: http://www.ccohs.ca/oshanswers/legisl/ whmis_classifi.html. Reproduced with the permission of the Minister of Public Works and Government Services Canada, 2013.

of a supplier label.) The supplier label must have a black-and-white border and must contain the following information (in both English and French):

- The product identifier (Controlled Products Regulations, s. 2(1)), including the brand name or code number. Information may include the chemical name, generic name, or trade name.

FIGURE (2.2)

Example of a Supplier Label

ISOPROPYL ALCOHOL

FLAMMABLE
HARMFUL IF INHALED
HARMFUL IF SWALLOWED
MAY CAUSE SKIN IRRITATION
MAY CAUSE EYE IRRITATION

First Aid: Obtain medical attention. Induce vomiting by sticking finger down throat. If breathing stopped, begin artificial respiration. If inhaled, remove victim to fresh air. For skin contact, wash with soap and water while removing contaminated clothing. For eye contact, flush with running water for at least 15 minutes, call physician.

Precautions: Wear chemical goggles. Wear resistant gloves. Do not take internally. Do not inhale vapour or mist. Use with enough ventilation to keep below TLV. Avoid skin or eye contact. Wash hands thoroughly after use. Keep container closed. Never use pressure to empty container. Do not reuse container for any purpose until commercially cleaned. Container must be grounded when emptied. Use explosion-proof equipment. Keep away from heat, sparks, and flame. No smoking. Do not keep near foodstuffs.

ALCOOL D'ISOPROPYLE

INFLAMMABLE
NOCIF SI INHALÉ
NOCIF SI AVALÉ
RISQUE D'IRRITATION CUTANÉE
RISQUE D'IRRITER LES YEUX

Premiers soins: Obtenir des soins médicaux. Faire vomir en enfonçant le doigt dans la gorge. En cas d'arrêt respiratoire, pratiquer la respiration artificielle. En cas d'inhalation, transporter la victime à l'air frais. En cas de contact avec la peau, laver au savon et `à l'eau tout en retirant les vêtements souillés. En cas de contact avec les yeux, laver à l'eau courante pendant au moins 15 minutes. Appeler un médecin.

Mise en garde: Porter des lunettes antiproduits chimiques. Porter des gants résistants. Pour usage externe. Ne pas inhaler les vapeurs et les bruines. Utiliser avec assez de ventilation pour ne pas dépasser la QLP. Éviter tout contact avec la peau ou les yeux. Bien se laver les mains après utilisation. Garder le contenant ferme. Ne jamais utiliser de la pression pour vider le contenant. Ne pas réutiliser le contenant pour n'importe quel usage avant de l'avoir nettoyé professionnellement. Effectuer la prise de terre du contenant avant de le vider. Utiliser un equipment à l'épreuve des explosions. Tenir à l'écart des étincelles, des flammes et de la chaleur. Interdit de fumer. Ne pas garder à proximité d'aliments.

SEE MATERIAL SAFETY DATA SHEET FOR PRODUCT/
VOIR FICHE SIGNALÉTIQUE

Company X
Brampton, Ontario

- The supplier identifier (Controlled Products Regulations, s. 2(1))—that is, the name of the manufacturer or supplier.

- A statement that the MSDS is to be referred to for more information.

- Hazard symbol(s) (Controlled Products Regulations, s. 11) that correspond to the class and division that allocates the product as a controlled substance.

- Risk phrases (Controlled Products Regulations, s. 2(1)) that correspond to the class and division to which the product is allocated.

- Precautionary measures to be followed when handling or using the controlled product.

- First aid measures to be taken in the event of exposure to a controlled product.

The requirement for workplace labels takes effect when the product is removed from its original container to be used or distributed. Workplace labels are also required for storage tanks or large in-house containers. The workplace label must contain a product identifier, instructions for safe handling, and the location of an MSDS. (See Figure 2.3 for an example of a workplace label.)

Material Safety Data Sheets

The objective of safety data information is to identify potentially harmful ingredients in products that the worker may be handling, to present factual information about the nature of the harmful ingredients, and to provide guidance in the use and disposal of the product.

FIGURE 2.3

Example of a Workplace Label

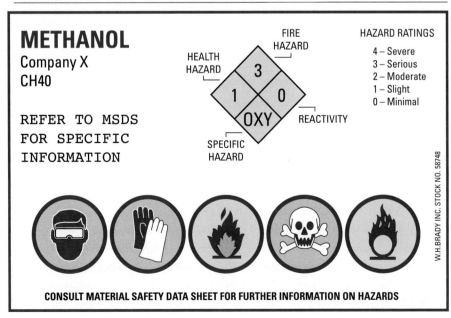

CONSULT MATERIAL SAFETY DATA SHEET FOR FURTHER INFORMATION ON HAZARDS

The MSDS must contain information as set out by the Hazardous Products Act, s. 11(1), and the Controlled Products Regulations, ss. 12 and 13. (See Figure 2.4 for an example.) The information must be comprehensive, up-to-date (revisions are required every three years), and made available in the two official languages. The following nine sections form the minimum standard:

1. Product information including the name, address, and phone number of the supplier or manufacturer and the product identifier and use.
2. A hazardous ingredients list, including all controlled substances in the product and their concentrations. The list generally includes the chemical abstract number (when available); the allowable concentration limits, known as threshold limit values (TLVs), set by the American Conference of Governmental Industrial Hygienists (ACGIH); the lethal dose range tested for a specific animal population; and routes of entry.
3. Physical data including information on appearance: odour, density, boiling point, corrosiveness, and so on.
4. Fire and explosion information, including data on the flammability of the hazardous ingredients.
5. Reactivity information outlining the conditions under which the material may react with other chemicals or materials. The section will also identify the hazardous products produced by decomposition in a fire situation.
6. Toxicological data, including all available information on the possible health effects from chronic or acute exposure.
7. Preventive measures to be used while dealing with the product, including information on personal protective equipment, ventilation requirements, storage, handling, and waste disposal.
8. First aid measures, providing specific recommendations for treatment for exposure to the material.
9. Preparation information, including the name of the person(s) who prepared the MSDS, a phone number for contact, and the date of issue of the MSDS.

The manufacturer or supplier must develop or cause to be developed an MSDS for each product supplied for use in the workplace. The MSDS must be transmitted to the purchaser on or before the date of sale or delivery of the product. The information on the MSDS must be current at the time of sale or delivery, and the MSDS must be dated no more than three years before the date of sale or delivery.

The requirement for supplying MSDSs is twofold. Suppliers are regulated by the federal legislation under the Controlled Products Act and provincial or territorial regulations, while employers are regulated only under provincial or territorial regulations. Should an employer also be a manufacturer or produce research products not intended for sale, the responsibility for creating an MSDS becomes the employer's.

Training

Education in WHMIS is commonly defined as the process of acquiring knowledge through systematic instruction. By contrast, training is defined as bringing a person to a desired state or standard of efficiency by instruction and practice. One area that often escapes scrutiny when the inspector/officer applies a performance-based regulation is the application of the education received. A worker

FIGURE (2.4)

Material Safety Data Sheet

Page 1

Safety Data Sheet

 **Dow AgroSciences**

Garlon™ RTU Herbicide
™Trademark of Dow AgroSciences LLC

1. PRODUCT AND COMPANY IDENTIFICATION:

PRODUCT: Garlon RTU Herbicide

COMPANY/SUPPLIER IDENTIFICATION:
Dow AgroSciences Canada Inc.
Suite 2100 450 - 1 ST SW
Calgary, Alberta
Canada, T2P 5H1
www.dowagro.ca
Effective date: November 28, 2012

2. HAZARDOUS IDENTIFICATIONS:

EMERGENCY OVERVIEW

Pale yellow liquid. May cause eye and skin irritation. Toxic to aquatic organisms and birds.

EMERGENCY PHONE NUMBER: 800-992-5994

3. COMPOSITION/INFORMATION ON INGREDIENTS:

COMPONENT	CAS NUMBER	W/W%
Triclopyr-butotyl	64700-56-7	23.2
Balance		76.8

4. FIRST AID:

EYE: Hold eyes open and rinse slowly and gently with water for 15-20 minutes. Remove contact lenses, if present, after the first 5 minutes, and then continue rinsing eyes. Call a poison control center or doctor for treatment advice.

SKIN: Take off contaminated clothing. Wash skin with soap and plenty of water for 15-20 minutes. Call a poison control center or doctor for treatment advice. Wash clothing before reuse. Shoes and other leather items which cannot be decontaminated should be disposed of properly.

INGESTION: Call a poison control center or doctor immediately for treatment advice. Have person sip a glass of water if able to swallow. Do not induce vomiting unless told to do so by the poison control center or doctor. Never give anything by mouth to an unconscious person.

INHALATION: Move person to fresh air. If person is not breathing, call an emergency responder or ambulance, and then give artificial respiration; if by mouth to mouth use rescuer protection (pocket mask etc). Call a poison control center or doctor for treatment advice.

NOTE TO PHYSICIAN: No specific antidote. Treatment of exposure should be directed at the control of symptoms and the clinical condition of the patient. Have the MSDS, and if available, the product container or label with you when calling a poison control center or doctor, or going for treatment.

5. FIRE FIGHTING MEASURES:

FLASH POINT: >200°F (>93.3°C)
METHOD USED: Not applicable

FLAMMABLE LIMITS
LFL: Not determined
UFL: Not determined

EXTINGUISHING MEDIA: Foam, CO_2, or Dry chemical

FIRE AND EXPLOSION HAZARDS: Foam fire extinguishing system is preferred because uncontrolled water can spread possible contamination. Toxic irritating gases may be formed under fire conditions.

FIRE-FIGHTING EQUIPMENT: Use positive-pressure, self-contained breathing apparatus and full protective equipment.

6. ACCIDENTAL RELEASE MEASURES:

ACTION TO TAKE FOR SPILLS: Absorb small spills with materials such as sand, sawdust, Zorball, or dirt. Wash exposed body areas thoroughly after handling. Report large spills to Dow AgroSciences at 800-992-5994.

7. HANDLING AND STORAGE:

PRECAUTIONS TO BE TAKEN IN HANDLING AND STORAGE: Keep out of reach of children. Do not swallow. Avoid contact with eyes, skin, and clothing. Avoid breathing vapors and spray mist. Handle concentrate in ventilated area. Wash thoroughly with soap and water after handling and before eating, chewing gum, using tobacco, using the toilet or smoking. Keep away from food, feedstuffs, and water supplies. Store in original container in a well-ventilated area.

FIGURE (2.4)

Material Safety Data Sheet (*continued*)

Safety Data Sheet

 Dow AgroSciences

Garlon™ RTU Herbicide
™Trademark of Dow AgroSciences LLC

8. EXPOSURE CONTROLS/PERSONAL PROTECTION:

These precautions are suggested for conditions where the potential for exposure exists. Emergency conditions may require additional precautions.

EXPOSURE GUIDELINES:
Triclopyr Acid: Dow AgroSciences Industrial Hygiene Guide is 2 mg/M3 as acid equivalent, Skin.

A "skin" notation following the exposure guideline refers to the potential for dermal absorption of the material including mucous membranes and the eyes either by contact with vapors or by direct skin contact. It is intended to alert the reader that inhalation may not be the only route of exposure and that measures to minimize dermal exposures should be considered.

ENGINEERING CONTROLS: Provide general and/or local exhaust ventilation to control airborne levels below the exposure guidelines.

RECOMMENDATIONS FOR MANUFACTURING, COMMERCIAL BLENDING, AND PACKAGING WORKERS:

EYE/FACE PROTECTION: Use chemical goggles.

SKIN PROTECTION: Use chemical protective clothing resistant to this material, when there is any possibility of skin contact. Use protective clothing chemically resistant to this material. Selection of specific items such as face shield, boots, apron, or full body suit will depend on the task. Wear a face-shield which allows use of chemical goggles, or wear a full-face respirator, to protect face and eyes when there is any likelihood of splashes. Safety shower should be located in immediate work area. Remove contaminated clothing immediately, wash skin area with soap and water, and launder clothing before reuse or dispose of properly. Items which cannot be decontaminated, such as shoes, belts and watchbands, should be removed and disposed of properly.
HAND PROTECTION: Use gloves chemically resistant to this material when prolonged or frequently repeated contact could occur. Examples of preferred glove barrier materials include: Butyl rubber, Polyethylene, Neoprene, Chlorinated polyethylene, Ethyl vinyl alcohol laminate ("EVAL"). Examples of acceptable glove barrier materials include: Viton, Natural rubber ("Latex"), Polyvinyl chloride ("PVC" or "vinyl"), Nitrile/butadiene rubber ("Nitrile" or "NBR"). NOTICE: the selection of a specific glove for a particular application and duration of use in a workplace should also take into account all relevant workplace factors such as, but not limited to: other chemicals which may be handled, physical requirements (cut/puncture protection, dexterity,

thermal protection), potential body reactions to glove materials, as well as the instructions/specifications provided by the glove supplier.

RESPIRATORY PROTECTION: Atmospheric levels should be maintained below the exposure guideline. When respiratory protection is required for certain operations, use an approved air-purifying or positive-pressure supplied-air respirator depending on the potential airborne concentration. For emergency and other conditions where the exposure guideline may be exceeded, use an approved positive-pressure self-contained breathing apparatus or positive-pressure air line with auxiliary self-contained air supply. The following should be effective types of air-purifying respirators: organic vapor cartridge with a particulate pre-filter.

APPLICATORS AND ALL OTHER HANDLERS: Refer to the product label for personal protective clothing and equipment.

9. PHYSICAL AND CHEMICAL PROPERTIES:

APPEARANCE: Pale yellow liquid
ODOR: None
DENSITY: 0.865 g/mL

10. STABILITY AND REACTIVITY:

STABILITY: (CONDITIONS TO AVOID) Combustible. Stable under normal storage conditions.

INCOMPATIBILITY: (SPECIFIC MATERIALS TO AVOID) Acids, bases and oxidizing materials.

HAZARDOUS DECOMPOSITION PRODUCTS: Nitrogen oxides, hydrogen chloride, and phosgene may result under fire conditions.

HAZARDOUS POLYMERIZATION: Not known to occur.

11. TOXICOLOGICAL INFORMATION:

EYE: May cause eye irritation. Corneal injury is unlikely.

SKIN: Brief contact may cause slight skin irritation with local redness. Prolonged skin contact is unlikely to result in absorption of harmful amounts. Has caused allergic skin reactions when tested in mice. The dermal LD_{50} for male and female rats is >5,000 mg/kg.

INGESTION: Low toxicity if swallowed. Small amounts swallowed incidentally as a result of normal handling operations are not likely to cause injury; however, swallowing larger amounts may cause injury. The oral LD_{50} for rats, female, is 3,200 mg/kg.

FIGURE 2.4

Material Safety Data Sheet (*continued*)

Safety Data Sheet

 **Dow AgroSciences**

Garlon™ RTU Herbicide
™Trademark of Dow AgroSciences LLC

INHALATION: No adverse effects are anticipated from single exposure to mist. The aerosol LC_{50} for male and female rats, 4 hr., is >5.37 mg/l.

SYSTEMIC (OTHER TARGET ORGAN) EFFECTS: For the active ingredient, in animals, effects have been reported on the following organs: blood, kidney and liver.

CANCER INFORMATION: Similar active ingredient(s) did not cause cancer in laboratory animals.

TERATOLOGY (BIRTH DEFECTS): The active ingredient did not cause birth defects in laboratory animals. Has been toxic to the fetus in laboratory animals only at doses toxic to the mother.

REPRODUCTIVE EFFECTS: For a similar active ingredient, in laboratory animal studies, effects on reproduction have been seen only at doses that produced significant toxicity to the parent animals.

MUTAGENICITY: For the active ingredient, in-vitro and animal genetic toxicity studies were negative.

12. ECOLOGICAL INFORMATION:

ENVIRONMENTAL FATE:

MOVEMENT & PARTITIONING:
Bioconcentration potential is moderate (BCF is between 100 and 3000 or Log Pow between 3 and 5).
DEGRADATION & PERSISTENCE:
Based largely or completely on information for triclopyr-butotyl.
Material is expected to biodegrade only very slowly (in the environment). Fails to pass OECD/EEC tests for ready biodegradability.

ECOTOXICOLOGY:
Based largely or completely on information for triclopyr-butotyl.
Material is highly toxic to aquatic organisms on an acute basis (LC_{50} or EC_{50} is between 0.1 and 1 mg/L in the most sensitive species tested).
Material is slightly toxic to birds on an acute basis (LD_{50} is between 501 and 2000 mg/kg).
Material is practically non-toxic to birds on a dietary basis (LC_{50} is >5000 ppm).

13. DISPOSAL CONSIDERATIONS:

DISPOSAL METHOD: If wastes and/or containers cannot be disposed of according to the product label directions, disposal of this material must be in accordance with your local or area regulatory authorities.

This information presented below only applies to the material as supplied. The identification based on characteristic(s) or listing may not apply if the material has been used or otherwise contaminated. It is the responsibility of the waste generator to determine the toxicity and physical properties of the material generated to determine the proper waste identification and disposal methods in compliance with applicable regulations.

If the material as supplied becomes a waste, follow all applicable regional, national and local laws and regulations.

14. TRANSPORT INFORMATION:

TRANSPORTATION OF DANGEROUS GOODS INFORMATION:

For all shipments: This material is not regulated for transport.

15. REGULATORY INFORMATION:

Pest Control Products Act registration number:29334
For information phone: 800 667 3852

16. Other Information:
National Fire Code classification: Not applicable

Notice: The information contained in this Safety Data Sheet ("SDS") is current as of the effective date shown in Section 1 of this SDS and may be subject to amendment by Dow AgroSciences Canada Inc. ("DASCI") at any time. DASCI accepts no liability whatsoever which results in any way from the use of SDS that are not published by DASCI, or have been amended without DASCI express written authorization. Users of this SDS must satisfy themselves that they have the most recent and authorized version of this SDS and shall bear all responsibility and liability with respect thereto. Any conflict or inconsistencies as to the contents of this SDS shall be resolved in favor of DASCI by the most recent version of the SDS published by DASCI.

This SDS based on GF2059 US RSSDS SDS

may know to check for labels, know where to find the MSDS, and know the employer's procedures for handling a spill; however, the same worker may not know how to read the MSDS or understand it in sufficient depth to apply it in the workplace. Training and education should include a practical process to ensure that the worker understands how to apply the knowledge acquired.

After completing a training program, the worker should understand the purpose and origin of WHMIS and be able to

- identify WHMIS hazard symbols
- read WHMIS supplier and workplace labels
- read and apply the applicable information on an MSDS

The WHMIS program must be reviewed annually or as changes occur in products or processes in the workplace.

ENVIRONMENTAL LEGISLATION

Environmental and occupational health and safety laws are closely linked. In recognition of this fact, many companies and institutions have occupational environmental health and safety departments. The health and safety professional will be aware of the overlap in environmental and OH&S statutes and regulations. Chemicals that can cause damage to a worker may also cause damage to the ecosystem if released into the environment. Federal and provincial or territorial statutes relating to some aspect of environmental or health and safety management are listed in **OH&S Notebooks 2.7** and **2.8.**

Regulatory laws related to environmental assessment, public health, waste disposal, buried fuel tanks, and storage or use of pesticides have an impact on the environment, the public, and the occupational health and safety of employees. As the following scenario indicates, the practitioner is required to understand environmental and OH&S jurisdictions and the potential for overlap.

If a release of a potentially hazardous substance occurs within a building (other than residential) it falls under the jurisdiction of the authority enforcing the health and safety legislation. If the release is outside the building, or if the potentially hazardous substance is released into the sewer, storm system, water, or air, it falls under the jurisdiction of the authority enforcing the environmental legislation. Any single occurrence may involve both authorities.

OH&S Notebook 2.7

FEDERAL STATUTES RELEVANT TO OH&S

Canadian Environmental Protection Act, R.S.C. 1985	Radiation Protection Act, R.S.C. 1985
Hazardous Products Act, R.S.C. 1985	Radiation Emitting Devices Act, R.S.C. 1985
Canadian Charter of Rights and Freedoms, Part I of the Constitution Act, 1982	Transportation of Dangerous Goods Act, 1992, S.C. as amended
Pest Control Products Act, R.S.C. 1985	Canada Labour Code, Part IV

OH&S Notebook 2.8

PROVINCIAL AND TERRITORIAL STATUTES

Province	Transportation	Environment	Other
Alberta	Transportation of Dangerous Goods Act, S.A. 1982	Environmental Protection and Enhancement Act, S.A. 1992	
British Columbia	Transportation of Dangerous Goods Act, S.B.C. 1985	Waste Management Act, S.B.C. 1982/Amended 1990, 1992	
Manitoba	Dangerous Goods Handling and Transportation Act, R.S.M. 1987	Environment Act, S.M. 1987–88/Waste Reduction and Prevention Act, S.M. 1989–90	
New Brunswick	Transportation of Dangerous Goods Act, S.N.B. 1988		
Newfoundland and Labrador	Dangerous Goods Transportation Act, R.S.N. 1990	Department of Environment and Lands Act, R.S.N. 1990/ Waste Material Disposal Act, R.S.N. 1990/Water Protection Act, R.S.N. 1990	
Northwest Territories and Nunavut	Transportation of Dangerous Goods Act, 1990, S.N.W.T.		
Nova Scotia	Dangerous Goods Transportation Act, R.S.N.S. 1989	Environment Act (draft)/Litter Abatement Act, S.N.S. 1989	
Ontario	Dangerous Goods Transportation Act, R.S.O. 1990	Environmental Protection Act, R.S.O. 1990 as amended/Environmental Bill of Rights, 1993, S.O. 1993/ Ontario Water Resources Act, R.S.O. 1990/Waste Management Act, R.S.O. 1992/Environmental Assessment Act	Gasoline Handling Act, S.O. 1990/ Health Protection and Promotion Act, R.S.O. 1990/Municipal Act, R.S.O. 1990/Pesticides Act, R.S.O. 1990/Public Health Act, R.S.O. 1980/ Energy Act, R.S.O. 1990
Prince Edward Island	Dangerous Goods Transportation Act, R.S.P.E.I. 1988	Environmental Protection Act, R.S.P.E.I. 1988	
Quebec		Environmental Quality Act, R.S.Q. 1990	
Saskatchewan	Dangerous Goods Transportation Act, S.S. 1984–85–86	Litter Control Act, R.S.S. 1978	
Yukon	Dangerous Goods Transportation Act, R.S.Y.T. 1986	Environment Act, S.Y. 1991	

The parallels between environmental and OH&S legislation have extended to the courts. In *R. v. Bata Industries Ltd., Bata, Marchant and Weston*, Bata Industries Ltd. and three of its directors were charged with allowing a large chemical waste storage site containing many deteriorating and leaking containers to discharge known toxic industrial chemicals into the ground environment. The defendants used the defence of due diligence, arguing that the legislation was vague and imprecise and contrary to the Canadian Charter of Rights and Freedoms. The company was convicted, as were two of the directors (the third director was acquitted). The court found that the two defendants had not exercised due diligence. The court stated that though it did not expect a board of directors to make all environmental decisions, these decisions were too important to be delegated to subordinates.

TRANSPORTATION OF DANGEROUS GOODS

The regulation of environmental hazards, occupational health and safety, and transportation of dangerous goods is not the exclusive domain of either the federal, provincial, or territorial governments. Therefore, the practitioner should be familiar with the statutes relevant to his or her particular jurisdiction. In essence, the environmental and transportation legislation seeks to supply the framework within which society can protect itself from the risk that attends the transportation of inherently dangerous materials.

The federal legislation governing the transportation of dangerous goods applies to all persons who handle, offer for transport, transport, or import any dangerous goods. The provincial or territorial legislation does not always go this far, making it sometimes impossible to determine which statutes apply. Notwithstanding some provincial or territorial limitations, dangerous goods legislation applies to carriers, shippers, and transportation intermediaries such as freight forwarders and customs brokers. Various regulations exist with respect to identifying and placarding dangerous goods, controlling quantities, and training and certifying workers. The regulatory wording complements the WHMIS requirements and the OH&S responsibility of employers and supervisors to educate and train workers.

In *R. v. Midland Transport Ltd.* (1991) the New Brunswick Provincial Court made the following observation about the legislation: "The Transportation of Dangerous Goods Act and the Regulations thereunder with the act fall in the category of legislation which creates public welfare offences. Recognizing the potential dangers, it establishes safety guidelines for the handling of hazardous materials to ensure the protection of the public and the environment."

CORPORATE LIABILITY

Whereas in the past, directors and officers of incorporated entities were responsible solely to the corporation and shareholders, their zone of accountability now extends to the public at large. Environmental and OH&S statutes have been amended to include broad responsibilities for directors and officers. The liabilities that directors and officers now face include the following:

- fines or imprisonment for corporate pollution—e.g., causing or permitting the discharge of liquid industrial waste into the ground

- cleanup costs associated with a property the corporation owns, controls, or occupies

- fines for failing to comply with regulatory legislation

Canadian jurisprudence has followed the lead of the United States in extending legal responsibility to the boardroom. The executives of a company are no longer permitted to hide behind the laws of incorporation (see **OH&S Today 2.3**).

OH&S Today (2.3

Corporate Killing: The Westray Legislation

Bill C-45 deals with issues of corporate liability with respect to both fraud and occupational health and safety; the bill was passed by Parliament in 2003 and became law in March 2004. The so-called "Westray legislation" makes company executives more accountable when workers are killed or injured on the job as a result of management negligence. It is named after the Westray tragedy, in which a mine explosion that killed 26 miners was attributed to corporate negligence (see Chapter 1). Ultimately, the new law could lead to a corporation and its managers being criminally prosecuted for failing to provide an appropriate standard of occupational health and safety in the workplace if an employee died or was injured as a result of that negligence. This brings the notion of "corporate homicide" into the Canadian Criminal Code for the first time.

The act makes a company responsible for

- the actions of those who oversee day-to-day operations (e.g., supervisors and mid-level managers)
- managers (executive *or* operational) who intentionally commit, or have employees commit, crimes to benefit the organization
- managers who do not take action when they become aware of offences being committed
- the actions of managers who demonstrate a criminal lack of care (i.e., criminal negligence)

Passage of the Westray legislation substantially raises the stakes for managers and corporations. Besides introducing criminal liability into the OH&S arena, the act takes away the ability of the company to shift blame to frontline managers. That is, companies are now responsible for ensuring not only that frontline staff know the appropriate rules, regulations, and working procedures, but also that

employees follow the procedures. It is no longer possible to claim that employees were derelict in their responsibility—even if they were, the company is liable.

The passage of Bill C-45 was greeted with great fanfare; the first charges (relating to the death of a construction worker) were laid in 2004 but were subsequently withdrawn in 2005. There is some concern that the law has no "teeth" in practice. Whenever charges could be laid under either the safety legislation (provincial) or the Criminal Code (federal), the preference seems to be for safety legislation to prevail. C-45 is likely to be invoked in only the most severe, egregious, and atypical cases. As a result, many who heralded the new stricter legislation are now expressing disappointment in the actual functioning of the law.

Nonetheless, there have now been several convictions under the act leading some to claim that the "sleeping giant has awoken." In one case, Transpave Inc., pled guilty to criminal negligence relating to a death of an employee and was fined $110,000. In a second case, a landscape contractor (Pasquale Scrocca) was sentenced to two years less a day to be served in the community for criminal negligence causing death when one of his employees was crushed by an improperly maintained backhoe. Merton Construction pled guilty to criminal negligence charges in relation to the staging collapse that killed four workers in Toronto on Christmas Eve, 2009. The company received fines of $230,000 with an additional $90,000 fine for the president of the firm. Several other charges have been filed under Bill C-45 although critics point to the fact that the penalties still do not reflect the seriousness of the charges.

Sources: Summary of Bill C-45, An Act to Amend the Criminal Code (Criminal Liability of Corporations). Found at: http://parl.gc.ca/HousePublications/Publication.aspx?DocId=5765988&File=19&Col=1 (Accessed May 25, 2010); U. Vu, "Unions Decry Lack of Charges Under `Corporate Killing' Law," *Canadian HR Reporter*, June 29, 2006.

SUMMARY

The complexities associated with OH&S legislation in Canada continue to increase. This chapter has outlined the scope of this legislation and the changing climate surrounding it. We began by reviewing the legislative framework of OH&S legislation and in doing so identified the duties of major stakeholders (employers, supervisors, employees). We discussed the three principal rights of employees (the right to know, the right to participate, and the right to refuse) and how they are enacted in health and safety programs. Work refusals and work stoppages were reviewed as concrete enactments of the right to refuse unsafe work. JHSCs were discussed as exemplifications of the right to participate in decision making around occupational health and safety. The elements composing the WHMIS were reviewed, and some consideration was given to ancillary legislation (e.g., environmental, transportation of dangerous goods). These are all examples of the workers' right to know about occupational health and safety issues (and hazards) in the workplace.

Key Terms

act 26
constructor 30
guidelines and policies 26

prescribed 29
regulations 26
standards and codes 26

Weblinks

American National Standards Institute
http://www.ansi.org

American Society for Testing and Materials
http://www.astm.org

Canadian General Standards Board
http://www.pwgsc.gc.ca/cgsb/home/index-e.html

Canadian Standards Association
http://www.csa.ca

Health Canada, "Workplace Hazardous Materials Information System (WHMIS)"
http://www.hc-sc.gc.ca/hecs-sesc/whmis

International Organization for Standardization
http://www.iso.org/iso/en/ISOOnline.frontpage

MSDS, searchable databases of MSDS
https://services.shell.ca/llutilsp/searchMSDS/Search.do?lang=en
https://www.vwrsp.com/search/index.cgi?tmpl=msds&src=topnav-msds

Ontario Ministry of Labour
http://www.labour.gov.on.ca

Standards Council of Canada
http://www.scc.ca

Underwriters' Laboratories of Canada
http://www.ulc.ca

Required Professional Capabilities (RPCs)

The following RPCs, listed by their CCHRA number, are relevant to the material covered in this chapter. All RPCS can be found at http://www.chrp.ca/rpc/body-of-knowledge.

RPC:170 Develops, implements, and ensures the application of policies, regulations, and standards relating to occupational health and safety.

RPC:171 Ensures compliance with legislated reporting requirements.

RPC:172 Ensures due diligence and liability requirements are met.

RPC:173 Ensures that policies for required medical testing fall within the limits of statute & contract.

RPC:174 Develops and implements policies on the workplace environment.

RPC:175 Ensures adequate accommodation, modified work and graduated return to work programs are in place.

RPC:176 Ensures that modifications to the work environment are consistent with worker limitations.

RPC:177 Develops or provides for wellness and employee assistance programs to support organizational effectiveness.

RPC:178 Provides information to employees and managers on available programs.

RPC:179 Ensures that mechanisms are in place for responding to crises in the workplace, including critical incident stress management.

RPC:180 Establishes a joint Health & Safety Committee as required by law.[*]

RPC:181 Responds to any refusals to perform work believed to be unsafe.[*]

RPC:182 Responds to serious injury or fatality in the workplace.

RPC:183 Analyzes risks to employee health & safety and develops preventive programs.[*]

RPC:184 Establishes an investigation process for incidents and accidents in the workplace.

RPC:185 Ensures that security programs and policies minimize risks while considering the obligation of the employer and the rights of employees, union, and third parties.[*]

RPC:186 Establishes and implements strategies to minimize workers' compensation costs.

RPC:187 Prepares Organizational Health & Safety files for investigation and/or for litigation.

---

[*] Canadian Council of Human Resources Associations, Human Resources Professionals in Canada: Revised Body of Knowledge and Required Professional Capabilities (RPCs ®), 2007.

Discussion Questions

1. What are the three fundamental workers' rights that underlie most health and safety legislation?
2. What is the difference between the responsibilities assigned to companies under occupational health and safety and those assigned under environmental legislation?
3. What three components make up WHMIS compliance?
4. Describe the structure and role of joint health and safety committees.

Using the Internet

1. What legislation applies in your jurisdiction? Find the body responsible for occupational health and safety and review the legislation. What are the major provisions and their implications for employers? for employees? for human resource managers?
2. WHMIS training is widely available online. Using a search engine and keywords such as "WHMIS online training," find a local provider of online WHMIS training.

Exercise

Health and safety legislation can be crafted following different approaches. One approach is to "force" compliance by establishing standards, conducting rigorous inspections on a regular basis, and harshly punishing failures to meet the established standards. A second approach is to facilitate self-reliance by providing the parties with the information and resources necessary to monitor and enhance health and safety in their workplaces. What are the relative merits of these two approaches? What advantages and disadvantages accrue under each system? What is the appropriate balance between enforcement and encouragement?

Case 1 WORKPLACE TRAGEDY

An auto parts manufacturer employs 500 workers. The plant operates on three shifts, and its various lines include large punch presses, conveyors, paint spray booths, and overhead cranes. A worker has been killed following an accident on the overhead crane line. The worker was guiding the load hoisted by the crane when the load slipped, causing a failure of the supporting cables. The worker was killed when the falling load struck him. Though this is the most serious accident, there have been several others at the plant in the past. As plant manager, you are responsible for ensuring the safety of your employees. Outline the steps you plan to take to improve health and safety in the plant.

Case 2   WORK REFUSAL AT REGIONAL HOSPITAL

Regional Hospital is a 100-bed acute care facility providing services to a mid-sized Canadian city. Recently, the hospital took advantage of a special government grant to develop and operate an HIV treatment ward. Though the ward is now open, there is considerable disquiet among the staff. Two nurses have refused to work their assigned shifts on the ward, claiming that it is their right to refuse unsafe work. Moreover, workers have been petitioning their certified representative on the Joint Health and Safety Committee to close the workplace because of the safety standard. As the HR representative for Regional Hospital, what is your planned response? How do you balance the workers' right to refuse unsafe work against the need to staff the ward?

WHMIS Regulations Consulted Model OH&S Regulations

Alberta	Chemical Hazards Regulation
British Columbia	Workplace Hazardous Materials Information System Regulations
Manitoba	Workplace Hazardous Materials Information System Regulations
New Brunswick	Workplace Hazardous Materials Information System Regulations
Newfoundland and Labrador	Workplace Hazardous Materials Information System Regulations
Northwest Territories/ Nunavut	Work Site Hazardous Materials Information System Regulations
Nova Scotia	Workplace Hazardous Materials Information System Regulations
Ontario	Workplace Hazardous Materials Information System Regulations
Prince Edward Island	Workplace Hazardous Materials Information System Regulations
Quebec	An Act to Amend the Act respecting Occupational Health and Safety
Saskatchewan	Occupational Health and Safety Act 1993, Part IV, Workplace Hazardous Materials Information System
Yukon	Workplace Hazardous Materials Information System Regulations

NOTES

1. P. Strahlendorf, "Is Your Committee Effective?" *OH&S Canada* 23 (2007): 24–31.
2. E.K. Kelloway, "Labor Unions and Safety," in J. Barling and M. Frone, eds., *Psychology of Occupational Safety* (Washington: APA, 2003).

3. B. Reilly, P. Paci, and P. Holl, "Unions, Safety Committees, and Workplace Injuries," *British Journal of Industrial Relations* 33 (1995): 275–88.

4. D. Weil, "Are Mandated Health and Safety Committees Substitutes for or Supplements to Labor Unions?" *Industrial and Labor Relations Review* 52 (1999): 339–61.

5. Idem, "Mandating Safety and Health Committees: Lessons from the United States," *Proceedings of the 47th Annual Meeting of the Industrial Relations Research Association*, Madison, WI, 1995, pp. 273–81.

Workers' Compensation

CHAPTER LEARNING OBJECTIVES

After reading this chapter, you should be able to:

- outline the goals and methods of Workers' Compensation Boards (WCBs)
- discuss the problems associated with compensating for psychological conditions and occupational illnesses
- describe the assessment methods of WCBs
- understand the methods of calculating injury frequency and severity rates

INJURED WORKERS, PRESCRIPTION PAINKILLERS, AND ADDICTIONS: A COMPENSATION CONCERN

Following a painful workplace injury, workers can be prescribed various medications to help them manage their pain and suffering. In some cases workers can be prescribed powerful drugs including opioids or narcotic-based medicines (e.g., morphine, oxycodone, and codeine). Prescription painkillers that include narcotics are not medications that come without risk; because of the addictive nature of narcotics, workers who are prescribed opioids for pain management run the risk of developing an addiction. WSIB data indicates that claimants prescribed narcotics has increased by 40% compared to 10 years ago and since 2006 the doses physicians prescribe has increased.

Workers who are addicted to painkillers are now raising concerns among Workers' Compensation Boards. In February 2010 the Ontario Workplace Safety and Insurance Board (WSIB) enhanced the way in which it manages claimants who become addicted to narcotics prescribed for non-cancer pain. The newly developed narcotics strategy targets the potential for claimants to become addicted to prescription painkillers by implementing decision support mechanisms for WSIB clinical staff and enhancing communications between WSIB

physicians and prescribing physicians. Specifically this strategy outlines maximum dosing allowances for short-acting and long-acting narcotics, increasing the amount of contact between the community and physicians and communications that manage the resources for addicted workers.

Support for this new strategy is mixed and does not come without concerns on behalf of workers. Some feel that this new strategy infringes on physicians independence and will hinder their ability to appropriately treat a worker's pain, others worry that the new strategy is a financially driven method for managing costs. Despite these concerns, this new strategy highlights the need for more research and work to be done in regards to defining the roles and responsibilities for Compensation Boards. In order to understand the roles and responsibilities Compensation Boards play in emerging workplace issues we must have a solid understanding of the basic and general principles of Workers' Compensation. This chapter reviews the history of Workers' Compensation and the basic principles and tenets of the various Compensation Boards from across Canada.

Source: WSIB CSPAAT Ontario, "Enhanced narcotics management for injured workers." Found at: http://www.wsib.on.ca/en/community/WSIB/230/ArticleDetail/24338?vgnextoid=3fc84c23529d7210VgnVCM100000449c710aRCRD; Dan Birch, "The Long and the Short of It," *OHS Canada*, Aug. 15, 2010. Found at: http://www.ohscanada.com/news/the-long-and-short-of-it/1000382014/.

Workers' Compensation is a form of insurance governed by an act of Parliament to help workers who are injured on the job return to work. Consider the example of a construction labourer who has sustained an injury on the job and is now unable to work because of a disability. Workers' Compensation will ensure that the injured worker receives (1) first aid treatment, either on the job or at the nearest local treatment facility, (2) benefits while at home recuperating, and (3) proper treatment for any injuries. If necessary, rehabilitation will be provided to help the worker return to his or her former job or some modified version of it, if circumstances dictate.

HISTORICAL ROOTS

Workers' Compensation originated in Germany in 1884 but was not established in Canada until 1914, when the Ontario Workmen's Compensation Act was passed by the provincial Parliament. This time lag was something of an advantage, because it allowed for consideration of the American and European experience (the federal Employers' Liability Act had been passed in the United States in 1908). In 1900 the Ontario government inquired into the German system. This was followed between 1912 and 1914 by an intensive and prolonged study of existing laws in other European countries and in the United States, under the guidance of Sir William Ralph Meredith, Chief Justice of Ontario. On the basis of his findings, the first act in Canada was passed.

Acts were subsequently passed in all provinces and territories, and though they have been amended many times (largely for the purpose of increasing coverage and benefits), they have retained many of the principles set forth in the Ontario act of 1914:

- **collective liability** for employers, with some recognition of risk in the amount of contribution paid by individual employers

- compensation for workers regardless of the financial condition of the employer

- compensation based on loss of earnings

- a "no fault" system

- a nonadversarial process: little or no recourse to the courts (in Ontario, Schedule 2 can allow legal recourse)

collective liability
where all employers in a class or other rate group are liable for the costs of any or all accidents and occupational diseases that occur in the operations of those employers

---

OH&S Notebook 3.1

OVERVIEW OF WORKERS' COMPENSATION

Essentially, Workers' Compensation is an insurance plan in which the premiums (i.e., the cost of insurance) are paid by the employer. The plan is administered by a board typically known as the Workers' Compensation Board. Each year the WCB sets a premium rate for each industry. The rate is usually expressed per $100 of payroll. For example, if you own a construction-based company that specializes in roofing and has an annual payroll of $175,000 in Ontario, you can use the calculator provided by the WSIB at http://www.wsib.on.ca/en/community/WSIB/230/PremiumEstimator/24343?vgnextoid=7b10fbc5cecd0310VgnVCM100000469c710aRCRD by first selecting the construction sector (or industry) from the drop-down menu and then choosing the specific rate group titled roofing (Rate group 728) to derive your 2012 premium as $25,270 paid in quarterly installments. A rate group is a method for categorizing companies based on the nature of their business (e.g., roofing). In some provinces a company's premium rate may be increased or decreased depending on their specific safety record. WCBs use this money to compensate injured workers, pay for medical treatment, engage in prevention activities, and fund safety associations (i.e., industry associations whose focus is promoting occupational health and safety).

If you are a worker who is injured in the workplace, your employer is required to file a report of the injury with the WCB. Assuming that your injury requires you to miss time from work, you will receive compensation to make up for lost income while you are off. Though the details vary by jurisdiction, the compensation is usually based on a percentage of your salary to a specified maximum. For example, in Ontario the 2012 maximum earning is $81,700.

A Workers' Compensation system amounts to a tradeoff for both workers and employers. Workers know they will be compensated for injury without having to undertake expensive and lengthy lawsuits; in return they accept the WCB's authority to determine the amount of compensation. Employers are obliged to pay for the Workers' Compensation system but are also protected from litigation that could drive them into bankruptcy.[1]

WORKERS' COMPENSATION IN CANADA

Administration and Responsibilities

The provincial and territorial acts throughout Canada are administered by the members of the Workers' Compensation Board, who are appointed by the lieutenant governor in council. The provincial boards are empowered to fix and collect assessments, determine the right to compensation, and pay the amount due to the injured worker. In all these matters, the Workers' Compensation system has exclusive and final jurisdiction. In terms of its authority and power, the Ontario act is representative of the legislation that exists in all jurisdictions. The regulations and responsibilities of Workers' Compensation Boards are as follows:

- The injured worker will receive payment while off work and will have all medical bills paid if the injury happened at work and because of work.

- The injured worker will receive a pension if the disability is or becomes permanent.

- The injured worker will receive benefits if he or she cannot earn the same amount of money earned before the incident.

- The injured worker's immediate family and dependants will be entitled to benefits if the worker is killed or dies as a result of an injury on the job.

- The Workers' Compensation Boards classify employers to ensure consistency.

- The Workers' Compensation Boards decide whether an individual is classified as a worker, a subcontractor, or an employer, as each class has different conditions.

- The Workers' Compensation system can pay benefits if a worker is affected by an industrial disease that has resulted from his or her occupation.

In relation to most of the industries within the scope of the provincial or territorial acts, the system of compensation is one of compulsory and collective liability. Under collective liability, the various industries are classified according to their size and end product, and each employer is assessed a rate that is a percentage of its payroll. The percentage is determined by the injury cost of its classification. From the incident fund thus collected, payments are made for compensation, medical aid, rehabilitation, incident prevention, and administrative expenses. Each employer is liable for assessment, whatever the cost of injuries sustained by its workers. As a result, each is relieved of individual liability. In most jurisdictions, liability is further distributed by a disaster reserve fund.

Public authorities and certain large corporations such as railways and shipping or telegraph companies have a different liability approach from the collective liabilities scheme and are individually liable for compensation; however, all disputes are settled by the WCB. Such corporations contribute their portion of the cost of administering the various acts.

Because jurisdictions sometimes provide different benefits, most WCBs in Canada have entered into agreements among themselves to avoid duplicate assessments and to help the worker claim and receive compensation when two or more jurisdictions are involved. These agreements are intended to ensure that the worker receives the best possible benefits and that coverage is extended in a province or territory, often at the request of the injured worker.

The provincial and territorial acts generally cover all employment in industries such as lumbering, mining, fishing, manufacturing, construction, engineering, and transportation. Covered occupations include operation of electrical power lines, employment in waterworks and other public utilities, navigation, operation of boats and ships, operation of elevators and warehousing, street cleaning, painting, decorating, renovating, and cleaning. Those types of employment that are exempted from this list may be admitted at their own request.

Personal injuries resulting from incidents arising out of and in the course of employment are compensated, except when the incident is attributed to the worker's serious and willful misconduct does not result in serious disablement. Workers' Compensation systems also compensate for certain specified occupational diseases. For example on July 25, 2012 the premier of British Columbia announced that esophageal cancer has been added to the list of cancers covered by the Workers' Compensation Act[2] (see **OH&S Today 3.1**).

OH&S Today 3.1

Legislative Updates

In July 2011, the Yukon Workers' Compensation Health and Safety Board (YWCHSB) amended the Workers' Compensation Act to include "presumptive provisions" for existing and former firefighters. Presumptive provisions means that the usual requirements for determining whether an injury/illness is work-related is not required in special acknowledged or presumed circumstances (e.g., cancer).

Similarly, in Alberta four new cancers (prostate, breast, skin, and multiple myeloma) were added to the list of cancers with presumptive WCB coverage, while in 2010 Manitoba also proposed adding breast cancer and three other cancers to the list of those covered under presumptive provisions. In November 2011, British Columbia proposed changes to the WCB Act, which would add to the list of cancers with presumptive coverage as well as provide broader compensation coverage of mental stress. On November 2, 2011, the Minister of Labour, Citizens' Services and Open Government, introduced the following amendments to the British Columbia Workers' Compensation Act:

- Broader compensation coverage for mental stress conditions resulting from the work environment
- Adjustment to the compensation provided to injured apprentices to a level that fairly represents their loss of earnings
- Grant survivor benefits to common-law couples without children after two years of cohabitation (previously three years[3])

Prevention

Most WCBs, at one time, were responsible for the incident prevention or OH&S aspects of Workers' Compensation. In the 1970s and 1980s the combined role was seen as a conflict of interest by some governments, and these WCB functions were placed under a government department in most provinces and territories (e.g., the Department of Labour). Though the OH&S function is separate in most jurisdictions (with B.C. being an exception), all WCBs cooperate with the responsible government department by sharing information.

The Ontario board—now called the Workplace Safety and Insurance Board (WSIB) since the passage of the Workers' Compensation Reform Act in 1998—has recently added a prevention function to its traditional compensation functions. Indeed, that shift in emphasis is increasingly common across Canada. For example, various Workers' Compensation Boards are now offering premium reductions based on safety records. Thus, Alberta reduced premiums in 2009 to a provincial average of $1.32/$100 of payroll, with a further reduction to $1.22 in 2012. Most jurisdictions are either reducing their rates or holding them steady (see **OH&S Today 3.2**). In addition to this general premium reduction, employers in Alberta (and in some other provinces— see the discussion in this chapter on experience ratings) can achieve further premium reductions of up to 20% from the industry rate based on their safety performance. Conversely, organizations with a poor safety record may be charged a surcharge to reflect the increased costs of insurance. In Nova Scotia the surcharge program is a rate-setting model that responds to the safety performance of individual employers. This program is designed to place the onus of prevention and reducing rates on employers by encouraging them

OH&S Today 3.2

Workers' Compensation Premiums (Averages per $100 of Payroll)

	2009	2012
Alberta	1.32	1.22
British Columbia	1.51	1.54
Manitoba	1.60	1.50
New Brunswick	2.03	1.70
Newfoundland and Labrador	2.75	2.75
Northwest Territories/Nunavut	1.71	1.77
Nova Scotia	2.65	2.65
Ontario	2.26	2.40
Prince Edward Island	2.16	1.99
Quebec	2.10	2.13
Saskatchewan	1.66	1.60
Yukon	3.00	2.39

Source: Association of Workers' Compensation Boards of Canada, "Provisional Average Assessment Rates, Per $100.00 Payroll." Found at: http://www.awcbc.org/english/Assessment_provisional_rates.asp. (Accessed Feb. 7, 2007).

to take the necessary steps required to create a safe and healthy workplace. Employers who improve their safety records by preventing and reducing injuries will see a reduction rate and those who do not could be required to pay a surcharge.

A mandate for prevention also means that WCBs are actively involved in trying to prevent incidents and reduce costs to employers. WCBs provide a wide range of information for employers and employees regarding safety-related matters. For example, WorkSafeBC maintains a large online library of safety-related publications; the WCB of Nova Scotia and Newfoundland and Labrador provide workshops on how to prevent workplace injuries while the New Brunswick WCB has developed the 5*22 Health and Safety Resources program. The WCB in Alberta and Nova Scotia offers a Certificate of Recognition (COR) to organizations that have implemented safety programs that meet its standards. In many jurisdictions in Canada, Workers' Compensation Boards provide extensive resources to both employers and individuals interested in health and safety issues. (See **OH&S Notebook 3.2** for individual WCB contact information.)

Compensation Rates and Methods

Two standards are in place for determining the amount of compensation. Eight jurisdictions base the payment on a percentage (generally 90%) of **net earnings**; the other four base payments on 75% of average earnings. Jurisdictions like Nova Scotia have used both methods depending on the date of the incident. A worker's average earnings are generally calculated on the basis of his or her earnings during the past 12 months. Since a large number of workers have not worked for the same employer for 12 months, other ways of establishing earnings are sanctioned. Each act also stipulates a maximum amount of earnings that can be used to determine the maximum amount of compensation. Though there are procedural variations across jurisdictions, Workers' Compensation is based on the individual's past salary record, not on the loss or potential loss of future earnings.

net earnings
salary after mandatory deductions (income tax, Canada Pension, and Employment Insurance)

One of the underlying premises of Workers' Compensation systems is that people do not want to work.[4] As a result, boards try to provide reasonable compensation without creating an incentive for individuals to stay off work. There is some empirical evidence that raising benefit rates does lead to longer absences from work.[5]

The method used for determining the average wage of a worker is the one that gives the best representation of the worker's weekly earnings and that seems fair and reasonable. When work is made available and the worker still suffers an earnings loss, the payment for the continuing disability may be adjusted, whether or not the worker accepts the work. A payment for non-economic loss (functional impairment) is also made in several jurisdictions. This figure is based on such factors as the worker's age, degree of impairment, and number of dependants. For example, a 40-year-old worker with three children would receive a larger payment than a 60-year-old worker with no children.

OH&S Notebook 3.2

CONTACT INFORMATION FOR THE PROVINCIAL AND TERRITORIAL WORKERS' COMPENSATION BOARDS

Workers' Compensation Board of Alberta
9912–107 Street
P.O. Box 2415
Edmonton AB T5J 2S5
Tel: 780-498-3999
Fax: 780-498-7999
http://www.wcb.ab.ca

WorkSafeBC
P.O. Box 5350
Vancouver BC V6B 5L5
Tel: 604-231-8888
Fax: 604-233-9777
http://www.worksafebc.com

Workers' Compensation Board of Manitoba
333 Broadway
Winnipeg MB R3C 4W3
Tel: 204-954-4321
Fax: 204-954-4999
http://www.wcb.mb.ca

WorkSafe/Travail Sécuritaire New Brunswick
1 Portland Street
P.O. Box 160
Saint John NB E2L 3X9
Tel: 506-632-2200
Fax: 506-632-4999
http://www.worksafenb.ca

Workplace Health, Safety, and Compensation Commission of Newfoundland and Labrador
146-148 Forest Road
P.O. Box 9000
St. John's NL A1A 3B8
Tel: 709-778-1000
Fax: 709-738-1714
http://www.whscc.nf.ca

Workers' Safety and Compensation Commission of the Northwest Territories and Nunavut
P.O. Box 8888
Yellowknife NT X1A 2R3
Tel: 867-920-3888
Fax: 867-873-4596
http://www.wcb.nt.ca

Source: Association of Workers' Compensation Boards of Canada, "Provisional Average Assessment Rates, Per $100.00 Payroll." Found at: http://www.awcbc.org/english/Assessment_provisional_rates.asp. (Accessed July 19, 2012).

Workers' Compensation Board of Nova Scotia
5668 South Street
P.O. Box 1150
Halifax NS B3J 2Y2
Tel: 902-491-8999
Fax: 902-491-8001
http://www.wcb.ns.ca

Workplace Safety and Insurance Board of Ontario
200 Front Street West
Toronto ON M5V 3J1
Tel: 416-344-1000
Fax: 416-344-4684
http://www.wsib.on.ca

Workers' Compensation Board of Prince Edward Island
14 Weymouth Street
P.O. Box 757
Charlottetown PEI C1A 7L7
Tel: 902-368-5680
Fax: 902-368-5705
http://www.wcb.pe.ca

Commission de la santé et de la sécurité du travail
1, complexe Desjardins
Tour Sud, 31e étage
Case postale 3
Succursale Place-Desjardins
Montréal QC H5B 1H1
Tel: 1-866-302-2778
Fax: 514-906-3133
http://www.csst.qc.ca

Saskatchewan Workers' Compensation Board
200–1881 Scarth Street
Regina SK S4P 4L1
Tel: 306-787-4370
Fax: 306-787-4311
http://www.wcbsask.com

Yukon Workers' Compensation Health and Safety Board
401 Strickland Street
Whitehorse YK Y1A 5N8
Tel: 867-667-5645
Fax: 867-393-6279
http://www.wcb.yk.ca

Compensation to employees can be provided using different methods including wage loss benefits, permanent disability benefits, dependency benefits, and rehabilitation.

Wage loss benefits means that an injured employee receives a specific percentage of their typical wages (this varies by province). An employee typically receives permanent disability benefits if they are determined to have a permanent disability because of his or her work injury; he or she may receive additional or varied compensation depending on the province. In the event that an individual dies while on the job their dependants (e.g., spouse or children) may be eligible to receive benefits. Finally, rehabilitation services and programs are provided to help workers get back to their pre-injury health and to get injured workers back to work.

Depending on the type of compensation, for example, wage loss, payments continue as long as a disability lasts, in accordance with the entitlement established by the province or territory. In cases of permanent partial impairment, the worker receives a life pension based on rating scales established by the boards. There are allowances for economic losses and non-economic losses. An injured worker could receive non-economic loss that is based on a percentage of impairment of the total person.

Wage or earnings loss refers to situations in which workers can no longer earn the same amount of money that they were earning before the incident as a result of their impairment. For a worker who was earning $20 per hour before the incident and now, as a result of the injury, is capable of earning only $10 per hour, the potential compensation is $10 per hour. The earnings loss is calculated and paid as long as the worker is unable to return to work paying the same wages as before the incident.

In the event of the death of a worker, the spouse may receive a pension in accordance with the schedules established by the various jurisdictions, and allowances are given to children. In addition, most provincial and territorial boards may allow an immediate lump sum payment and variable expenses (see **OH&S Today 3.3**).

OH&S Today (3.3

Spiralling Disability Costs

An aging workforce and an expanded definition of "disabling condition" have resulted in far more individuals receiving disability compensation. Employee illness and disability is estimated to cost Canadian employers $16 billion a year.

Changes in the composition of the workforce—in particular, the elimination of mandatory retirement—are expected to affect these already escalating costs, and organizations need to consider how they will approach this new class of older workers.

Sources: T. Clark, "Benefit Trends: Will You Still Need Me?" *Benefits Canada*, Jan. 2007, Pg. 33; A. Sharratt, "In the Balance," *Benefits Canada*, April 2006, Pg. 65–77.

Employers or injured workers who disagree with a WCB decision can turn to various appeal bodies and mechanisms. In Prince Edward Island, Saskatchewan, and Yukon, however, the WCB is the final level of appeal.

MEDICAL AID AND INCIDENT PREVENTION

Accompanying compensation in all cases is the provision of medical aid. This aid includes medical and surgical care, hospitalization, nursing care, drugs and supplies, physical and occupational therapy, and the provision and maintenance of prostheses. An employee who sustains a work-related injury is compensated not only for loss of earnings but also for **loss of functional capacity**. Workers who, as a result of their injury, are no longer able to perform some of their duties on the job, such as lifting, twisting, or bending, are considered to have suffered loss of functional capacity for which benefits are payable.

Employers within a particular industry may form safety associations and make rules for incident prevention that, on approval of the WCB and the lieutenant governor, are binding on all employers in that industry. WCBs pay the expenses of these associations out of the incident fund and have the authority to investigate the premises of employers to ensure compliance with safeguards required by law. The goal of safety associations is to provide training in the area of incident prevention and health and safety (see **OH&S Today 3.4**).

SOCIAL GOALS OF WORKERS' COMPENSATION

Workers' Compensation is driven by two main social goals: (1) to provide services intended to prevent injuries or reduce the psychological impact of injuries when they occur, and (2) to provide the training and development necessary to prepare an injured worker to return to work. The various WCBs have come to look on compensation as a means for society to share with the worker the consequences of industrial incidents and to ensure the restoration of the worker to

loss of functional capacity
limit of ability or dexterity depending on the seriousness of an injury

OH&S Today 3.4

Safety Associations

Health and safety associations are industry groups funded at least in part through the Workers' Compensation Board (employers pay a levy or surcharge as part of their premium to fund the association). Associations provide training programs, and other health and safety related services (e.g., safety audits, certificates of recognition), to members of their industry, typically charging a fee for these services. They are not responsible for regulation, nor are they a government agency—rather, a safety association represents a specific industry and provides general and industry-specific safety knowledge to its members. Because Workers' Compensation premiums are initially set by industry, all employers in a given industry benefit if safety improves within that industry. This is the goal of safety associations. For more information about provincial safety associations, visit http://www.awcbc.org/en/safetyassociations.asp.

active participation in the life of the community. The focus is more on restoring earning power than on paying for its loss. In no sense is compensation considered a reward for being injured.

This social conception of compensation is grounded in the following standard provisions contained in the various acts:

- unlimited medical aid

- artificial prostheses

- a fund to encourage re-employment (known as the Second Injury and Enhancement Fund [SIEF] in some jurisdictions)

- liberal compensation

- rehabilitation maintenance income

Canada's compensation system provides greater benefits than those of most other countries; it also ensures that benefits are not prejudiced by earnings after rehabilitation. In Canada, a permanently injured worker draws compensation for life and is able to keep his or her pension, even if the sum of the pension and the earnings supplements amounts to more than the wages earned before the injury. In contrast, many compensation laws in the United States hinder rehabilitation, either by cutting off compensation for permanent injury as soon as workers begin to earn as much money as they did before the injury or by paying compensation for only a limited period (which can leave workers stranded before they can be retrained).

Provision for Second Injuries

In some provinces (e.g., Ontario) provisions may be provided to an employee who receives a second injury. The purpose of which is to facilitate the re-employment of disabled workers. Without a provision for multiple injuries, employers might be tempted to discriminate against workers with disabilities, as an additional injury could make the employer responsible for a far more serious disability than if the worker had not had a prior injury. Thus, a worker who has lost one arm will be given a total disability rating if he or she loses the second arm. By charging the excess liability resulting from the cumulative effect of a prior disability and the subsequent injury to a disaster reserve fund, the various acts distribute the burden throughout industry as a whole rather than letting it rest on one particular class. In this way, employers are relieved of the extra risks associated with the employment of workers with disabilities.

Rehabilitation

Before the First World War, persons with disabilities were left to fend for themselves. Some were placed in poorhouses; others survived through begging. Gradually, society realized that just because people had disabilities did not mean they could not be productive; however, the first attempts at drafting people with disabilities into the workplace proved to be difficult and frustrating for those so drafted. People with disabilities found that though they

vocational rehabilitation
the steps undertaken by WCBs to help injured workers return to their place of employment or find similar or suitable work elsewhere

physical rehabilitation
the steps taken to restore, fully or partially, the worker's physical function

social rehabilitation
the psychological and practical services that help workers with severe disabilities cope with daily life

were given an opportunity to earn a living, they could do so only by accepting menial jobs that no one else wanted. When thousands of injured soldiers returned from the First World War, the need to provide rehabilitation programs was finally recognized. Rehabilitation is a financial necessity as well as a moral and social obligation. Only through effective rehabilitation can the future cost of the Workers' Compensation system be maintained at a reasonable level.

There are three types of rehabilitation. **Vocational rehabilitation** refers to the steps undertaken by WCBs to help injured workers return to their place of employment or find similar or suitable work elsewhere. Placement services, vocational testing, and retraining or training may all be part of this process. **Physical rehabilitation** refers to the steps taken to restore, fully or partially, the worker's physical function. **Social rehabilitation** refers to the psychological and practical services that help workers with severe disabilities cope with daily life (e.g., assistance with cooking, bathing, and household chores). An example of the full range of compensation benefits being provided to an injured worker is outlined in **OH&S Today 3.5**.

OH&S Today 3.5

Workers' Compensation at Work

In 1987, an employee lost his left hand in an industrial incident. Over the previous 10 years, he had risen from the position of delivery truck driver to plant manager at a small aluminum fabricator in northwest Toronto.

Robert Smith* recalled the incident. "We were having problems with the alignment. The mechanic was on lunch and repairs had to be made. I had done the same thing a thousand times before. It was a stupid incident. There was a piece of paper on the floor, and I instinctively kicked it out of the way. Unfortunately, I didn't know that the foot pedal was beneath the paper. The press came down in the blink of an eye and my hand was left attached to my wrist by a single tendon."

Mr. Smith had been thinking about a career change before the incident. Besides his duties as plant manager, he had begun to do some selling and marketing and found it was something he enjoyed. After the incident, he knew he would not be able to work in the plant again, so he began to consider retraining.

After his surgery, Mr. Smith spent four weeks in hospital recovering. A WCB representative came to see him two days after the incident and initiated his claim so that he could continue to pay his bills. Before Mr. Smith could be fitted with a prosthesis, his physical wounds had to heal. He spent the next couple of months getting better and receiving treatment.

Around this time, Mr. Smith decided to pursue a marketing career. Thanks to the sponsorship of the WCB, he enrolled in a marketing program. On graduation, Mr. Smith received further assistance from a WCB placement adviser. Within months, a job was located. After completing a training program with his new employer, Mr. Smith began work as a full-time marketing representative.

In this scenario the full range of compensation benefits was provided, including monetary benefits, medical aid, prosthetic device, vocational rehabilitation, placement services, and counselling in social services.

*Name has been changed.

OCCUPATIONAL DISEASES AND WORKPLACE STRESS

A significant issue facing Workers' Compensation today concerns occupational diseases and the degree to which they are work related. Occupational diseases include various cancers, skin diseases, and allergic reactions to materials and components in the workplace. Occupational disease compensation has been part of Workers' Compensation ever since six specific diseases were cited in Ontario's act of 1914. The past 30 years have seen a broadening of the definitions of "incident" and "injury," and this has allowed for greater consideration of occupational disease claims. Today many occupational disease claims can be considered in the same way as any other claim. The requirement to isolate the point at which the disease was contracted has given way to a recognition that the disease could be the result of exposure or injury over time. Occupational disease claims, unless very straightforward, are often adjudicated by a special claim unit and may require additional expert medical opinion as well as exposure and employment histories. Some WCBs use separate claim forms for specific occupational diseases. The **latency period** is quite often a major factor in determining the acceptability of the claim.

latency period
the time between exposure to a cause and development of a disease

Stress-related disabilities can be divided into three groups: (1) physical injury or occupational disease leading to a mental disability, (2) mental stress resulting in a physical disability, traumatic occurrence, or series of occurrences, and (3) mental stress resulting in a mental condition. Generally, stress claims in the first group have been dealt with in the same way as any other claims. Those in the second group have been subject to some selection. If the disability (say, a cardiac attack) is acute, it will be considered for compensation. If the disability (say, an ulcer) is a result of accumulated stress, it will likely not be considered for compensation. With respect to the third group, an unusual incident that provokes the mental reaction and results in a disability will probably be considered for compensation; chronic stress resulting in a mental disability is seldom compensated. The adjudication of stress claims is currently receiving a great deal of attention from all insurance parties. The courts and human rights tribunals have consistently maintained that stress-related disorders or other psychological disabilities are to be treated the same as physical disabilities in employment settings.[6] It remains to be seen whether Workers' Compensation schemes can defend their exclusion of some stress-related disorders in the face of this accumulated experience.

ASSESSMENTS

Employers are grouped together according to the type of operation or industry in which they are engaged, and they are assessed on that basis. The groups are referred to as industries, classes, subclasses, or classifications. In some jurisdictions, the terms "unit" and "sector" are used; employers are not grouped by occupation, though occupation may help determine a subdivision of an industry or class.

Separate accounts are generally used when an employer is involved in more than one industry or when an industry or employer's operation includes several departments. Assessments are determined by the WCB at least once a year when the board sets a percentage or rate to be applied to the payroll of the employer. Payrolls are estimated; the employer is then required to submit a certified payroll statement (see **OH&S Notebook 3.3**).

> ## OH&S Notebook 3.3
> ### ILLUSTRATIVE INDUSTRY ASSESSMENT RATES
>
> The average Workers' Compensation assessment in Ontario for 2012 was $2.40 for every $100 in insurable earnings. However, there are dramatic differences in assessment across occupational groups. For some sample rates, see the table below.
>
> | Rate Group | Description | Assessment per $100 of Insurable Earnings |
> | --- | --- | --- |
> | 030 | Logging | $10.99 |
> | 728 | Roofing | $14.44 |
> | 875 | Professional Offices and Agencies | $0.72 |
> | 335 | Publishing | $0.55 |
>
> Source: Workplace Safety and Insurance Board of Ontario, "2012 Premium Rates." Found at: http://www.wsib.on.ca/en/community/WSIB/230/ArticleDetail/24338?vgnextoid=b15b55c37a2c0310VgnVCM100000469c710aRCRD#table. (Accessed Aug. 2, 2012).

The Workers' Compensation system in Canada is based on the concept of dividing employers into three categories: (1) those who contribute to the incident fund and benefit from its collective liability, (2) those who are individually liable for their own employees' incidents, and (3) those in certain low-risk industries, who are excluded under various acts across the country. Employers who pay directly for the incidents of their employees are generally public enterprises such as provincial or territorial and municipal governments and certain transportation and communication companies within Crown corporations.

All employers within a particular industry group are assessed at the same rate based on the injury experience of the group as a whole. In most jurisdictions, within the general incident fund, a provision is made for a rate stabilization and disaster reserve fund. One group by itself cannot sustain the heavy costs associated with a major disaster that might occur in any one year, or with a sharp decline in assessable payroll owing to massive layoffs in the industry. Continued financing can be provided by the rate stabilization and disaster funds, which are maintained by the various WCBs.

Calculating Injury Frequency and Severity Rates

Following a workplace injury, a copy of the incident analysis report about the injury should accompany the firm's Workers' Compensation claim form. Compensation Boards issue injury frequency and severity rates for injuries resulting from incidents in order to determine the assessment for the organization. These indices may also be used by organizations as benchmarks or targets to manage their own health and safety performance (e.g., http://www.bchydro.com/etc/medialib/internet/documents/info/pdf/2003_annual_report_social_performance_indicators.Par.0001.File.2003_annual_report_social_performance_indicators.pdf).

To determine the frequency injury ratio, consider that the term frequency is the number of medical aid injuries relative to the number of hours worked expressed in a ratio of 200,000. Some firms and jurisdictions use a factor of 1,000,000 rather than 200,000. Using the 200,000 figure, the relationship becomes

$$\text{frequency} = \frac{\text{number of injuries}}{\text{total hours worked}} \times 200,000$$

Take, as an example, a company that employs 300 people who work 8-hour shifts for 250 days in one year. The total number of hours worked is

$$250 \times 300 \times 8 = 600,000$$

This company has a record of 6 medical-aid injuries with no lost time, 15 minor injuries with 5 days lost, 3 major injuries with 55 days lost, and 6 property damage incidents with no lost time. The total number of injuries is

$$(6 + 15 + 3) = 24$$

The frequency is calculated as

$$\text{frequency} = \frac{24}{600,000} \times 200,000 = 8$$

Therefore, this organization has an injury frequency ratio of 8 per 200,000, or 8.

Property damage incidents are not considered, since there is no associated injury.

Severity of work-related injuries is the ratio of the number of days lost due to injuries to a factor of 200,000. Severity is calculated by using the relationship

$$\text{severity} = \frac{\text{number of days lost to injuries}}{\text{total hours worked}} \times 200,000$$

The severity, based on the total number of days lost due to injury in the above example, would be calculated as

$$\text{total lost days} = (5 + 55) = 60$$

$$\text{severity} = \frac{60}{600,000} \times 200,000 = 20$$

The injury severity for this company is 20, or a ratio of 20:200,000. If the company works two or three shifts instead of one, as the examples show, then the total hours worked will be increased twofold or threefold and the relationship will be the same.

These figures facilitate comparisons between various years of the company and among companies within the same product and size group. These values can help identify trends. Records of injuries caused by incidents can also be used as a basis for risk and fault tree analyses.

EXPERIENCE RATING

Experience rating in Workers' Compensation refers to an incident insurance premium pricing scheme that takes into account the clear cost experience of the individual employer. Under experience rating, the assessment for each firm may be higher or lower than the basic rate for the relative industry group. Firms with lower-than-average incident costs per worker pay lower premiums than firms with above-average incident costs. In essence, experience rating reduces or eliminates the cross-subsidization of relatively unsafe firms by relatively safe firms. Given two otherwise similar firms, a safer employer will face lower Workers' Compensation costs and hence lower production costs. Thus, the primary effect of the experience rating is to create a financial incentive for relatively unsafe firms to begin caring for their workforces (see **OH&S Notebook 3.4**).

Experience rating is intended to offer an incentive to employers to reduce injuries and to return workers to their jobs as early as possible. In this way, employers benefit because the amount of money spent on compensation is reduced; workers benefit because they return to their jobs quickly. Experience rating is thus a process of rewarding good performers and penalizing those organizations that are not making efforts to reduce incidents and return workers back to work as quickly as possible.

Generally, if an employer has an experience rating of a three-year average injury cost lower than that of the entire group, that employer will receive a rebate on the annual assessment. Conversely, employers who have an average injury cost higher than the group will receive demerit charges on top of their regular assessments.

One of the most important reasons for mandatory experience rating is to reduce industrial incidents and injuries and their costs. The profit-maximizing, cost-minimizing firm will respond to the incentive by investing in activities that reduce

---

 OH&S Notebook 3.4

EXPERIENCE RATING PROGRAMS IN ONTARIO

New Experimental Experience Rating Program (NEER)

NEER automatically applies to companies that pay more than $25,000 per year in premiums and that are not in a construction rate group. NEER allows companies to earn rebates on premiums by maintaining a good health and safety record. Alternatively, companies that have a poor health and safety record will be assessed a surcharge. To establish whether a company's record is better or worse than average, it is compared with similar companies (i.e., a company's costs are compared within its rate group over the past four years). Companies are not penalized for long-term conditions such as hearing loss or asbestosis.

CAD-7

CAD-7 applies to employers in the construction sector whose average annual premiums are more than $25,000. Similar to NEER, a company's claim history is compared with that of similar firms within a rate group to determine whether a surcharge or rebate is applicable.

Merit Adjusted Premium (MAP) Plan for Small Business

MAP is similar to the foregoing programs but applies to small businesses (those paying between $1,000 and $25,000 in annual WCB premiums). Generally, MAP decreases or increases to premiums do not take effect until after three years of continuous operations (though increases may be applied earlier if a significant number of claims are filed).

Sources: Workplace Safety and Insurance Board of Ontario, "2012 Premium Rates." Found at: http://www.wsib.on.ca/en/community/WSIB/230/ArticleDetail/24338?vgnextoid=b15b55c37a2c0310VgnVCM100000469c710aRCRD#table. (Accessed Aug. 2, 2012).

its Workers' Compensation claim costs to the point where the expected marginal benefits (i.e., incremental reduction in the expected cost of injuries and incidents) equal the marginal costs. Given the existence of workplace risk, and assuming full information about such risk, the firm may allocate resources to safety practices or pay the costs associated with work injury. Profit-maximizing firms operating in competitive markets will strive to minimize some of the costs associated with workplace injuries and incidents, such as Workers' Compensation premium payments (including experience rating service charges/refunds as well as material costs), fixed employment costs, lost production time, and damage to equipment, by preventing incidents (i.e., reducing the probability of a hazardous state) as well as by engaging in activities that minimize costs when incidents do occur. Post-incident employer actions that can result in claim cost reduction include implementing early return-to-work programs and appealing WCB decisions on workers' benefits.

The Workers' Compensation Boards in several jurisdictions (e.g., Ontario, Alberta, B.C.) operate experience rating plans with the goal of creating incentives for firms to reduce their claim rates. That is, the experience rating systems attempt to reward safe firms (through a rebate of assessment premiums) and to penalize unsafe firms (through a surcharge on premiums). Such programs provide some leverage to firms seeking to reduce their Workers' Compensation costs—to the extent that firms can establish and maintain better-than-average safety records, costs will be decreased.

Empirically, then, the question is whether experience rating schemes actually work. That is, do they decrease incidents or injuries in the workplace? This is an exceedingly complex question, and there does not appear to be a clear answer thus far.[7] However, the best evidence to date suggests that such plans are effective in improving workplace safety.[8]

REPORTING REQUIREMENTS

In most jurisdictions, employers are required to report all workplace injuries to the Workers' Compensation Board within a certain time. In Manitoba, for example, the requirement is to report within five days of learning of an injury. In New Brunswick, employers must report serious (e.g., fatality, loss of limb) incidents immediately, other incidents within 24 hours or, if neither of these applies, within three days of learning of the incident. Each board provides a form for employer reporting. Figure 3.1 shows the form used for employer reporting in Manitoba (note that each board has its own form, though all are very similar). Essentially the employer report is designed to collect information about (a) the nature of the employment relationship, (b) the employee's salary and hours of work, (c) the nature of the incident and injury, and (d) the extent of time loss and medical treatment. These elements will then enter into the determination of whether the employee is eligible for compensation and, if so, the amount and duration of this compensation.

Employees are also required to report to the WCB if they want to open a claim for compensation. Employees often do not want to complete an incident report if they do not plan to open a claim (e.g., have not incurred medical expenses, do not intend to miss time). Though not a requirement, it is a good idea to encourage employees to file a report—one never knows when a seemingly minor injury will become something much more serious later on, and having the paper work filed

FIGURE (3.1)

Employer Incident Report, Manitoba

WCB
Workers Compensation Board of Manitoba

Please FAX this form IMMEDIATELY to:
954-4999 (Toll-free 1-877-872-3804)

or report this claim by calling:
954-4100 (Toll-free 1-800-362-3340)
333 Broadway • Winnipeg R3C 4W3

EMPLOYER'S INCIDENT REPORT

Claim No.		**2**

Employer Information

Business Name	Address (include Branch where applicable)		
City	Province	Postal Code	Firm Number	Industry Code	Telephone No. ( )

Worker Information

Last Name	First Name
Address	City
Province	Postal Code	Telephone No. ( )	Date of Birth DD / MM / YYYY
Social Insurance Number	Male ☐ Female ☐	Job Title

Incident Details

Date of Incident DD / MM / YYYY	Area(s) of Injury
Date Reported to Employer DD / MM / YYYY	Name and position of person to whom incident was reported.

Please describe the incident in as much detail as possible. (Use separate sheet if necessary)

City and province where incident occurred.

If the incident occurred out of province, is the worker's usual place of employment in Manitoba? ☐ yes ☐ no   Had the worker been employed outside of Manitoba for 6 months or longer at the time of the incident? ☐ yes ☐ no

Did the incident occur on your premises? ☐ yes ☐ no   If no, specify name and address of premises where incident happened.

Name and Address of Doctor(s) and/or Hospital(s) who Provided Treatment (If known)

Name	Address
Name	Address

Time Loss & Wages (Only complete this section if the worker missed time from work beyond the date of the incident)

What was the last day and hour worked following the incident?	DD / MM / YYYY at HOUR ☐AM ☐PM
Has the worker returned to work? ☐ yes ☐ no If yes, when?	DD / MM / YYYY at HOUR ☐AM ☐PM
Are you continuing to pay the worker during time loss? ☐ yes ☐ no	What wages were paid to the worker on the last date worked? $
How many hours does the worker work per week? If it varies, please describe.	What are the worker's regular days off? If it varies, please describe.
What are the worker's regular gross earnings? (Specify weekly, bi-weekly, etc.) $	What are the worker's total gross earnings for the last calendar year? $
What date did the worker begin employment with your firm? DD / MM / YYYY	If employed less than one year, what are the worker's gross earnings for the period from the date of employment to the date of the incident? $
If employed more than one year, what are the worker's gross earnings during the twelve months prior to the date of the incident? $	Are you able to accommodate worker in alternate duties? ☐ yes ☐ no

WCB 2009   Aussi disponible en français

For Faster Claim Reporting, Please Call 954-4100

Page 1 of 2

NEL

FIGURE 3.1

Employer Incident Report, Manitoba (*continued*)

Worker's Name	Claim No.	**2**

Coverage

Was anyone not employed by you involved in the incident? ☐ yes ☐ no	If yes, give name and address.
Is the worker a partner, director or sole proprietor of the company? ☐ yes ☐ no	

Please answer these questions if the incident occurred between Jan. 1, 1992 and Dec. 31, 2005

Is the worker a member of the employer's family (or if the employer is a corporation, a family member of the director of the corporation)? ☐ yes ☐ no

If yes, does the worker reside with the employer or director? ☐ yes ☐ no

Is the worker a sub-contractor? ☐ yes ☐ no   If yes, specify: ☐ Construction ☐ Logging   (Complete appropriate sections below)

Is the worker an owner operator? ☐ yes ☐ no   If yes, specify: ☐ Courier ☐ Trucking ☐ Towing   (Complete appropriate sections below)

Farming:

Is the worker related to the farm owner? ☐ yes ☐ no

Sub-Contractor or Owner Operator: (only complete if worker is a sub-contractor or owner operator)

Are you covering the worker under your WCB coverage? ☐ yes ☐ no	If no, is the worker registered with WCB? ☐ yes ☐ no		
Does the worker work in a partnership? ☐ yes ☐ no	Does the worker employ other workers? ☐ yes ☐ no		

Sub-Contractor in Construction

Does the worker supply any materials or equipment? ☐ yes ☐ no   If yes, please specify.

Sub-Contractor in Logging

Does the worker supply any materials or equipment? ☐ yes ☐ no   If yes, please specify.

Was the worker cutting on the firm's timber sale, timber permit or sawmill license? ☐ yes ☐ no   If no, on whose timber sale, timber permit or sawmill license was the worker cutting?

Owner Operator is a Courier

What is the gross vehicle weight? (This can be obtained from the Autopac registration)

Owner Operator in Trucking

Does the worker haul within a 16 km radius of the city or town in which the home terminal is located? ☐ yes ☐ no   Is the worker a long distance driver? ☐ yes ☐ no

Does the worker provide a vehicle? ☐ yes ☐ no   If yes, how many vehicles?

Name and Position of Person Completing Report	Date DD / MM / YYYY

Page 2 of 2

Source: Workers Compensation Board of Manitoba.

FIGURE 3.2

Worker Incident Report, Manitoba

WCB
Workers Compensation
Board of Manitoba

To report your claim faster, please CALL:
954-4100   (Toll-free 1-800-362-3340)

or fax this form to:
954-4999   (Toll-free 1-877-872-3804)
333 Broadway • Winnipeg R3C 4W3

WORKER INCIDENT REPORT

Claim No.	3

Worker Information

Last Name	First Name

Address	City

Province	Postal Code	Telephone No. ( )	Date of Birth DD / MM / YYYY	PHIN ___ - ___ - ___

Social Insurance Number	Male ☐ Female ☐	Job Title

Employer Information

Business Name	Address (include Branch where applicable)

City	Province	Postal Code	Telephone No. ( )

Incident Details

Date of Incident DD / MM / YYYY	Area(s) of Injury
Date Reported to Employer DD / MM / YYYY	Name and position of person to whom incident was reported.

Please describe the incident in as much detail as possible. (Use separate sheet if necessary. If applicable, identify any witnesses.)

City and province where incident occurred.

Did the incident occur on your employer's premises? ☐ yes ☐ no	If no, specify name and address of premises where incident happened.

Name and Address of Doctor(s) and/or Hospital(s) that Provided Treatment (Attach separate sheet if necessary)

Name	Address	Date of Visit DD / MM / YYYY
Name	Address	Date of Visit DD / MM / YYYY

Time Loss & Wages (Only complete this section if you have missed time from work beyond the date of the incident)

What was the last day and hour you worked following the incident?	DD / MM / YYYY at HOUR ☐ AM ☐ PM

Have you returned to work? ☐ yes ☐ no   If yes, when?   DD / MM / YYYY   at   HOUR   ☐ AM ☐ PM

Were you paid wages by your employer while you were off work? ☐ yes ☐ no	Do you have other sources of employment income? ☐ yes ☐ no
How many hours do you work per week? If it varies, please describe.	What are your regular days off? If it varies, please describe.
What is your current hourly wage? $	What are your regular gross earnings? (Specify weekly, bi-weekly, etc.) $

What is your marital status?
☐ Single ☐ Common-law ☐ Married ☐ Separated ☐ Divorced   If married/common-law, is your spouse/partner working? ☐ yes ☐ no

Are you personally allowed to claim a deduction on your current year Income Tax Return for:

Dependant children age 18 years or younger? ☐ yes ☐ no   If yes, how many dependants? _____
Disabled dependants age 18 years or older? ☐ yes ☐ no   If yes, how many dependants? _____
Child care expenses? ☐ yes ☐ no   If yes, estimate total deduction for current tax year $ _____
Child support payments? ☐ yes ☐ no   If yes, state monthly amount $ _____   Total for the year $ _____
Spousal support payments? ☐ yes ☐ no   If yes, state monthly amount $ _____   Total for the year $ _____

Have you applied for income from other sources? ☐ yes ☐ no   If yes, please describe.
(e.g. EI, CPP, Social Insurance, Co. Disability Plan, etc.)

WCB 2009

For Faster Claim Reporting, Please Call 954-4100

Aussi disponible en français

Page 1 of 2

FIGURE 3.2

Worker Incident Report, Manitoba (*continued*)

Worker's Name	Claim No.	3

Coverage

Was anyone not employed by your employer involved in the incident?	☐ yes ☐ no	If yes, give name and address.

Are you a partner, director or sole proprietor of the company? ☐ yes ☐ no

Are you a sub-contractor? ☐ yes ☐ no   If yes, specify: ☐ construction ☐ logging   (Complete appropriate sections below)

Are you an owner operator? ☐ yes ☐ no   If yes, specify: ☐ courier ☐ trucking ☐ towing   (Complete appropriate sections below)

Please answer these questions if the incident occurred between Jan. 1, 1992 and Dec. 31, 2005

Are you a member of the family of your employer (or if the employer is a corporation, a family member of the director of the corporation)? ☐ yes ☐ no

If yes, do you reside with the employer or director? ☐ yes ☐ no

Farming:

Are you related to the farm owner? ☐ yes ☐ no

Sub-Contractor or Owner Operator: (only complete if you are a sub-contractor or owner operator)

Is your employer covering you under their WCB coverage? ☐ yes ☐ no   If no, are you registered with WCB? ☐ yes ☐ no

Do you work in a partnership? ☐ yes ☐ no   Do you employ other workers? ☐ yes ☐ no

Sub-Contractor in Construction

Do you supply any materials or equipment? ☐ yes ☐ no   If yes, please specify.

Sub-Contractor in Logging

Do you supply any materials or equipment? ☐ yes ☐ no   If yes, please specify.

Were you cutting on the firm's timber sale, timber permit or sawmill license? ☐ yes ☐ no   If no, on whose timber sale, timber permit or sawmill license were you cutting?

Owner Operator is a Courier

What is the gross vehicle weight? (This can be obtained from the Autopac registration)

Owner Operator in Trucking

Do you haul within a 16 km radius of the city or town in which the home terminal is located? ☐ yes ☐ no   Are you a long distance driver? ☐ yes ☐ no

Do you provide a vehicle? ☐ yes ☐ no   If yes, how many vehicles do you provide?

I understand that under *The Workers Compensation Act* the WCB can collect information about me to adjudicate and manage my claim and that information from my claim may be disclosed to my employer or employer representative for WCB program purposes, or may be released to others as authorized by legislation, including *The Workers Compensation Act*, *The Personal Health Information Act* and *The Freedom of Information and Protection of Privacy Act*. The information collected may be used to conduct WCB evaluations and surveys.

If you have any questions regarding the collection, use or disclosure of information on your claim, please contact the WCB's Access and Privacy Officer at 954-4557 or toll free at 1-800-362-3340 extension 4557.

Release for Medical Information
I authorize persons in possession of medical and other information that the WCB determines relevant to this claim to release same to the WCB upon request.

Release for Income Information from Canada Customs and Revenue Agency
This is your authorization to provide the Workers Compensation Board of Manitoba with copies of my complete income tax return(s) and other taxpayer information including all supporting information slips, schedules and financial statements. The information will be used:

(1) to assist in establishing my net average earnings and
(2) to determine and verify eligibility for benefits under the Workers Compensation Act.

This authorization is valid for the two taxation years prior to the year it was signed, the year it was signed, and each following taxation year where benefits are provided.

Signature of Worker X	Date DD / MM / YYYY

Page 2 of 2

Source: Workers Compensation Board of Manitoba.

NEL

will make subsequent claims easier to file. A typical employee report is presented in Figure 3.2; it collects basically the same information as the employer report.

SUMMARY

Workers' Compensation was established in Canada in 1914 with the passage of Ontario's Workmen's Compensation Act. Since then, coverage and benefits have increased, as have the associated costs. Though the primary goal of Workers' Compensation is to ensure that injured workers receive appropriate treatment, compensation, and rehabilitation, WCBs often engage in promoting occupational health and safety and trying to prevent occupational injuries. WCBs fund these activities by collecting a premium (based on industry, amount of payroll, and previous claim history) from employers. Compensation for stress-related and chronic conditions remains a particular challenge for WCBs.

Key Terms

collective liability 55
latency period 65
loss of functional capacity 62
net earnings 59

physical rehabilitation 64
social rehabilitation 64
vocational rehabilitation 64

Weblinks

"Workers' Compensation Past, Present and Future—A Historical Overview"
http://www.awcbc.org/en/historyofworkerscompensation.asp

"Workers Compensation Timeline"
http://www.awcbc.org/en/workerscompensationtimeline.asp

Required Professional Capabilities (RPCs)

The following RPCs, listed by their CCHRA number, are relevant to the material covered in this chapter. All RPCS can be found at http://www.chrp.ca/rpc/body-of-knowledge.
RPC:171 Ensures compliance with legislated reporting requirements.*
RPC:186 Establishes and implements strategies to minimize workers' compensation costs.*

Discussion Questions

1. Outline the responsibilities of WCBs today. Describe how these responsibilities have changed over the years since the inception of Workers' Compensation in 1914.

* Canadian Council of Human Resources Associations, Human Resources Professionals in Canada: Revised Body of Knowledge and Required Professional Capabilities (RPCs ®), 2007.

2. Imagine you are a truck driver. An accident on the road has left you with two broken legs and a head concussion. What type of assistance might you expect from Workers' Compensation? What could your manager do to expedite your return to work?

3. If you are employed, talk with the health and safety manager in your organization. (If you are a student, ask to speak to the safety officer at your school.) Obtain information about the organization's sector, assessment, and record-of-experience ratings.

Using the Internet

1. Check the Workers' Compensation Board in your area. What cost savings are available to firms that improve their health and safety record? What obligations exist to implement return-to-work procedures?

2. Most WCBs publish their current rates online. Pick a single industry and find the appropriate rate group assessment across the provinces and territories. Who pays the highest assessments? Who pays the lowest?

Exercises

1. Various jurisdictions have struggled with how employees should be compensated for stress-related disabilities. Using the Workers' Compensation websites listed in **OH&S Notebook 2.3** in the preceding chapter, check to see how the following scenarios are handled in your jurisdiction:

   a. mental—mental stress at work results in a psychological disorder (e.g., depression)

   b. mental/physical—mental stress at work results in a physical disorder (e.g., heart attack)

   c. physical/mental—an incident at work results in a psychological disorder (e.g., anxiety attacks)

2. Company X operates one 12-hour shift per day for 220 days per year. It employs 315 people. The company records show a history of incidents and injuries:

   • 3 medical aid injuries with no days lost

   • 15 property damage incidents with a total of 35 days lost

   • 11 equipment failures that caused a total of 20 days lost

   • 19 injuries requiring medical attention with a total of 75 days lost

3. Calculate the following (refer to page 67 for the formulas):

   a. frequency

   b. severity

4. Explain how the company's severity rate can have a significant increase while the frequency rate has a very minor increase.

Case 1 THE EMPLOYER'S DUTY

Sulleman has worked for Speedy Courier for the past three years. Last Tuesday he was loading his truck when he suddenly screamed in pain. Apparently, he had injured his back while lifting a box that exceeded the weight limits. Sulleman was rushed to the hospital, where they could find no evidence of injury other than the pain expressed by Sulleman. Knowing that a lack of hard evidence is common in these types of injuries, you can assume that Sulleman will be off work for a considerable period. As the HR representative for Speedy Courier, you have been charged with fulfilling the company's responsibilities under the act. In this regard, senior management has expressed concern about the number of disability claims and the fact that most recent claims have been for extended periods (e.g., several exceeding 12 months). What do you need to do?

Case 2 A STRESSFUL JOB

Joan is an emergency room nurse at a busy city hospital. She has always enjoyed the hustle of working with emergencies and the challenges of dealing with the unexpected. Lately, though, she has been worried about her own well-being. She has been very abrupt with her coworkers on several occasions and has had difficulty concentrating on her job. Though there have been no problems to date, she is worried that her deteriorating performance might cause a problem, given the critical nature of her work. Her doctor has suggested that she take an extended leave because of her "nerves" and has assured her that Workers' Compensation would cover her lost salary. As an HR person, what would you advise Joan?

NOTES

1. K. Roberts, "Using Workers' Compensation to Promote a Healthy Workplace," in D.A. Hoffman and L.E. Tetrick, eds., *Health and Safety in Organizations: A Multi-Level Perspective* (San Francisco: Jossey Bass, 2003). 367.
2. "B.C. Expands Cancer Benefit Coverage for Firefighters," Government of British Columbia, accessed July 19, 2012, http://www2.news.gov.bc.ca/news_releases_2009-2013/2011PREM0087-000878.pdf
3. Ministry of Labour, Citizens' Services and Open, "Workers' Compensation Act Expands Mental Stress Coverage," accessed July 23, 2021, http://www2.news.gov.bc.ca/news_releases_2009-2013//2011LCITZ0021-001395.HTM.
4. K. Roberts, "Using Workers' Compensation to Promote a Healthy Workplace," in D.A. Hoffman and L.E. Tetrick, eds., *Health and Safety in Organizations: A Multi-Level Perspective* (San Francisco: Jossey Bass, 2003). 369.
5. D.E. Hyatt, "Work Disincentives of Workers' Compensation Permanent Partial Disability Benefits: Evidence for Canada," *Canadian Journal of Economics* 29 (1996): 289–308;

B. Meyer, W.K. Viscusi, and D. Durbin, "Workers' Compensation and Injury Duration: Evidence from a Natural Experiment," *American Economic Review* 85 (1996): 322–40.

6. E.K. Kelloway, L. Francis, V.M. Catano, J. Cameron, and A. Day, *Psychological Disorders in the Canadian Forces: Legal and Social Issues—Contractor's Report* (Ottawa: National Defence Headquarters, Director Human Resources Research and Evaluation, 2004).

7. K. Roberts, "Using Workers' Compensation to Promote a Healthy Workplace," in D.A. Hoffman and L.E. Tetrick, eds., *Health and Safety in Organizations: A Multi-Level Perspective* (San Francisco: Jossey Bass, 2003).

8. D. Durbin and R. Butler, "Prevention of Disability for Work-Related Sources: The Roles of Risk Management, Government Intervention, and Insurance," in T. Thomason, J.F. Burton, and D.E. Hyatt, eds., *New Approaches to Disability in the Workplace* (Madison: IRRA, 1998).

PART 2

Jill Wachter/Getty Images

Hazards and Agents

Hazard Recognition, Risk Assessment, and Control

CHAPTER LEARNING OBJECTIVES

After reading this chapter, you should be able to:

- define key terms used in the field of occupational health and safety
- identify the sources of workplace hazards
- describe the types of injuries caused by workplace hazards
- identify types of workplace hazards
- describe methods for systematically examining workplace hazards and risk
- describe the processes for controlling hazards and managing risk

NUCLEAR TRAGEDY

In March 2011 the world witnessed the second worst nuclear power disaster unfold as a 15- metre tsunami caused by an earthquake approximately 130 kilometres off the coast of Japan destroyed the Fukushima Daiichi and Daini Nuclear Power Plants of Tokyo Electric Power Company. The International Atomic Energy Agency (IAEA) classified it as a level 7 out of 7 (major accident) on the International Nuclear Event Scale (INES) due to the high amounts of radioactive material released into the environment. On May 24, 2011 a committee was created to determine whether the proper precautions were in place at Tokyo Electric. Upon investigation into the incident the committee determined much of the damage at the company was the result of a number of causes, citing a lack of preventative measures, disaster preparedness, and accident emergency responses. A final report into the accident makes a number of recommendations to ensure that Tokyo Electric is better prepared for such natural disasters. Specifically the committee made recommendations that Tokyo Electric reevaluate their attitudes towards the assessment of the risks posed by natural disasters, in particular the risks posed by hazards that are viewed to have a low probability of occurrence or considered to be difficult to predict. While a final report has been released, the tragedy emphasizes the need to properly assess and control hazards and risks within the workplace, as well as maintain a positive and proactive culture of safety. Hazard recognition and risk assessment and control are the backbone of workplace OH&S programs and is the focus of this chapter.

Source: Secretariat of the National Diet of Japan Fukushima Nuclear Accident Independent Investigation Commission. Found at: http://naiic.go.jp/wp-content/uploads/2012/07/NAIIC_report_hi_res4.pdf; http://icanps.go.jp/eng/SaishyuRecommendation.pdf.

Almost every workplace has recognizable hazards to which people are exposed. There are many different definitions of the term hazard however, the term is typically defined as any source of potential adverse health effects, damage, or harm to something or someone under certain conditions at work.[1] Hazards within the work environment pose a risk to those within that environment and in order to manage that risk, the hazard and its potential must be properly understood, assessed, and controlled using a systematic process known as hazard/risk assessment and control.

TERMINOLOGY

Hazard identification and risk assessment and control involve very specific terms, some of which are incorrectly used interchangeably. Though the following terms seem similar to one another, each has a distinctive use in the OH&S field:

hazard
any source of potential adverse health effect, damage, or harm on something or someone under certain conditions at work

- A **hazard** is any object, action, or condition that can be a source of potential adverse health effect, damage, or harm to people, processes, or equipment within the workplace. Examples of objects that can be considered workplace hazards are chemicals used to disinfect a surface, or sharp objects and machinery. Examples of hazardous conditions are icy steps, or an understaffed shift rotation. Examples of hazardous actions are not wearing personal protective equipment (e.g., gloves), or not following safety procedures.

OH&S Today (4.1

A Controversial Term

Though the term "accident" is commonly used to refer to an unwanted event that causes harm, more and more health and safety professionals avoid using it, preferring the term "incident." This preference is based on two observations. First, effective health and safety management is more appropriately focused on understanding incidents and the root cause(s). Second, some health and safety professionals suggest the term accident implies the event was unavoidable and uncontrollable and as such there are no "accidents" in this sense. They reject the view that "accidents will happen," relying instead on effective means of hazard recognition, risk assessment, and control whereby we can prevent incidents and injury from occurring.

- Generally the term **incident** is defined as an event or occurrence that had or could have had a negative impact on people, property, or processes. Events which could have had a negative impact are frequently referred to as close calls or near-miss incidents. A close call or near-miss incident is any unplanned event wherein harm or equipment loss almost occurred but was successfully prevented or mitigated. Examples of close calls include not wearing safety glasses when operating a power saw and nearly being hit by flying debris, or brushing against hot objects with unprotected hands without getting burned. Close calls or near-miss incidents involve the presence of a hazard but may or may not result in harm or loss.

- **Risk** is typically defined in terms of the probability or the extent to which a hazard is likely to cause harm to people, processes, or equipment. The concept of **risk perception** is based on the individual's interpretation of the potential for harm and their concern for the consequences based on social, physical, political, cultural, and psychological factors that then influence how an individual behaves in response to that hazard.[2]

incident
an event or occurrence that had or could have had a negative impact on people, property, or processes

risk
the probability or the extent to which a hazard is likely to cause harm to people, processes, or equipment

risk perception
an individual's interpretation of the potential for harm based on values, beliefs, and experience with a hazard

HAZARD RECOGNITION AND IDENTIFICATION

Broadly speaking, when hazards are being identified, one considers the sources: biological, chemical, ergonomic, physical, and psychosocial (discussed in detail in following chapters) followed by the specific type of hazard. There are five categories of hazard types: people, equipment, environment, materials, and processes that should be considered during the hazard identification process.

People

Humans create hazards in the workplace by their actions or inactions. Proper training, administration, leadership, and supervision are required to ensure that employees engage in the appropriate workplace behaviours. Incidents involving humans are referred to as unsafe acts. An **unsafe act** generally refers to a deviation from standard job procedures or practices that increases the potential for an incident and harm. A human action that may cause an immediate event of any type, and

unsafe act
a deviation from standard job procedures or practices that increases a worker's exposure to a hazard

over which the person has control, is considered a direct, unsafe act (sometimes referred to as a *substandard practice*). An example would be improper modifications to a respirator used in a paint booth to allow a cigarette to be smoked through the filter cassette. An indirect, unsafe act is one in which the human action is only indirectly involved. Consider the following example. A designer of a machine alters a braking system on a punch press that allows the machine to complete its operating cycle after the emergency stop is activated instead of immediately stopping. In this instance there is overlap between an indirect unsafe act and an unsafe condition. The machine defect started as an indirect unsafe act but resulted in an unsafe condition for the operators using the machine.

Unsafe acts are observable behaviours that are the direct outcome of a decision made by an individual. Unsafe acts that contribute to or cause an incident are labelled as human factors.

human factor

when a person causes an accident by commission, poor judgment, or omission (failing to do something)

When a worker or another person causes an incident by commission (doing something), poor judgment, or omission (failing to do something), the cause is labelled a **human factor**. However, when conducting an incident investigation and determining the role of human factors there is a distinction between fact finding and fault finding. A human action may have been directly or indirectly involved in the event, but "human error" or blame should never be used nor implied. In a similar vein, no one would willingly or intentionally injure himself or herself, which tends to support the idea that a human action should not be considered "human error" and have blame assigned. No matter how many backup systems are in place, some shortcut or personal foible can cause the system to fail. The intent of hazard recognition, risk assessment, and control is not to find a scapegoat, but to correct procedures and behaviours so that the likelihood of the incident occurring again is reduced. Similarly, there are techniques that can permit a professional to identify hazardous conditions or activities and implement correct procedures before hazardous events occur.

Equipment

Under certain conditions or situations the tools, machines, or equipment people use and work near can be hazardous. Examples of equipment that can be hazardous include defective tools (broken ladder), unguarded moving machinery (unguarded saw blades in a butcher shop). When considering the equipment in the workplace that can be hazardous it is important to carefully consider what falls under workplace equipment and to make sure that everyday equipment like office, lunchroom , or kitchen equipment are considered.

Environment

Some hazards can be created by the work environment and can be either naturally occurring (e.g., weather in outdoor work environments) or the result of an unsafe condition caused by poorly maintained equipment, tools, or facilities.

The following are examples of an unsafe work environment:

- Improper illumination—too dark or too much glare

- Poor exhaust or ventilation systems—the toxic vapours from a process hang in the air rather than being removed

- Defective equipment and materials—not to the required specifications

- Adverse temperature conditions—working around a furnace on a hot summer day

- Poor indoor air quality—odours and stuffiness

Environmental factors, which are encompassed sources of hazards like physical, chemical, biological factors, and ergonomic factors, can play a direct *or* indirect role in incidents. For example, physical factors such as noise, vibration, illumination, and temperature extremes have an obvious relation to safety and exist within certain work environment. A noisy work environment may prevent a worker from hearing approaching vehicles or may damage hearing over time. Similarly, chemical factors such as airborne toxic gases not only may cause illness, but also may impair a worker's reaction, judgment, or concentration. Contact with biological agents such as viruses or parasites may cause either minor illness—a cold—or something more serious—hepatitis B.

Materials

Materials are any workplace substance, matter, or provisions used for production that have the potential to cause harm or loss especially if handled improperly. Examples of materials include supplies and raw materials such as wood within a carpentry shop, dry cleaning chemicals, paint, or cleaning chemicals. When materials are improperly handled or misused or if the wrong materials are used during production they can become a hazard or create hazardous conditions. For instance certain cleaning materials such as ammonia and bleach should never be mixed together because the mixture results in a toxic chemical reaction. Ensuring the proper handling and use of workplace materials is very important and requires training (e.g., WHIMIS training).

Processes

When combining people, equipment, environment, and materials with the purpose of production of a good or service a process is involved. Processes involve the flow of work and include factors such as design, pace, and organization of the various types of work via policies, procedures, and work processes. Work processes can result in various hazardous byproducts when combined with people, equipment, environment, and materials. While the objects and equipment in and of themselves are types of hazards, when combined with using a poor process or procedure then the process or procedure itself is a hazard.

HAZARD IDENTIFICATION PROGRAMS

A hazard identification program (or hazard recognition) is simply a systematic means of identifying and recording hazards in the workplace. They are designed to integrate safe and healthy procedures into job tasks and procedures. The process of hazard identification should be completed by safety experts or employees who are trained to recognize hazards that might not be readily apparent to the casual observer. The hazard identification process can be as simple as a visible inspection of the workplace or as complex as taking air samples to test for suspected contaminants. There are various methodologies available for conducting a hazard identification however, it is critical that a sequential and systematic process is used to ensure that no hazard is overlooked.

Components of the Hazard Identification Program

walk-through survey
a survey in which a safety professional walks through a worksite and notes hazards

safety sampling
a systematic survey procedure undertaken by safety personnel who record their observations of unsafe practices on a sampling document

A safety professional can enter a worksite and, by walking through, note hazards. The utility of a **walk-through survey** is increased when the supervisor and a worker member of the Joint Health and Safety Committee (JHSC) accompany the safety expert. **Safety sampling**, often referred to as *behaviour* or *activity sampling,* is a systematic survey procedure undertaken by safety personnel, who record their observations of unsafe practices on a sampling document. They might observe, for example, workers without hardhats where they are required.

Actual and observable exposures to hazards are the focus of the survey. Following the walk-through survey, the safety personnel encode and count their observations. A report is then submitted to management to provide an objective evaluation of the type and number of unsafe acts and conditions.

Management can ask workers who represent a variety of tasks and jobs to identify hazards and unsafe conditions. Employees might report that they are required to adapt tools (thus rendering them potentially hazardous) in order to meet production quotas, or that a machine is dripping oil, rendering a corridor slippery and treacherous. Discussions with both the experts and the employees should be supplemented by an analysis of the job site and the work performed.

The company should have a detailed layout of the plant or premises, showing the location of processes, machinery, materials storage, shipping, and so forth. WHMIS requires that a drawing showing the location of any toxic materials and storage arrangement is available.

Task and Job Inventory

job description
the content and hierarchy specific to a particular job

job specifications
the requirements necessary to perform the various functions of a job (e.g., ability to lift weight, education level)

A description of the job and its associated tasks should be obtained and organized by department, operation, or product. The human resource department can assist by providing **job descriptions** and **job specifications**.

Task analysis refers to the systematic examination of a job's many components. It consists of a list of tasks and the job of which they are a part, the number of workers who perform the same or similar tasks, the time spent on each task, the importance of the task to the job, the complexity and criticality of the job, the learning curve if complicated and repetitive, and the effort required. The analysis identifies the various demands on the worker, the tasks that are susceptible to worker error and stress, and potentially hazardous conditions. Industrial engineering methods are best for performing this kind of analysis.

Reports and Audits

A review of the reports filed after an incident, accident, or injury or as part of a safety inspection will provide valuable information on hazards. Also, OH&S departments and safety associations can provide written information about the types of accidents in similar industries. Accident and injury rates published by governments are another source of information. For example, most Workers' Compensation Boards (for a complete list, see Chapter 3) publish regular reports on accident statistics. Audit information, which is obtained by reviewing records of all injuries, accidents, incidents, workplace design changes, and environmental sampling, is an extremely useful source for cataloguing hazards. Most large organizations use computers to store, analyze, and report on hazards and incidents, thus facilitating the identification of hazards by type or department.[3]

Hazard Analysis

Hazard analysis is used to acquire specific hazard and failure information about a given system.[4] Hazard analysis is an orderly, analytical technique that examines a system for the most probable hazards having the severest consequences, for the purpose of establishing corrective or control mechanisms. The most common form of hazard analysis is the analytical tree, of which there are two types. The **positive tree** shows, graphically, how a job should be done. The more frequently used tree is the **fault tree**, which illustrates things that can go wrong. A typical fault tree structure is shown in Figure 4.1.

Risk Assessment

Once hazards have been identified, the risk of an incident or injury must be determined. Risk assessments are a critical aspect of occupational health and safety by making employees aware of the hazards and risks they are exposed to and what they should be doing to manage the risk. Determining risk is difficult due to the nature of how it is defined and because there are various methods for assessing it. It is important at this point to consider the concept of risk perceptions and the relationship between the actual risk of a hazard and an individual's perception of the risk. Risk

hazard analysis
an orderly, analytical technique that examines a system for the most probable hazards having the severest consequences, for the purpose of establishing corrective or control mechanisms

positive tree
shows, graphically, how a job should be done

fault tree
an illustration of things that can go wrong

FIGURE 4.1

Example of a Fault Tree

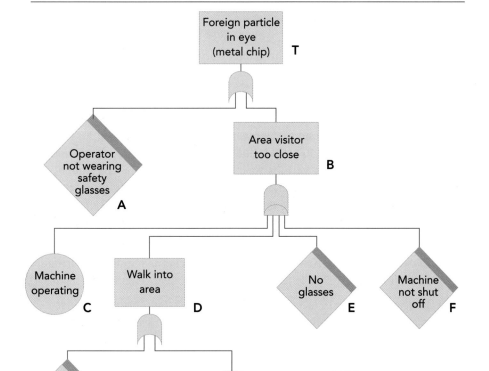

can be assessed by rating the probability of an incident followed by rating the consequences and assigning a level of priority (e.g., very high risk). It can also be measured by consulting statistics (e.g., accident statistics) and calculating the probability of an event. Risk assessment methods that are based on numerical calculations are sometimes referred to as quantitative risk assessments while those not based on numerical calculations are referred to as subjective risk assessments. An argument can be made for choosing one type of risk assessment method over another given the subjective nature of risk perceptions however, there is evidence to support that the actual or objective level risk and an individual's interpretation are not always disparate. Research involving offshore oil and gas platform employees showed that workers had "reasonably accurate perceptions of risk" and suggest that the factors that influence risk perceptions are similar to those which influence more objective assessment methods (i.e., quantitative risk assessment[5]). Regardless of the assessment method chosen the necessity of conducting a risk assessment cannot be negated.

probability

the chance or likelihood that an event will occur and will result in harm or loss

Probability refers to the chance or likelihood that an event will happen and will result in harm or loss. Within the context of workplace safety and risk assessments probability is typically expressed in terms describing the likelihood (e.g., very unlikely, likely, very likely) however there are numerous ways to express probability and it is up to the organization to ensure they are appropriate within a particular context, environment, or situation. The Canadian Centre for Occupational Health and Safety (CCOHS) provides the following terminology for probability:

- *Very likely*—Typically experienced at least once every six months by an individual.

- *Likely*—Typically experienced once every five years by an individual.

- *Unlikely*—Typically experienced once during the working lifetime of an individual.

- *Very unlikely*—Less than 1% chance of being experienced by an individual during their working lifetime.[6]*

consequences

the results or severity of the injury

Consequences correspond to the severity of the injury, harm, or loss and can range from dust in the eye, to amputation of a finger, to death. Consequences of hazard can be expressed in various ways and can include the consequences of harm and or the loss to equipment. It is important for organizations to select terminology that is appropriate for a given job, situation, or context. Consequences are often expressed in terms of severity of harm or loss (e.g., slight harm, moderate, or extreme). CCOHS provides the following indicators of severity of consequences:

- *Slightly harmful* (e.g., superficial injuries; minor cuts and bruises; eye irritation from dust; nuisance and irritation; ill-health leading to temporary discomfort).

- *Moderate harm* (e.g., lacerations; burns; concussion; serious sprains; minor fractures; deafness; dermatitis; asthma; work-related upper limb disorders; ill-health).

- *Extremely harmful* (e.g., amputations; major fractures; poisonings; multiple injuries; fatal injuries; occupational cancer; other severely life-shortening diseases; acute fatal diseases).[7]*

*CCOHS, "Risk Assessment." Found at: http://www.ccohs.ca/oshanswers/hsprograms/risk_assessment.html.

Determining the risk level of hazard is done by gauging likelihood and the consequence of a hazard and assigning it a rating. Risk can be rated as very low, moderate, high, or very high. The rating or priority of risk can be determined by an organization however, it is extremely important that each ranking or priority rating of risk be clear to all those who conduct risk assessments. In other words, employees conducting risk assessments should be clear on what is defined as "low risk." CCOHS provides guidance on defining risk and is a useful resource that is based on the British Standards Institute (UK equivalent of ISO) (see Table 4.1). For example, very low risk is defined as acceptable and does not require further action other than ensuring existing controls are maintained. CCOHS (see Table 4.2) provides a sample layout that can be used for hazard inventory and risk evaluation, which is also based on the British Standards Institute.

Follow-Up

The information obtained through hazard identification and risk assessment should be communicated to the appropriate manager, the immediate supervisor, and the health and safety committee. Some reports may be forwarded to the Ministry of Labour (if the substance is under assessment) or the Ministry of Environment, or

TABLE 4.1

Risk Assessment

Likelihood of Harm	Severity of Harm		
	Slight Harm	Moderate Harm	Extreme Harm
Very unlikely	Very low risk	Very low risk	High risk
Unlikely	Very low risk	Medium risk	Very high risk
Likely	Low risk	High risk	Very high risk
Very likely	Low risk	Very high risk	Very high risk

Source: CCOHS, "Risk Assessment," Table 2. Found at: http://www.ccohs.ca/oshanswers/hsprograms/risk_assessment.html.

TABLE 4.2

Sample Hazard Inventory and Risk Evaluation

EXAMPLE OF RISK ASSESSMENT

Task	Hazard	Risk	Priority	Control
Delivering product to customers	Drivers work alone	May be unable to call for help if needed		
	Drivers have to occasionally work long hours	Fatigue, short rest time between shifts		
	Drivers are often in very congested traffic	Increased chance of collision		
		Longer working hours		
	Drivers have to lift boxes when delivering product	Injury to back from lifting, reaching, carrying, etc.		

Source: CCOHS, "Risk Assessment," Table 1. Found at: http://www.ccohs.ca/oshanswers/hsprograms/risk_assessment.html.

to the corporation's lawyers. Safety professionals and supervisors who do not pass on information about unsafe conditions to a responsible manager could be charged under the jurisdiction's occupational health and safety act.

When presented with information about hazards, management may decide to (1) take no action, (2) take corrective action, or (3) consider a cost–benefit analysis to determine whether the anticipated losses are worth the cost of correcting the problem.

TYPES OF INJURIES

A look at the nature of workplace injuries will help us identify the types of workplace hazards we are concerned with. There are at least two broad classes of **injuries** in workplaces. **Overt traumatic injuries** (e.g., cuts, fractures, burns) typically result from coming into contact with an energy source (e.g., falling, being struck by material). In contrast, **overexertion injuries** (e.g., sprains, back pain, tendonitis, carpal tunnel syndrome) typically are caused by excessive physical effort, repetitive motions, and, possibly, awkward working positions. From this observation it follows that hazard identification and control should focus on identifying and controlling sources of energy that can result in injury as well as in conditions of work that may lead to overexertion.

Overt Traumatic Injuries

One of the most common causes of workplace accidents is individuals coming into contact with objects and equipment. For example, individuals may be struck by objects that are falling from overhead or may drop materials on themselves, resulting in crush injuries. Material may be flying through the air because of grinding or cutting operations. The use of compressed air in many industrial settings is a particular hazard, as the stream of compressed air may cause small particles of material to accelerate rapidly through the work environment. Individuals may also be struck by moving equipment (e.g., vehicles, forklifts).

Another form of contact with equipment occurs when individuals become caught in, under, or between (CIUB) machinery. Industrial presses, for example, are often associated with crush injuries when individuals who are feeding the machine stock get their hands caught in the machinery as it presses. Conveyer belts and other power transmission systems (e.g., belts, pulleys) may have "pinch points" in which individuals can become entangled.

Falls are another significant source of workplace injury. This category includes falls from a height (e.g., off a ladder, or down a set of stairs) as well as falls on the same level (e.g., slipping on the floor). As we might expect, falls from a height are common in construction, where ladders and other temporary structures (e.g., scaffolding) are frequently used. Falls on the same level often result from spilled material (e.g., oil) or from tripping over poorly placed material, uneven surfaces, and so on.

Overt traumatic injuries also result from coming into contact with sources of energy such as electricity, chemicals (e.g., chemical burns), and heat (e.g., touching a hot surface results in a burn). Prolonged kneeling and the use of abrasives can result in abrasive injuries in which the skin is torn or rubbed raw.

In all situations, prevention focuses on (1) recognizing the source of the hazard (i.e., the potential energy source), (2) eliminating the hazard, and (3) protecting workers from exposure to the energy source (e.g., through personal protective equipment).

injury
any trauma, physical or mental, direct or indirect, acute or chronic, experienced by a human being

overt traumatic injuries
injuries resulting from coming into contact with an energy source

overexertion injuries
injuries resulting from excessive physical effort, repetitive motions, and, possibly, awkward working positions

Overexertion Injuries

There are many types of overexertion or repetitive strain injuries. Most of them, though, have one of three basic causes: lifting, working in an awkward position, or repetition.

Materials handling, which involves lifting, carrying, and lowering, is an often-performed operation in many organizations that can result in high-risk injuries through overexertion and poor posture, both of which are the primary cause of low back pain. Lifting tolerances can be estimated using formulae developed by the National Institute for Occupational Safety and Health (NIOSH) in the United States.[8] Back injuries —from stabbing pain to total disability—can have far-reaching effects for the worker, the worker's family, and the company. Low back pain, often associated with materials handling, accounts for more than 50% of all musculoskeletal complaints and is the fastest growing category of disability (see **OH&S Notebook 4.1**).[9]

 OH&S Notebook 4.1

TWELVE RULES FOR PROPER LIFTING

1. *Size up the load and check the overall conditions:* Is the load being picked up in the open, or is it surrounded by other boxes? Is it too large to grasp? How far does it *have* to be carried? How high does it have to be lifted? Is the floor dry or slippery?

2. *Choose the lifting position that feels the best:* There are several "correct" ways to lift a load. Figure 4.2 illustrates two of the more common ones: the straight-back leg lift and the stoop lift.

3. *Check for slivers, nails, sharp edges, and so on:* Sustaining a penetration injury while lifting is both painful and awkward.

4. *Lift by gripping the load with both the fingers and the palms of the hand:* The more the hand is in contact with the object, the better the control and the more positive the application of the lifting force.

5. *Keep the back straight:* A straight back (not a vertical back) will reduce stress on the spine and make the load distribution on each vertebral disc uniform.

6. *Maintain good balance:* If you are not steady on your feet, an off-balance motion can impose significant stress on the discs.

7. *Avoid any unnecessary bending:* Do not place loads on the floor but on a platform or rack if they have to be picked up again later. Bend the knees, and do not stoop.

8. *Avoid unnecessary twisting:* No twisting is acceptable. Turn the feet, not the hips or shoulders.

9. *Avoid reaching out:* Keep all loads as close to the body as possible. The farther away from the body centre, the greater the disc load and hence the greater the stress (see Figure 4.3).

10. *Avoid excessive weight:* If the load is too heavy or too awkward, get help. The definition of "excessive" will depend on the individual and his or her physical condition and training.

11. *Lift slowly and smoothly:* Use your body weight to start the load moving, and then lift using your legs and arms.

12. *Keep in good physical shape:* The better your physical condition, the easier lifting will be and the lower the risk of sustaining a lower-back injury.

Sources: WorkSafe Alberta, "Lifting and Handling Loads." Found at: http://www.hre.gov.ab.ca/documents/WHS/WHS-PUB_bcl001. pdf (Accessed Feb. 7, 2007); North American Occupational Safety and Health, "Preventing Back Injury in Manual Materials Handling." Found at: http://www.naosh.org/english/documents/mmh.html (Accessed Feb. 7, 2007); WorkSafeBC, "Top Seven Dangers for Young Workers." Found at: http://youngworker.healthandsafetycentre.org/s/Top-Seven-Dangers.asp?ReportID533144 (Accessed Feb. 7, 2007).

FIGURE 4.2

Lift Positions

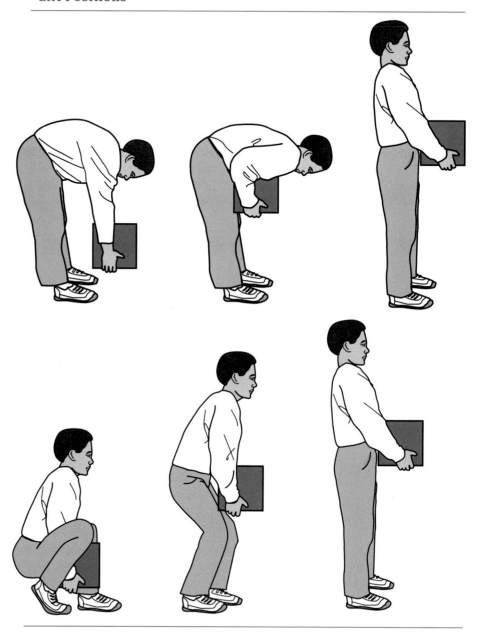

When lifting activities are identified as a workplace hazard, materials handling can be mechanized through the use of conveyors and forklift trucks or other lifting devices; or it can be automated through the use of guided vehicles, which follow sensor lines on the floor, stopping as required to transfer their loads; or inventory systems can be installed that allow computer-controlled machines to pick up or stock inventory. In these ways, many of the risks associated with

FIGURE (4.3)

Relationship between Load Position and Lower Back Stress

LOWER BACK STRESS = (A + B) × C

where A = distance from front of body to rotation point of spine, approximately 20 cm

B = distance in front of body to load centre of mass

C = load weight

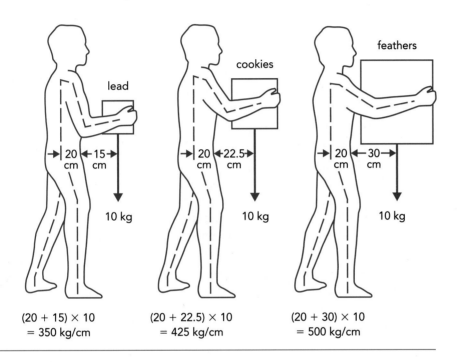

$$(20 + 15) \times 10 = 350 \text{ kg/cm}$$

$$(20 + 22.5) \times 10 = 425 \text{ kg/cm}$$

$$(20 + 30) \times 10 = 500 \text{ kg/cm}$$

lifting can be greatly reduced. Some workers use supports that force the back to remain straight but do not prevent the worker from lifting or handling heavier loads. Though the logic of using back supports is appealing, agencies such as NIOSH in the United States have suggested that there is no scientific evidence in favour of the use of such devices. The Canadian Task Force on Preventive Health Care found that randomized control trials did not support the use of back supports.[10] Of the five trials reviewed, three found no effect and the remaining two found marginal effects.

Repetitive Strain Injuries

Tennis elbow, golfer's elbow, telephone operator's elbow, writer's cramp, and postal worker's shoulder are well-known examples of what is known as repetitive strain injury (RSI). More recently named conditions include carpal tunnel syndrome, thoracic outlet syndrome, and white fingers disease or Raynaud's syndrome (see **OH&S Today 4.2**).

RSI is fast becoming the most common occupational injury. Data from the Canadian Community Health Survey suggest that 1 in 20 Canadians over the age of 20 have experienced RSI.[11] This translates into 2.3 million cases, most of which result from work activities. The origins of RSI can be traced to the following four general conditions:

- *Unnatural joint position or posture.* Whenever a joint is forced to work in a position that is unnatural or stressed, the risk of RSI is increased. For instance, during keyboarding the wrists are forced out of axial alignment with the arm. The use of a hand tool such as a pair of pliers can force the wrist-arm axes out of line, creating a stress condition that could eventually cause joint irritation.

- *Force application to hinge joints.* When hinge joints are forced to carry applied loading, particularly when flexed, the joint load distribution of the cartilage is uneven, causing excessive stress in a small area of the joint. The wrist is a good example of a hinge joint. When performing a task such as lifting while bent, this joint can begin to ache. Repetition of the activity can result in a loss of strength.

- *Activity repetition.* Tasks such as keyboarding (computer operator) or using a hammer (carpenter) involve a repetitive flexing of the fingers and wrists. The action of typing applies low-load repetition to the fingers (touching the keys) and medium loading to the wrist (supporting the hand). The action of hammering applies a high-impact loading to the wrist, which is flexed into a nonaligned axis on impact. The shock effect increases the potential risk of tissue damage.

- *Pre-existing conditions.* Ailments such as arthritis and circulation disorders can have a synergistic effect on RSI conditions. For example, arthritis—an inflammation condition of the joints—can be aggravated by the stress associated with hammering or keyboarding.

OH&S Today 4.2

Artistic Occupations at Risk

If you search for RSI on the Web, you will mostly find articles focused on the hazards of computer work and industrial jobs that involve repetitive motions. It may surprise you to know that people in other occupations—such as dancers and musicians—are also at risk for RSI. These occupations involve considerable repetition (practice, practice, practice) and often involve awkward hand or body positions. Intense preparation for a performance, learning new pieces (requiring extensive practice and repetition), changes in techniques or instruments, and prolonged performances are all risk factors for performing artists. Dancers are at risk because of these factors but also because forceful exertions can lead to stress fractures and similar injuries.

Source: Safety and Health in Arts, Production, and Entertainment, "Preventing Musculoskeletal Injury (MSI) for Musicians and Dancers." Found at: http://www.shape.bc.ca/resources/pdf/msi.pdf (Accessed Feb. 7, 2007); NOASH, "Health, Preventing Back Injury in Manual Materials Handling." Found at: http://www.naosh.org/english/documents/mmh.html (Accessed Feb. 7, 2007); WorkSafeBC, "Top Seven Dangers for Young Workers." Found at: http://youngworker.healthandsafetycentre.org/s/Top-Seven-Dangers. asp?ReportID533144 (Accessed Feb. 7, 2007).

Awkward Working Positions

Strains and sprains can result from bending, twisting, and working in a variety of awkward positions. Frequently, the work position may compound or interact with other factors. For example, an individual may be lifting a load that normally would present no problem but be working in a confined space that prohibits following safe lifting procedures, resulting in an injury.

Perhaps the most common types of injury result from bending or twisting the torso, extending the reach beyond the body, and working overhead with the hands and arms. As a general guideline, individuals should not have to reach below the knees or raise their arms above the shoulder for any length of time. Workstations and work procedures should be designed to ensure that individuals work in a comfortable position. Moreover, equipment and machinery should be adjustable to accommodate differences in body size.

HAZARD CONTROL

Hazard control refers to the program or process used to establish preventive and corrective measures as the final stage of hazard recognition, risk assessment, and control. The goal is to eliminate, reduce, or control hazards so as to minimize injuries and losses, including accidents, property damage, and time lost. It is useful to think of hazard control as comprising three levels of intervention (1) **precontact control** (addressing issues before an incident or accident occurs), (2) **contact control** (identifying ways in which a hazardous situation can be prevented from becoming worse and harming workers), and (3) **post-contact control** (putting in place medical and cleanup operations and ensuring that the event cannot be repeated). Controls at each of these levels could comprise engineering controls, administrative controls, and control through personal protective equipment.

Precontact Control

Precontact control is the first method of controlling hazards by preventing hazards from reaching individuals within the workplace. Precontact control means using methods such as isolation, housekeeping, safe work policies and procedures, machine guarding, and replacing or retrofitting hazardous equipment. Precontact control of hazards involves various engineering, administrative, and personal protective equipment based controls. It is important that organizations consult with their provincial occupational health and safety act and regulations because many precontact controls are legislated, for example the Nova Scotia Department of Labour and Advanced Education provides information within the general occupational health and safety regulations for housekeeping and other methods for preventing contact with various hazards.

When precontact control measures are not feasible or practical given the work environment then employers must engage point of contact controls that mitigate the risk associated with that hazard (e.g., using personal protective equipment). In some situations hazards result in an incident in which case contact control must be implemented.

hazard control
the program or process used to establish preventative and corrective measures

precontact control
addressing issues before an incident or accident occurs

contact control
identifying ways in which a hazardous situation can be prevented from becoming worse and harming workers

postcontact control
putting in place medical and cleanup operations and ensuring that the event cannot be repeated

Contact Control

If workplace, equipment, machines, or buildings are damaged as a result of an incident or if a hazard results in an emergency, then control of the hazard site is necessary so that the worker can be protected. Many contact controls fall under the engineering, administrative and PPE categories.

The main purpose of contact control is to ensure that the workers and emergency crews—firefighters—are not added to the injury list. Steps to be taken can be grouped into the five following categories:

- *Suppression.* Reduce or eliminate the ongoing hazard condition by using standard firefighting techniques: install fans to help clear the contaminants from the surrounding air, and turn off the power and utilities to the area. Another example: dust from an explosion in a mining operation can be controlled by spraying water at the rock surface.

- *Barriers.* Install barriers between workers and sources of the emergency to keep unauthorized personnel out of the area.

- *Modifications.* Identify and modify equipment or structures that need to be strengthened in order to prevent further damage from occurring, such as adding shoring to weakened walls to prevent collapse.

- *Substitution.* Eliminate potentially harmful energies that have been unleashed by the event and replace them with safer, independent devices. For example, use portable floodlighting to replace the existing plant lighting if there is a possibility that damaged electrical equipment could cause a fire.

- *Isolation.* Isolate energy sources from the emergency personnel and plant workers. Shut off all energy sources in the plant to prevent additional problems, and replace with outside equipment if possible, such as a portable air compressor to replace the one in the damage area. Shut down any expensive equipment that could be damaged by energy surges.

Postcontact Control

The following are some steps that should be taken in the aftermath of an event:

1. Ensure that any injured worker receives immediate and thorough emergency care. The injury could be anything from a blow to the head to exposure to a hazardous chemical. Provisions for first aid and emergency care should have been made during the precontact control process. The extent of these provisions will depend on the number of workers in an organization and the types of hazards they face.
2. Lock out the machinery involved until the accident investigation is complete and the damage is repaired.
3. Keep unauthorized people out of the area.
4. Determine what can be salvaged and what waste must be disposed of. Environmental regulations may prohibit the easy removal of certain hazardous wastes (e.g., PCB-contaminated oils from a damaged power transformer).

5. Apprise the JHSC, affected managers, and government agencies of the event—fire, police, and paramedics will probably already know.

6. Complete all accident reports to determine what happened. Use report recommendations to ensure that the accident will not be repeated.

7. Review all company procedures and revise where appropriate.

8. Communicate with workers about the event. If necessary, implement safety retraining and possibly trauma counselling depending on the seriousness of the event.

Points 2 to 5 are requirements of the Ministry of Labour in most provinces and territories, and the Workers' Compensation Board in B.C.

ENGINEERING CONTROL

Engineering control refers to the modification of work processes, equipment, and materials in order to reduce exposure to hazards.[12] Hazard control should be built into the design of the work itself. Before equipment and materials are purchased, specifications for efficient and safe operations should be determined. For example, noise emission limits for noisy equipment can be specified before the equipment is purchased, thus reducing possible worker exposure. Engineering control also refers to the installation of auxiliary equipment, such as physical barriers and ventilation systems, in order to reduce hazards dealing with the source and path. Because engineering controls avoid hazards or eliminate them entirely, they are always the first (i.e., most preferred) way to deal with hazards. The redesign of common hand tools is a good example of engineering control.

> **engineering control** modification of work processes, equipment, and materials to reduce exposure to hazards

The common in-line screwdriver configuration, for example, requires that the hand and wrist be forced out of line. In contrast, the T-bar handle in the ergonomic screwdriver allows the hand and arm to be kept in alignment by producing a lower wrist–arm angle (see Figure 4.4). The key to effective hand tool design is to maintain natural joint alignment such as that illustrated by the ergonomic hammer in Figure 4.5.

Safety professionals can sometimes replace hazardous equipment or materials with those that are less hazardous. For example, replacing a light, fluffy powder with the same material in granular form will result in a reduction of airborne dust levels. Lead paints can be replaced with less toxic materials such as water-based coatings. Similarly, electric trucks can be substituted for gasoline-powered ones, with a resultant decrease in exposure to carbon monoxide. The substitute should, of course, be checked for other types of hazards. The introduction of electric trucks will reduce the serious risk of carbon monoxide exposure but increase less serious exposure to flammable hydrogen or electric shock from batteries.

Controls and displays can be designed to reduce confusion. Automobile instrument panels and machine operating panels should exhibit the following four characteristics:

- *Visibility*. The display must be within the worker's field of vision, with no obstructions. Characters should be of a readable size, with high contrast.

- *Legibility*. Characters must be adequately spaced as well as distinguishable (a "3" should not look like an "8"). No more than one line or pointer should appear on each display.

FIGURE 4.4

Screwdriver Configurations

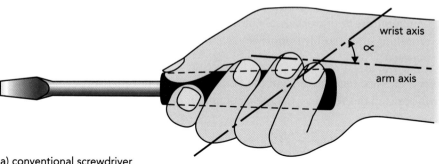

a) conventional screwdriver

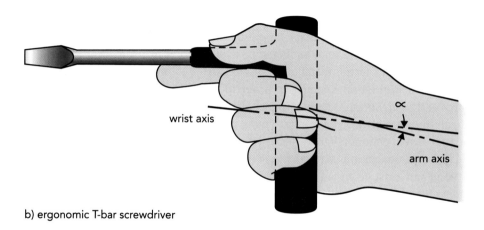

b) ergonomic T-bar screwdriver

- *Interpretability*. The displays must be interpreted in the same way by all observers. Universal symbols help but can lead to misunderstandings. For example, the red exit symbols may be confused with the red glow that means "stop." In Europe, exit symbols are green.

- *User-friendliness*. Each control must be a different shape and have a different operating direction in order to be easily distinguished from adjacent controls. Picture the controls in your car: the radio volume rotates, while the station change button is pushed; the most important controls—the fuel gauge and the speedometer—are displayed most prominently.

Engineering controls can also be applied in the office environment. Many employees spend long periods seated at their workstations. A poor sitting position or posture can restrict blood circulation, increase blood pooling in the legs and feet, and add to the compressive load on the spine. Correct chair design will minimize the concentration of pressures under the thigh and the back of the

FIGURE 4.5

Hammer Configurations

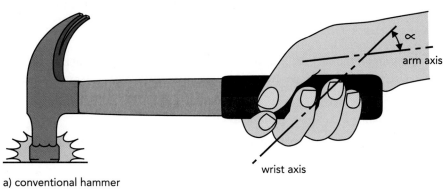

a) conventional hammer

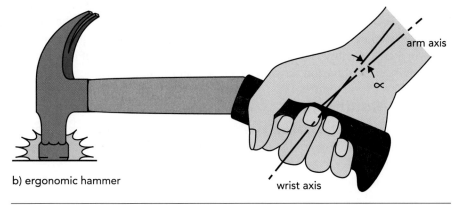

b) ergonomic hammer

knee. Work seating must be completely adjustable in all directions and planes. A forward-tilting seat may be preferred by employees who must lean over a workstation. (Interestingly, a study by Ontario Hydro revealed that only 5% of users adjust their furniture.[13]) Seat cushions should have about a 2.5 cm compression, with minimal contouring to allow ease of position shift. Permeable fabrics allow ventilation and absorption of perspiration.

The backrest should be curved on the vertical and horizontal planes. It should also be vertically adjustable (so that the point of contact fits the small of the back in the lumbar region) as well as horizontally adjustable. Armrests are recommended unless a wide variety of arm movements are required. The chair base should provide stability and mobility. Five casters with a wide spread will prevent tipping.[14] Visit http://www.ccohs.ca/oshanswers/ergonomics/sitting/sitting_position.html for illustrations and information on recommended chair settings and body positions.

Lighting within an office environment is also extremely important and has two main purposes: to illuminate the tasks, and to increase the safety and comfort of the worker. Bright overhead lighting can produce glare and annoying reflections on a computer screen, resulting in eyestrain and headaches. Choosing the correct lighting for a workplace will involve consideration of the following factors:

- *Intensity:* the amount of light given off by a source

- *Luminance:* the amount of light uniformly reflected or emitted from a surface and the background

- *Reflectance:* the amount of light reflected from a surface (luminance) and the amount of light falling on the surface (illuminance). A dull black surface has 9% reflectance, while a shiny white surface has closer to 100% reflectance.

- *Luminaire:* a complete lighting device

- *Contrast:* the relationship between the amount of light from a surface and the background

- *Glare:* the reduction of visibility caused by brightness differences between an object and its background

Both the quantity and the quality of light must be considered. In the context of workstation design, quantity refers to the correct amount of light needed to perform a task. Quality is more complex and includes measures of distribution (or spread), glare, diffusion, shadows, contrast, and colour.

Process Modification

Sometimes changing the manner in which the work is done can increase safety. Moving from a manual operation to an automated one, or from batch processes to continuous processes, may result in fewer hazards.

Effective job design is key to worker safety and efficiency. Frederick Taylor (1856–1915), the founder of industrial engineering, tried to increase both by breaking a job into its basic components and then assigning to each task specific times and methods (motions). Taylor's ideas were applied to the shovelling of coal at the Bethlehem Steel Company in what was to become a classic motion study. This application demonstrated that a stoker could shovel more coal into the blast furnace by using a larger shovel and engaging in fewer work cycles. Decreasing the repetition of the task reduced fatigue and back strain.

Subsequent efficiency experts addressed the tedium associated with simple task repetition. Inspired by the Hawthorne studies of the 1920s, the socio-technological approach to work design was concerned with enhancing worker involvement and satisfaction. What has this to do with health and safety? The more interested and motivated the worker, the lower the probability of a serious accident or injury.

Isolation or Segregation

In this approach, the hazardous job or task is isolated from the employees in order to reduce their exposure. Isolation strategies may be as simple as putting a physical barrier around a chemical or noise source, or it can involve removing a hazardous operation to a separate facility. Robots can handle tasks that are too dangerous for humans.

Segregating the hazardous operation in time as well as space is also advisable. Cleanups, maintenance, and especially hazardous tasks such as spray painting can be done on weekends or at night, when fewer workers are present.

Machine Guarding

Machine guarding is necessary to protect a worker from the hazards and energies created by moving machinery. According to Ontario's Ministry of Labour, more orders citing problems are written for nonexistent or improper guarding than for any other.[15] The problem is serious enough to have prompted the Canadian Standards Association to issue standard Z432–94, *Safeguarding of Machinery*,[16] which thoroughly covers the topic of machine guarding.

machine guarding protection for workers from the hazards and energies created by moving machinery

The following basic guidelines for machine guarding apply, regardless of the type or operation of the equipment:

- The guard must be sturdy enough to resist external source damage that would interfere with the operation of the machine, such as being struck by a forklift truck.

- The guard must permit required maintenance tasks without excessive dismantling or reassembly labour.

- The guard must be properly and securely mounted to prevent rattling, which is a distraction, or part interference, which can cause snags and force the operator to attempt to free them, possibly without proper precautions.

- There should be no parts that, if removed, would compromise the protection provided by the guard—there should always be some guarding left.

- Construction should be relatively simple so that problems can be immediately identified and corrected during an inspection.*

Thoroughness in guard design is essential. An incomplete guard may be as much of a hazard as no guard at all. The guard must not create a false sense of security that may cause accidents and possible injuries. When the guard is in operation, all parts of the body must be excluded, and no access is permitted. The barrier or guard will prevent a worker from being caught in, on, or between moving equipment (kinetic energy), or from being struck by flying, sliding, or falling objects (gravity energy).

Floor barriers installed around pumps and other hazardous equipment must be strong enough to resist damage by, for example, forklift truck impact (mechanical energy), and high enough that a worker will not trip or fall over them. Expanded metal should fill the open spaces to prevent parts from rolling into the hazard area and fingers from being poked through.

Several devices can be used to control point-of-operation hazards. *Barrier* or *enclosure guards* prevent workers from entering a hazardous area. The barrier may be mechanical (a cage that covers the work action) or electrical (a photocell that will not permit the machine to cycle while the beam is broken). The

---

*CCOHS, "Risk Assessment," Table 2. Found at: http://www.ccohs.ca/oshanswers/hsprograms/risk_assessment.html.

emergency stop button is another form of guard; for it to be effective, the machine must be equipped with a braking system that will stop the machine in mid-cycle.

Guarding by distance involves keeping workers physically removed from the machine hazard. One of the most common methods is the two-handed trip guard or control, which is located near but not in the midst of the hazard site. Both hands are required to press each button simultaneously for the machine to cycle.

Hand-removal devices are designed to physically remove the worker's hands and arms from the activated machine. The "hand pullout" is a harness-like system fastened to the worker's wrists at one end and to the machine at the other end. When the machine (say a punch press) is activated, the harness mechanism physically pulls the worker's hands out of the way. Short of removing the harness, the worker cannot win the ensuing tug of war.

The *sweep away* is a device with one or two arms (single sweep or double sweep) that, when activated by the machine cycle, will swing across in front of the worker, forcibly removing his or her hands from the danger area. A small panel attached to each arm screens the swept area to keep the worker's hands from re-entering the danger zone after the sweep arm passes. The sweep-away device is not a recommended guard.

The *photoelectric eye* is a light beam that, when broken, will not allow the machine to cycle. This type of device has the advantage of not adding to the machine any obstructions that can make maintenance difficult. It is generally expensive to install and maintain but very effective.

Feeding tools include hand-held tongs, push sticks, or clamps that allow the operator access to the machine while keeping his or her hands out of the way. Metal tools are usually made of aluminum or magnesium, which will crush easily if caught in the machine, thereby saving the die sets and not allowing the type of **kickback** that could direct the worker's hands into the machine. A press forge operator will use a set of special tongs to hold a red-hot piece of metal in place in the dies while the machine forms the part. In a similar manner, a set of handles secured to sheet glass or metal by vacuum will permit a worker to handle the material without being cut by sharp edges.

kickback
action of having a work piece suddenly thrown backward into the operator

ADMINISTRATIVE CONTROL

administrative control
management involvement, training of employees, rotation of employees, environmental sampling, and medical surveillance to protect individuals

Administrative control is the use of management involvement, employee training, employee rotation, environmental sampling, and medical surveillance to protect individuals.[17] Administrative control is the second level of priority for worker protection, after engineering controls but before personal protective equipment. Against some negative attitudes, administrative controls can have some effect in minimizing hazardous conditions. The most serious failure of this method relates to a company's reluctance or lack of appreciation. Using administrative controls, the HR practitioner can be effective by (1) introducing preplacement examinations so that employees are chosen who have suitable characteristics for the job (e.g., the ability to lift materials), (2) scheduling job rotations so that workers spend time in less hazardous jobs, thereby reducing exposures (e.g., working with toxic materials in the morning and with nontoxic materials in the afternoon), (3) moving workers to other permanent jobs after exposure to toxic materials, and (4) performing periodic monitoring.

Some common examples of administrative control include safety awareness programs, incentive programs, housekeeping programs, preventive maintenance, and the development of policies and training modules for unique situations such as confined space entry.

Safety Awareness

Safety awareness refers to programs that attempt to inform workers about health and safety issues and to remind them of the importance of health and safety.

Visible Reminders

Posters and signs at worker entrances and other points of entry are one way to promote safety awareness. A company-designed booklet dealing with health and safety issues can be issued to employees. Safety message inserts can be added to paycheques. Place mats and napkins in the dining area can be imprinted with safety messages. Decals (self-adhesive or magnetic) can be applied to specific objects as safety reminders. In addition, safety displays can be set up at entrances and in cafeterias. These displays can feature photographs of the Safe Employee of the Month or brief statements by workers who were saved from injury by, for example, correct use of personal protective equipment (e.g., safety glasses). Newsletters, bulletin boards, and billboards are other vehicles for promoting safety awareness. Finally, safety campaigns can be used to target specific hazards or unsafe practices. These efforts and presentations, though, will not be effective unless the senior managers are fully behind the programs.

Special Events

Numerous special events and campaigns have been developed to promote safety awareness in the workplace (e.g., National Safe Driving Week). In general, the intent of these special events is to increase awareness of safety issues in the workplace by focusing on safety or a specific element of safety in the workplace (see **OH&S Today 4.3**).

OH&S Today 4.3

Young Worker Awareness Program

In response to the high rate of injuries among young workers, almost every jurisdiction has begun to address the issue of young workers' health and safety. The Young Worker Awareness Program in Ontario is funded by the Workplace Safety and Insurance Board and is delivered through various agencies. The intent of the program is to increase young people's awareness of health and safety issues, the importance of health and safety, and their rights under the law.

Source: Workplace Safety and Insurance Board of Ontario, "Young Worker Awareness Program." Found at: http://ywap.ca/english (Accessed Feb. 7, 2007).

Awards and Incentives

Safety awards are another vehicle for increasing awareness of safety. By establishing an award, the sponsoring agency or company creates an "event" comprising a presentation and a media announcement. The resulting publicity can be used to raise safety awareness. Safety award programs have been created by industrial associations, governments, and agencies to recognize achievements in safety (see the Weblinks section at the end of the chapter).

Within organizations, individual employees can be given incentives to maintain good safety performance. These incentives can range from individual payments to team rewards. For example, DuPont Canada employees were given special scratch-and-win lottery tickets.[18] Other organizations recognize good safety performance through incentives such as private parking spaces or dinners (see Chapter 10 for a discussion of behaviour-based safety programs, which often involve incentives). In addition, supervisors may receive rewards based on the number of employees who attended safety talks or the number of safety deficiencies that were corrected expeditiously. Contests can be held in which employees compete to produce the best safety slogan. Finally, safety records can be used as a criterion when evaluating supervisory and managerial performance. Care must be taken with this approach, since some supervisors may be tempted to hide problems and serious hazards.

Housekeeping

Ensuring that the worksite is clean and that workers have access to cleaning facilities will contribute to the control of hazards. A clean, orderly workplace can reduce hazards and at the same time increase efficiency. Every worksite contains potentially hazardous tools and equipment. For example, a plant site may have containers of chemicals such as solvents, tools such as drills, and processes that generate dust or scrap material. Maintaining a clean and orderly job site reduces the risk of injury due to falls, fires, and so forth. Furthermore, it is easier to locate first aid equipment or exits in an environment in which all tools and equipment are in their assigned places (see **OH&S Notebook 4.2**).

Housekeeping is not just a good practice—it is a legal requirement under most health and safety legislation. Though legislation varies across jurisdictions,

---

▶ OH&S Notebook 4.2

PREVENTING SLIPS AND FALLS THROUGH HOUSEKEEPING

Good housekeeping practices are perhaps the simplest and most effective way to prevent slips and falls in the workplace. These include the following:

- Keeping walkways and stairwells clear of clutter
- Closing drawers, doors, and storage bins after use
- Keeping floors free of debris or spills
- Marking hazards (e.g., spills, debris) until they can be cleaned up
- Ensuring adequate lighting

Source: CCOHS, "Why should we pay attention to housekeeping at work?" Found at: http://www.ccohs.ca/oshanswers /hsprograms/house.html (Accessed Feb. 7, 2007).

the Canadian Health and Safety Regulations under the Canada Labour Code (see the Weblink) are typical:

1. Every exterior stairway, walkway, ramp, and passageway that may be used by employees shall be kept free of accumulations of ice and snow or other slipping or tripping hazards.
2. All dust, dirt, waste, and scrap material in every workplace in a building shall be removed as often as is necessary to protect the health and safety of employees and shall be disposed of in such a manner that the health and safety of employees is not endangered.
3. Every travelled surface in a workplace shall be
   a. slip resistant; and
   b. kept free of splinters, holes, loose boards and tiles, and similar defects. (SOR/2000-374, s. 2; SOR/2002-208, s. 6.)*

The cleaning process itself should be evaluated. Besides the obvious hazards posed by solvents used for cleaning, other hazards may be involved in operations such as dust removal. Workers using compressed air may be tempted to blow dust off work surfaces and even clothing; however, compressed air can be forced through the skin, enter the bloodstream, and cause death.

Organizations that employ workers who handle toxic materials should ensure that washing facilities are located close to the work area. Workers should wash before drinking or eating to prevent the ingestion of toxic materials. No food or drink should be permitted at the worksite. Workers exposed to chemicals should have showers and change clothes before leaving the worksite. Where appropriate, hazardous material (hazmat) suits should be available and workers should be trained in their use.

Preventive Maintenance

Preventive maintenance refers to the orderly, continuous, and scheduled protection and repair of equipment and buildings. The primary goals of preventive maintenance are to determine potential problems and to implement corrective actions. The main benefits of this process are uninterrupted production and the reduction of potential hazards caused by equipment failure.

Generally speaking, equipment failures do not happen without warning. We are all familiar with the atypical noises that our cars or air conditioners produce as signals that something needs to be fixed. However, maintenance should enter the picture before warning signs emerge. It is more cost effective to perform maintenance routinely while the equipment or machines are still operating than it is after they have failed, necessitating shutdown of the entire operation. Checking the level of oil in your car at every second fuel stop is preventive maintenance. To let the oil level drop and the engine seize is expensive and unnecessary.

Recordkeeping is essential to any preventive maintenance program. Maintenance information should be recorded at the time the maintenance work is done. Pertinent data will include part replacement and frequency, lubrication, bearings and drive repairs, electrical failures, and cleanliness. Once the historical information is

preventive maintenance
the orderly, continuous, and scheduled protection and repair of equipment and buildings

---

* Canada Occupational Health and Safety Regulations (SOR/86-304). Found at: http://laws-lois.justice. gc.ca/eng/regulations/SOR-86-304/page-7.html#h-20.

OH&S Notebook 4.3

ADMINISTRATIVE CONTROLS FOR STRUCK-BY-OBJECT INJURIES

To reduce injuries attributable to falling objects:

- Provide and require the use of safety helmets.
- Provide safety signage and warning where overhead hazards are present.
- Train and ensure the use of safe-rigging and safe-storage procedures.
- Provide and require the use of safety shoes.

To reduce "caught in, under, or between" (CIUB) injuries:

- Use lockout procedures that require the operator or maintenance provider to turn the power off and to lock the switch in the off position using a personal padlock. Because each worker is the only one with the key to his or her lock, it is impossible to inadvertently start the machine during maintenance.

Source: CCOHS. Found at: http://www.ccohs.ca (Accessed Oct. 10, 2004).

available, failure trends can be anticipated and addressed. (This approach is often referred to as failure mode analysis or maintenance hazard analysis.)

Work Permits

Before any high-risk work is undertaken, a series of work permits must be in place, one for each type of activity. These permits are, in effect, in-house licences to perform dangerous work. Permits are required for confined space entry, electrical work, excavation work, safety valve work, scaffolding work, radiation work, and equipment-disconnecting work (lockout procedures). "Hot work" permits may be required for activities such as cutting, welding, and soldering wherein the heat involved may trigger the fire alarm system or present a fire hazard. A sample work permit for scaffolding is shown in Figure 4.6.

Lockout Procedures

When maintenance or adjustment is performed on any machine, the machine must be shut off and locked out. For example, replacing the signal light on a residential stove involves accessing the appliance's interior. Shutting off the stove entails turning off the switches; locking it out entails turning off the power at the main fuse box or circuit breaker and removing the appropriate fuses in either the power panel or the stove. With these precautions, no one can turn the stove on and cause an electrical shock or burn injury. For a more complicated appliance such as a furnace, not only must the fuses be removed, but also the fuel lines must be shut off, and the supply flange joint must be disassembled.

The following are some of the precautions that must be taken during the lockout process:

- Only one person should be in charge of the lockout procedure.

- The worker must ensure that the machine is shut off completely, that all internal pressure sources (hydraulic, air, steam) are bled off to atmospheric levels, that the valves are locked open, and that any movable parts, such as flywheels or rams, are immobilized.

FIGURE 4.6

Example of Scaffold Use Permit

SIRTE OIL COMPANY	SCAFFOLDING PERMIT		
DATE	TIME FROM:		TO:

PLANT:

EQUIPMENT & LOCATION:

DESCRIPTION OF WORK TO BE DONE:
☐ ERECTION
☐ REMOVAL

SCAFFOLD DUTY: ☐ LIGHT   ☐ GENERAL   ☐ HEAVY

HEIGHT = ___ M   WIDTH = ___ M   ☐ CONSULT CIVIL ENG. GROUP

ANSWER WITH (X) WHERE APPLICABLE: YES
1. FAMILIAR WITH AREA HAZARDS/SAF. RULES?   ☐
2. SCAFFOLD TYPE/MATERIAL AGREED TO?   ☐
3. SCAFFOLD ANCHORING POINTS APPROVED?   ☐
4. FOUNDATION/FOOTING PREPARED?   ☐
5. HAZARD CREATED TO/FROM TRAFFIC?   ☐
6. AREA FREE OF COMB./TOXIC GAS?   ☐
7. ACCEPTANCE APPROVAL NEEDED?   ☐

SPECIAL PROTECTION REQUIRED
☐ MONITOR FOR _____   ☐ SAFETY BELTS/LINE
☐ LIFTING DEVICE APPROVAL   ☐ STANDBYS
☐ BARRIERS/ROPING OFF   ☐ (SPECIFY)

THE EQUIPMENT AND/OR LOCATION WHERE THE WORK IS TO BE DONE HAS BEEN INSPECTED & POINTS 1-7 ABOVE HAVE BEEN INVESTIGATED TO MY SATISFACTION.

_____
SIGNATURE OF PERSON AUTHORIZING THIS PERMIT

I UNDERSTAND THE HAZARDS INVOLVED IN THE ABOVE PERMITTED WORK AND THE LIMITATIONS REQUIRED HAVE BEEN EXPLAINED TO ME.

7-3 SHIFT   11-7 SHIFT

SIGNATURE OF AUTHORIZED CRAFTSMAN

PERMIT CLOSED OUT	WORK COMPLETED	
DATE TIME	☐ NO ☐	
AUTHORIZED CRAFTSMAN	OPERATING SUPERVISOR	
APPROVAL FOR USE OF COMPLETED SCAFFOLD	NAME	SIGNATURE	DATE

SIDE 1

CHECKLIST FOR THE AUTHORIZED CRAFTSMAN
PREPARATIONS
☐ SPECIFICATIONS/DRAWING PROVIDED?
☐ FOUNDATIONS/FOOTING PREPARED?
☐ LIFTING DEVICES NEEDED?
☐ ERECTION PERSONNEL EXPERIENCED?
☐ SUPERVISION APPOINTED? COMPETENT?
☐ AREA HAZARDS/SAF. RULES KNOWN?
☐ ADDITIONAL JOB DEMONSTRATION NEEDED?
☐ STRUCTURE INSPECTION/APPROVAL BY A COMPETENT PERSON NEEDED?

STABILITY & CONSTRUCTION
☐ ANCHORING POINTS SELECTED? APPROVED? SUFFICIENT?
☐ SCAFF. MATERIAL INSPECTED? SELECTED? IN GOOD CONDITION?
☐ FOOTING FIRM?
☐ STANDARDS SPACING ADEQUATE?
☐ BRACING USED? SUFFICIENT?
☐ PLATFORMS FULL? TRIPPING? OPENINGS?
☐ GUARDRAILS? TOE BOARDS?
☐ ACCESS ADEQUATE? LADDERS FIXED?

IN USE
☐ STRUCTURE INSPECTED DAILY?
☐ TRAFFIC HAZARDS?
☐ OVERLOADING?
☐ USE OF PERSONAL PROTECTION?
☐ RESPONSE TO EMERGENCY KNOWN?

DISMANTLING
☐ METHOD AGREED TO?
☐ HAZARD CREATED TO SURROUNDING?
☐ FINAL SITE CLEARING ENSURED?

SPECIAL INSTRUCTIONS

SIDE 2

- After the machine has been shut down, all the disconnect points, such as the electrical panel, must be left open.
- Before work begins, complete testing must be undertaken to ensure that all energy sources are inoperative.
- The worker must use an approved lockout tag and single-key padlock to secure the equipment.
- Only the workers who installed each lock are permitted to remove that lock, in the reverse order to the lock installation, beginning and ending with the project manager.
- Each worker must sign off the work permit as his or her lock is removed.

When the project is finished, the equipment will be activated in the reverse sequence to the shutdown. Checks must be made to ensure that guards are in place, isolation devices have been removed, all tools are accounted for, energy controls have been closed and put back into operating condition, and tags and locks have been removed. The last lock removed is that of the manager of the project from the shift on which the lock was applied.

Confined-Space Entry

Confined space refers to a space that is potentially deficient in oxygen and that could contain toxic aerosols. Sewers, tanks, and boilers are all examples of confined spaces. Other examples include any long, small tunnel, a shower stall, and some specialty rooms such as computer equipment rooms that are completely independent from any adjacent spaces.

At home, cleaning the bathroom shower stall with the door closed and using a tile cleaner will trap the vapours from the cleanser. These vapours may accumulate near the floor where the work is being done, displace oxygen, and cause drowsiness or fainting.

Entry into industrial confined spaces is addressed in various OH&S regulations. One of the first things to determine is whether the space to be entered is in fact a confined space. CCOHS provides helpful information on identification of a confined space, how to manage the space, and how to develop a confined-space safety program.

Once it has been established that a confined space exists, the following steps should be taken:

1. Issue a proper work permit and follow all the lockout procedures.
2. Determine the ease of access to and from the space and develop appropriate contingency plans for worker emergencies.
3. Make sure that all the proper tools and equipment are on hand to do the job.
4. Communicate to workers that no smoking or open flames are to be permitted at or near the worksite.
5. Purge the space of all contaminants and test the air quality several times to ensure that all impurities have been removed.
6. Ensure that a constant forced airflow into the space is provided.
7. Clean the interior of the space to ensure that no hazardous scale or deposits are present.
8. Post a trained safety lookout outside the space. (The inside workers should be kept in full view at all times.)
9. Attach a lifeline to each worker in the space. (The free end should be controlled by the safety lookout.)

On completion of the confined-space work, equipment start-up can be undertaken in the reverse order to the shutdown. The permit and lockout systems should be followed without deviation.

PERSONAL PROTECTIVE EQUIPMENT

In some cases it is not possible to fully protect individuals by applying engineering and administrative controls. The third line of defence in occupational health and safety is the use of personal protective equipment (PPE). PPE consists of clothing, helmets, goggles, and other devices designed to protect the individual from specific hazards. A construction worker, for example, might wear steel-toed safety boots (typically with a nonconductive, nonslip sole), a helmet, safety glasses or goggles, work gloves, and hearing protection.

It is relatively easy to control the wearing of some PPE. For example, in many industries the use of steel-toed safety boots/shoes is a standard policy. Since most of us don't remove or change our shoes during the working day, a worker who puts on safety boots is likely to continue to wear them. The use of other PPE can be more variable. Safety goggles or glasses (for example) can steam up on a hot day, and workers may find that they are uncomfortable. Hearing protection can make it difficult to converse with coworkers. Moreover, workers can simply forget. For example, when working on a construction site it is easy to "forget" to put on your safety glasses before using a saw. Individuals may opt for "style" that reduces the effectiveness of some PPE. One often sees construction workers wearing helmets with the peak to the back or perched improperly on the head. Helmets worn in an improper position do not provide the same level of protection as when properly worn.

Though PPE offers protection to workers, its use can be highly variable because of factors like this. As a result, the use of PPE is recognized as the least preferred means of controlling hazards. Though PPE of one sort or another is required in many workplaces, it is most properly considered to be an adjunct or "backup" to other methods of control. It should never be the sole means of protecting workers from hazards.

SOURCE–PATH–HUMAN CONTROLS

Hazards can be controlled or eliminated by identifying and attacking the source of the hazard, the path it travels, and the employee or recipient of the hazard. The strategies discussed in this chapter can be regrouped along these lines, as shown in Figure 4.7. This schematic provides a useful summary of the information on hazard control. Placing control strategies in categories is less important than having a thorough understanding that hazard control is necessary and possible.

FIGURE **4.7**

Source–Path–Human Controls

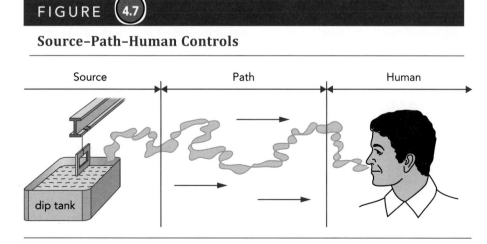

MONITORING/AUDITING

Monitoring is an important part of hazard control. Audits are done to ensure that hazard controls are functioning effectively and to identify new hazards. Monitoring can be done daily by supervisors and maintenance personnel, weekly by department heads, monthly by health and safety committees, and as needed by compliance officers.[19] The auditing process itself affects safety. A 50% decrease in accidents in one organization over a two-year period was attributed to the fact that managers began to audit.[20]

An audit program can be used to evaluate health and safety performance in the workplace. A number of audit methods are available. One very effective technique, which involves applying total quality control methodologies and trend analysis, relates the number of incidents to some predetermined goal. If it seems from the number of events in a particular time frame that a safety goal failure is imminent, steps can be taken to prevent the occurrence. The audit program should:

a. ensure that safety programs are being carried out without restrictions;
b. ensure that safety programs are up- to-date and that deficiencies are documented;
c. be carried out by people with some understanding of both the audit methods and the material being examined (the various members of the JHSC should be able to carry out this inspection);
d. stimulate discussion among all managers and workers, and ultimately produce conclusions and recommendations;
e. be conducted at least annually by companies with high-risk hazards; *and*
f. include all documentation (WSIB/WCB statements, Ministry of Labour citations, air sampling results, first aid and incident reports, hazard analyses, discipline records, cost–benefit studies, etc.).

RECORDKEEPING

Information obtained at all stages of the hazard control process should be stored in a database. These records are used to identify frequency of events as well as trends in hazards. They are also a source of information on worker training and equipment maintenance. The provision of monthly updates to managers will assist them in their efforts at ongoing hazard control. The length of time that records should be kept varies with the nature of the record. Records on individual employees should be kept for as long as that individual is with the company. In some cases (e.g., individual records of exposure to radiation) records may have to be kept for the length of employment plus an additional period (e.g., 10 years).

SUMMARY

In this chapter we introduced the concept of hazard recognition, risk assessment, and control. A hazard was defined as any source of potential damage, harm or adverse health effects on something or someone under certain conditions at work. Hazards typically involve exposure to some kind of energy, and hazard recognition involves the systematic identification of the hazards and risks associated with them. We discussed various tools for hazard recognition. Risk assessment refers to the evaluation of the likelihood of harm posed by the hazard. Such an assessment needs to consider the probability of an adverse event, and the potential consequences. If the decision is made to control the hazard, there are three basic approaches: engineering, administrative, and PPE. Engineering controls typically involve redesigning the work (e.g., the tools, machines, or substances) so as to reduce or eliminate the hazard. Administrative controls involve strategies such as training, education, and management techniques to reduce exposure to the hazard. In this case the hazard is still present but the exposure of the individual worker is substantially reduced or controlled. PPE includes items such as helmets, safety glasses, and hearing protection. These devices do not reduce exposure but do reduce the probable consequences of being exposed to a hazard. There is a hierarchy of hazard control such that engineering controls are the preferred solution (i.e., reduce or eliminate the hazard), administrative controls are the second line of defence (i.e., reduce exposure to the hazard), and PPE is the last option (i.e., reduce the consequences). That said, all three forms of control have a place in OH&S programs and can be thought of as providing multiple layers of protection for workers.

Key Terms

administrative control 102	kickback 102
confined space 108	machine guarding 101
consequences 88	overexertion injuries 90
contact control 95	overt traumatic injuries 90
engineering control 97	positive tree 87
fault tree 87	postcontact control 95
hazard 82	precontact control 95
hazard analysis 87	preventive maintenance 105
hazard control 95	probability 88
human factor 84	risk 83
incident 83	risk perception 83
injury 90	safety sampling 86
job description 86	unsafe act 83
job specifications 86	walk-through survey 86

Weblinks

Association for Mineral Exploration in British Columbia, "Canadian Mineral Exploration Health & Safety Awards"
http://www.amebc.ca/policy/health-and-safety/ame-bc-health-and-safety-awards.aspx

Canada's Occupational Health and Safety Magazine
http://www.ohscanada.com/news/alberta-worker-suffers-finger-injuries-in-press-accident/1001059825

Canada Safety Council 2012 Safety Campaigns
https://canadasafetycouncil.org/campaigns

Canadian Centre of Occupational Health and Safety, OHS Answers, Confined Space
http://www.ccohs.ca/oshanswers/hsprograms/confinedspace_intro.html

Canadian Construction Association, "Awards"
http://www.cca-acc.com/en/about-cca/awards

Canadian Society of Safety Engineering, "National Safety Awards Programs"
http://csse-lmc.org/wp/national-safety-awards-program

Infrastructure Health and Safety Association "Auditing"
http://www.ihsa.ca/auditing/index.cfm

Infrastructure Health and Safety Association, "Heavy Equipment"
http://www.ihsa.ca/topics_hazards/heavy_equipment.cfm

Infrastructure Health and Safety Association, "New and Young Workers"
http://www.ihsa.ca/new_experienced_workers/new_young_workers.cfm

National Institute for Occupational Safety and Health, "Back Belts: Do They Prevent Injury?"
http://www.cdc.gov/niosh/backbelt.html

Nova Scotia Department of Labour and Advanced Education, "General Occupational Health Safety Regulations"
http://www.gov.ns.ca/just/regulations/regs/ohsgensf.htm

Shelter Online, "Online RSI Resources"
http://www.shelterpub.com/_fitness/_office_fitness_clinic/OFC_clinic.html

WorkSafeBC, "Injury Prevention Resources for Performing Arts and Film—Music"
http://artsandfilm.healthandsafetycentre.org/s/Music.asp

WorkSafe Saskatchewan, "Fall Arrest Systems"
http://www.worksafesask.ca/Fall-Arrest-Systems

Required Professional Capabilities (RPCs)

The following RPCs, listed by their CCHRA number, are relevant to the material covered in this chapter. All RPCS can be found at http://www.chrp.ca/rpc/body-of-knowledge.

RPC:170 Develops, implements, and ensures the application of policies, regulations, and standards relating to occupational health and safety.*
RPC:171 Ensures compliance with legislated reporting requirements.*
RPC:179 Ensures that mechanisms are in place for responding to crises in the workplace, including critical incident stress management.*
RPC:183 Analyzes risks to employee health & safety and develops preventive programs.*
RPC:185 Ensures that security programs and policies minimize risks while considering the obligation of the employer and the rights of employees, union, and third parties.*

Discussion Questions

1. Explain why hazard control at the precontact stage is better than hazard control at the other stages.
2. In recent years there has been a move to make ergonomic design and ergonomic standards mandatory in workplaces. Should your jurisdiction

*Canadian Council of Human Resources Associations, Human Resources Professionals in Canada: Revised Body of Knowledge and Required Professional Capabilities (RPCs ®), 2007.

implement legislation requiring ergonomic analysis and design of work processes? Why or why not?

3. A maintenance crew has been hired to enter an underground sewer line to do some minor repair work. They call and ask you for advice about necessary equipment and procedures. Briefly outline your response.

4. When a worker does not wear PPE or wears it incorrectly, who is responsible? The company? The individual?

5. Examine available literature and catalogues to determine how many methods and accessories are available to prevent keyboard-related RSI. How many of these devices do you have in your own workstation?

6. Outline all of the methods that a manager of a small plant could use to identify hazards. What could a safety professional add to this manager's hazard identification program?

7. Choose any operation in your workplace or at school and identify the hazards associated with it. Perform a risk assessment to determine whether these hazards are dangerous. Outline the changes that could be made to reduce the level of risk associated with the hazards.

Using the Internet

1. Human resources managers are responsible for ensuring that workplace safety inspections take place regularly. Using your text and online resources, describe how you would conduct an effective safety inspection program. (*Hint*: Go to http://www.worksafebc.com/publications/health_and_safety/by_topic/assets/pdf/safety_inspections.pdf).

2. Using the Web, determine (a) how safety awareness events are celebrated or implemented in your local area, and (b) what other safety awareness events are held in your area.

3. Lifting limits can be established by calculations developed by the National Institute for Occupational Safety and Health (NIOSH) in the United States. An online calculator for the equations is found at http://www.ccohs.ca/oshanswers/ergonomics/niosh/calculating_rwl.html. Use the calculator to assess the lifting limits for a worker who has to lift a package weighing approximately 16 kg onto a shelf that is 60 cm from where he or she is standing. The worker picks up the load from a point 30 cm from the floor; the final position on the shelf is 170 cm from the floor. The lift is repeated once each minute. Calculate the AL and the MPL, and determine the acceptability of the operation.

Exercises

1. In law, the "thin skull argument" refers to a perfectly healthy person whose minor trauma resulted in serious injury. Were it not for the trauma, the individual would not have been hurt. However, other individuals who experience the trauma are not hurt. Imagine, for example, four workers who are struck on the head by flying objects. Three workers suffer no injury whatsoever; the other (perhaps because of an abnormally thin skull) suffers serious brain damage. Is the damage a result of the hazard or the

individual's pre-existing condition? How should health and safety programs account for individual variability like this?

2. Identify a hazard at your workplace (or a workplace with which you are familiar). List all the approaches you could undertake to control or minimize the hazard.

Case 1   INDUSTRIAL HAZARD ASSESSMENT

The plant is experiencing some difficulties with a clamping device on a holding fixture that keeps a metal part in position while it is fed into an automatic stamping machine. The clamp does not always allow the metal part to be fed into the machine properly aligned. The worker who was operating the machine had 32 years' experience with this type of equipment. While attempting to make the necessary adjustments for smooth operation without shutting off the power, she had to reach into the machine. She placed her left hand between the feed-in mechanism levers while her right hand was positioning the misaligned part between the open clamps of the fixture.

Unfortunately, the one-button actuating control was located immediately to the left of the worker's body, about hip level. The worker inadvertently depressed the button with her leg while reaching into the machine. The machine cycled—the feed mechanism slid forward while the fixture clamps closed. The worker had a portion of her left middle finger amputated.

List the following:
a. the unsafe acts
b. the unsafe conditions
c. the energies involved
d. the steps to be taken to prevent this situation from recurring

Case 2   DANGER IN THE GROCERY STORE

Tadao works as a butcher in a large chain grocery store. His primary responsibility is cutting up meat using large (and very sharp) knives. He's been on the job now for four years and has never had a health and safety complaint. Lately, though, he's been experiencing some difficulties. Actually, it started a couple of years ago when Tadao noticed that his right hand was painful at the end of the day and that he was unable to use the hand for several hours after work. The pain and fatigue didn't last long, and Tadao assumed that he was just overworking the hand (Tadao is right-handed). In the past month or so, the pain has escalated—it often lasts all night and makes sleep difficult. Tadao also experiences numbness and tingling in the hand. Tadao has begun to avoid activities that require using his right hand, including shaking hands with people.

Last Tuesday, Tadao came to work and could not pick up the knife in his right hand—he had to pick up the knife with his left hand and place it in his right hand to begin work. Watching him go through this procedure, a coworker observed, "Well, it looks like you've developed butcher's claw—it comes from doing the same motion over and over again. It happens to us all and there's not much you can do about it." As an HR professional responsible for health and safety, do you have a better answer for Tadao?

Case 3 HAZARD CONTROL

A new plating machine had been installed and was being checked for proper operation. During this check it was discovered that the bearings on the caustic solution circulating pump were defective and had to be replaced. The pump was removed and repaired and was being reinstalled. An electrician was assigned to make the electrical connections, while a plumber performed the necessary pipe connections on the same pump.

The electrician finished the assignment except for checking the direction of shaft rotation. Since the plumber was out of the area, the electrician asked the company representative supplying the equipment if the pump was ready to be tried out. The representative stated that it was. The electrician walked to the end of the plater to start the motor, just as the plumber appeared. The plumber's shouts to the electrician not to start the pump were too late—the pump had already been turned on. At that moment, hot caustic solution showered out of the pipe flange, which had not been tightened after reassembly. The solution splashed onto the plumber, two engineers in the area, another plant engineering employee, and the vendor representative. The plumber received burns requiring immediate hospitalization and was off work for about two months. One engineer required subsequent hospitalization for eye burns and was off work for more than a week. The other three involved received minor burns. The accident occurred at 10:45 a.m. on a Wednesday.

What would you recommend for contact and postcontact control?

NOTES

1. Canadian Centre for Occupational Health and Safety, OHS Answers, "Hazard and Risk," accessed September 19, 2012, http://www.ccohs.ca/oshanswers/hsprograms/hazard_risk.html.

2. M. Fleming, R. Flin, K. Mearns, and R. Gordon, "Risk Perceptions of Offshore Workers on UK Oil and Gas Platforms," *Risk Analysis* 18: 103–10.

3. G. Rampton, I. Turnbull, and G. Doran, *Human Resources Management Systems,* (Toronto: Nelson, 1996).

4. R.J. Firenze, *The Process of Hazard Control* (Dubuque: Kendall/Hunt, 1978).

5. M. Fleming, R. Flin, K. Mearns, and R. Gordon, "Risk Perceptions of Offshore Workers on UK Oil and Gas Platforms," *Risk Analysis* 18: 103–10.

6. Canadian Centre for Occupational Health and Safety, OHS Answers "Risk Assessment," accessed September 19, 2012, http://www.ccohs.ca/oshanswers/hsprograms/risk_assessment.html.

7. Ibid.

8. National Institute of Occupational Safety and Health, *A Work Practices Guide for Manual Lifting: Technical Report 81–122* (Cincinnati: U.S. Department of Health and Human Services, 1983).

9. P. Kim, J.A. Hayden, and S.A. Mior, "The Cost-Effectiveness of a Back Education Program for Firefighters: A Case Study," *Journal of the Canadian Chiropractic Association* 48, no. 1: (2004): 13–19.

10. C. Ammendolia, M.S. Kerr, and C. Bombardier, "The Use of Back Belts for Prevention of Occupational Low Back Pain: Systematic Review and Recommendations," *CTFPHC Technical Report* 02-1, London, ON, 2002.

11. Statistics Canada, *Canadian Community Health Survey* (Ottawa: 2001).

12. C.W. Pilger, "Hazard Control Procedures," presentation to the 23rd Intensive Workshop in Industrial Hygiene, September 27, 1994.

13. H. McDonald, "Know Thy Users," *Accident Prevention*, March–April 1995, 11–12.

14. Canadian Standards Association, "Office Ergonomics," CSA Standard, CAN/CSAZ412-M89, section 5, 1995.

15. S. Somasunder, "Machine Safeguarding," *OH&S Canada* 9, no. 5 (September–October 1993): 30–31.

16. Canadian Standards Association, "Safeguarding of Machinery," Standard Z432–94, 1995.

17. S. DiNardi, ed., *The Occupational Environment—Its Evaluation and Control*, 2nd ed. (Fairfax: American Industrial Hygiene Association, 1997).

18. S.L. Dolan and R.S. Schuler, *Human Resources Management: A Canadian Perspective* (Toronto: Nelson, 1994).

19. P.M. Laing, ed., *Accident Prevention Manual for Business and Industry: Administration and Programs*, 10th ed. (Washington: National Safety Council, 1992).

20. J. Taylor, "Guide to Health and Safety Management: 20 proven programs," *Safety Auditing* (Toronto: Southam Business Communications, 1991).

CHAPTER 5

Physical Agents

CHAPTER LEARNING OBJECTIVES

After reading this chapter, you should be able to:

- identify common physical agents within the workplace
- explain how and when many of the commonly found physical agents can be considered hazardous
- identify methods of controlling physical agents within the workplace

ARE CELLPHONES SAFE?

Look around your workplace, the bus you take to school, the supermarket where you shop, and count the number of people you see with a cellphone. Health Canada indicates that by the end of 2010 the number of cellphone users in Canada reached 24 million people. In 1987 the number of users in Canada was 100,000. Now, consider how much time during the day those 24 million users spend on their cellphone talking, texting, surfing the Internet, or even playing games. What, if any impact does using a cellphone have on your health? Cellphones give off what is referred to as non-ionizing radiation, which does not break down chemical bonds in your body unlike other forms of radiation but, does that mean there are no harmful effects? According to the Canadian Centre for Occupational Health and Safety (CCOHS) and Health Canada, the jury is still out on whether the radiation emitted from cellphones is hazardous. Health Canada indicates there is research to support that brain cancer rates "may be elevated in long term/heavy cell phone users," while at the same time there are studies that do not support these findings.

Health Canada also indicates that while health risks associated with the non-ionizing radiation emitted from cellphones is debated, there are other risks associated with using them. Cellphones can be a distraction, and can interfere with important equipment (e.g., pacemakers and hearing aids) as well technology (e.g., aircraft communication and navigation systems). The risks associated with many of the physical agents we are exposed to on a daily basis, such as cellphones, is complex. Consequently, mitigating the risks associated with them can also be complex. The first step in managing these risks is ensuring that all employees are able to identify physical agents within the workplace and the danger they pose to their health and safety.

Sources: Health Canada, "Safety of Cell Phones and Cell Phone Towers," *It's Your Health*, October 2011. Found at: http://www.hc-sc.gc.ca/hl-vs/alt_formats/pacrb-dgapcr/pdf/iyh-vsv/prod/cell-eng.pdf; CCOHS.

physical agents
sources of energy that may cause injury or disease

ambient
all-encompassing condition associated with a given environment, being usually a composite of inputs from sources all around us

In this chapter we consider the effects of physical agents in the workplace and how best to control them. **Physical agents** are sources of energy that may cause injury or disease if they are not controlled or managed properly. Examples include noise, vibration, radiation, and extremes in temperature and pressure. Each of these agents may be **ambient** or acute (i.e., resulting from a single exposure).

NOISE

Noise is defined as any unwanted sound and is often referred to as the most common workplace hazard. Technically, it refers to "the auditory sensation evoked by the oscillations in pressure in a medium with elasticity and viscosity," such as air.[1] Sound and noise differ by definition in that that noise is unwanted sound. It would be difficult to find a profession where employees are not exposed to some type of sound or noise; however construction workers, cafeteria workers, and farmers are among some of the professions most at risk for hearing damage, specifically, **early warning change**, as a result of noise. One Canadian study reported that approximately 95% of construction workers were exposed to high levels of noise on a daily basis.[2] Even in office settings and computer labs, annoyance, stress, and interfering with communicating are some of the concerns associated with noise.

early warning change
a deterioration of hearing in the upper frequency—the earliest detectable sign of noise-induced hearing loss

What makes the issue of noise within the workplace so complex, is the fact that a sound considered to be noise by one individual, may not be considered to be noise by another, meaning various circumstances can change whether a sound is considered to be noise and therefore harmful. Furthermore there are characteristics about the ear which add to the complexity of managing noise in the workplace. For instance, one major characteristic of the human ear and hearing is that we do not hear everything in a nice, neat fashion. If sound were measured electronically, the sound spectrum might appear more or less as a straight line. However, what the human ear hears or perceives is significantly different. Sound is often assessed using a unit of measurement known as Hertz or Hz (equal to one cycle per second). The human hearing range of frequencies is approximately 20 Hz to 20,000 Hz. Thus, a person can hear a bass note from a tuba or a shrill note from a piccolo, but not a dog whistle. This has direct implications for human hearing problems. Just because we cannot hear the sound does not mean that it is not present and possibly causing hearing damage.

The response of the human ear to sound is usually represented as a graph that illustrates the threshold of hearing. The term *threshold of hearing* refers to the envelope or range of sound that the human ear can perceive or hear. The standards for the measurement of noise use the unit of a decibel, or dB (also referred to as sound pressure level). Decibels are measured on a logarithmic scale so that very small differences in the numbers can translate into very large actual differences. For example, a 3 dB difference (e.g., going from 80 to 83 dB) represents a doubling of the "loudness" (83 dB is twice as loud as 80 dB), and a 10 dB difference represents a tenfold difference (90 dB is 10 times louder than 80 dB). A 20 dB difference is a 100-fold increase (90 dB is 100 times louder than 70 dB). Thus what may seem to be a very small numeric difference actually represents a very large difference in loudness. When the human response is involved, the unit becomes dB (A) or A-weighted decibel. This response is built into the sound meters used for measuring noise exposure in the workplace.

Human hearing response is conditional on three characteristics: frequency, duration, and loudness. Any noise level investigation must take into account these three elements. Most noise sources and sounds, such as music, are made up of a variety of frequencies, which the ear blends to create a pleasant or not-so-pleasant sound. As noted previously, noise beyond the range of human hearing response can be damaging even though not "heard." Similarly, certain frequencies in a noise that is made up of a variety of frequencies can be extra-loud and thus damaging without being noticed, even within the human range. It is important to consider frequency response when dealing with hearing protection.

The duration of the sound is one of those conditions that the human ear responds to in a strange way. A loud noise of very short duration, like a gunshot, is perceived to be "quieter" than the same sound level heard for a longer duration. They can both be damaging, but only the latter one "sounds" like it. The short-duration noise is referred to as impact or impulse noise, which has a duration of about 1 millisecond (1/1000th of a second). The third characteristic of human response is loudness. This term is self-explanatory. The louder (volume) the noise, the more problems it can cause.

TYPES OF HEARING LOSS

Noise can affect humans in three ways: by causing physiological damage that affects hearing, by causing more general physiological effects in some cases referred to as sociological, and by causing psychological effects. In terms of the first effect, physiological damage, there are two basic types of hearing loss. The first is *conductive*, and restricts the transmission of sound to the cochlea or inner ear (see Figure 5.1); the second is *sensorineural* (sometimes referred to as nerve deafness), and affects the cochlea and is usually irreversible. Conductive hearing loss can be caused by wax buildup, infection, or trauma. From an industrial standpoint, it can be caused by the nonhygienic application of hearing protectors or the improper cleaning of these devices.

More prevalent in industry, however, is the sensorineural type of hearing loss. Two indications of exposure to excessive noise levels at work are ringing in the ears (tinnitus) and raising the volume on the radio or television after work. The volume of the radio or television will seem very high the next morning because temporary hearing loss diminishes with rest and removal from exposure.

Gradual hearing loss, known as temporary threshold shift (TTS), can sometimes be reversed by removal from the noise source. Permanent threshold shift (PTS) identifies a hearing disability that is permanent and may not be correctable. In many cases, a hearing aid can bring about some improvement. However,

FIGURE 5.1

The Auditory System

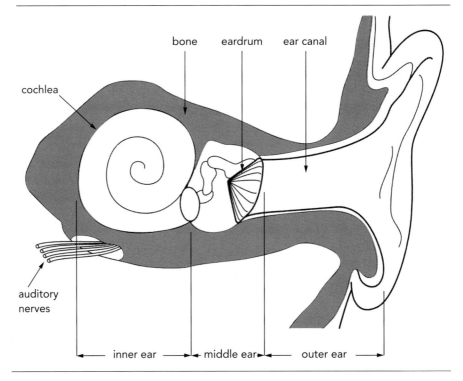

OH&S Notebook 5.1

NOISE EXPOSURE STANDARDS

Noise exposure standards vary across provinces and territories in terms of their relative stringency. The standards are based on worker exposure during a defined time frame. This relationship is referred to as *dose*, which describes the amount of noise absorbed by or impinged on an organ (the ear or the body) in a given unit of time. The exposure limits in Canadian jurisdictions are available at: http://www.ccohs.ca/oshanswers/phys_agents/exposure_can.html.

Sources: CCOHS, "Noise - Occupational Exposure Limits in Canada." Found at: http://www.ccohs.ca/oshanswers/phys_agents/exposure_can.html.

such a device is of little assistance when the hearing loss has been caused by noise exposure or sensorineural loss, because the hair cells in the cochlea have been destroyed.

The second effect of noise is also physiological but a slightly different category of physiological in that it is more general. It is sometimes referred to as sociological hearing loss and causes extra-auditory effects such as a startled response to a loud, unexpected noise; cardiovascular, neurologic, endocrine, and biochemical changes; and nausea, malaise, and headaches.[3] Other laboratory and field studies have demonstrated **vasoconstriction**, **hyperreflexia**, fluctuations in hormonal secretions, and disturbances in equilibrium and visual functions. In the past companies would hire workers with hearing loss to work in high noise environments on the notion that the damage was done, however it is now known that noise can cause more general physiological effects.

The third effect deals with human psychology. Many people are affected and disturbed by certain sounds that are not loud enough to present any serious physiological problem. These are day-to-day noises that tend to bug us, such as a patron talking during a movie, a helicopter flying overhead, or a tap dripping. Though the actual noise level may be well below acceptable standards and may not be measurable with a sound level meter, it is nonetheless very real (often referred to as "selective hearing") and can cause stress and other possible non-auditory effects.

vasoconstriction
the process of causing a constriction of the blood vessels

hyperreflexia
the condition of unusually quick reaction by the nerves to some external stimulus

NOISE CONTROL

Noise can be controlled by using various methods, but the process for control follows the source–path–human strategies used by health and safety professionals. The first strategy for reducing noise is to make the *source* quieter. There are a number of possible approaches. If the problem consists of a noisy machine, for instance, it may be possible to make the machine quieter by adding sound-absorbing materials, placing vibration padding under it, redesigning the operation so that the machine performs in a different manner, isolating the machine in a separate room or sound-deadening enclosure, or purchasing a new machine.

OH&S Notebook 5.2

NOISE IN THE WORKPLACE: SIGNS AND LEVELS

Though nothing will replace accurate measurement of noise levels in the workplace, the Canadian Centre for Occupational Health and Safety suggests that a workplace might be too noisy if

- people have to raise their voices to be understood
- employees have ringing in the ears at the end of the workday
- employees find that they have to turn their radio up on the drive home (compared with the volume on the way to work)
- individuals who have worked in the workplace for years have difficulty understanding conversations at parties or restaurants

If any of the above statements are true, a noise assessment or survey of the workplace should be undertaken. Noise exposure tests can be done by an outside specialist or by a trained person on staff using various pieces of equipment including:

- sound pressure level meter—measures gross noise levels
- octave band analyzer—measures noise level in each frequency range
- a dosimeter—measures a person's exposure to noise as a percentage for one shift
- or an audiometer—determines the sensitivity of a person's hearing or degree of hearing loss

Source: CCOHS, "Noise - Basic Information." Found at: http://www.ccohs.ca/oshanswers/phys_agents/noise_basic.html#_1_3.

---

attenuated or attenuation

reduction of noise at one location compared to another farther from the source

The second strategy—*path*—involves moving the worker away from the source or erecting sound barriers between the noise and the worker, or both. Based on the physics of noise, as the distance from the sound source is doubled, the noise level will drop by a fixed amount. For example, if a noise level of 90 dB is measured 5 metres away from a machine (a point source) and the distance is increased to 10 metres, the noise level will be **attenuated** or lowered by 6 dB. This is called a "free field effect," which simply means that nothing like a wall is around to reflect the sound back on the worker. Objects such as the walls of the building and other machines will cause reflections that can reduce the amount of attenuation from this fixed amount. Nevertheless, the principle is still valid, and this process is usually less costly than the source approach.

The third strategy—*human*—involves the use of personal protective equipment (PPE). This approach is the least costly and the one that is most commonly used. It is not always the best method, but in many cases some companies are not well enough informed to undertake other approaches such as job rotation, relocation, isolation, automation, rest periods, and site design. The two basic classes of hearing protection available are earplugs, which are inserted into the ears, and circumaural muffs or earmuffs, which are worn over the ears. A description of the various types of industrial hearing protection is provided in Table 5.3 in the chapter appendix. Note that whatever strategies are used to decrease noise exposure, personal protective devices may still be necessary in conjunction with other methods (see **OH&S Notebook 5.3**).

OH&S Notebook 5.3

CHOOSING HEARING PROTECTORS

For each application and to be properly fitted for maximum protection, there are 10 factors to consider when deciding on the most effective hearing protection.

1. *Comfort:* Earmuffs in particular can be hot in warm *conditions.* The spring band can generate a feeling of the head being squashed. Workers who are claustrophobic may experience feelings of confinement.

2. *Visibility:* It is important that hearing protection be visible so that supervisors can ensure that the worker is wearing the protection and using it in the required manner.

3. *Size:* People have heads of different sizes and shapes. It is imperative that hearing protective devices be fitted properly. Additional types of paraphernalia such as face shields used in conjunction with hearing protection must also be examined.

4. *Weight:* Generally, the lighter the protection, the greater the comfort.

5. *Ease of donning:* A device that is easy to put on will gain more acceptance among workers.

6. *Cost:* The actual dollar cost will depend on the application, the required degree of attenuation, and the style of device. Earmuffs are more costly than earplugs. The specific noise protection required could necessitate both plugs and muffs.

7. *Effective attenuation:* Most modern hearing protection devices use a noise reduction rating (NRR) system to indicate the degree of attenuation based on laboratory evaluation. The NRR value is usually accompanied by a chart showing attenuation by octave band frequencies. Generally, the higher the number, the greater the level of attenuation. A good rule of thumb relationship is expressed with the equation below:

$$NRR = L_{actual} - L_{standard} + 7$$

where L_{actual} is the noise level measured in the workplace and $L_{standard}$ is the noise standard for an eight-hour period. Thus, if a worksite has a noise level of 97 dB(A) and the standard is 90 dB(A) for eight hours, the required NRR for hearing protectors would be 97 – 90 + 7, or 14 dB(A).

8. *Hygiene:* This requirement is the most critical and most abused. It is not uncommon to observe a hearing protection device hanging from a hook in a dirty environment. Care must be taken to keep the personal item clean and stored in a sanitary location to avoid ear infections, which could cause more damage than the noise does.

9. *Useful life:* Disposable plugs or inserts do not last long but require no maintenance; muffs last longer but require maintenance.

10. *Maintenance:* All nondisposable hearing protection devices require ongoing maintenance and care. They must be cleaned regularly with soap and warm water, not alcohol, and checked periodically for wear. The foam seal pads on circumaural units must be regularly maintained because skin oils and sweat will cause embrittlement and surface failure. Once the seal is damaged, the attenuation effectiveness is reduced.

Sources: E.H. Berger, W.D. Ward, J.C. Morrill, and L.H. Royster, eds., *Noise and Hearing Conservation Manual, 4th ed.* (Akron: American Industrial Hygiene Association, 1988); CCOHS, "What Is Personal Protective Equipment?" Found at: http://www.ccohs.ca/oshanswers/prevention/ppe/designin.html (Accessed May 29, 2010).

VIBRATION

Another physical agent within the workplace that can be hazardous, but may not be thought about as often, is vibration. Vibration refers to the oscillating motion of a particle or body moving about a reference position.[4] Vibration is measured by examining the frequency, amplitude, and acceleration of an object. Vibration has a number of mechanical causes, including the dynamic effects from machine tolerances, clearances, rolling or rubbing contact, and out-of-balance conditions with rotary or reciprocating parts.

Vibrations are often easily detectable but determining the amount that is hazardous is difficult and because of that, vibration exposure must be measured and carefully monitored. Vibration enters the body from the part in contact with the vibrating equipment. Vibrations are classified into two categories: low frequency (discussed above) and high frequency. Vibrating effects fall into two separate conditions. As noted, the first concerns low-frequency vibrations. The second deals with higher frequency vibrations, which can happen so fast that the body cannot respond. When the higher frequencies occur, the effects of wave velocity and acceleration take precedence. Vibratory effects are evaluated using measurements of velocity and acceleration caused by the source, with a vibration meter, which is often a variation on a sound-level meter.

Health Effects of Vibration

An employee who is required to operate a handheld piece of equipment that vibrates (e.g., jackhammer) typically feels it in the hands and arms. This is often known as **segmental vibration** or in many situations hand–arm vibration. An employee who is required to sit or stand on a vibrating floor area such as a seat or piece of equipment will experience vibration in their entire body, known as **whole-body vibration**. The impact on health is largely dependent upon the average amount of exposure and must be properly assessed. An evaluation takes into account the intensity and frequency of the vibration, the duration (years) of exposure, and the part of the body that receives the vibration energy.

Vibration can be a health hazard for three reasons. As mentioned above, it can cause whole body-vibration, segmental vibration, and noise. Similar to noise, vibration is transmitted through a medium, though in this case the medium is usually solid (e.g., steel or brick). The health effects will vary with the frequency and amplitude of the vibration. At low frequencies—say, up to 15 Hz—the body will experience whole-body vibration. In this instance, the complete human body will "shake" with the source. We have all experienced or witnessed this condition in an automobile or on board a ship when an individual experiences motion sickness. Whole-body vibration can also result in fatigue, nausea, stomach problems,

segmental vibration affects only parts of the body

whole-body vibration affects the whole body as a unit

OH&S Today 5.1

When Vibrations Help

Can you think of an object you use on a daily basis that vibrates and when it does, it is helpful to you? Consider when you put your cellphone on vibrate; this allows you to take phone calls without requiring the use of the ringer thus minimizing any annoyance or disturbance to others. On some highways in Nova Scotia "rumble" strips have been cut along the sides of highways and along the centre line to warn drivers of when they are dangerously close to the edge or middle of the roads. Have you ever played a video game and had the controller vibrate, warning that you are about to go off course or lose control? All these are ways in which vibrations can be helpful; the difficult aspect is knowing how much vibration is too much.

headache, and "shakiness" and some situations may be connected to bowel, respiratory, circulatory, and back disorders.[5] Additionally, health effects of whole-body vibration can also include inhibition of muscular reflexes, impaired or blurred vision, and alterations of brain electrical activity. Whole-body vibration effects can result from driving a motorcycle, truck, or tractor, or from working near large machines such as air compressors or punch presses.

As the frequency of vibration increases, parts of the body—not the whole body—will be affected by a process called segmental vibration. Segmental vibration effects include sore neck and shoulder muscles and sore joints; Raynaud's phenomenon, or white fingers, caused by restricted blood circulation in the fingers; neuritis and degenerative alterations of the central nervous system; fragmentation, **necrosis**, and **decalcification** of the carpal bones; and muscle atrophy and tenosynovitis (see **OH&S Notebook 5.4**).

One term that often arises in discussions of vibration is **resonance**, which refers to the effect that occurs when an object reacts strongly to some particular frequency. If you sing in a tiled shower stall, you will occasionally hear a note that sounds louder than most, which means that the space is resonant to that note. Parts of the human body can resonate when exposed to some lower frequencies. For instance, the head and shoulders can resonate at 20 Hz to 30 Hz, while the eyeballs resonate at 60 Hz to 90 Hz.[6] If your vision becomes blurry when you have been working with a power tool such as a belt sander, you are experiencing minor levels of eyeball resonance, which is harmless unless prolonged.

necrosis
death or decay of tissue

decalcification
loss of lime salts (calcium) in the bones

resonance
the effect that occurs when an object reacts strongly to some particular frequency

Controlling Vibration

The first step in controlling vibration in the workplace is being knowledgeable about the standards or exposure limits. The CCOHS website contains information about exposure limits and can be found at: http://www.ccohs.ca/oshanswers/phys_agents/vibration/vibration_effects.html.

 OH&S Notebook 5.4

HAND–ARM VIBRATION SYNDROME (HAVS)

Working with handheld power tools (particularly in cold weather) can result in vibration-induced white finger (VWF)—or, more generally, hand–arm vibration syndrome (HAVS). HAVS results from changes in blood circulation and the nervous system associated with vibration and is characterized by

- tingling in the fingers;
- loss of sensation in the fingers (numbness);
- loss of sense of light touch;
- whitening (blanching) of the fingers when exposed to cold;
- loss of grip strength; and
- development of cysts in fingers and wrists.

HAVS is a progressive disorder and is also known as Raynaud's phenomenon. Prevention efforts focus on reducing vibration, using ergonomically designed tools, keeping hands warm and dry, and taking rest breaks.

Sources: J. Mason, " Bad Vibrations," *Occupational Health*, Vol. 55, No. 7 (2003) Pg. 24; E. Weir and L. Lander, "Hand–Arm Vibration Syndrome," *Canadian Medical Association Journal*, Vol. 172, No. 8 (2005) Pg. 1000–1.

Being knowledgeable of the standards helps you to determine which control mechanisms are required for minimizing any negative impact. By using the proper engineering and administrative controls as well as the correct personal protective equipment the impact of vibration, whether it be whole body or segmental can be greatly reduced.

One example of an engineering control includes ergonomically designed equipment or equipment features such as special grips or properly designed seating that helps to absorb or decrease the vibrations felt by the worker. The frequency response associated with vibrating systems is directly related to the system's mass. In the simplest terms, vibration can be dampened by increasing mass or weight. An example: the increased weight on the outer flange of a flywheel (typically a large wheel designed to regulate the speed of machinery) smoothes out much of a machine's vibration. A flywheel is one method for reducing health effects of vibrations. Segmental vibration effects are caused by vibrating tools such as riveters, sanders, saws, air hammers, or hammer drills. The most serious segmental effects are those associated with hand–arm vibrations. Vibrating hand tools produce a Catch-22 situation. To properly control a vibrating hand tool, one must grip it securely; but the tighter the hand grips the tool, the more severe the effects of segmental damage from vibration. The human resource professional should also be aware that vibration has chronic effects that must be managed.

Examples of administrative controls include policies or rules around the duration and amount of exposure (e.g., shift rotations) as well as regular maintenance of equipment. Finally personal protective equipment like padding, gloves, or floor mats can help to reduce the amount of vibration that is felt by the individual. For more specific methods for controlling vibrations see **OH&S Notebook 5.5**.

THERMAL STRESS

homeostasis
the balance of heat
generation

Thermal stress conditions involve cold and hot temperature extremes. The human body can be seen as a machine that takes in chemical energy (food) and converts it to mechanical energy (muscles) and heat (see Figure 5.2). The balance of this heat generation, referred to as **homeostasis**, is the basis for examining the effects

---

OH&S Notebook 5.5
CONTROLLING VIBRATION

Strategies for whole body and segmental vibration control include

- avoiding the source by revising the task;
- using equipment that produces lower vibrations;

- adding dampening devices to equipment to reduce vibrations;
- decreasing worker exposure time; *and*
- isolating the worker from the source.

Source: CCOHS, "How can you measure vibration?" Found at: http:// www.ccohs.ca/oshanswers/phys_agents/vibration /vibration_ measure.html (Accessed Feb. 7, 2007).

FIGURE (5.2)

The Body as a Machine System

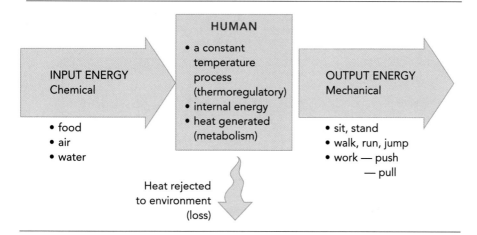

of heat and cold on the body. Simple thermodynamic theory shows that temperature, like water, flows from the high point to the low point. Thus, in cold climates, heat will flow from the body into the surrounding environment, making the person feel cold. Similarly, in hot climates, heat will be absorbed by the body, making the person feel hot. Adding physical work to either of these situations will increase body heat and shift the thermal balance. When an imbalance occurs, the body is stressed thermally. This body thermal balance can be illustrated by the mathematical model below:[7]

$$S = (M - W) \pm R \pm C \pm V - E$$

where S is the body heat storage or loss, M is the metabolic heat production of the body, W is the work output, R is the radiative heat gain or loss, C is the convective heat gain or loss, V is the respiratory heat gain or loss, and E is the evaporative heat loss.

When there is heat, the body will gain heat if R, C, and V are positive; similarly, when there is heat loss, then R, C, V, and E are negative. In medical terms, heat gain is referred to as *hyperthermic*; heat loss is referred to as *hypothermic*; and a condition of neither gain nor loss is known as balance (see **OH&S Notebook 5.6**).

There are three methods of heat transfer that apply to the body, as well as to any other thermal condition. The first method, **conduction**, occurs when two surfaces are in contact (e.g., the skin touches a hot stove, resulting in a local burn). The second method, **convection**, occurs when one surface adds heat to the surroundings (e.g., the skin is close to air flow emanating from a flame or a heater). The third method, **radiation**, occurs when energy is transmitted by electromagnetic waves (e.g., the skin is exposed to sunlight).

The body has remarkable temperature control, with the blood system and the skin being the major players. As body heat increases, blood flow increases, capillaries move closer to the surface of the skin (they actually open up), and sweating increases, thereby allowing increased heat exchange to the atmosphere. As body heat decreases, blood flow slows and the capillaries withdraw from the skin surface, thus reducing the amount of heat transferred to the atmosphere.

conduction
heat transfer occurring when two surfaces are in contact

convection
heat transfer occurring when one surface adds heat to the surroundings

radiation
heat transfer occurring when energy is transmitted by electromagnetic waves

OH&S Notebook 5.6

MEASURING THERMAL STRESS

Thermal stress is measured using the wet bulb globe temperature (WBGT) index. This index measures the effect of heat and humidity on a worker.

Humidex Range (°C)	Comfort
20–29	Comfortable
30–39	Varying degrees of discomfort
40–45	Uncomfortable
46 and over	Many types of labour must be restricted

Source: CCOHS, "Humidex Rating and Work," Table 1. Found at: http://www.ccohs.ca/oshanswers/phys_agents/humidex.html.

The effects of heat and cold on health are well recognized by anyone who spends a lot of time outside in summer and winter. The focal point of most thermal stress and control is at the body core—from the neck to the groin and between the shoulders. The body core temperature range is 35°C to 38.5°C, with "normal" being 37°C. Fluctuations in the body's core temperature typically stay within 1°C and occur during various times of the day or when engaged in a physical activity or an emotionally arousing situation. In some situations the environment can cause the body's core temperature to increase more than 1°C. We typically see greater changes in the body's core temperature when an individual is ill. When the core temperature goes outside the normal range, serious problems can result.

Heat-Related Illnesses

There are a number of factors that influence the risk that heat poses to an individual. For instance health, weight, age, low fitness level, and medical conditions such as high blood pressure are factors that influence the risk that heat poses to an individual.[8] There are a number of heat-related illnesses. Heat edema occurs most often in individuals who are not acclimatized to working in hot environments and typically results in parts of the body swelling (e.g., ankles). Heat rash is one of the first signs of the body's intolerance to heat and results in the sweat glands becoming swollen and plugged. Small red spots appear on the skin and cause an individual to feel a tingling sensation or itchiness. Heat cramps occur in the muscles of the body and may or may not occur in conjunction with other heat-related illnesses such as heat rash. Heat cramps are the result of an imbalance of salt in the body and are often felt in the arms and legs first. Heat syncope or fainting is the result of an inadequate amount of blood in the brain due to lowered blood pressure and often occurs while an individual is standing or working. Fainting as a result of heat often occurs in individuals who are not acclimatized however, recovery is typically rapid after a period of rest in a cool area. Heat exhaustion occurs when an individual is sweating excessively and loses too much body water. Individuals suffering from heat exhaustion exhibit one or more of the following symptoms: excessive sweating, dizziness, blurred vision, nausea, headache, vomiting, heart palpitations, and numbness in the hands and or feet. Heat stroke and heat hyperpyrexia occur when the body is unable to control its thermal balance resulting in a dangerous rise in core temperature (above 41°C). Symptoms of heat stroke include either a partial or complete loss of consciousness while the symptoms of heat hyperpyrexia are similar but the skin remains moist or wet. Heat stroke and heat hyperpyrexia are the most serious of heat-related illnesses and require immediate first aid and if left untreated can result in damage to the brain, kidneys and heart.

Controlling Heat

Provincial legislation requires that employers take every reasonable precaution to prevent heat-related illnesses and the risks of heat exposure. If employees are at risk for heat-related illnesses the employer is required to conduct heat assessments and implement the proper controls.[9] Engineering controls are the most effective method for controlling heat exposure however, they are often impractical in certain environments such as outdoors. Examples of engineering controls include reducing worker activity, insulating heat sources or hot surfaces, shielding or protecting workers, providing air conditioning, or increased ventilation. When engineering controls are not feasible then administrative controls should be put into place. Administrative controls include proper supervision, arranging for work–rest cycles, and implementing work methods or requirements that help to acclimatize workers (e.g., physical fitness, water drinking). Personal protective equipment including proper clothing, such as proper eye protection, cooling vests, hats, and sunblock are also useful and effective methods for minimizing the risk of heat-related illnesses however, they should be used in combination with other administrative and engineering control mechanisms.

Cold Environments

Cold environments can be very hazardous to an individual's health and require similar precautions as hot environments. Cold work environments include not only outdoor environments exposed to weather but also environments that are refrigerated such as large industrial freezers and pools.

OH&S Today 5.2

Men and Women in the Cold

How we react to cold temperatures varies not only from person to person but varies between men and women.[10] CCOHS studies have demonstrated that while women's core body temperature decreases more slowly than men's, they are not able to create as much body heat through activities like exercise and shivering. This is an important consideration for both employees and employers.

Source: Adapted from: CCOHS, "Cold Environments - General." Found at: http://www.ccohs.ca/oshanswers/phys_agents/cold_general.html (Accessed Jan. 19, 2013).

Cold-Related Injuries and Illnesses

Similar to heat-related illnesses there are a number of factors or conditions that influence the extent to which you are at risk for cold-related illnesses. For example, age, gender, fatigue, diseases, health conditions such as Reynaud's syndrome, consuming drugs, alcohol, or smoking are all factors that increase the risk of suffering from a cold-related illness. Interestingly, the human body does not become acclimatized to the cold in the same way it does in hot environments however, certain body parts are able to develop a tolerance to the cold (e.g., hands).[11] Furthermore there are key factors that influence the human body's response to the cold: air temperature, wind speed, humidity, physical activity, work schedule, and protective clothing.

Cold-related injuries are labelled as nonfreezing injuries or freezing injuries. Nonfreezing injuries happen when body parts such as hands and feet cool but do not freeze. Nonfreezing injuries can occur in temperatures above the freezing mark and include chilblains, immersion foot, and trench foot. Chilblains are a mild injury caused by reduced circulation in the extremities after prolonged exposure to temperatures above freezing. Chilblains result in redness, swelling, and tingling in the hands and feet. Immersion foot is an injury that occurs after an individual's foot or feet have been wet but not frozen for prolonged periods of time (e.g., days, weeks). Similar to chilblains, immersion foot results in tingling, numbness, itching, pain, swelling in the feet and legs, and the skin may turn blue or purple. Trench foot is similar to immersion foot and is caused by prolonged exposure to colder (up to 10°C) wet conditions. The onset of symptoms can be hours or days and are similar to immersion foot and if left untreated can result in muscle tissue or nerve damage.[12]

Freezing injuries occur in colder temperatures and are caused by local freezing of muscles and tissues. Examples of freezing cold injuries include frostnip and frostbite. Frostnip is the mildest form of a cold injury and can affect the ear lobes, nose, cheeks, fingers, and toes after exposure to temperatures below the freezing mark. Symptoms of frostnip include the top layer of skin freezing, which results in numbness, tingling, and the skin turning white and hard. Frostbite is similar to frostnip except the underlying tissues freeze in addition to the outer layer of skin. Frostbite occurs after exposure to freezing temperatures, frozen objects, or cold compressed gases. Frostbite results in restricted blood flow to the tissue and in severe cases can cause permanent tissue damage, blisters, infection, and gangrene if left untreated.

Hypothermia occurs when cold causes the body's ability to regulate its thermal temperature fails and is not able to compensate for the loss of heat. Hypothermia sets in after the body's core temperature falls below 33°C and is a life-threatening illness if left untreated. Hypothermia requires immediate first aid and treatment of symptoms. The first signs and symptoms of mild hypothermia include an overall feeling of cold and pain in exposed extremities. As time passes moderate hypothermia sets in and feelings of cold and pain subside due to an increase in numbness. This is followed by muscle weakness and drowsiness. Eventually, severe hypothermia sets in resulting in heart and respiratory failure and eventually death. See Table 5.1 for the signs and symptoms of hypothermia.

TABLE 5.1

Signs and Symptoms of Hypothermia

Stage	Core Temperature	Signs and Symptoms
Mild hypothermia	37.2–36.1°C (99–97°F)	Normal, shivering may begin.
	36.1–35°C (97–95°F)	Cold sensation, goose bumps, unable to perform complex tasks with hands, shivering can be mild to severe, hands numb.
Moderate hypothermia	35–33.9°C (95–93°F)	Shivering, intense, muscle incoordination becomes apparent, movements slow and laboured, stumbling pace, mild confusion, may appear alert. Use sobriety test, if unable to walk a 9-metre (30-foot) straight line, the person is hypothermic.
	33.9–32.2°C (93–90°F)	Violent shivering persists, difficulty speaking, sluggish thinking, amnesia starts to appear, gross muscle movements sluggish, unable to use hands, stumbles frequently, difficulty speaking, signs of depression, withdrawn.
Severe hypothermia	32.2–30°C (90–86°F)	Shivering stops, exposed skin blue or puffy, muscle coordination very poor, inability to walk, confusion, incoherent/irrational behaviour, but may be able to maintain posture and appearance of awareness
	30–27.8°C (86–82°F)	Muscle rigidity, semiconscious, stupor, loss of awareness of others, pulse and respiration rate decrease, possible heart fibrillation.
	27.8–25.6°C (82–78°F)	Unconscious, a heartbeat and respiration erratic, a pulse may not be obvious.
	25.6–23.9°C (78–75°F)	Pulmonary edema, cardiac and respiratory failure, death. Death may occur before this temperature is reached.

Source: CCOHS, "Cold Environments - Health Effects and First Aid." Found at: http://www.ccohs.ca/oshanswers/phys_agents/cold_health.html.

Controlling Cold

Similar to heat there are engineering, administrative, and PPE mechanisms that reduce the risk of suffering from a cold-related injury or illness. Engineering controls include equipment like heaters and shields that protect an individual from the cold environment or object. Administrative controls include work and rest schedules and cold weather procedures such as shut down or closure requirements. Clothing is one of the most effective methods for reducing the risk of a cold-related injury or illness. Protective clothing should be carefully selected based on what is required by legislation, the conditions of the environment, as well as the nature of the work being performed.

RADIATION

Radiation is divided into two distinct groups—ionizing and non-ionizing. These two types of radiation are identified primarily by wavelength range—short for ionizing and long for non-ionizing—and by their action on tissue. This section will be general since any worker employed by a company involved in radiative processes or materials must undergo extensive, specialized training.

Ionizing Radiation

Ionizing radiation is any form of electromagnetic energy capable of producing ions through interaction with matter. Types of ionizing radiation include X-rays, gamma rays, alpha particles, beta particles, and neutrons. X-radiation is most commonly found in medical facilities. The other forms of ionizing radiation are commonly found in nuclear operations or research companies. All of these forms, except X-rays, occur naturally as well as in manufactured states. Natural radiation is found in ground-grown food, cosmic bombardment, building materials such as concrete, and fertilizers such as phosphorus. Most of these sources are measurable with very sensitive instruments but are insignificant from a health standpoint. Some harmful ionizing radiation, which might occur in basements and mines, is radon gas.

Radiation exposure or dosage is usually measured in a unit called a rem (*r*oentgen *e*quivalent *m*an). Natural radiation is approximately 125 mrem (millirem) per year. A dose of approximately 75 rem (75,000 mrem) per year can cause serious health effects.

Manufactured ionizing radiation can be found in a number of products or operations other than nuclear energy. Most home smoke detectors use a source that emits alpha particles, which are harmless; older "glow in the dark" watch faces were painted with very low radioactive paint. In industry, ionizing radiation can be found in bulk-material measuring devices, high-voltage electronic devices, and medical equipment such as X-ray machines or scanners; none of these poses a health hazard to the general population.

The biological effects of equal amounts of different radiations depend on several factors, including whether the exposure is whole body or local (for example, the arm), acute, or chronic. Genetic effects can include cell mutation, burns, and radiation sickness. Control of exposure will include regular monitoring, shielding, job rotation, protective equipment, and extensive training. This is why the dentist places a lead apron over your body and neck when taking X-rays.

Non-Ionizing Radiation

Non-ionizing radiation refers to electromagnetic radiation that does not have energies great enough to ionize matter. Types of non-ionizing radiation include ultraviolet radiation, visible (white light) radiation, infrared radiation, microwave radiation, and radio waves. The sun can be a source of all these radiations. The eye is the primary organ at risk from non-ionizing radiation (see Figure 5.3).

Control of non-ionizing radiation exposures usually includes isolation or separation, protective equipment, and training. With respect to separation, a pregnant computer worker should be offered another job where she is not exposed to a VDT. Even though there is no hard evidence of fetal risk,

Chapter 5: Physical Agents   **133**

General Absorption Properties of the Eye for Electromagnetic Radiation

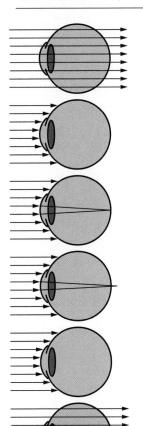

High-energy X-rays, gamma rays; 99% pass completely through the eye. 1% is absorbed.

Short UV; absorption principally at cornea. (Intermediate UV; absorption at cornea and lens.)

Long UV, visible; transmitted through eye and focused on retina.

Near IR; partially absorbed by lens, iris, and media; partially focused at retina.

Far IR; absorption localized at cornea for sharp H20 absorption wavelengths; other wavelengths absorbed also by lens and iris.

Microwave; generally transmitted with partial absorption in all parts of the eye.

and such a move may be impractical in a small firm, the company should not put itself in the position of subjecting one of its employees to a possible health risk.

Controlling Radiation

Controlling or mitigating the health risks of radiation using specially designed equipment that prevents access to radiation include various types of engineering controls. Engineering controls include specially designed equipment such as shields, walls, locked doors, warning indicators, displays, and ventilation systems. Typically in an environment wherein the risk of exposure is high there are multiple engineering controls in place in order to protect a worker should one of those control mechanisms fail or be bypassed. Administrative controls include regular inspections and

OH&S Notebook 5.7

EFFECTS OF NON-IONIZING RADIATION

Specific health effects of non-ionizing radiation forms can be itemized as follows:

- *Ultraviolet radiation* (originating from mercury vapour lamps and fluorescent tubes): conjunctivitis and keratitis (inflammation of the cornea), reddening of the skin (sunburn), skin cancer.
- *Infrared radiation* (originating from incandescent, fluorescent, high-intensity discharge lights, and hot metals and glass): corneal and retinal burns, overheating of the iris, cataracts, skin burns.

- *Microwave radiation* (originating from microwave ovens, radar, induction heating equipment, and diathermy equipment): deep tissue damage (cooking), surface skin rash, cataracts and eye lens opacities, biochemical changes and central nervous effects, pacemaker interference.
- *Radio waves* (originating from radio and television broadcasting, most electronic devices—e.g., video-display terminals [VDTs] and power lines): a number of conditions, including tumours, none of which have been conclusively proven.

Source: Ontario Ministry of Labour, "Radiofrequency and Microwave Radiation in the Workplace." Found at: http://www.labour.gov.on.ca/english/hs/guidelines/radiation/index.html (Accessed Feb. 7, 2007).

maintenance schedules, operating procedures, as well as proper labelling and inventory of any radioactive devices or materials. Personal protective equipment includes lead aprons, vests or air purifying respirators as well as eye protection. In the event that an incident has occurred and an employee is exposed to a radioactive source, it is important to consider how that source remains a hazard. The intensity of a radioactive source diminishes over time and as a result radioactive atoms decay and eventually form more stable atoms. To measure the amount of time that is required for the intensity of a radiation from a radioactive source to be reduced in half is referred to as radiation half-life. This measure tells us the amount of radioactivity that is left in a substance or object thereby indicating the level of risk or danger that is associated with it.

SUMMARY

This chapter has focused on four physical agents that are commonly encountered in industry—noise, vibration, thermal stress, and radiation. Industries in which agents such as ionizing radiation are encountered have implemented extensive, specialized training programs and procedures. In most situations, however, simple prevention policies and programs are adequate for reducing and controlling worker exposure to physical agents.

Key Terms

ambient 118
attenuated or attenuation 122
conduction 127
convection 127
decalcification 125
early warning change 118
homeostasis 126
hyperreflexia 121

necrosis 125
physical agents 118
radiation 127
resonance 125
segmental vibration 124
vasoconstriction 121
whole body vibration 124

Weblinks

Canadian Centre for Occupational Health and Safety Answers "Cold Environments—Health Effects and First Aid"
http://www.ccohs.ca/oshanswers/phys_agents/cold_health.html

Canadian Centre for Occupational Health and Safety Answers "Hearing Protectors"
http://www.ccohs.ca/oshanswers/prevention/ppe/ear_prot.html

Canadian Centre for Occupational Health and Safety Answers "Working in the Cold"
http://www.ccohs.ca/oshanswers/phys_agents/cold_general.html

CBC News Marketplace, "How Loud Is Your House? A Look at the Dangers of 'Noise'"
http://www.cbc.ca/marketplace/pre-2007/files/home/noise

Hearing Center Online, "Name That Sound—What Does Hearing Loss Sound Like?"
http://www.hearingcenteronline.com/sound.shtml

Radiation Safety Institute of Canada, "Issues in Radiation Safety"
http://www.radiationsafety.ca/community/issues

WorkSafeBC, "Part 7: Noise, Vibration, Radiation, and Temperature"
http://regulation.healthandsafetycentre.org/s/Part7.asp

Required Professional Capabilities (RPCS)

The following RPCs, listed by their CCHRA number, are relevant to the material covered in this chapter. All RPCS can be found at http://www.chrp.ca/rpc/body-of-knowledge.

RPC:172 Ensures due diligence and liability requirements are met.*
RPC:174 Develops and implements policies on the workplace environment.*
RPC:183 Analyzes risks to employee health & safety and develops preventive programs.*

---

*Canadian Council of Human Resources Associations, Human Resources Professionals in Canada: Revised Body of Knowledge and Required Professional Capabilities (RPCs ®), 2007.

Discussion Questions

1. Workers in a manufacturing division in your jurisdiction have made a formal complaint that three machines are too noisy. Noise measurements are taken: the results are 83 dB, 87 dB, and 88 dB. Do the workers have a legitimate complaint?
2. What are the health risks associated with vibrations?
3. All jurisdictions in Canada have access to the same science. Yet jurisdictions vary in legislated standards. Why might different standards apply in different jurisdictions?
4. Many occupations involve inherent exposure to a physical agent resulting in excessive exposure to noise, vibration, thermal conditions, and so on. Outline the steps an employer can take to protect employees when avoiding the exposure is not possible.

Using the Internet

Working outside in the Canadian winter can be a hazard for many workers. Using Internet resources, determine the health and safety regulations and guidelines for outdoor work in your jurisdiction. Compare regulations across several provinces or territories. Which jurisdictions have developed the most extensive sets of guidelines for outdoor work?

Exercise

OH&S legislation establishes standards for exposure to various forms of physical agents in the workplace. Think of common forms of after-work entertainment (e.g., movies, bars, restaurants, malls). What physical agents are present in these settings? What risks do they pose for customers? What about the employees of these establishments?

Case 1   MONTY'S PROBLEM

The newly appointed corporate medical director, a physician, paid an initial visit to one of the company's branch plants. For the first time, he met the occupational health nurse, an RN and recent CCOHN, who had been appointed from the local community some years previously. Occupational hygiene and safety at the plant was the responsibility of one of the senior production engineers, a P.Eng. who had been at the plant for many years. Neither of these individuals had received any formal instruction in occupational health nursing or occupational health and safety, respectively, since such training had not been available when they were appointed to these positions. The director was disturbed to note that medical records maintained by the nurse appeared to be available to the personnel department and that there was no defined OH&S program. The plant manager was absent on the day of the director's visit and unavailable to discuss these concerns.

On returning to corporate headquarters, the physician sent a directive to the occupational health nurse instructing her that medical records were to be regarded as private and that information was not to be released without his express permission. He also asked the OH&S person to purchase a simple class 2 sound level meter and to carry out a survey of noise levels at the branch plant. This information was to be available for discussion when the director next visited the operation.

Unfortunately, these requests caused considerable difficulties. The nurse had an argument with the personnel department over the availability of medical records, and this led to strong internal friction. The production engineer/health and safety specialist resented the physician's interference and complained to the plant manager, whom he had known personally for many years. The plant manager, Monty James, called head office to ensure that the director did not visit the plant without his permission or without at least giving notification so that Monty would be available.

In reply, the physician pointed out that the noise levels at the site were clearly excessive and that the so-called OH&S specialist was not capable of carrying out his duties.

When Monty James heard this response, he telephoned his superior, the general manager at corporate. If you were Monty, what would you say to your superior and how would you go about resolving the situation?

Case 2 EXPENSIVE JEWELLERY

As a newly hired HR specialist, you are touring the floor of the manufacturing plant. You are surprised to see that many workers are wearing their hearing protectors around the neck like a necklace instead of covering their ears. Moreover, the style seems to be to wear safety glasses perched on top of the head rather than in a position that would protect eyes. Employees working with acids are doing so in street clothes and barehanded even though rubber gloves and safety aprons are hanging on hooks next to the workstations. Even from your brief tour, it is clear that the company has invested in the best personal protective equipment available. Yet workers do not seem to be using the equipment to protect themselves. One of your new responsibilities is health and safety programming. What do you do?

APPENDIX

This appendix illustrates some of the techniques and calculations for noise and hearing protection that could prove useful to the HR practitioner when examining workplace conditions, adding new noise-generating equipment, or working with a consultant, government inspectors, or certified members of the JHSC. Noise calculations are pertinent to the combining of noise levels from various operating machines or the purchase of new equipment. Some of this material may be required by the student's specific course of study.

CALCULATING NOISE LEVELS

Noise level is measured in decibels or dB. This is a unit of measure for sound pressure level (SPL), which is the technical name for noise level or the "amount" of noise we hear. This relationship can be mathematically expressed as

$$dB = 20 \log (p/p0) \qquad \text{(equation 5.1)}$$

where dB is the sound pressure level (SPL), p is the sound pressure, and p_0 is a reference pressure, usually 0.00002 Pascal (N/m^2) or 0.0002 microbars.

Though equation 5.1 has little practical application other than to identify the basics of noise, a variation of it can assist in noise level evaluation. The variation is expressed as

$$\text{total dB} = 10 \log (10 \text{ dB1}/10 + 10 \text{ dB2}/10 + \cdots + 10 \text{ dBn}/10)$$

$$\text{(equation 5.2)}$$

where the various dB values are for any number of machines or noise sources in an area. For example, one manufacturer had a machine with a noise level, or SPL, of 88 dB. The manufacturer decided to purchase an additional machine. The supplier insisted that the noise level of the new machine was 85 dB, below the current noise standard. However, when the values for each of these machines were entered into the relationship expressed in equation 5.2, the result was a total dB = 10 log ($10^{88/10} + 10^{85/10}$) = 89.8 or 90 dB, which reached the current limit and could possibly create

some hearing problems. Any other ambient noise in this workplace could cause the noise level to exceed the safety standards. This calculation can be used for decibels (dB) as above, or for A-weighted decibels (dB[A]).

An easier way to make this same calculation is shown in Table 5.2. In our example, the difference in noise level between the two machines is 88 – 85, or 3 dB. Using the table, find the line that shows a difference of 3. The line at which the difference ranges from 2.8 to 3.0 gives a factor of 1.8, which is to be added to the highest noise level. Thus, 88 + 1.8 gives a total of 89.8, or 90 dB, as before.[13]

This table can be used for more than two sound sources. When there are more than two, the sound sources must be dealt with in pairs. For example, there are four machines in an area that are running and causing noise. The ratings are 82, 85, 88, and 88 dB. Take these noise levels in pairs, 82 and 85, 88 and 88. In the first instance, the difference is 3 dB, which from the table, as above, gives a factor of 1.8, which is added to the highest value. Thus 85 + 1.8 = 86.8. Perform this same operation with the second pair, 88 and 88. The difference between these is 0. From the table for 0.00 to 0.1, the factor is 3.0, which when added to the highest value gives 88 + 3.0 = 91.3. Now we have two new pairs—86.8 and 91.3. The same operation is again performed. The difference is 4.5. From the table for 4.4 to 4.7, the factor is 1.3, which is added to the higher of the two values. Thus 91.3 + 1.3 = 92.6. The total noise level in this example becomes 92.6 dB, which by any standard is too high.

If equation 5.2 is used, then

$$\text{total dB} = 10 \log (1082/10 + 1085/10 + 1088/10 + 1088/10)$$

$$= 92.4 \text{ dB}$$

SHIFT ADJUSTMENT FOR NOISE EXPOSURE

All of the TLV values for chemical and noise exposure are based on an eight-hour shift. If the shift is longer,

TABLE 5.2

Measuring Noise Levels

Difference between High and Low Noise Level	Amount to be Added to Higher Noise Levels	Difference between High and Low Noise Level	Amount to be Added to Higher Noise Level
0.0 to 0.1	3.0	4.1 to 4.3	1.4
0.2 to 0.3	2.9	4.4 to 4.7	1.3
0.4 to 0.5	2.8	4.8 to 5.1	1.2
0.6 to 0.7	2.7	5.2 to 5.6	1.1
0.8 to 0.9	2.6	5.7 to 6.1	1.0
1.0 to 1.2	2.5	6.2 to 6.6	0.9
1.3 to 1.4	2.4	6.7 to 7.2	0.8
1.5 to 1.6	2.3	7.3 to 7.9	0.7
1.7 to 1.9	2.2	8.0 to 8.6	0.6
2.0 to 2.1	2.1	8.7 to 9.6	0.5
2.2 to 2.4	2.0	9.7 to 10.7	0.4
2.5 to 2.7	1.9	10.8 to 12.2	0.3
2.8 to 3.0	1.8	12.3 to 14.5	0.2
3.1 to 3.3	1.6	14.6 to 19.3	0.1
3.4 to 3.6	1.5	19.4 to ∞	0.0
3.7 to 4.0	1.5		

say 12 hours, or shorter, say four hours, then the time weighted average (TWA) should be adjusted. This adjustment for noise uses the equation:

$$L_{eq}t = L_{eq} - 10 \log T_1/T \qquad \text{(equation 5.3)}$$

where L_{eq} is the noise exposure level limit for an 8-hour shift; L_{eq}, t is the noise exposure level limit for the time exposure t; T_1 is the time period worked; and T is the nominal time period.

Example: If a worker works a 12-hour shift at a location where the limit for an eight-hour period is 85 dB(A), then the exposure limit for the 12-hour shift will be

$$L_{eq}12 = 85 - 10 \log 12/8 = 83.2 \text{ dB(A)}$$

In a similar fashion, if the worker spent only four hours at the job, then the new TWA will become

$$L_{eq}4 = 85 - 10 \log 4/8 = 88.0 \text{ dB(A)}$$

These calculations are mathematically correct. However, conditions such as long-term exposure, physical condition, and a 40-hour workweek must be considered.

HEARING PROTECTION TYPES OR CLASSIFICATIONS

The early part of this chapter noted that there are two basic styles of hearing protection devices—plugs and muffs. Table 5.3 shows a more detailed breakdown of the styles and their designations.

TABLE 5.3

Types of Industrial Hearing Protection

Class	Type	Description
Earplugs	A1	Preformed earplug, the fitting of which should be done professionally.
	A2	User-formable earplug made of soft spongelike materials that the user rolls between the fingers for insertion into the ear canal.
	B1	A stethoscope configuration with the spring headband holding earplugs in position in the ears. Easy to observe, and the band may be worn in several positions on the head.
Circumaural	D1	An earmuff that surrounds the complete ear with a headband that sits only on the top of the head. Often best for comfort and optimum attenuation.
	D2	An earmuff similar to D1 but with a headband system that can be worn in many positions on the head. Attenuation may vary with headband position.
	D3	An earmuff attachment for a hardhat, which can be permanently attached or field applied. Usually used in construction settings.
Nonlinear protectors	F1	A specialty device with an electronic amplifier. A system that allows only certain sound levels and frequencies to pass unimpeded.
	F2	A specialty device with a mechanical "ear valve" on each ear that responds to impact noise and causes attenuation.
Combination		Many of the above types may be used in combination.

NOTES

1. E.H. Berger, W.D. Ward, J.C. Morrill, and L.H. Royster, eds., *Noise and Hearing Conservation Manual*, 4th ed. (Akron: American Industrial Hygiene Association, 1988).
2. A. Tidsskrift, "Hearing Loss Among Construction Workers in Edmonton," *Journal of Occupational and Environmental Medicine* 42 (2000): 57–63; WorkSafeBC Health and Safety Centre, *Hearing Conservation in British Columbia—2003*, http://www2.worksafebc.com/PDFs/hearing/statistics/annual_update_2003.pdf.
3. M.M. Key, A.F. Henschel, J. Butler, R.N. Ligo, I.R. Tabershaw, and L. Ede, *Occupational Diseases: A Guide to Their Recognition*, rev. ed. (Cincinnati: U.S. Department of Health, Education, and Welfare, 1977).
4. J.T. Broch, *Mechanical Vibration and Shock Measurements*, 2nd ed. (Naerum: Brüel and Kjær, 1980).
5. "Vibration Health Effects," Canadian Centre for Occupational Health and Safety Answers, accessed January 19, 2013, http://www.ccohs.ca/oshanswers/phys_agents/vibration/vibration_effects.html.

6. R.D. Soule, "Vibration," in *The Industrial Environment—Its Evaluation and Control* (Cincinnati: U.S. Department of Health, Education, and Welfare, 1973).

7. W. Hammer, *Occupational Safety Management and Engineering*, 4th ed. (Englewood Cliffs: Prentice Hall, 1989).

8. "Hot Environments: Health Effects," Canadian Centre for Occupational Health and Safety Answers, accessed January 19, 2013, http://www.ccohs.ca/oshanswers/phys_agents /heat_health.html.

9. "Hot Environments: Control Measures," Canadian Centre for Occupational Health and Safety Answers, accessed January 19, 2013, http://www.ccohs.ca/oshanswers/phys_agents /heat_control.html.

10. "Cold Environments—General," Canadian Centre for Occupational Health and Safety Answers, accessed January 19, 2013, http://www.ccohs.ca/oshanswers/phys_agents /cold_general.html.

11. "Cold Environments—General," Canadian Centre for Occupational Health and Safety Answers, accessed January 19, 2013, http://www.ccohs.ca/oshanswers/phys_agents /cold_general.html.

12. "Cold Environments—Health Effects and First Aid," Canadian Centre for Occupational Health and Safety Answers, accessed January 19, 2013, http://www.ccohs.ca/oshanswers /phys_agents/cold_health.html.

13. P.L. Michael, "Physics of Sound," in *The Industrial Environment—Its Evaluation and Control*, 2nd ed. (Cincinnati: U.S. Department of Health, Education, and Welfare, 1988).

Chemical and Biological Agents

CHAPTER LEARNING OBJECTIVES

After reading this chapter, you should be able to:

- define the numerous terms relating to chemical and biological agents
- discuss the management of chemical and biological agents
- outline the actions of chemical and biological agents on human physiology
- outline control mechanisms

LYME DISEASE IN CANADA

According to the Canadian Lyme Disease Foundation (CanLyme), Lyme disease is on the rise in Canada. The Canadian Centre for Occupational Health and Safety indicates that Lyme disease is the most common disease transmitted by insect. Lyme disease is caused by bacteria known as *borrelia burgdorferi* and is carried by particular ticks found outdoors. Various types of ticks carry the bacteria however, it is most often found on the "black legged" or "deer tick." Ticks carrying the bacteria spread it by biting hosts such as mice, squirrels, deer, and in some cases humans. When an individual become infected with Lyme disease, the effects can vary from one individual to the next thus making it difficult to detect. Symptoms can range from rashes and flu-like symptoms in one individual to more serious symptoms such as arthritis, cardiac, and neurological problems. In terms of treatment, Lyme disease can often be treated with antibiotics so long as it is detected in the early stages. If left untreated for too long it becomes increasingly difficult to treat and can result in chronic diseases. Lyme disease is and should be a concern to individuals who work outdoors as they are at risk of contracting the disease. In some locations across Canada the disease has been established thus making it continually present in that area, resulting in higher infection rates. This does not mean however, that you must be in one of these areas to contract the disease as these ticks can be found in any area.

CCOHS lists the following areas in Canada:

- Ontario—Point Pelee National Park, Presqu'ile Provincial Park, Prince Edward Point National Area

- Nova Scotia—Lunenburg and Bedford areas

- Manitoba—Buffalo Point area

- British Columbia—most of the province, but largest tick populations are on the lower mainland, Vancouver Island, and Fraser Valley.

Wearing appropriate protective clothing such as socks, long pants, long-sleeved shirts, insect repellant containing DEET, and avoiding contact with tall grasses and low bushes are some of the ways in which the risk of infection can be reduced.

Source: Canadian Lyme Disease Foundation. Found at: http://canlyme.com/; CCOHS, "Lyme Disease." Found at: http://www.ccohs.ca /oshanswers/diseases/lyme.html.

As noted in Chapter 2, most OH&S legislation now includes specific sections dealing with chemical and biological agents. These agents are also dealt with under WHMIS regulations. Almost all occupational diseases, such as asbestosis, silicosis, various types of dermatitis, and respiratory problems, and many occupational injuries, such as chemical splashes, spills, and burns, are related to chemical or biological exposures. The results of these exposures can range from minor irritation to death. Dealing with these materials requires complete training. There have been too many deaths, among young people in particular, to ignore these facts. This chapter provides an overview of the problems associated with chemical and biological substances and the requirements for managing and controlling them. The term **chemical agents** is used to describe hazards that are created by any one or any combination of a very large number of chemicals and their physical reactions. A *biological agent* or **biohazard** can be as subtle and as deadly as some chemical agents. Biological agents include hazards such as mould, fungus, bacteria, and viruses. Each of these agents may be ambient or acute (i.e., a single exposure).

chemical agents
hazards created by one or more chemicals

biohazard
hazard created by exposure to biological material

CHEMICAL AGENTS

More than 70,000 different chemicals are currently in use in North America, and approximately 800 new ones are introduced every year. No toxicity data are available for about 80% of the chemicals that are used commercially.[1] Increasingly, physicians are seeing patients who complain of physiological reactions to low-level chemical exposures in the environment—reactions such as headaches, dry nasal passages, and nausea, to name but a few. These complaints have been variously labelled as multiple chemical sensitivity (MCS), "twentieth-century disease," total allergy syndrome, and environmental illness.[2] Certain industrial chemicals have been linked to cancer, lung disease, blood abnormalities, nervous system disorders, birth defects, sterility, and skin problems. The specific effects of some chemicals are well documented, while those of many others are still unknown (see **OH&S Today 6.1**).

Vapours entering the atmosphere from solvents such as paint thinners are included in the chemical reaction category, because the vapours from the solvents can react to such things as heat and pressure. In this vein,

OH&S Today 6.1

Deadly Fires Burning: Firefighters at High Risk for Occupational Cancer

Each day Canadian firefighters risk their lives in flaming buildings as a service to their community. Though the immediate risk of death from an injury sustained during an active fire is obvious, other health risks associated with firefighting may not be as obvious. In reality, firefighters are also at high risk for certain types of cancer because of long-term exposure to carcinogenic chemical fumes and smoke. For instance, the chemical fumes released from burning plastic are toxic. Indeed, some relatively rare forms of cancer are far more common among firefighters than among the general population. For instance, glial blastoma, a primary brain cancer, is three times more likely among firefighters than among the general population.

Some provincial and territorial jurisdictions recognize particular forms of cancer as an occupational illness stemming from fighting fires. In 2002, Manitoba became the first province to pass legislation linking cancer to full-time firefighting. Such legislation is called *presumptive*—if workers in a certain occupation develop a disease, it is presumed to have been caused by their occupation and there is no need for the worker to prove the link.

Manitoba has set a high bar for other jurisdictions. Since the Manitoba legislation passed, other provinces have followed with legislation linking firefighting to certain forms of cancer. For example in 2011, Alberta added primary prostate cancer; primary site skin cancer; primary breast cancer and multiple myeloma to the existing list of presumptive cancers. This amendment means that firefighters who suffer these conditions and their families are qualified to receive Workers' Compensation.

The availability of financial compensation for firefighters suffering from cancer is certainly a large move forward—in this regard, the Manitoba legislation followed years of lobbying on the part of the Manitoba Professional Firefighters Association. However, firefighters are also focused on preventing occupational cancers. In terms of chemical exposure, the most dangerous time is when the flames have been put out but the fire is smouldering and firefighters are engaged in site cleanup. This is a time when individuals may be less vigilant about the use of protective breathing apparatus. Education programs about the importance of protective equipment may help reduce the incidence of these deadly cancers.

Source: Legislative Assembly of Manitoba. Found at: http://www.gov.mb.ca/legislature/hansard/5th-39th/sed_03/sed_03.html (Accessed Jan. 19, 2013); Workers' Compensation Board Alberta. Found at: http://www.wcb.ab.ca/pdfs/workers/WFS_Firefighters_with_cancer.pdf (Accessed Jan. 19, 2013); Alberta Firefighters Association. Found at: http://www.albertafirefighters.com/news/page/2/ (Accessed Jan. 19, 2013).

airborne particulates (e.g., dust created by mechanical means such as sanding or grinding) are included in the physical reaction category because the contaminant is caused by an expenditure of energy or work. These categories account for most of the health hazards found in industry and at home (see **OH&S Notebook 6.1**).[3]

Such agents may be hazards in and of themselves, but they can also interact *synergistically* with lifestyle or environmental factors. Synergistic effects occur when the result of two factors taken together is greater than the sum of the two. For example, a lifestyle factor such as smoking can have a synergistic effect on some materials. An asbestos worker is four times more likely than a non-asbestos worker to develop lung cancer; the probability rises to 80 to 90 times more likely if the asbestos worker smokes.

It has been estimated that 80% of all occupational illnesses are the result of chemical exposures.[4] Health problems created by chemical exposures are

---

OH&S Notebook 6.1

TYPES OF CONTAMINANTS

Listed below are seven types of contaminants:

1. *Dust:* Airborne respirable particulate that is solid particles generated by some mechanical means such as grinding, crushing, or sanding. The heavier particles tend to settle out of the air under the influence of gravity. The lighter or smaller the particle, the longer or greater the settling rate.

2. *Fume:* Airborne respirable particulate formed by the evaporation of some solid materials (e.g., steel, where the parent metal will vaporize on the application of weld-level heat and the vaporized metal will condense on contact with cooler ambient air). This condensed particulate is a fume. (This term is often confused with vapour.) Particle size is usually less than 1 micron or micrometre in diameter. Other examples of fume include plastic extrusion and automobile exhaust, which can include fumes (from the metallic additives) and vapours (from the unburned fuel).

3. *Smoke:* Airborne respirable particulate originating from the products of combustion, usually less than 0.1 micron in size. An example would be tobacco smoke or smoke from a fire.

4. *Mist:* Airborne respirable particulate in the form of liquid droplets generated by condensation from the gas state or by the breaking up of a liquid into a dispersed state of finely divided droplets. Spray paint and hair spray are two sources of mist generation.

5. *Vapour:* The airborne respirable contaminants in a gaseous form of any substances that are normally in the solid or liquid state at room temperature and pressure. Usually caused by evaporation. An example would be the airborne contaminant present above any solvent.

6. *Gas:* An airborne respirable contaminant that is one of the three states of matter created where the temperature is above the boiling point. Carbon dioxide and oxygen are two examples.

7. *Liquid:* Chemicals are sometimes found in a liquid form that, though not airborne respirable particulate, can come in contact with the skin and the eyes—for instance, when there is a splash or spill during manual mixing or pouring operations.

Source: J. B. Olishifsky, "Overview of Industrial Hygiene," *Fundamentals of Industrial Hygiene*, 4th ed. (Chicago: National Safety Council) 1995.

more prevalent in the workplace than in any other location. Though for the sake of simplicity this chapter will discuss single chemical exposures, most of the exposures that take place in the workplace are more complex.

To understand chemical agents, we must be familiar with the associated hazards each possesses. The hazard associated with a material is defined as the likelihood that it will cause injury in a given environment or situation. The potential degree of seriousness of the hazard is determined by its **toxicity** (i.e., its ability to cause injury to human biological tissue) or its explosive properties, which are defined in terms of flammability and reactivity. The extent to which a potentially toxic substance is an actual health hazard will depend on other factors, such as the concentration of the chemical and the length of time the employee is exposed to it.

Chemicals exist in three main states: solid, liquid, and gas. Having knowledge of the physical state of a chemical helps you to understand the health risks it poses to the human body. The physical state of a chemical determines its route of entry into the body for example; chemicals in a gaseous state are more likely to enter the human body via inhalation whereas liquids and solids are more likely to enter the body via skin absorption or ingestion. Throughout a work process the physical state of a chemical can change (e.g., liquid to a gas) and therefore change the health risks associated with that chemical. Consequently it is extremely important to take into consideration the physical state of a chemical in the context of routes of entry into the human body.[5]

Every chemical has its own melting, freezing, and boiling points. Typically, more than one of these states is present at the same time. Consider an open container of boiling water: the water is in the liquid state, while the steam is entering the gas

toxicity
ability to cause injury to human biological tissue

OH&S Today 6.2

Globally Harmonized System of Classification and Labelling Chemicals

The classification and labelling of chemical products differ by country and in some cases differs within a country despite the fact that many of the chemicals are used worldwide. These different classification and labelling systems create a number of difficulties for governments responsible for regulation and enforcement, companies who must comply with different systems, and of course for the workers who must clearly understand the chemicals they are exposed to. The Globally Harmonized System (GHS) is a system that would provide a systematic and consistent method for defining and classifying the hazards associated with chemical agents. The general purpose is to provide a consistent set of rules for classifying, labelling, and communicating about hazards. The idea behind the GHS is that it will help to reduce costs, promote and facilitate regulatory compliance and efficiency, and provide clear and consistent hazard information that would support safety transport and more efficient emergency response. Currently Canada, the United States, and countries in Europe are working on the implementation of GHS however, each are at varying stages of development and implementation. The goal is to have the system adopted worldwide. Implementation of GHS in Canada appears to be stalled with no specific deadline for full implementation. Other countries have identified specific dates, which can be found at: http://www.ccohs.ca/oshanswers/chemicals/ghs.html.

Source: CCOHS, "Globally Harmonized System." Found at: http://www.ccohs.ca/oshanswers/chemicals/ghs.html (Accessed Jan. 19, 2013).

aerosols

airborne respirable con-taminants, such as liquid droplets or solid particulate, dispersed in air, that are of a fine enough particle size (0.01 to 100 micrometres) to remain suspended for a time

state. Similarly, ice will feel hard (solid), be wet (liquid), and actually have evaporated water surrounding it (vapour). Most chemical-related health problems result from contact with chemicals in the liquid or gas (vapour) state. Most of the negative effects of exposure are derived from airborne respiratory contaminants known as **aerosols**.

A workplace health hazard is posed by exposure to one or more of these airborne respirable particulate forms. For instance, the white cloud that rises from a welding operation usually consists of the following: fumes resulting from the condensation of the parent metal and the weld rod metal and coating; smoke resulting from combustion of oil and other surface contamination; and vapours resulting from the evaporation of some of the oils and solvents on the metal surface (see **OH&S Today 6.3**).

TOXICOLOGY: AN OVERVIEW

Toxicology is the scientific study of poisons. For the purposes of this chapter, toxicology is the study of chemical-related occupational illnesses.

routes of entry

respiration (inhalation), skin absorption, ingestion, and skin penetration

Chemicals may enter the body by one of four **routes of entry**. In order of risk and normal contact, they are respiration (inhalation), skin absorption, ingestion, and skin penetration.

OH&S Today 6.3

Occupational Asthma: The Case of Snow Crab Workers

If we asked you to think about someone with a shellfish allergy, you would likely recall a person with a food allergy diagnosed in childhood, rather than a person with an adult-onset occupational illness. However, this less well-known reaction to shellfish is a reality for many people who work in snow crab processing plants. These employees are at risk for developing a specific type of occupational asthma called crab asthma. This form of asthma may develop following exposure to airborne dust and fumes that materialize when processing (cooking, crushing, or cutting) crab. SafetyNet, a community research alliance on health and safety in coastal and marine work, led by Memorial University of Newfoundland researchers Dr. Barbara Neis and Dr. Stephen Bornstein, has launched a long-term research program on crab asthma.

The symptoms have two major categories: asthma symptoms and allergy symptoms. The asthma symptoms

include coughing, wheezing, tightness of the chest, and shortness of breath. The allergy-type symptoms include itchy, watery eyes, running nose, and skin rash. These symptoms are strongest while employees are at work but can persist when the person goes home at night or takes vacations.

Though not all processing workers develop crab asthma, it can be a devastating diagnosis for those who do develop it. The symptoms, which can occur anywhere from a few weeks after starting work in a plant to a few years after exposure, can mean that the individual has to leave the job. In many coastal communities, the crab processing plant may be the only employment option. As such, alternative employment is difficult to find and unemployment may follow. Due to this, some individuals with crab asthma may continue to work in crab processing plants while their condition worsens. As an occupational illness, crab asthma is a compensable claim.

Sources: SafetyNet. Found at: http://www.safetynet.mun.ca (Accessed Feb. 7, 2007); D. Howse, B. Neis, and L. Horth-Susin, "All Out of Breath and Nowhere to Go: The Social, Economic, and Quality of Life Impacts of Occupational Asthma to Snow Crab," paper presented at the SafetyNet Conference, St. John's, October 2003.

Respiration (Inhalation)

An average-sized human breathes approximately eight litres of air per minute while at rest; this quantity increases with any activity.[6] Most human exposure to chemicals comes from breathing airborne contaminants. The respiratory system (see Figure 6.1) does a very efficient job of distributing these contaminants throughout the body during the normal air exchange process.

FIGURE 6.1

The Respiratory System

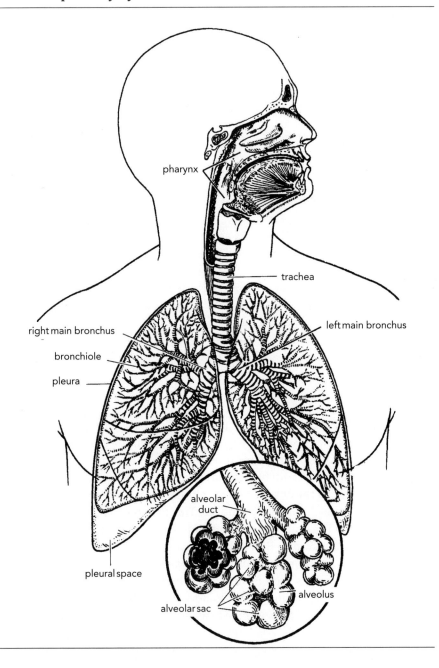

OH&S Today 6.4

Good Scents?

Environmental illness (EI) involves seemingly healthy individuals experiencing long-lasting symptoms of physical distress in their work settings. EI contaminants are estimated to exist in 20% to 30% of all work settings in North America. This illness has generally been associated with newly constructed and renovated buildings designed for energy efficiency and, until recently, was thought to be related solely to the inadequacy of mechanical ventilation systems. Recent findings suggest that other factors contribute to poor indoor air quality (e.g., car exhaust fumes from indoor garages, and heat and chemicals released by laser printers, computers, and photocopiers).

The effects of EI are variable and nonspecific, affecting building occupants both physically and psychologically. Physical symptoms include mucous membrane irritation affecting the eyes, nose, and throat; skin ailments; and unpleasant odour and taste perceptions. Other commonly reported symptoms include fatigue, headaches, nausea, confusion, and dizziness, as well as asthma-like symptoms. Typically, symptoms increase with exposure to the affected environment but usually dissipate once the occupant leaves the building (i.e., evenings, weekends, and holidays). In some cases symptoms do not abate. They may recur on exposure to chemicals found in home products and in nonwork environments. Moreover, an increasing number of individuals have developed sensitivities to fragrances such as perfumes, scented deodorants, and hair spray.

In recognition of this growing phenomenon, an increasing number of organizations are adopting scent-free policies. Typically, workplaces post notices asking both employees and visitors to refrain from using scented products while on the premises. Though aimed at a health and safety issue, such policies can be quite controversial, with some individuals maintaining their right to wear fragrances of their choice. Adopting a scent-free workplace policy should be preceded and accompanied by an educational campaign pointing out the reality of EI chemical/fragrance sensitivities and the types of physical symptoms some individuals experience when exposed to such fragrances. Employers and employees need to keep in mind that individuals with environmental sensitivities are entitled to protection under the Canadian Human Rights Act and an employer is obligated to ensure that employees are not discriminated against as a result of their disability.

Source: CCOHS, "Can scents cause health problems?" Found at: http://www.ccohs.ca/oshanswers/hsprograms/scent_free.html (Accessed Jan. 19, 2013).

There are five basic levels of protection or defence within the respiratory tract. The first is the nose. The nose, or upper respiratory tract, is lined with hairs, or *cilia*, which act as a coarse filter medium. The second is the interior of the nasal passage, where **turbinates** are found, which act as humidifiers and heat exchangers. The third is farther back in the throat, where the hairs or cilia are coated with a thick fluid called mucus. This mucus/cilia system entraps the finer particulate. The trapped contaminant is removed by blowing the nose and/or clearing the throat. Everyone has experienced these conditions after cleaning the garage, dusting a room, or sanding wood for refinishing. The fourth level is the lung passages such as the bronchi and the bronchiole. Here, the flow of air and its turbulence from breathing allow much of the larger particulate that bypassed the earlier defences to be expelled with normal exhalation. The fifth level of defence consists of myriad tiny air sacs, called **alveoli**, located at the ends of the lungs' air passages, called the alveolar ducts. These sacs (which are the

turbinates

spiral or spongy sections of the respiratory system that have a centrifugal effect to help remove aerosols

alveoli

tiny air sacs

source of oxygen transfer from the lungs to the bloodstream) contain small cells called macrophages (Greek for "big eater"), which dispose of any impurities via the lymph system.

Skin Absorption

In many workplaces and at home, chemical contact with the skin is a common occurrence. Many fat-soluble chemicals are readily absorbed, and most gases can pass through the skin very quickly. Chlorinated solvents such as carbon tetrachloride can pass through the skin into the blood and eventually reach the liver, where tissue damage may occur. Dimethyl sulphoxide can be absorbed through the skin in less than a minute following contact, and most people can detect a garlic-like taste in the back of the throat from this exposure.

A chemical's ability to easily pass through the skin is often closely associated with its level of toxicity. For example, the toxicity of DDT is about the same for insects and humans when it is injected. However, it is much less toxic to a person when applied to the skin, because it is poorly absorbed through the skin. Other pesticides are much more rapidly absorbed through human skin. Many agricultural workers have died following skin absorption of pesticides, particularly the organophosphate insecticides.

Chemicals that are not rapidly absorbed through the skin may produce a localized irritation (dermatitis) at the point of contact through a process called defatting, which causes the skin to become white and dry (e.g., when cleaning your hands with paint remover) and thus more permeable to water vapour, leading to tissue water loss and cracking. Burns or blisters can result from contact with acids or alkalis (chemical action). Skin disorders can result from contact with certain plants (biological action). Skin damage can result from contact with radiation or heat (physical action).

Ingestion

For many solvents, entry through the mouth and digestive system is not as major an issue as entry through the skin or the lungs. That said, poor personal hygiene can contribute to poisoning, as can eating, drinking, or smoking in an area where solvents are used. Ingestion of most solvents will cause damage to the lining of the digestive system. The ingested solvent may also be absorbed into the bloodstream and carried to **target organs**, where it will produce toxic effects. Worse still, the ingested solvent may be aspirated into the lungs where it can destroy the **surfactant layer**, cause a chemical pneumonitis, and collapse the alveoli.[7]

Penetration

Penetration occurs when the skin is cut or punctured by any sharp object. The type of contamination on the source, such as a knife or needle, will determine the possible trauma or illness. Cuts can occur when contact is made with sharp metal, glass materials, or other pointed instruments. Workers such as doctors, nurses, and veterinarians can easily be punctured by a hypodermic needle. The disorders range in seriousness from low-grade infections to HIV (human immunodeficiency virus).

target organs
tissues or organs that are most affected by exposure to a particular substance

surfactant layer
layer of liquids in the digestive tract and elsewhere (e.g., the cardiovascular system) that modify or reduce the surface tension within the conductors—intestine, blood vessels—to allow material—blood, food, stools, and so on—to move easily

OH&S Notebook 6.2

OTOTOXIC EFFECTS OF WORKPLACE CHEMICALS

When you consider typical causes of hearing loss, most individual would think of noise; however certain chemicals are known to have ototoxic effects. Ototoxicity is defined as having an adverse or harmful effect on the nerves and or bones required for hearing and balance. Chemicals known to have ototoxic effects include those used in the manufacturing of plastics, perfumes, dyes, and certain medications (e.g., antibiotics) can also cause hearing loss or damage (e.g., tinnitus or ringing in the ears). A proper assessment of the work environment should be conducted if there are concerns about possible noise or ototoxic hazards.

Source: Isaac Rudik, "Chemicals linked to hearing loss," *Canadian Occupational Safety*. Found at: http://www.cos-mag.com/PPE /PPE-Stories/Chemicals-linked-to-hearing-loss.html.

OH&S Notebook 6.3

TOXICITY TERMINOLOGY

- *Dose.* The degree of exposure and possible reaction with time. The dose is usually the basis for the values that are developed for threshold limit values (TLVs), which are used as a control measure in the workplace. For example, the TLV for carbon dioxide is 5,000 parts per million (ppm), based on an eight-hour exposure time.
- *Acute toxicity.* An effect that manifests itself immediately following exposure or very shortly thereafter. Burning your hand on a hot surface, for example, results in immediate pain and discoloration, and, later, blisters.
- *Chronic toxicity.* An effect that manifests itself some time after the exposure (possibly months or even years). Examples include cirrhosis of the liver from prolonged alcohol exposure; sensitization from isocyanates; occupational cancer, such as leukemia, from benzene exposure; and mesothelioma from asbestos exposure.
- *Local toxicity. The effect of an exposure at the point of contact. Cleaning your hands with paint thinner will cause dry, grey skin at the point of contact; this will be an immediate reaction.*
- *Systemic toxicity.* An effect that occurs at some location remote from the point of contact. For example, inhaling a chlorinated solvent such as trichloroethylene can cause damage to the liver; and inhaling carbon monoxide, which interrupts oxygen transfer to the blood, can cause asphyxiation and death.

Source: *Threshold Values for Chemical Substances and Physical Agents in the Workplace.* Cincinnati: American Conference of Governmental Industrial Hygienists, 1994.

CHARACTERISTICS AND PROPERTIES OF SOLVENTS

The majority of solvents were developed by the science of organic chemistry, and they are the most common of those products used both at work and at home. There are eight general characteristics or properties that make solvents effective but at the same time hazardous and toxic (see **OH&S Notebook 6.4**).

1. *Low surface tension.* This property allows a solvent to spread evenly and quickly and to provide excellent wetting of the contact surface. The higher the wetting factor, the better the wetting effect. But the wetting factor allows a spilled solvent to flow into cracks and joints and remain there, creating vapours that may be toxic. It also allows for more effective skin absorption.

2. *High vapour pressure.* Vapour pressure increases with temperature; this in turn increases the volume or concentration of a generated vapour or gas. This property of solvents allows efficient cleaning in processes such as degreasing systems because of the high vapour generation at the high operating temperatures. It can, however, create an inhalation hazard, the risk of which increases with temperature. This is not considered a problem as long as the container is kept closed. In a fire situation, the pressure increase can cause an explosion.

3. *Low boiling point.* The lower the **boiling point**, the greater the rate of evaporation or generation of vapours from a liquid. This property is useful when cleaning or painting because the solvents can evaporate quickly at room temperature, allowing the article to dry or tack off efficiently. The lower the boiling point, the greater the health risk since vapour can be generated at lower temperatures. Chemicals with boiling points close to room temperature or lower, such as ammonia (BP = 22°C) or hydrogen cyanide (BP = 25°C), can be a special problem since they can evaporate readily and are highly toxic.

boiling point
temperature at which the vapour pressure of a liquid equals atmospheric pressure

4. *Low heat of vaporization.* This relates to the amount of heat or energy required to change a liquid into a gas or vapour. The less heat required, the less costly the process in an industrial environment. But similarly, the lower the amount of heat necessary, the greater the risk of exposure if the material is not properly controlled.

5. *High volatility.* The main test of a solvent's effectiveness is the speed at which it will evaporate. The greater the volatility, the faster the evaporation, and the greater the health and fire risk.

6. *Ability to dissolve fats.* The more effectively a solvent dissolves fats or oils, the more useful it can be. However, when solvents are in contact with the skin, the skin's surface oils are dissolved. The unprotected skin then becomes susceptible to infection and other trauma. Skin contact with solvents is one of the major causes of **dermatitis**.

dermatitis
the inflammation of the skin from any cause

7. *Flammability.* This is one of the main hazards associated with solvent use, since all organic solvents are flammable. Care must be taken to ensure that there are no sources of ignition present during use. Chemical specifications usually list four characteristics that relate to flammability.

   (a) *Flash point.* Defined as the lowest temperature at which a liquid gives off enough vapour to form an ignitable mixture with air and produce a flame with a source of ignition. If the flash point is close to room temperature, the danger of ignition can be very great.

   (b) *Lower explosion limit* (LEL; also known as lower flammability limit, LFL). Defined as the smallest fuel–air mixture that is ignitable, expressed as a percentage. Carbon monoxide has an LEL of 12.5% by volume, which is equivalent to 125,000 parts per million (ppm). The upper exposure value for health exposure is 50 ppm, as shown in various standards. If the exposure to carbon monoxide in the workplace is maintained well below the health limit, there is no risk of ignition from that source.

OH&S Notebook 6.4

CLASSIFICATION OF TOXIC SUBSTANCES

Toxic materials are many and varied and have a variety of health effects on humans. In this section, organic and inorganic solvents are enumerated, because they are common at home and at work, and because they can have widespread health effects based on their properties. The overall effects of toxic materials can be grouped under the following 12 classifications.

1. **Irritants.** Irritants, sometimes referred to as "primary irritants," produce tissue or other damage at the point of contact. They are divided by route of entry into two groups:

   a. *Inhaled irritants.* These refer to airborne respirable contaminants or aerosols (including vapours, gases, and solid particulate) that are inhaled into the lungs causing damage wherever they settle. Ammonia is dissolved into body fluids and absorbed by the mucous membranes of the upper airways and can result in symptoms such as headache, nausea, salivation, and burning of the throat. Bronchitis may follow a very severe exposure, if the patient survives.

   b. *Contact irritant.* A contact irritant is any material that causes some sort of irritation, such as a rash or itch, at the point of contact. An example would be using Varsol to clean paint from your hands or coming into contact with poison ivy. In most cases, the skin is the organ most affected.

2. **Asphyxiants.** Any material that interferes with the oxygen supply to the blood and body tissues is referred to as an asphyxiant. Normal air contains approximately 21% oxygen and 79% nitrogen. The average person uses about 3% of the oxygen in air when breathing. If the oxygen content of the air falls below 15%, the body will be asphyxiated. There are two major types of asphyxiants:

   a. *Simple asphyxiants.* Any airborne respirable chemical that reduces the quantity of oxygen in the inhaled air by displacement is referred to as a simple asphyxiant. Examples are methane, propane, and nitrogen.

   b. *Chemical asphyxiants.* If an airborne and inhaled chemical interferes with the transport of oxygen by the blood hemoglobin or with the ability of the body cells to use oxygen, it is called a chemical asphyxiant. Examples of such chemicals are carbon monoxide, which interferes with the ability of the hemoglobin to transport oxygen and can result in tissue hypoxia and death, and hydrogen sulphide (rotten gas), which can interfere with the ability of the body cells to use oxygen and can result in immediate coma with acute exposure and possible death.

3. **Anesthetics and narcotics.** Any chemical that affects the central nervous system (CNS) can be considered to belong to this class. Most of these chemicals can, on exposure, cause headaches, interfere with the ability to concentrate, and act as a depressant. Examples include ethyl alcohol, acetylene, acetone, and toluene. In fact, all organic solvents can produce narcotic effects. Many of us have experienced some of these symptoms after consuming alcohol.

4. **Systemic poisons.** Systemic poisons can cause damage to one or more internal organs, as well as cell and neuron damage. Chlorinated materials

(c) *Upper explosion limit* (UEL; also known as the upper flammability limit, UFL). Defined as the highest fuel–air mixture that is ignitable, expressed as a percentage. Carbon monoxide has a UEL of 74% by volume, or 740,000 ppm. The LEL and UEL spread indicates that carbon monoxide could be ignited through a wide range of fuel–air mixtures, which could be an advantage if the gas were to be used for some heat applications.

such as DDT, endrin, chloroform, and trichloroethylene can cause damage to the liver and kidneys, usually as a result of chronic exposure. Benzene can cause damage to the blood-forming cells (the homeopathic system). Carbon disulphide is believed to damage the neurons. Other common systemic poisons include heavy metals such as lead, cadmium, and mercury, and chemicals such as arsenic and fluoride.

5. *Liver toxicants.* This grouping includes any chemical that will cause direct damage to the liver. The toxic action may be chemical (caused by alcohol) or metabolic (caused by benzene). In most instances, slight damage can be repaired. Cirrhosis is the most common disease.

6. *Kidney toxicants.* Kidney toxicants, like liver toxicants, include chemicals that cause damage to the kidneys, usually through the process of metabolic-transformation whereby harmless chemicals are rendered harmful or vice versa. Heavy metals such as lead, cadmium, and mercury, in addition to some solvents, can have this effect.

7. *Neurotoxins.* As the name indicates, these chemicals can cause damage to the nerves in the body. Hexane, a component of gasoline, can produce a condition called peripheral neuropathy—a disease affecting the nerves of the extremities—that can result in numbness and loss of feeling. This condition is dose related.

8. *Sensitizers.* Sensitizers, which can be chemical or biological, cause the body's immune system to respond abnormally by producing antibodies. Examples of sensitizers are isocyanates and poison ivy. The result is an allergy to the specific chemical whereby even casual exposure will cause an allergic reaction. Workers thus affected may have to change jobs, if not employers. Though sensitization is usually chronic, a very large acute exposure can sometimes bring it on. Farmer's lung, humidifier fever, nickel itch, and nickel fume fever are common examples of sensitization.

9. *Lung toxicants.* Toxic chemicals that can affect the lungs include irritant gases such as hydrogen chloride and ammonia, vapours such as isocyanates, and respirable solids such as asbestos, platinum, and silica. These materials can cause a variety of diseases, from simple pneumoconiosis (an accumulation of dust in the lungs and the tissue reaction to the presence of such dust) to cancer.

10. *Mutagens.* These include any chemicals that can lead to changes or mutations in DNA. The actions of chemicals such as lead, nickel, zinc, and manganese usually cause the death of cells but may in some cases allow the distorted cells to multiply, creating a potentially malignant tumour.

11. *Teratogens.* Chemicals such as lead, DDT, and PCB can damage germ cells or create defects in a developing fetus. The most infamous of these chemicals, thalidomide, is a well-known cause of gross abnormalities or birth defects in the fetus.

12. *Carcinogens.* Carcinogens are agents that cause or promote the formation of cancers. Well-known carcinogens include vinyl chloride, which can cause a liver cancer called angiosarcoma; benzene, which can result in leukemia; and asbestos, which can lead to mesothelioma. Following exposure to the carcinogenic chemical, there can be a latency period of five to 15 or more years.

Sources: M.M. Key et al., eds., *Occupational Diseases: A Guide to Their Recognition*, rev. ed. (Cincinnati: U.S. Department of Health, Education, and Welfare, 1977); WorkSafe Saskatchewan, "Chemical Hazards," in Ontario's Basic Certification Training Program Participant's Manual. Found at: http://www.worksafesask.ca/files/ont_wsib/certmanual/ ch_08.html?noframe (Accessed Feb. 7, 2007).

(d) *Auto-ignition temperature.* Defined as the lowest temperature at which a flammable fuel–air mixture will ignite from its own heat source. An example is spontaneous combustion in moist hay in a barn or in paint-soaked rags stuffed in a pail.

8. *Vaporization.* Most solvents will form very large volumes of vapour from a small amount of liquid. For instance, turpentine can form 112 litres of vapour for each litre of liquid at standard temperature and pressure conditions.

Inorganic Solvents

Inorganic solvents fall into two classes: acids and bases. These are the simplest of chemical groups and are the oldest known such groups. The difference between an acid and a base is expressed in terms of pH, a unit that notes the degree of acidity or alkalinity of a solution, having a scale of 1 to 14. A pH value of 7 is considered neutral (i.e., neither an acid nor a base). A pH of 1 indicates extreme acidity, while a pH of 14 indicates extreme alkalinity.

1. *Acids.* Materials such as hydrochloric acid (HCl), sulphuric acid (H_2SO_4), and chromic acid (H_2CrO_4) are some of the most common. All are highly corrosive and are used for refining and processing metals. The plating process makes extensive use of these acids. The health effects are predominantly burns resulting from inhalation and skin contact. The eyes are the most susceptible body part and are exposed usually as a result of splashing. Chromic acid is a known carcinogen and a sensitizer. The most common indicator of chromic acid exposure is the presence of chrome holes in the surface of the skin. These are ugly, black holes left when the skin has been corrosively attacked. Their size depends on the amount of exposure and personal hygiene practices.

2. *Bases.* Sometimes referred to as alkalines, these chemicals include potassium hydroxide (KOH), sodium hydroxide (NaOH), and sodium chloride (NaCl; also known as table salt). Sodium chloride in its refined state is a requirement of a normal diet. In its less refined form, it is used to keep roads free of ice. The other two alkalines are used to etch or dissolve a variety of materials. All are toxic in certain concentrations.

Organic Solvents

Organic solvents, which are petrochemically based, are manufactured by combining the carbon atom with a great many other elements. These solvents can be identified by their molecular structure and can be grouped under 10 classifications (see Table 6.1).

Biological Agents

biological agents
natural organisms or products of organisms that present a risk to humans

Biological agents or *biohazards* are natural organisms or products of organisms that present a risk to humans. Two of the better known diseases resulting from biological agents are Legionnaires' disease (*Legionella pneumophilia*) and AIDS (acquired immunodeficiency syndrome). Though exposure to biohazards is not as common as exposure to chemical agents, the results can be just as deadly. The acute and chronic exposure effects described previously for chemical agents apply to biohazards as well, though the sources of exposure are different and the physiological reactions vary. Most exposures occur through inhalation.

Most biohazards encountered in the workplace fall into Biosafety Level 1 (BSL 1. See **OH&S Notebook 6.5**.) Viral agents such as hepatitis B would be included in BSL 2. The people most at risk of exposure to biohazards tend to be employed in unique or specialized fields, such as medicine, research, and farming.

TABLE 6.1

Organic Solvents

Number	Classification	Example	Toxic Effects	Uses
1	Aliphatic hydrocarbons	Paraffin, acetylene, methane	Simple asphyxiants, CNS, irritants	Fuels, refrigerants, dry cleaning, propellants
2	Aromatic hydrocarbons	Benzene, toluene, xylene	CNS, dermatitis, leukemia (benzene)	Plastics, resins, dyes, pharmaceuticals
3	Halogenated hydrocarbons	Chlorine, iodine, fluorine, carbon tetrachloride	CNS, dermatitis, cancer (carbon tetrachloride)	Fire extinguishers, fumigants, aerosol propellants
4	Nitro-hydrocarbons	Nitroglycerin, pitric acid	Irritants, skin sensitizers	Explosives
5	Esters	Methyl acetate, banana oil	Irritants	Plastics, resins, artificial flavours, perfumes
6	Ethers	Ethylene oxide	Irritants, anesthetics, nausea, respiratory difficulties	Antifreeze, chemical synthesizers, cancer treatment (ethyl ether—anesthetic)
7	Ketones	Acetone, methyl ethyl ketone (MEK)	Narcotic, irritants, vertigo, nausea	Acetate rayon, artificial silk, lubricants
8	Alcohols	Ethyl alcohol (grain alcohol), methyl alcohol (wood alcohol)	Narcotic, dermatitis, headache, nausea, tremors, blindness	Ethyl—liquors; methyl—solvent for inks, embalming fluids
9	Glycols	Ethylene glycol, cellosolve	Intoxication; blood, brain, and kidney disorder	Antifreeze, disinfectants, drugs
10	Aldehydes	Formaldehyde	Sensitizers, CNS, allergic response	Dyes, perfumes, flavourings, vinegar

In the case of salmonella food poisoning, however, members of the general public could be at risk through food contamination (see Table 6.2).

CONTROL OF EXPOSURES

The safe use and handling of chemical and biological agents can be ensured only through the active employment of a variety of control measures. Figure 6.2 (p. 160) outlines the various control measures used to ensure the safe handling of solvents. Controls for low-level biohazards can follow similar measures. These controls are the subject of the sections that follow.

Engineering Controls

One of the best ways to reduce the risks associated with handling solvents is to find alternatives. A thorough investigation should be conducted to ensure that the proposed substitute meets the intended purpose, does not contain dangerous properties, and is compatible with existing materials in use. If solvents *are* being

OH&S Notebook 6.5

CLASSIFICATION OF BIOLOGICAL AGENTS

All biological agents are classified into four groups on the basis of their degree of risk to humans. The higher the class number, the greater the risk.

- *Biosafety Level 1 (BSL 1):* Agents of no or minimal hazard that are harmless to healthy humans and that can be handled safely using techniques for nonpathogenic materials. An example is *E. coli* K-12. Effective control is maintained through cleanliness and through ventilation—that is, air is conducted through a high-efficiency particulate air (HEPA) filter in a biological safety cabinet (a well-ventilated room or space in which a worker is isolated from contact with biological agents). The degree of sophistication of the biological safety cabinet depends on the biosafety level.
- *Biosafety Level 2 (BSL 2):* Agents that may produce diseases of varying degrees of seriousness through accidental skin penetration and for which preventive or therapeutic interventions are often available. Examples are bacteria such as salmonella, legionella, and streptococcus; fungi; parasites; and viruses such as hepatitis A, B, C, and D. Control involves the use of a well-ventilated, sealed, filtered space with an air wall to keep workers from contacting the biohazard.

- *Biosafety Level 3 (BSL 3):* Agents involving special hazards that require special conditions for containment. Agents are indigenous or exotic, with potential for infection following aerosol transmission. Agents are associated with serious or lethal disease for which preventive or therapeutic interventions may be available. These agents can pose a high risk to the individual but not to the community. Examples include rabies, yellow fever, and HIV types 1 and 2. Containment involves specialized facility design and equipment, with cabinets with HEPA filters externally exhausted back to the room and containment spaces under negative pressure.
- *Biosafety Level 4 (BSL 4):* Organisms that are extremely dangerous or exotic, that pose a life-threatening disease, and for which preventive or therapeutic interventions are usually not available. Examples include Lassa fever virus, Ebola virus, and tick-borne encephalitis virus. Containment locations are rare and usually involve a totally enclosed room that is gas-tight and well ventilated. OH&S practitioners should not be involved at this level.

Sources: S.R. DiNardi, *The Occupational Environment -- Its Evaluation and Control* (Fairfax: AIHA, 1977); Canadian Council on Animal Care, "Biosafety Guidelines and Levels of Containment." Found at: http://www.ccac.ca/Documents/Standards/lbg_2004_e.pdf (Accessed Jan. 19, 2013); Office of the Auditor General of Canada, "Biosafety and Laboratory Containment Levels." Found at: http://www.oag-bvg.gc.ca/internet/English/att_9807xe01_e_9055.html (Accessed Jan. 19, 2013).

used, areas should be properly enclosed to prevent or minimize the escape of vapours, and an effective exhaust system should be in place. Because some of the chemicals used may be a source of ignition, it is equally important to ensure that appropriate fire-extinguishing equipment is on hand and that combustibles are isolated from sources of ignition. Materials should not be stored adjacent to highly reactive chemicals.

Work Practices and Procedures

All employees must be properly trained in the identification and handling of dangerous substances. Senior management must ensure that policies and procedures are accompanied by an appropriate discipline system for dealing

TABLE 6.2

Biological Agents

Agent Group	Agent	Source	Occupation
Bacterial	Anthrax (*bacillus anthracis*)	Direct contact with infected animals, hides, and wool	Veterinarians, farmers, butchers, wool workers
	Brucellosis (*brucella* species)	Exposure by ingestion or cuts from excretions or secretions of infected animals, microbiology	Livestock handlers, meat inspectors, farmers, lab workers
	Salmonellosis (*salmonella* species)	Oral exposure, usually from unsanitary food conditions (food poisoning)	Travellers, patient-care workers, amateur chefs
	Staphylococcal food poisoning (*staphylococcus* species)	Ingestion of improperly stored or leftover food or food infected by workers	Food workers, health care workers, home storage
	Lyme disease (*borrelia burgdorferi*)	Tick bites	Outdoor workers
Chlamydiae	Psittacosis or ornithsis (*chlamydia psittaci*)	Inhalation or exposure to infected bird droppings	Zoo workers, taxidermists, pet owners
Rickettsia	Q fever (*coxiella burneth*)	Contact with sheep, cattle, goats, birth byproducts, and contaminated dusts	Farmers, veterinarians, slaughterhouse workers, laboratory workers
	Rocky Mountain spotted fever (*rickettsia rickettsii*)	Tick bites	Outdoor workers—lumberjacks, ranchers
Viruses	Cat scratch disease	Breaks in skin, usually from animal scratch	Pet owners and breeders
	Serum hepatitis (hepatitis B virus—HBV)	Direct contact with infected material by puncture, abraded skin, or onto mucous membrane surfaces	Hemodialysis workers, surgeons, dentists, health care workers
	Infectious hepatitis (hepatitis A virus—HAV)	Fecal–oral transmission (from contaminated water)	Travellers, primate handlers, dentists
Fungal	Dermatophytosis (*trichophyton* species)	Contact with people infected by soil, animals, or humans	Gardeners, military personnel (athlete's foot), farm workers (cattle ringworm), health care workers
	Histoplasmosis (*histoplasma capsulatum*)	Inhalation or ingestion of dust from areas that have been bat or bird habitats	Construction workers, bird or chicken farm workers
	Farmer's lung (*aspergillus* species)	Inhalation or ingestion of dusts containing spores from mouldy hay or grain or compost piles	Mushroom workers, brewery workers, bird hobbyists
	Humidifier lung (*penicillium* species)	Inhalation of airborne spores from sources of mould such as cheese, wood, HVAC system water	Cheese workers, HVAC (heating, ventilating, air conditioning) workers, tree cutters

FIGURE 6.2

Engineering, Work Practices, and Medical Control Measures

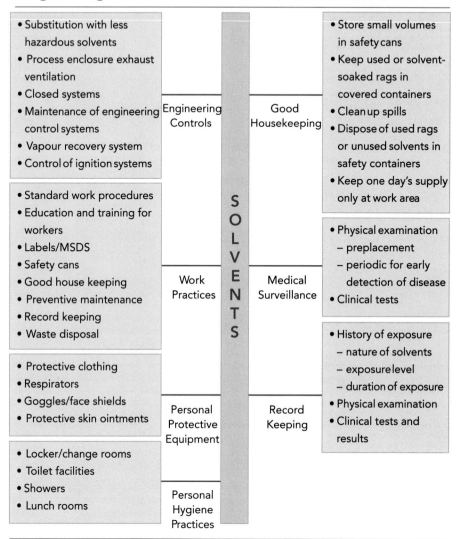

with those employees who willfully neglect these practices. Standards must be communicated, in writing, to all employees (**OH&S Today 6.5**). (This is also a requirement of WHMIS.)

Good housekeeping is essential when handling, storing, or using **agents**. If containers are leaking, the agents they contain must be transferred immediately to sound containers. Spills must be cleaned up properly, and employees who may be exposed to the hazard must wear protective equipment. Solvent-soaked rags should be disposed of in airtight, all-metal containers and removed daily. Each municipality has its own guidelines for the disposal of wastes, and employees must be familiar with the guidelines that apply to them.

Preventive maintenance must be conducted regularly to ensure that no potential dangers exist. For example, air filters on exhaust or ventilation equipment may become damaged or plugged and pose a potential danger in an enclosed

agents

any substances—chemical, biological, or physical—to which a human may be exposed at work or at home

OH&S Today (6.5

Needlestick Injuries: A Spreading Health and Safety Concern

Needlestick injuries have been a health and safety concern for many years. A needlestick injury occurs when a sharp object, such as a needle, which is potentially carrying blood-borne pathogens, punctures the skin of a care provider. For example, a nurse changing an intravenous (IV) may inadvertently stick the used needle in her own hand. It is estimated that more than 800,000 needlestick injuries occur each year in North American health care systems and that about 30% of such injuries carry the potential of transmitting diseases such as hepatitis or HIV.

Health care workers have developed procedures for handling and disposing of "sharps" in order to minimize the chance of a needlestick injury. However, needlestick injuries are now spreading to a new occupation—workers at recycling centres.

Many communities have adopted recycling programs that involve (at least in part) individuals working at a recycling centre sorting through various types of recyclable material (glass, plastic, etc.). Items such as syringes are often discarded in the recycling bins, and recycling plant workers run the risk of a needlestick injury as they sort through the material to identify what can be recycled.

The solution to the problem involves both prevention and protection. First, communities with recycling programs must educate citizens in the proper procedures for disposing of needles and similar items. Second, employees should be provided with protective gear (e.g., heavy leather gloves over latex) to offset the exposure to needles.

Source: CCOHS, "What are needlestick injuries?" Found at: http://www.ccohs.ca/ ohsanswers/diseases/needlestick_injuries.html (Accessed Feb. 7, 2007).

area in which solvents or biohazards are used. Employees should understand the procedures for maintaining equipment and documenting all repairs.

Thorough record keeping is essential. Though provinces and territories vary in terms of requirements for record keeping, all demand that records be kept of employee exposure, workplace air monitoring, and equipment breakdowns and repairs.

Administrative Controls

Perhaps the single most important administrative function is the education and training of all employees in safe work practices. Employees should receive training in safe operating and emergency procedures, in the use and care of PPE, and in the handling and control of agents. Training must be conducted on an ongoing basis, given that new solvents and other agents are continually entering the workplace. Finally, workers must be familiar with all aspects of WHMIS legislation (see Chapter 2).

Personal Protective Equipment (PPE)

Because inhalation is the most common and hazardous route of entry, the most commonly used protection device is a respirator. Respiratory protection is more specialized for biohazards than it is for chemical agents, since a biological airborne contaminant can be much smaller than a chemical one. PPE for hands, face, and other body parts must be provided where necessary. No single protective device, such as a facemask, will adequately address all conditions for all workers. Each device must be matched to the chemical or biological exposure, and it is imperative that the device be properly fitted to the individual. (One size does not fit all!)

Personal Hygiene Practices

The ingestion of chemicals or biological particulate is often the result of poor hygiene. Individuals who handle agents without wearing proper protective gear, such as gloves, are at risk of food contamination. In other instances, chemicals that are not adequately removed at the workplace can be transferred to the worker's home. To ensure that this and similar incidents do not occur, individuals who handle toxic substances must adhere to the following:

- Remove outer protective clothing, and clean hands, arms, face, and nails before entering rest areas or lunchrooms.

- Avoid touching lips, nose, and eyes with contaminated hands.

- Wash hands before eating, drinking, or smoking, and eat, drink, and smoke only in designated areas.

- Remove work clothes and wash or shower before leaving work.

Medical Surveillance

Medical surveillance programs, an administrative control, are implemented to ensure that employees who are exposed to agents are not subjected to situations in which their health will be jeopardized. For such programs to be effective, pre-employment and preplacement medical examinations should be conducted to establish a baseline of the employee's health *and* exposure to agents in previous workplaces. Follow-up medical examinations should be conducted periodically. Examinations may include chest X-ray, pulmonary function tests, and blood workups. Finally, record keeping is an important aspect of medical surveillance programs. The types of exposures employees face and their health records before and after exposure should be included in this process.

SUMMARY

This chapter has focused on the types, characteristics, measurement, and control of chemical and biological agents. All workers who are exposed to these agents should be knowledgeable about their potential health effects as well as trained in their proper use and handling. Chemical agents and, to a lesser extent, biological agents are the major causes of occupational diseases. Much of the required knowledge is highly technical, and there is a lot of terminology to understand. HR practitioners should be sensitive to the potential effects of a broad array of health-related effects that can occur. Most important, the focus of an OH&S program should be on the appropriate management of exposure to these agents.

Key Terms

aerosols 148
agents 160
alveoli 150
biohazard 144
biological agents 156
boiling point 153
chemical agents 144

dermatitis 153
routes of entry 148
surfactant layer 151
target organs 151
toxicity 147
turbinates 150

Weblinks

Canadian Association of Poison Control Centres
http://www.capcc.ca

Office of Health and Safety, "The 1, 2, 3's of Biosafety Levels"
http://www.cdc.gov/od/ohs/symp5/jyrtext.htm

Pesticide Safety Canada
http://www.pesticidesafety.ca

Toxicology Resources
http://www.toxicology.org

WorkSafeBC, "Resources—Fungi and Microorganisms"
http://indoorair.healthandsafetycentre.org/s/FungiandMicroorganisms.asp

Required Professional Capabilities (RPCs)

The following RPCs, listed by their CCHRA number, are relevant to the material covered in this chapter. All RPCS can be found at http://www.chrp.ca/rpc/body-of-knowledge.

RPC:172 Ensures due diligence and liability requirements are met.*
RPC:174 Develops and implements policies on the workplace environment.*
RPC:183 Analyzes risks to employee health & safety and develops preventive programs.*

Discussion Questions

1. This chapter lists the types of contaminants found in industrial workplaces. Consider the typical office setting—to what types of chemical hazards might office workers be exposed?
2. Explain the concept of a "synergistic effect" as used in this chapter.
3. What are the major ways of controlling the potential adverse effects of exposure to chemical and biological agents?
4. What is the Globally Harmonized System and what is its goal?

Using the Internet

1. Using a search engine, such as Google, find reports detailing the flu season in Canadian cities (especially Newfoundland) during 2013. What procedures or measures did workplaces and individuals (e.g., hospitals) implement to minimize exposure or reaction to this biological hazard?

---

*Canadian Council of Human Resources Associations, Human Resources Professionals in Canada: Revised Body of Knowledge and Required Professional Capabilities (RPCs ®), 2007.

2. Cases of environmental illness or environmental sensitivity seem to be becoming more common. Search out contemporary cases in which employees have been exposed to chemical or biological agents with long-term consequences. Could these exposures have been prevented? Could the workers have been protected?

Exercises

Though exposure to various workplace hazards is never a good thing, some individuals may be more sensitive to some exposures than others. For example, pregnant women may be more at risk when exposed to certain chemicals than are other employees. To what extent can we use HR tools such as selection and placement to offset this problem? Is it appropriate to refuse to hire women of childbearing age to work in environments in which exposures are possible?

Case 1 MASS HYSTERIA?

It's the first week of the semester in the new school building, and already Principal LeBlanc is ready to quit. For years, parents in her district have been campaigning for a new school and teachers have been complaining about outdated classrooms. Now they have a new multimillion-dollar building with all the latest technology.

"You'd think that everyone would be happy," grouses LeBlanc to her vice principal, "but all I've heard all day are complaints."

"What kind of complaints?"

"Well, for starters, we have five teachers off sick claiming that they get migraines every time they enter their classrooms. And now parents have started to complain that their kids have sore eyes and are feeling nauseated all the time they're in the building."

"Maybe they're really sick," states the concerned vice principal.

"Yeah, sick of school," replies LeBlanc. "At least that's what I think."

As a health and safety expert, what do you think? What actions would you take?

Case 2 UNEXPECTED GAS

A man was killed by an explosion when another worker attempted to cut through the top of one of two old steel drums using a handheld grinder. Both barrels had contained a fruit concentrate but were never cleaned. The sparks generated by the grinder ignited hydrogen gas that had been generated from the contents' residue after standing for many years. Because there was a defective sterile coating separating the walls of the drum from the concentrate, the acid in the fruit concentrate reacted with the metal of the drum and formed hydrogen gas. The gas accumulated and the pressure caused the drum ends to bulge. This deformation made it impossible to open the drum with the drum opener, and a hole was punched into the top of each drum. One worker was attempting to add water to one drum in order to displace the remaining gas, while another worker attempted to open the other drum with a grinder. Sparks ignited the hydrogen gas, causing an explosion and a fire. The fire was extinguished, but one worker lost his life. The defective drums had been recalled years before by the supplier, and only three remained unaccounted for before the accident.

What steps would you take to ensure that this event was never repeated?

NOTES

1. Workplace Safety and Insurance Board of Ontario, *Annual Report* (Toronto: WSIB, 2000).
2. L. Genesove, *Multiple Chemical Sensitivity Syndrome* (Toronto: Healthwise, Accident Prevention, 1995).
3. S.R. DiNardi, ed., The *Occupational Environment—Its Evaluation and Control* (Fairfax: AIHA, 1997).
4. WSIB, *Annual Report* (2000).
5. http://www.takeonestep.org/pages/yoursafety/safenotsorry/chemicalhazards.aspx, January 20 2013.
6. P.L. Williams and J.L. Burson, eds., *Industrial Toxicology—Safety and Health Applications in the Workplace* (New York: Van Nostrand Reinhold, 1985).
7. C.W. Pilger, "Toxic Solvents," 23rd Intensive Workshop in Industrial Hygiene, Toronto, 1994.

Psychosocial Hazards

CHAPTER LEARNING OBJECTIVES

After reading this chapter, you should be able to:

- describe and distinguish among the concepts of stressor, stress, and strain
- explain the transactional model of stress and its implications
- identify major sources of stress in the workplace
- discuss the psychological, physical, behavioural, and organizational consequences of stress
- discuss ways to recognize and assess psychosocial hazards at work
- describe and distinguish among primary, secondary, and tertiary stress interventions
- describe injustice, technology, and work–life conflict as prevalent workplace stressors

PRESENTEEISM: AT WORK IN BODY, BUT NOT IN MIND

We've likely all done it—pulled ourselves out of bed in spite of a cold, a fever, allergies, or perhaps an emotional crisis to get to work or school because of a meeting, project, or exam that simply can't be missed. Or perhaps it was because you didn't have the necessary sick time to take a day off without penalty. When we get to work or class we can't focus, lose track of what we're supposed to be doing, and have trouble getting work done. And our performance at that all-important meeting, project, or exam is likely less than stellar. This is *presenteeism* in action.

Presenteeism, sometimes cast as the opposite of absenteeism, is a growing phenomenon where workers show up for work, but because of their symptoms, conditions, or feelings are not fully functioning. Not surprisingly, presenteeism is associated with reduced individual productivity. Some estimates suggest that attending work when sick reduces individual productivity by about one-third and is perhaps more costly to the organization than actual absenteeism.

Presenteeism has become a more pressing concern during the recent economic recession. Faced with extreme job insecurity, workers are afraid to take time away from work, even when they are sick, lest they be viewed as uncommitted or nonessential to their organizations. Furthermore, the recession has placed many families under financial pressure, which may contribute to problems such as insomnia and depression, thus increasing symptoms among workers and prompting still more presenteeism.

Organizations need to be aware of presenteeism as a possible outcome of workplace stress. This includes providing support and understanding to stressed workers who suffer insomnia, psychological symptoms, or physical illness. Services like an Employee and Family Assistance Program can help employees find solutions. In addition, a supportive organizational culture and managers who are sensitive to employees' well-being can go a long way to reduce presenteeism.

Sources: P. Hemp, "Presenteeism: At Work—But Out of it," *Harvard Business Review*, Vol. 82, No. 10, Pg. 49–58, 2004; Rosie Lombardi, "Absent-Minded Workers Show Signs of Presenteeism," *Canadian Occupational Safety* (Jan. 20, 2010). Found at: http://www.cos-mag.com/201001201781/health-page/health-page-stories/absent-minded-workers-show-signs-of-presenteeism.html (Accessed Feb. 8, 2013); Esther Huberman, "Addressing the Presenteeism Issue," *Benefits Canada* (Oct. 15, 2012). Found at: http://www.benefitscanada.com/benefits/health-wellness/addressing-the-presenteeism-issue-33190 (Accessed Feb. 8, 2013).

In 1990, the United States' National Institute of Occupational Safety and Health (NIOSH) declared occupational stress to be one of the 10 leading causes of workplace death, and it is now common to speak of occupational stress as an epidemic.[1] Estimates suggest that workplace stress costs the Canadian economy anywhere from $12 to 33 billion annually. In the United States this figure rises to a staggering $300 billion.[2] Mental illness is prevalent. Each year, 1 in 5 Canadians will experience a mental health problem. The associated cost to the economy exceeds $50 billion per year. Specific to workplace productivity, mental health problems cost organizations $6 billion annually in absenteeism and presenteeism.[3] Some estimates of the total costs to workplaces are closer to $20 billion annually.[4]

Though we recognize that estimates of the cost of work stress involve considerable guesswork, it is clear that workplace stress is a large and growing problem with considerable consequences for individuals and organizations. The workplace is replete with factors that contribute to stress, and many Canadian workers experience the reality of stress. The results of the 2010 General Social

Survey on Time Use show that 27% of Canadian workers report being quite a bit or extremely stressed in their daily lives. Among those highly stressed workers, 60% identify work as their major source of stress.[5] A recent survey of employed Nova Scotians found that a large percentage of them experienced such stressors as high workloads (60%), role conflict (70%), and work–family conflict (50%). Furthermore, about 20% of the sample reported health-related symptoms that commonly manifest themselves after the experience of stress.[6]

There are several reasons for organizations to address issues of mental health at work. From the statistics presented above, the economic drivers are clear. Further, given the prevalence of workplace stressors and the number of employees affected, one might also consider a moral incentive for workplaces to focus on creating psychologically healthy work. Beyond these reasons, there are legal motivations for Canadian employers to focus on creating psychologically healthy workplaces.[7] For instance, Canadian human rights tribunals are explicating the responsibility to accommodate mental illness at work. Workers' compensation boards are increasingly addressing claims related to mental stress. Occupational health and safety acts are recognizing that psychological safety is part of a safe workplace. And cases across jurisdictions show that managers are being held accountable to understand how their actions affect others.

Reflecting this increased focus on mental health at work, the Canadian Standards Association, with the support of the Mental Health Commission of Canada, published a voluntary workplace standard, CSA-Z1003-13, for **psychological health and safety in the workplace**. This standard provides guidance for employers on developing a Psychological Health and Safety Management System in the workplace.[8] The standard aims to help employers create psychologically healthy and safe workplaces. A psychologically healthy and safe workplace "promotes workers' psychological well-being and actively works to prevent harm to worker psychological health including in negligent, reckless, or intentional ways."[9] Although voluntary, the standard is a way for employers to demonstrate due diligence when it comes to issues of psychological health at work.

So, what exactly is stress? One way to discuss stress is in terms of the **psychosocial model of health**. The term *psychosocial* highlights the importance of both the social environment and the psychological or individual factors that affect a person's health and well-being. Social factors that influence a person's health include family circumstances, exposure to violence, and workplace policies. Psychological factors that affect a person's health include levels of self-esteem and anxiety, as well as the ability to cope with pressure.

In everyday conversation, we use the term stress in several different ways. We talk about feeling stress and about stress as something we're exposed to. Even the scientific literature demonstrates considerable confusion over the precise meanings of stress-related terms.[10] Most researchers now agree on a general stress model that distinguishes among three closely related terms: stressors, stress, and strain.

STRESSORS

A **stressor** is an objectively verifiable event in the environment that has the potential to cause stress. For example, congested traffic is a stressor. Stressors,

psychologically healthy and safe workplace
a workplace that promotes workers' psychological well-being and actively works to prevent harm to workers' psychological health including in negligent, reckless, or intentional ways

psychosocial model of health
approach to the study of health that highlights the importance of both the social environment and psychological factors

stressor
an objectively verifiable event that occurs outside the individual that has the potential to cause stress

then, exist outside the individual and reflect some of the social factors that affect a person's health. Stressors vary along several dimensions, including frequency of occurrence, intensity, duration, and predictability (time of onset).[11] These dimensions have led researchers to distinguish among four categories of stressors: acute, chronic, daily, and catastrophic (see Table 7.1).

Acute stressors have a specific time onset (i.e., you know exactly when it began), are typically of short duration and high intensity, and have a low frequency. For example, a traffic accident is an acute stressor. In terms of the work environment, a performance review meeting or a conflict with a supervisor may be an acute stressor. In contrast, a *chronic* stressor has no specific time onset, may be of short or long duration, repeats frequently, and may be of low *or* high intensity. Many individuals today are experiencing job insecurity as a chronic stressor. Most cannot point to a specific event or time that triggered the insecurity, but the nagging worry that their job is at risk is always with them.

Daily stressors have a specific onset, are of short duration, are low in intensity, and are typically infrequent. Dealing with a broken piece of office equipment may be a daily stressor for some employees. Finally, we need to recognize the existence of *catastrophic* stressors or disasters. Much like acute stressors, catastrophic stressors have a specific onset, occur infrequently, have a high intensity, and may be of long *or* short duration. The main distinction between acute and catastrophic stressors relates to the intensity of the stressor. Catastrophic stressors typically involve a direct threat to life, loss of life, or major property damage. Again, the complexities involved in categorizing stressors are indicated by the observation that catastrophic stressors can become chronic over time. For example, the events of September 11, 2001, constituted a catastrophic stressor for those directly involved, but also have had long-term consequences for those individuals who live with the fear of terrorism.

Stressors in the Workplace

The above categorization (as seen in Table 7.1) provides a general overview of stressors. Other researchers have focused on the content or sources of workplace stressors.[12] The NIOSH model identifies the following major categories of workplace stressors:

- *Workload and work pace.* This refers to the amount of work that must be completed and the speed at which employees must work to complete their tasks.

TABLE 7.1

Categories of Stressors

Type	Frequency	Duration	Intensity	Time of Onset
Acute	Rare	Short	High	Specific
Chronic	Frequent	Short or long	Low or high	Nonspecific
Daily	Infrequent	Short	Low	Specific
Catastrophic	Very rare	Short or long	Extremely high	Specific

- *Role stressors* (conflict, ambiguity, inter-role conflict). Role *conflict* exists when individuals face incompatible demands from two or more sources. Role *ambiguity* reflects the uncertainty that employees experience about what is expected from them in their work; the opposite of role ambiguity is role clarity. *Inter-role conflict* exists when employees face incompatible demands from two or more roles. The most common form of inter-role conflict is work–family conflict, in which the demands of work conflict with the role of parent or spouse. We'll learn more about work–family conflict later in this chapter.

- *Career concerns*. This includes worries about job security, fear of job obsolescence, underpromotion and overpromotion, and, more generally, concerns about career progression.

- *Work scheduling*. Working rotating shifts or permanent night shifts results in a disruption of physiological circadian rhythms, as well as a disruption of social activities.

- *Interpersonal relations*. Poor interpersonal relations in the workplace are consistently identified as a source of stress. Poor interpersonal relationships can range from experiencing rude treatment to a variety of more intense experiences such as bullying or violence. Chapter 8 focuses exclusively on workplace violence as a psychosocial hazard in the workplace. Having well-established sources of social support (i.e., receiving support from coworkers and supervisors) may *reduce* the effects of other workplace stressors.

- *Job content and control*. Jobs that are highly repetitive, or that do not make use of a variety of workers' skills or give workers a measure of control over how and when they complete their tasks, can be a source of stress.

The Canadian standard for psychological health and safety at work (CSA-Z1003-13) identifies 13 organizational factors that affect psychological health at work. All these factors are in the control of the organization and when met, provide sources of psychological safety for employees. However, when not met, the factors identified in this inventory represent workplace stressors. Managing these factors effectively should contribute to positive experiences and mental health for workers. The factors, along with their desired state, identified in the standard are:[13]

- *Organizational culture.* A culture that reflects trust, respect, civility, and fairness.

- *Psychological and social support.* Supportive social interactions from coworkers and supervisors.

- *Clear leadership and expectations.* Leadership communicates clear expectations to employees about their work roles and organizational change.

- *Civility and respect.* Workers are respectful and considerate of each other and with clients.

- *Psychological demands.* The psychological demands of the job are recognized and assessed with respect to their potential impact on worker well-being.

- *Growth and development.* Employees are supported to develop skills.
- *Recognition and reward.* Workers' efforts are acknowledged and appreciated.
- *Involvement and influence.* Workers are able to influence the work process and important work decisions.
- *Workload management.* Tasks can be accomplished within the available timeframe.
- *Engagement.* Workers feel motivated and connected to their work.
- *Balance.* The workplace accepts that there needs to be balance between personal, family, and work aspects of life.
- *Psychological protection.* Workers feel they can ask questions, report mistakes, or propose ideas without fear of reprisal.
- *Protection of physical safety.* Workers are protected from risks in the physical environment.

STRESS

stress

an individual's internal response to, or evaluation of, stressors; often characterized by negative feelings of arousal

Stressors are objective events. However, the individual's response to or evaluation of these events also plays an important role. Researchers have typically referred to this response or evaluation as **stress**. Stress is an internal response to stressors and is often characterized by negative feelings of arousal. Stress, then, reflects some of the psychological factors that affect a person's health. In contrast to the objective stressors we have discussed, stress is an internal event that is subjectively defined. Stress is a consequence of any action, situation, or event that places special demands on a person. The stress response is an adaptive reaction to these demands and is influenced by differences between people.

general adaptation syndrome

the body's way of gearing up for fight or flight (i.e., to confront or run away from a predator)

Stress is an adaptive response. The stress response is our way of mobilizing resources to deal with stressors in the environment. Viewed in an evolutionary context, stress is the product of millions of years of evolution. The **general adaptation syndrome** (stress response) is the body's way of gearing up for fight or flight (i.e., to confront or run away from a predator).[14] Some of the physiological changes that occur as the body prepares for fight or flight include increased blood supply to the brain and major muscle groups, decreased blood supply to the digestive system and skin, increased heart rate and breathing, and increased activity in the stomach, bowels, and bladder. If the stress reaction is prolonged, the resulting symptoms include headaches, dry mouth, skin rashes, heartburn, hypertension, stomach ulcers, and asthma.

Stress is moderated by individual differences. Psychologists have recognized for many years that our responses to events in the environment are determined largely by our interpretations of those events. Some people are less vulnerable to stressors in their environment than others. In fact, one of the most popular models of stress, the transactional model, is based on the notion that individuals may perceive and respond differently to the same stressors.[15] According to this model, people appraise the stressors in their environment and assess their ability to manage them. For example, a person may determine that though work demands are heavy, he or she can manage the workload by setting up a comprehensive

OH&S Notebook 7.1

OCCUPATIONAL HEALTH PSYCHOLOGY

Occupational health psychology applies psychology to questions of occupational stress, illness, and injury. Having developed throughout the 1990s, this field has brought considerable attention to psychosocial risk factors for workplace injury and illness.

Occupational health psychology aims to improve quality of work life and *protect* and *promote* the safety, health, and well-being of workers. Occupational health psychologists consider both organizational and individual factors in occupational health. They believe that the transformation of the work environment can carry positive effects for employee health.

Researchers and practitioners of occupational health psychology rely on a four-component strategy to reduce work-related psychosocial disorders:

1. *A focus on organizational change:* Organizational change is possible and is at times necessary to reduce psychosocial hazards in the workplace.

2. *A focus on information:* Workers should be provided with information, education, and training regarding psychosocial hazards and psychological health at work.

3. *A focus on psychological health services:* Enriched services for the promotion of psychological well-being and the treatment of psychological symptoms (e.g., employee assistance programs, inclusion of preventive services in benefits plans) should be provided to employees.

4. *A focus on surveillance:* The surveillance and monitoring of psychosocial risk factors and psychological disorders should be routine in organizations.

Sources: CDC, "Occupational Health Psychology." Found at: http://www.cdc.gov/niosh/topics/stress/ohp/ohp.html (Accessed Apr. 23, 2010); S. L. Sauter, L.R. Murphy, and J.J. Hurrell, "Prevention of Work-Related Psychological Disorders: A National Strategy Proposed by the National Institute for Occupational Safety and Health (NIOSH)," *American Psychologist*, Vol. 45, Pg. 1146–58, 1990; L.E. Tetrick and J.C. Quick, "Prevention at Work: Public Health in Occupational Settings," in Quick and Tetrick, eds., *Handbook of Occupational Health Psychology* (Washington: APA, 2003) Pg. 3–17.

"to do" list and by delegating some of the tasks to coworkers. Stress occurs when an individual realizes that a pertinent stressor is present and that he or she does not have the resources or ability to manage that stressor. Thus it is clear that stress does not always follow exposure to a stressor; rather, it results when an appraisal process indicates that the stressor is indeed an unmanageable threat to the person's well-being.

Researchers often talk about stressors as events that have the potential to cause change, harm, or loss, or to pose a threat or a challenge. Even events that are viewed as positive can be stressors. For instance, a promotion can be a stressor because it involves considerable change (e.g., in job duties), challenge (e.g., increased job responsibilities), and threat (e.g., the potential to fail in the new job). Stress is the body's way of coping with the environment, and the response is the same whether these demands are positive or negative.

Stress Moderators

Many factors affect people's evaluations of stressors as well as how they react to them (i.e., degree of stress experienced). We often call these factors **moderators**. A moderator is a variable that changes the relationship between two other variables. Some moderators *aggravate* or increase the effects of stressors.

moderator

a variable that changes the relationship between two other variables

risk factor
a variable that increases the negative effects of stress

buffer
a variable that protects people from the negative effects of stress

These types of moderators are called **risk factors** for stress. Other moderators can *protect* an individual from the adverse effects of stressors. Because of their role in breaking the chain of response, these moderators are sometimes referred to as stress **buffers**.

Two well-accepted general classes of moderators in the stress process are the enduring properties of the individual (i.e., personality characteristics) and the social context (i.e., social support, individual relationships). We will consider each type of moderator.

The Individual—Personality

A considerable amount of research has examined the role that personality plays in stress. Personality is the relatively stable set of characteristics, responses, thoughts, and behaviours of a given individual.[16] Two personality characteristics of particular relevance in considerations of stress are the **Type A behaviour** pattern and **negative affectivity**.

Type A behaviour
action–emotion complex that can be observed in any person who is aggressively involved in a chronic, incessant struggle to achieve increasingly more in increasingly less time

negative affectivity
a dispositional dimension reflecting persistent individual differences in the experience of negative emotion

TYPE A BEHAVIOUR   Type A individuals try to achieve increasingly more in increasingly less time. Their struggle is chronic and, if necessary, is carried out against the will of others.[17] Individuals who exhibit Type A behaviour are hard driving, competitive, and time urgent. There are two components of Type A behaviour: achievement striving and impatience/irritability.[18] Someone who is high on achievement striving is typically very goal directed and action oriented. Individuals high on impatience/irritability are typically very time conscious, hostile, impatient, and irritable. In general, achievement striving is associated with performance outcomes but not health outcomes. That is, those high on achievement striving perform well, but this aspect of themselves is not related to their health. Conversely, impatience/irritability is associated with health outcomes. Those high on impatience/irritability experience more stress and have poorer health, but this is not related to their work performance.[19]

NEGATIVE AFFECTIVITY   Negative affectivity is a mood factor that reflects persistent individual differences in the experience of negative emotion. More simply—perhaps too simply—some people are optimists and others are pessimists. Pessimists demonstrate negative affectivity across situations; that is, they seem predisposed to see the negative side of everything. These individuals may react negatively or adversely to *all* stressors, and in this sense, negative affectivity may be a risk factor for stress.

The Social Context—Social Support

Social relationships are another important moderator of stress. Having sources of support can reduce a person's vulnerability to stressors.[20] In other words, people who provide support are a buffer against stress. For example, in an environment filled with challenging stressors (e.g., workload and time pressure), a high degree of organizational support can improve a person's performance at work.[21] Alternatively, a lack of social support can intensify the impact of stressors and may be a potential risk factor for stress.

Support can come from a number of sources, including supervisors, coworkers, and family members. Support can be offered in a number of ways. For instance, a coworker may provide *tangible* support by giving a new employee needed information about a job task. This same coworker may also show *emotional* support by offering positive feedback and encouragement to the new hire.

STRAIN

The result of stress is **strain**. When people encounter a stressor and experience persistent stress, ultimately strain will result. We will discuss four categories of strain reactions: psychological, physical, behavioural, and organizational.

Psychological Strain

Psychological strain reactions typically include either a disturbance in affect (e.g., mood) or a disturbance in cognition (e.g., concentration). Feeling irritable, anxious, overwhelmed, moody, depressed, and angry are all common *affective* strain reactions. Indeed, we often describe these moods as "feeling stressed out." Disturbances in mood resulting from stress range from short-lived periods of feeling blue, down, or irritable to longer term and more serious diagnoses of psychological disorders such as depression and anxiety.[22] Similarly, we often hear people colloquially talking about being "burnt out." More formally speaking, burnout has three dimensions: emotional exhaustion, cynicism about one's work, a sense of inefficacy about one's contributions. People who are burnt out may feel exhausted owing to prolonged exposure to stress, have negative perceptions about the value of their work, and feel incompetent or unproductive.[23]

Most people recognize the affective or emotional reactions to stress; cognitive reactions often go *un*noticed. Typical strain-related cognitive disturbances include difficulty making up your mind (often on trivial matters), difficulty concentrating and staying with one task, being unable to remember people's names even though you know them quite well, and other small mistakes. These small mistakes are generally not very important, but they can be devastating for an individual under considerable strain. For instance, even small mistakes in the workplace can sometimes have negative consequences for employee safety and performance.[24]

Physical Strain

Some physical symptoms of strain (e.g., stomach upsets, headaches) may seem quite trivial, but considerable evidence now suggests that stress is implicated in more serious physical conditions. Most prominently, coronary heart disease (CHD) has been consistently linked to increased stress; so has high blood pressure (hypertension), strokes, ulcers, asthma, and even some forms of cancer.[25]

The mechanisms through which strain manifests itself physically are not yet clearly understood, though it has long been known that changes in hormone and enzyme secretion occur under stress. Moreover, stress may play a dual role as a cause of serious physical illness. First, individuals exposed to a stressor may experience stress and ultimately develop a physical strain response—illness (e.g., you are constantly under pressure to meet deadlines and make clients happy; as a result, you have developed hypertension). Second, increased strain may lower the body's resistance by impairing the immune system, thereby opening the door to physical illness.[26] Indeed, evidence suggests that work-related stress is a risk factor for the common cold, such that those experiencing heavy psychological job demands have reported increased incidence of colds.[27]

strain
the result of stress; it is classified into four categories of reactions: psychological, physical, behavioural, and organizational

OH&S Today 7.1

Mental Health at Work: Prevalence and Impact

Questions pertaining to the prevalence and impact of mental illness have received considerable attention of late. And the answers that are emerging present a concerning picture. One report estimates that the burden of mental illness, in terms of premature mortality and reduced functioning, is 1.5 times that for all cancers. Conditions such as depression, bipolar disorder, alcohol use disorders, and social phobias decrease a person's ability to function in several ways, including their ability to participate fully in the workforce.

In a recent Canadian survey 14% of employees reported that they were clinically depressed with an additional 8% indicating that they would diagnosis themselves as depressed. One in 10 employees indicated that they had little pleasure or interest in doing things for more than half of the days in the previous two-week period. About 40% of the respondents indicated that they or someone they knew was stressed at work to the point of requiring time off work or had reduced productivity. Those who are depressed indicate that they feel a good deal of support from their coworkers, but report less support from human resources or their union. Interestingly, 84% of managers indicated that they feel it is their job to intervene when an employee is depressed, but most report that they need better training in this area. In terms of workplace accommodations, respondents largely perceived their employers as being more willing to provide accommodations for those with physical needs than for those with mental health concerns.

An analysis of the 2002 Canadian Community Health Survey found that 80% of those employees who experienced depression reported that their symptoms negatively affected their work performance; almost 20% of those indicated that the impairment was very severe. Common impairments associated with depression are trouble concentrating, reduced productivity, and poor time management. Workers who have recently experienced a depressive episode are twice as likely to have been absent from work in the prior week than those who have never experienced depression. These negative effects of depression can persist up to two years after the episode. Mental health problems are a commonly cited reason for workplace disability claims. More than 80% of employers report mental health concerns to be among the top three drivers of disability claims. Some estimates suggest that 30% of short- and long-term disability claims stem from mental health problems. Some in fact estimate that mental health problems are the cause of closer to three-quarters of short-term disability leaves.

It seems clear that mental health problems can negatively affect work. However, perhaps ironically, work itself can increase the risk of depression and other mental health concerns. Many workplace stressors are associated with depressive symptoms. For instance, those who work shift work, particularly evening and night shifts, are more likely to be depressed than others. Also, those who reported being exposed to many workplace stressors most days on the job were at increased risk for depression. Employee stressors such as work role conflict, workload, and work–life conflict appear to be on the rise. A 2011 survey reports that nearly 89% of Canadian employers indicate excessive workloads are a problem up from 63% in 2009.

Sources: Ipsos, *Great West Life Centre for Mental Health in the Workplace, Mental Health in the Workplace Research*, Aug. 2012. Found at: http://www.workplacestrategiesformentalhealth.com/pdf/GWLReleaseDeckDepressionintheWorkplace.pdf (Accessed Feb. 8, 2013); Public Health Ontario & Institute for Clinical Evaluative Sciences, *Opening Eyes, Opening Minds*, Oct. 2012. Found at: http://www.oahpp.ca/opening-eyes-opening-minds/index.html (Accessed Feb. 8, 2013); Mental Health Commission of Canada, "Mental Health Strategy for Canada," Apr. 24, 2012. Found at: http://www.fcmhs.ca/news/MHCC%20Strategy%20-%20FINAL%20 -%20april%2024%20FINAL%20PDF.pdf (Accessed Feb. 8, 2013); Towers Watson, "Pathway to Health and Productivity: 2011/2012 Staying@workTM survey report. North America," 2012. Found at: http://www.towerswatson.com/assets/pdf/6031/Towers-Watson-Staying-at-Work-Report.pdf (Accessed Feb. 8, 2013); Statistics Canada. 2007. "Study: Depression and work impairment." *The Daily*. Statistics Canada Catalogue No. 11-001. Found at: http://www.statcan.gc.ca/pub/82-003-x/2006001/article/9566-eng.htm (Accessed Feb. 8, 2013); K. Thorpe and L. Chénier, *Building Mentally Healthy Workplaces: Perspectives of Canadian Workers and Front-line Managers*. June 2011. Ottawa: The Conference Board of Canada.

Behavioural Strain

Behavioural strain reactions take a variety of forms. Individuals under increased stress may develop nervous habits (e.g., nail biting or nervous tics). Other behavioural strain reactions include avoidance of certain situations, or a reduction in individual involvement, either because of a lack of interest or as a means of reducing time demands. Individuals may also engage in aggressive or violent behaviour stemming from stress. Evidence also suggests that individuals may increase their smoking, consumption of alcohol, or reliance on psychotherapeutic drugs under periods of increased stress.[28] Given the known health outcomes associated with smoking, excessive alcohol consumption, and overmedication, these are very dangerous ways of coping with increased stress.

Organizational Strain

Stress researchers interested in organizations have identified increased absenteeism, decreased performance, disturbances of interpersonal relationships at work, and an increased likelihood of looking for alternative employment as some of the most common organizational outcomes of stress.[29] Consistent evidence suggests that high levels of stress are also associated with an increased risk of workplace accidents.[30] This increased risk may be a consequence of other strain reactions (e.g., increased cognitive failures, impaired ability to concentrate). Note also that the causal direction of this relationship is not certain. Though accidents and increased stress are certainly correlated, it may be that working in a dangerous or risky environment is in itself a stressor.

MANAGING PSYCHOSOCIAL HAZARDS

It is clear that work-related stressors, stress, and strain have substantial negative consequences for both employees and organizations. Organizations must learn to recognize and control psychological hazards in the workplace. Certainly, the new Canadian Standard for psychological health and safety in the workplace (CSA-Z1003-13) not only sets the expectation that Canadian organizations will strive for psychologically healthy work environments, but also helps to identify strategies to promote and sustain psychological health at work.

There are several means to identify psychosocial hazards:

- *Learn to identify stressors.* The NIOSH model identifies some stressors that can be recognized in job design. For example, any job that involves shift work places workers at risk for this psychosocial hazard. Air traffic control is widely recognized as a career that involves high cognitive demands and the associated stress. Transit operators are known to be targets of aggression from the public they serve. HR managers and OH&S professionals should acquaint themselves with the particular psychosocial risk factors that exist among the working population they serve.

- *Survey the employees.* Checking in with employees to gain their sense of the prevalent workplace stressors is a useful way to identify psychosocial hazards at work. An employee survey that asks employees about common stressors such as work overload, work–family conflict, and interpersonal conflict can identify problem areas in the workplace.

- *Look for telltale signs of stress.* As described earlier, there are organizational manifestations of strain. For example, if organizations are experiencing rates of absenteeism and turnover that are higher than the industry standard this may be a warning sign for high levels of stress.

- *Be attuned to individual employees.* Changes in employee behaviour may reflect work stress. If a person who has always submitted things on time and had an excellent attendance record is suddenly handing things in late and missing lots of work, that person may be under strain. A manager who has a good relationship with this employee may be able to inquire tactfully about the person's well-being or encourage the person to use organizational resources such as an Employee and Family Assistance Program.

preventive stress management

an approach to managing stress in the workplace that emphasizes that the health of an organization and its employees are interdependent; encourages the reduction of stressors in the workplace as well as the recognition and management of occupational stress and strain

Fortunately, individual employees and organizational management can work together to offset or avoid negative outcomes by taking an approach known as **preventive stress management**. The basic principle of preventive stress management is that the health of an organization and the health of its employees are interdependent.[31] In other words, organizations whose employees are in good health are more likely to succeed. Alternatively, employees who work for organizations that provide pleasant working conditions are more likely to be healthy, productive individuals.

The Canadian standard on psychological health and safety at work (CSA-Z1003-13) outlines how organizations can develop a psychological health and safety management system.[32] The recommended structure notes the importance of organizational commitment, leadership support, and employee involvement. It also outlines the value of careful planning of program implementation that involves the identification and prioritization of hazards and risks that is informed by organizational data. Once implemented, the psychological health and safety management system needs sustained and appropriate resources to engage in such programs as education, investigations, and critical event preparedness. Finally, the system should be the focus of management review and continual improvement.

Ideally, stress management programs will include both organizational and individual interventions designed to reduce exposure to stressors, reduce the experience of stress when stressors are unavoidable, and swiftly provide treatment options to those individuals who are experiencing the negative consequences of stress. In the following paragraphs, we describe three categories of interventions (primary, secondary, tertiary), providing illustrative examples for each of organizational and individual efforts to manage workplace stress.

Primary Interventions

primary interventions

stress interventions that involve the reduction or removal of actual stressors

Primary interventions involve reducing or removing the actual stressors and are highly effective in reducing work-related stress and strain.[33] The idea is that the removal of sources of stress from the workplace should reduce employee stress and strain. Despite the supporting evidence, primary prevention strategies have not been broadly implemented in Canadian organizations, presumably because organizational decision makers believe that the costs and logistics of primary preventive strategies would be excessive; so they prefer to focus on interventions that target the employees' ability to cope with existing stressors.[34] However, the costs associated with primary preventive efforts can be reasonable and, given the resulting reduction in employee stress, worth the effort involved to implement them. Tables 7.2 and 7.3 provide examples of primary stress prevention strategies at the individual and organizational levels.

Secondary Interventions

Secondary interventions focus on minimizing negative outcomes once a person is feeling stress. Techniques such as stress management and relaxation training help people identify the negative health effects of stress. This often involves teaching effective coping strategies, the premise being that appropriate strategies

secondary interventions stress intervention techniques that focus on minimizing negative consequences once a person is feeling stress

TABLE 7.2

Stress Intervention Strategies: Individual Level

Level of Intervention	Examples
Primary	Avoid taking on an overload of work Take adequate leisure time Try to reduce Type A behaviour
Secondary	Talk with friends and coworkers Make time to exercise Use relaxation techniques
Tertiary	Seek medical treatment Participate in psychological counselling

TABLE 7.3

Stress Intervention Strategies: Organizational Level

Level of Intervention	Examples
Primary	Redesign particularly demanding jobs Respect employees' opinions in management decision-making processes Provide flexible working conditions
Secondary	Provide comprehensive benefits programs that include provisions for such options as employee and family assistance programs (EFAPs), personal leave, massage therapy Offer on-site fitness centres Ensure balanced nutrition on the cafeteria menu
Tertiary	Offer benefits packages with sick days and leave options Provide counselling services following major stressors, such as a violent episode at work or a major act of terrorism Support employee efforts to find appropriate medical or psychological care

for managing stress can lessen the negative effects of stress on health.[35] Common interventions include relaxation training, stress management training and counselling, and programs in nutrition and physical fitness. We will explore some of these interventions in more detail in Chapter 14. Secondary interventions are more widely used than primary ones. However, secondary strategies are less desirable than primary ones because they target stress only after it has developed. See Tables 7.2 and 7.3 for examples of ways that organizations and individuals can engage in secondary stress interventions.

Tertiary Interventions

tertiary interventions

stress intervention techniques that are used to help those individuals who have not been able to manage workplace stress effectively and who are now experiencing symptoms of strain

Tertiary interventions include psychological therapy and medical attention—strategies, in other words, that are applied after the fact to help those individuals who have not been able to manage workplace stress effectively and who are now experiencing symptoms of strain.[36] In the "best of all organizations, primary and secondary prevention would be enough to manage the demands of work life."[37] However, in the event that stressors and stress are not adequately dealt with via primary and secondary efforts, it is important to consider tertiary intervention strategies that organizations and individuals could use to treat employees' symptoms of strain. What is important at the tertiary level is that individuals experiencing strain be aware that the symptoms pose a real threat to their overall health and well-being, and seek treatment. The organization can facilitate tertiary interventions by providing education about strain-related illnesses for employees. Tables 7.2 and 7.3 outline the individual and organizational strategies that contribute to successful tertiary stress interventions.

SPOTLIGHT ON A STRESSOR: INJUSTICE AT WORK

Recent studies show that employees who experience unfairness in the workplace report higher levels of strain.[38] Indeed, research now shows that exposure to injustice at work is associated with increased risk of death from a cardiac event as well as with increased insomnia.[39] Researchers have long known that unfairness negatively affects employee attitudes, including their commitment to the organization. However, investigations of the relationship between the experience of unfairness at work and employee health are relatively new.

distributive justice

the perceived fairness of outcomes

procedural justice

the perceived fairness of decision-making processes

interactional justice

the perceived fairness of interpersonal treatment

In organizational justice research, "fairness" is not treated as a one-dimensional construct. Researchers in this area focus on three separate categories of fairness judgments that a person can make: (1) the fairness of outcomes, or **distributive justice**, (2) the fairness of processes, or **procedural justice**, and (3) the fairness of interpersonal treatment, or **interactional justice**.[40] All three types of injustice have been associated with increased work stress and strain. Perceived injustice has been associated with increased risk of psychiatric symptoms, high blood pressure, and sickness-related absences from work.[41]

Employees are likely to judge an outcome as unfair when they do not receive a reward or the recognition they feel they deserve. For example, Joe, an employee who has recently put in many extra hours on a project at work, may feel that he deserves a bonus in recognition of his extra effort. If he does not receive it, he may feel that he has been the victim of a *distributive* injustice.

With respect to *procedural* injustice, people arrive at perceptions of fairness by examining several aspects of the process. Procedures that allow employee input; that are consistently implemented across conditions; that are unbiased, accurate, and ethical; that are subject to appeals on the part of those involved; and that are representative of all relevant parties, are viewed as more fair than those that are not.[42] For instance, Ellen would have judged the decision to change her work hours from 8 a.m. to 4 p.m. to 9 a.m. to 5 p.m. as more fair had she been told beforehand the reason for the decision and had she been permitted to give her opinion about the potential change.

In terms of *interactional* fairness, individuals judge the fairness of the interpersonal treatment they receive on several levels. For instance, they examine the extent to which their supervisors treat them with kindness and consideration, provide adequate explanations for decisions, and give useful and timely feedback. As an example, Tom is likely to have a better reaction to a negative performance review if his boss delivers that information in a sensitive manner and makes constructive suggestions on how he can improve his performance before the next performance appraisal.

Creating a Fair Workplace

Organizations can engage in primary stress interventions by working to reduce occurrences of injustice at work. Organizational leaders should be given training on the importance of fairness at work. Leadership training programs that include a discussion of the value of fair treatment are likely to help leaders see the value of fairness and the damage associated with injustice. The provision of appropriate feedback in a kind and sincere manner can go a long way toward improving an employee's perceptions of interactional justice at work and may have a positive impact on that individual's health.

Organizations can also try to follow decision-making processes that are procedurally fair. For example, they might consider allowing employee representation on committees or decision-making bodies for important organizational procedures. For instance, if an HR manager is considering changing the employee review process, striking a committee that includes representatives from the various stakeholder groups may increase the perceived fairness of the new evaluation process and ultimately the well-being of the employees who undergo the performance review.

SPOTLIGHT ON A STRESSOR: TECHNOLOGY

Innovations in computer hardware and software have profoundly changed the workplace, including how people do their work and interact with other employees.[43] Researchers in occupational health and safety recognize the health risks involved in the increasing presence of technology in the workplace. For instance, increased reliance on computers in the modern work environment has been associated with increased risk for physical health problems. The repetitive movements involved in keyboarding and cursor control place people at risk for musculoskeletal injuries. Carpal tunnel syndrome is an example of a common work-related musculoskeletal disorder that may stem from computer use. (In carpal tunnel syndrome, the median nerve of the arm and hand is compressed.)[44]

OH&S Today (7.2

Too Much Mail?

The advent of electronic mail was first hailed as a revolutionary tool that would save time and streamline organizational communication. Few could have predicted just how popular email would become. Daily, worldwide email traffic is now at 141 billion messages.

A Hewlett-Packard–sponsored survey found that workers are highly distracted and pressured by the onslaught of work-related email. The interruptions and information overload that come with large amounts of email can leave people exhausted and reduce their productivity. About two-thirds of the respondents indicated that they checked work email while out of the office and on vacation. About half reported responding to emails received within an hour of receipt. Some reported stepping out of social engagements to check email on handheld devices—others reported doing so while in face-to-face meetings. Checking email on

handheld devices in public is perceived by some as very rude indeed. Others prefer to use email to communicate with colleagues instead of picking up the phone or even walking to the next office.

Some companies are trying to combat the proliferation of email. Jon Coleman of Pfizer Canada has requested that staff in his department substantially reduce the number of emails they send over a one-year period. By providing tips on the appropriate and efficient use of electronic communication, email trainers are helping employees reach this challenging goal. Pfizer has also introduced a program called Freedom Six to Six, banning email messages between 6 p.m. and 6 a.m. and on weekends. The idea is to allow employees to really disengage from their work and to promote work–life balance—the idea being that employees will thus become more productive while at work.

Sources: CNN, "E-mails Hurt IQ More Than Pot." Found at: http://www.cnn.com/2005/WORLD/europe/04/22/text.iq (Accessed Feb. 8, 2013); Katherine Macklem, "You've Got Too Much Mail," *Maclean's*. Found at: http://www.macleans.ca/business/companies/article.jsp?content=20060130_120699_120699 (Accessed Feb. 8, 2013).

Musculoskeletal injuries are a prevalent and costly problem. Individuals with these injuries are sometimes in such chronic pain that they are forced to seek disability leave or early retirement.[45] Workers' Compensation claims relating to musculoskeletal disorders can place heavy financial demands on companies and government compensation systems. Preventive solutions are available to employers. A field of study called ergonomics emphasizes the importance of creating workstation arrangements that fit the needs of workers. For instance, computer keyboards and cursor controls are being redesigned with the aim of reducing the likelihood of musculoskeletal strain.

SPOTLIGHT ON A STRESSOR: WORK–FAMILY CONFLICT

For many people, work and family are life's central elements. Recent demographic shifts, such as those outlined in **OH&S Today 7.3**, have increased the extent to which responsibilities to work and those to family interfere with each other. For instance, more and more workers are facing childcare demands, and more and more families are dual-income, and these two circumstances together mean that working parents will sometimes be torn between work demands and childcare responsibilities. For example, a child who is home sick from school may prompt a working parent to miss work to care for the child. Studies suggest that work–family conflict is prevalent among Canadian workers.[46] For example, in one study

OH&S Notebook 7.2

TECHNOLOGY-RELATED STRESSORS

The increasing role of technology in the workplace affects the psychological as well as the physical well-being of workers. Several technology-related factors have been implicated as psychosocial stressors:

- *Malfunctions.* We have all likely experienced the frustration of an ill-timed computer crash. In these types of situations, our increasing reliance on technology to help us complete our work tasks can in fact be associated with reduced control at work. When our control over our work environment is reduced, increased stress and strain can result.
- *Isolation.* Our increasing reliance on technology has been associated with increased isolation in the workplace, reducing the incidence of positive social interactions among workers. For instance, employees who rely on computers are often "tied to their desks" to complete their work and thus are available for fewer social interactions with their coworkers.
- *Privacy.* The advanced state of technology in today's workplaces provides new means of employee surveillance and monitoring. Increasingly, organizations are turning to watchdog systems to keep track of such things as the amount of time an employee spends on the phone or email, the number of keystrokes a worker makes at the keyboard in a given amount of time, and the extent to which people use office technology (e.g., the Internet) for non–work-related tasks. In some cases these systems are used for performance monitoring.
- *Increased job demands.* The increasing role of technology in the workplace can also increase the demands associated with a job. (Recall that workload and work pace can be potent psychosocial stressors.) With respect to work pace, technological advances have increased the pace of many jobs. For example, the prevalence of technologies such as email and fax has shortened the expected turnaround times for work-related communications. Also, the need to keep pace with quickly advancing technology increases the workload of some employees.
- *Increased expectations for continuous learning.* Rapid changes in technology may require employees to learn new software, attend additional training, or change their work processes to incorporate new technology on a frequent basis. These changes may be particularly frustrating if employees are still mastering current systems.

Sources: Based on: M.D. Coovert and L.F. Thompson, "Technology and Workplace Health," in J.C. Quick and L.E. Tetrick, eds., *Handbook of Occupational Health Psychology* (Washington: APA, 2003) Pg. 223–48; A.L. Day, N. Scott, and E.K. Kelloway, "Information and Communication Technology: Implications for Job Stress and Employee Well-Being," in P.L. Perrewe and D.C. Ganster, eds., *New Developments in Theoretical and Conceptual Approaches to Job Stress: Research in Occupational Stress and Well Being*, Vol. 8 (Bingley: Emerald, 2010).

of the Nova Scotia workforce, half the respondents reported high work–family conflict.[47] Researchers are interested in the factors that contribute to **work–family conflict**, the outcomes of this type of conflict, and how organizations can help employees meet their multiple work and family roles.

Organizational experts define work–family conflict as a form of inter-role conflict. That is, it is a type of conflict in which the responsibilities of two separate roles are incompatible in some respects. In other words, pressures experienced in the work and family domains are in opposition.[48] Participation in one role is made more difficult by virtue of participation in the other.

work–family conflict
a type of inter-role conflict in which the role pressures experienced in the work and family domains are incompatible

work-to-family conflict
a form of work–family conflict in which work demands interfere with the fulfillment of family responsibilities

family-to-work conflict
a form of work–family conflict in which family demands interfere with the fulfillment of work responsibilities

Some experts in this area distinguish two categories of work–family conflict.[49] They note that work–family conflict is bi-directional: work may interfere with a person's ability to meet family demands, and family responsibilities may interfere with an individual's ability to keep pace with work demands. These two categories have been labelled **work-to-family conflict** and **family-to-work conflict**, respectively. Work-to-family conflict is a real problem for Canadian families. As indicated in **OH&S Today 7.3**, one in four respondents to a recent national survey reported that their work seriously interferes with their family responsibilities. Another 40% reported that work interferes with their family role to a moderate degree.[50]

OH&S Today 7.3

Work–Life Balance: Some Canadian Statistics

Balancing multiple commitments, including work and family, is a reality for Canadians. Here are some Canadian statistics on family, work, and well-being. In a study of more than 30,000 Canadian employees from 100 organizations:

- 58% reported high levels of role overload. This represented an increase of 11% in a single decade. Women reported more role overload than men.
- 25% of respondents indicated that their work seriously interferes with their family responsibilities. Another 40% reported a moderate degree of work-to-family interference. However, only 1 in 10 indicated that they allow family demands to interfere with their work responsibilities.
- Women spent more time per week than men in nonwork activities such as childcare and household tasks.
- About 25% experienced high levels of strain due to caring for an elderly or disabled person.
- One-third reported a high degree of job stress, and one-quarter of respondents were thinking of leaving their organization; almost half met the criteria for high absenteeism. Job stress and absenteeism appear to be on the rise in Canada. Almost three times as many respondents in this survey reported high stress than did so in a comparable study a decade prior.

- One in four Canadians work more than 50 hours per week.

Other important work–family facts include:

- The number of women in the workforce has increased. Women now account for 46% of the workforce, compared with 37% in 1976. In fact, in 1999, 61% of Canadian women with a child under the age of three worked (relative to only 28% in 1976).
- Both men and women in the Canadian labour force have childcare demands. Statistics from the mid-1990s suggest that nearly half of working Canadians have children living in the home. Furthermore, 15% of these individuals also care for elderly family members.
- Almost half of all Canadian children between the ages of one and five are in nonparental care.
- Family-friendly workplace policies are on the rise in Canadian organizations. A survey of Canadian employers found that 88% offer flextime, 50% make provisions for telework, and 63% offer family responsibility leave. However, other data suggest that there is limited access to flexible work arrangements even in organizations that offer this benefit and that the provision of childcare benefits in Canadian workplaces is low, with only 15% of companies indicating they provide on-site or near-site daycares.

Sources: L. Duxbury and C. Higgins, *Work–Life Conflict in Canada in the New Millennium: A Status Report* (Final Report; October 2003). Found at: http://www.phac-aspc.gc.ca/publicat/work-travail/report2/index-eng.php; C. Higgins, L. Duxbury, and S. Lyons, "Reducing Work–Life Conflict: What Works? What Doesn't?" (2008). Found at: http://www.phac-aspc.gc.ca/publicat/work-travail/index.html, (Accessed Apr. 21, 2010); K.L. Johnson, D.S. Lero, and J.A. Rooney, *Work -Life Compendium 2001: 150 Canadian Statistics on Work, Family and Well-Being* (Guelph: Centre for Families, Work, and Well-Being, 2001).

Causes of Work–Family Conflict

Several elements of work and family roles contribute to work–family conflict. One is the amount of time a person spends in each role, or **behavioural involvement** in the role. Generally, more time dedicated to one role means less time available to spend in the other role. Certainly, increased time devoted to work is associated with increased incidence of work-to-family conflict. Similarly, the more time a person spends on family pursuits and responsibilities in the home, the more likely that individual is to experience family-to-work conflict.[51]

A person's **psychological involvement** in work and family roles has also been implicated as a predictor of work–family conflict. Psychological involvement reflects the degree to which a person identifies with a particular role and sees the role as central to his or her self-concept. For example, a woman who considers her status as a mother to be the defining feature in her life has a high degree of psychological involvement in her mother role. A high degree of involvement in one role can cause it to conflict with other responsibilities.

Stress in either the work or the family role is also associated with work–family conflict. In particular, the experience of family-related stress, such as many family demands or dissatisfaction with family life, is associated with family-to-work conflict. Similarly, the experience of work-related stress, such as many work demands or job dissatisfaction, is associated with work-to-family conflict.[52]

Outcomes of Work–Family Conflict

Both work-to-family and family-to-work conflict are associated with negative consequences. Interestingly, the outcomes tend to be in the opposite domain from the cause of the conflict. That is, work-to-family conflict tends to affect family-related outcomes, and family-to-work conflict affects work-related outcomes. For instance, family-to-work conflict is linked with decreased work performance and absenteeism from work. Conversely, work-to-family conflict is associated with reduced performance in the family role and absences from family events.[53]

SUMMARY

In this chapter we have distinguished among the concepts of stressors in the work environment, the experience of stress, and the possible strain consequences. Whether or not someone perceives an event as stressful, or as a stressor, is individual. Not everyone will react to the same situation in the same way. People must perceive the event to be demanding in some way (e.g., a threat or a challenge) for it to be deemed stressful. As we've discussed, stress is an adaptive and individualistic response to the demands of the objective environment (i.e., stressors). We have also demonstrated that these demands take a variety of forms (acute, daily, chronic, catastrophic).

Stress can have serious consequences. Individuals exposed to continued or high levels of stress develop strain reactions that may be psychological, physical, behavioural, or organizational. In turn, these forms of strain reactions can affect the organization and people's lives. The human *and* the monetary costs of occupational stress warrant our attention.

Organizationally and individually driven interventions are important to reduce the extent to which stressors exist in the workplace, as well as to minimize the

behavioural involvement
the amount of time a person spends in a particular role

psychological involvement
the degree to which a person identifies with a particular role and sees the role as a central component of his or her self-concept

damage caused by unavoidable stressors. Such programs involve primary (preventive) techniques, secondary interventions (to help people avoid the negative consequences of stress), and tertiary programs (to help people find the appropriate treatment when they are experiencing strain). The most successful stress management initiatives involve both the individual employee and the organization as a whole. The organizational responsibility to promote psychologically healthy workplaces is increasingly recognized. For instance, the first Canadian standard on psychological health and safety at work (CSA-Z1003-13) was published in 2013. This standard defines a psychologically healthy workplace and articulates guidelines for management systems to promote and sustain psychological health at work.

Injustice, technology, and work–life conflict are relevant workplace stressors. When reflecting on these stressors, we highlight the individual nature of stress. Not all employees reach the same conclusions about the fairness of a given situation, some employees are not bothered by the increasing technological demands of modern workplaces, and some individuals do not experience high levels of work–life conflict. For others, though, one or more of these stressors present potential health and safety issues in the workplace.

Key Terms

behavioural involvement 185
buffer 174
distributive justice 180
family-to-work conflict 184
general adaptation syndrome 172
interactional justice 180
moderator 173
negative affectivity 174
preventive stress management 178
primary interventions 178
procedural justice 180
psychological involvement 185

psychologically healthy and safe workplace 169
psychosocial model of health 169
risk factor 174
secondary interventions 179
strain 175
stress 172
stressor 169
tertiary interventions 180
Type A behaviour 174
work–family conflict 183
work-to-family conflict 184

Weblinks

Canadian Centre for Occupational Health and Safety, "OSH Answers, Health Promotion/Wellness/Psychosocial"
http://www.ccohs.ca/oshanswers/psychosocial

Canadian Centre for Occupational Health and Safety, "OSH Answers, Work–Life Balance"
http://www.ccohs.ca/oshanswers/psychosocial/worklife_balance.html

Canadian Fitness and Lifestyle Research Institute
http://www.cflri.ca

Centre for Families, Work, and Well-Being, University of Guelph
http://www.uoguelph.ca/cfww

Mental Health Commission of Canada
http://www.mentalhealthcommission.ca/English/Pages/default.aspx

Required Professional Capabilities (RPCs)

The following RPCs, listed by their CCHRA number, are relevant to the material covered in this chapter. All RPCs can be found at http://www.chrp.ca/rpc/body-of-knowledge.

RPC:170 Develops, implements, and ensures the application of policies, regulations, and standards relating to occupational health and safety.*

RPC:172 Ensures due diligence and liability requirements are met.*

RPC:174 Develops and implements policies on the workplace environment.*

RPC:177 Develops or provides for wellness and employee assistance programs to support organizational effectiveness.*

RPC:179 Ensures that mechanisms are in place for responding to crises in the workplace, including critical incident stress management.*

RPC:183 Analyzes risks to employee health & safety and develops preventive programs.*

Discussion Questions

1. Think of five stressors you have experienced in the past 12 months. Using the guidelines presented in this chapter, categorize the stressors as daily, acute, chronic, or catastrophic. Which, if any, seemed to lead to strain?

2. If only one individual in a workplace is experiencing strain, are the causes of that strain likely to be in the workplace? Why or why not?

3. What are the major stressors in modern workplaces?

4. How does stress manifest itself in behaviour? In organizational functioning?

5. What are some actions that individuals can take to help manage stress? What can organizations do to help employees avoid or manage stress?

6. What are some of the ways in which evolving technology contributes to the experience of workplace stress? What are some interventions that employees and employers might attempt in order to avoid or manage the stress associated with technology?

7. Discuss some emerging stressors in the workplace. How might companies help employees deal with the changing demands of work?

Using the Internet

1. Psychological symptoms have been identified as a health-related outcome of stress. Individuals who feel prolonged stress may experience such symptoms as depression and anxiety. Many employees indicate that they would be uncomfortable telling their boss or coworkers that they are experiencing these types of psychological symptoms because of the associated stigma. Using the website resources of the Canadian Mental Health Association (http://www.cmha.ca), the Canadian Psychiatric Association (http://www.cpa-apc.org), the Canadian Psychological

*Canadian Council of Human Resources Associations, Human Resources Professionals in Canada: Revised Body of Knowledge and Required Professional Capabilities (RPCs ®), 2007.

Association (http://www.cpa.ca), the Canadian Centre for Occupational Health and Safety (http://www.ccohs.ca), the Mental Health Commission of Canada (www.mentalhealthcommission.ca), and other websites, design an awareness program that might help reduce the stigma associated with stress-related mental health issues in the workplace.

2. Use Internet resources to find out what you can about CSA-Z1003-13, the Canadian standard for psychological health and safety in the workplace. Some angles you might consider are the media's response to and coverage of the standard, the response by professional associations (for example HR, psychological, or safety associations), and the ways in which particular organizations are implementing the standard.

3. The "sandwich generation" is particularly exposed to issues of work–family conflict. Using Internet resources, define the sandwich generation. Why are they vulnerable to work–family conflict?

Exercises

1. Think about your current or most recent job. What are/were some of the pertinent stressors? What actions do/did you take to cope with them? How does/did the organization help you to deal with the stress? Talk to some of your friends or members of your family about the stressors they encounter at work and the strategies they and their employers use to manage workplace stress.

2. Returning to work after a stress-related leave can be difficult for both the individuals coming back to work and their coworkers. Create and enact two role plays in which you and your classmates are employees at an organization. In one of the scenarios, one of the employees is returning to work after a leave due to a stress-related mental health problem. In the second scenario, one of the coworkers is returning to work following a leave due to a car accident. Following the role plays, discuss each scenario. How did the returning employee feel? What were the responses of the coworkers? Was there a greater sense of discomfort in discussing the well-being of the person who had been on stress leave, relative to the person who was in the car accident? Do you think there are taboos about discussing mental health problems in the workplace? In your follow-up discussion, generate ways that organizations and individual employees might make the transition easier for the person returning to work from a stress-related leave.

3. Imagine you are the human resources director for a large organization. You have been given the job of designing and implementing a new performance review system. You know that the employees may find the shift to a new system stressful and that employees often think that performance review instruments are unfair. You are also aware that perceived injustice in the workplace is a stressor, and you would like to minimize the extent to which your employees are exposed to work stress. What might you do to maximize the perceived distributive, procedural, and interactional fairness of the performance review process?

4. Contact the human resources department of an organization. Interview the HR manager about psychosocial hazards in the workplace. Some of the things you should ask about are:

a. the extent to which he or she considers workplace stress to be a problem in that organization;

b. the types of stressors experienced by the employees in that organization;

c. the types of strain reported by employees;

d. the organizational outcomes of employee stress that the company experiences (e.g., turnover, absenteeism); *and*

e. the types of interventions the company has to help employees reduce or manage stress.

5. Issues of work–family conflict are highly prevalent for parents of young children. To find out more about the experience of work–family conflict, interview a working individual who also has responsibility for childcare. Some questions you might ask include the following:

a. How many hours per week does the individual spend on paid work?

b. How many hours per week does the individual spend on childcare activities?

c. How many hours per week does the individual spend on nonpaid household chores and errands?

d. If the individual has a spouse, in what ways does the spouse help him or her manage the multiple responsibilities of work and family commitments?

e. What are some of the special challenges the individual encounters in balancing work and family life?

f. What are some of the strategies the individual uses to meet all of his or her work and family demands?

g. What efforts does the individual's employer make to help him or her manage work and family demands?

Case 1 A STRESSFUL JOB

Joan is an Emergency Room nurse at a busy city hospital. She has always enjoyed the hustle of working Emergency and the challenges of dealing with the unexpected. Lately, Joan has been worried about her own well-being. She has been very abrupt with her coworkers on several occasions and has had difficulty concentrating on her job. Though there have been no problems to date, Joan is worried that her deteriorating performance might cause a problem, given the critical nature of her work. Her doctor suggested that she take an extended leave because of her "nerves." As the HR representative, what do you think is going on here? Are Joan's concerns likely to be a result of stress? What stressors are present in the environment? If there are 20 employees in Emergency and Joan is the only one complaining, does this mean that her complaints are not real?

Case 2 TECHNOLOGY AT WORK

SmithCorp is a quickly growing organization specializing in pharmaceuticals. The management of SmithCorp prides itself on being on the cutting edge. Accordingly, it ensures that all its employees are provided with the latest advances in technology. Employees have laptops, wireless Internet access, BlackBerry devices, and cellphones. SmithCorp also often upgrades its software and network systems. Many of the employees rely heavily on this technology and these programs in their daily work. Many of SmithCorp's staff work in sales and product management. They are often on the road visiting client sites and making sales calls. As such, much of the communication among coworkers and between coworkers and managers is technologically mediated. What are some of the potential psychosocial hazards that employees at SmithCorp might face? As an HR manager at SmithCorp's head office, what types of programs could you implement to help employees manage the stress and strain that may result from exposure to these psychosocial hazards?

Case 3 A TOXIC WORKPLACE

Tyrell is a sergeant with a regional police force. He's recently been given the commanding post at a large urban branch. Tyrell has 15 years' experience in the police services with many of those years in management roles. However, the situation he finds at this branch surprises and baffles him. Morale among the officers is extremely low. Several officers are off on long-term stress leave. Serving a high crime area, the officers in this branch often face challenging calls that also receive substantial press coverage. However, Tyrell senses that the problems run deeper than work overload or negative media attention. He notices that some of the male officers are noticeably disrespectful of their female colleagues. He also senses a good deal of animosity among some officers. Two in particular won't even work on the same shift. With some digging around he finds that one of the two officers in question has alleged harassment from another officer. Tyrell knows that the sergeant who previously had command of the branch took an autocratic approach to leadership and didn't get involved with interpersonal aspects of the workplace. Tyrell sees that his employees are suffering and wants to reach out to them and help improve the situation. He and his wife hosted a potluck for all the officers and staff at their home, but only a few showed up. Tyrell is not sure what to do. Imagine you work in the central office of the force as the HR officer with responsibility for implementing psychologically healthy workplace programs. What advice would you give to Tyrell?

NOTES

1. S.L. Sauter, L.R. Murphy, and J.J. Hurrell, "Prevention of Work-Related Psychological Disorders: A National Strategy Proposed by the National Institute for Occupational Safety and Health (NIOSH)," *American Psychologist* 45 (1990): 1146–58.
2. American Institute of Stress, *Job Stress* (New York: 2002).

3. Mental Health Commission of Canada, "Mental Health Strategy for Canada," April 24, 2012, http://www.fcmhs.ca/news/MHCC%20Strategy%20-%20FINAL%20-%20april%2024%20FINAL%20PDF.pdf, February 8, 2013; and P. Smetanin, D. Stiff, C. Briante, C. Adair, S. Ahmad, and M. Khan, "The Life and Economic Impact of Major Mental Illnesses in Canada: 2011 to 2041," RiskAnalytica, on behalf of the Mental Health Commission of Canada, 2011.

4. E. Anderssen, "Ottawa to Fund Mental-Health Strategy: First-Ever Canadian-wide Standards to Tackle Problem Estimated to Cost $20-Billion a Year in Workplace Losses Alone," *The Globe and Mail,* June 17, 2011.

5. S. Compton, "What's Stressing the Stressed? Main Sources of Stress Among Workers," October 13, 2011, Statistics Canada. Accessed at http://www.statcan.gc.ca/pub/11-008-x/2011002/article/11562-eng.pdf, February 11, 2013.

6. E.K. Kelloway and L. Francis, "Stress and Strain in Nova Scotia Organizations: Results of a Recent Province-Wide Study," paper presented at the Nova Scotia Psychologically Healthy Workplace Conference, Halifax, February 2006.

7. M. Shain, "Tracking the Perfect Legal Storm. Converging Systems Create Mounting Pressure to Create the Psychologically Healthy Workplace, 2010, Calgary, AB. Mental Health Commission of Canada, retrieved from http://www.mentalhealthcommission.ca/English/Pages/Mentalhealthintheworkplace.aspx, February 11, 2013.

8. CSA Group, "CAN/CSA-Z1003-13 Psychological Health and Safety in the Workplace—Prevention, Promotion, and Guidance to Staged Implementation," January 2013.

9. Ibid., p. 4.

10. L.I. Pratt and J. Barling, "Differentiating Between Daily Events, Acute and Chronic Stressors: A Framework and Its Implications," in J.J. Hurrell, L.R. Murphy, S.L. Sauter, and C.L. Cooper, eds., *Occupational Stress: Issues and Development in Research* (London: Taylor and Francis, 1988), 41–53.

11. Ibid.

12. Sauter et al., "Prevention of Work-Related Psychological Disorders."

13. CSA Group, "CAN/CSA-Z1003-13 Psychological Health and Safety in the Workplace—Prevention, Promotion, and Guidance to Staged Implementation," January 2013.

14. H. Selye, "The General Adaptation Syndrome and Diseases of Adaptation," *Journal of Clinical Endocrinology* 6 (1946): 117; T. Theorell, "To Be Able to Exert Control Over One's Situation: A Necessary Condition for Coping with Stressors," in J.C. Quick and L.E. Tetrick, eds., *Handbook of Occupational Health Psychology* (Washington: American Psychological Association, 2003), 201–20.

15. R.S. Lazarus and S. Folkman, *Stress, Appraisal, and Coping* (New York: Springer, 1984).

16. M.S. Gazzaniga and T.F. Heatherton, *Psychological Science* (New York: Norton, 2003).

17. M. Friedman and R. Rosenman, *Type A Behavior and Your Heart* (New York: Knopf, 1974).

18. R.L. Helmreich, J.T. Spence, and R.S. Pred, "Making It Without Losing It: Type A, Achievement Motivation, and Scientific Attainment Revisited," *Personality and Social Psychology Bulletin* 14 (1988): 495–504.

19. P.A. Landsbergis, P.L. Schnall, K.L. Belkic, D. Baker, J.E. Schwartz, and T.G. Pickering, "Workplace and Cardiovascular Disease: The Relevance and Potential Role for Occupational Health Psychology," in Quick and Tetrick, *Handbook of Occupational Health Psychology,* 2e (Washington: American Psychological Association, 2011) 243–64; S.D. Bluen, J. Barling, and W. Burns, "Predicting Sales Performance, Job Satisfaction, and Depression Using the Achievement Striving and Impatience-Irritability Dimensions of Type A Behavior," *Journal of Applied Psychology* 75 (1990): 212–16.

20. C.D. Speilberger, P.R. Vagg, and C.F. Wasala, "Occupational Stress: Job Pressures and Lack of Support," in Quick and Tetrick, *Handbook of Occupational Health Psychology,* 185–200.

21. J.C. Wallace, B.D. Edwards, T. Arnold, M.L. Frazier, and D.M. Finch, "Work Stressors, Role-Based Performance, and the Moderating Influence of Organizational Support," *Journal of Applied Psychology* 94 (2009): 254–62.

22. Sauter et al., "Prevention of Work-Related Psychological Disorders."

23. C. Rubino, A. Luksyte, S.J. Perry, and S.D. Volpone, "How Do Stressors Lead to Burnout? The Mediating Role of Motivation," *Journal of Occupational Health Psychology* 14 (2009): 289–304.

24. J.C. Wallace and S.J. Vodanovich, "Can Accidents and Industrial Accidents Be Predicted? Further Investigation into the Relationship Between Cognitive Failures and Reports of Accidents," *Journal of Business and Psychology* 17 (2003): 503–14.

25. T.S. Kristensen, "Job Stress and Cardiovascular Disease: A Theoretical Critical Review," *Journal of Occupational Health Psychology* 3 (1996): 246–60; N. Wager, G. Fieldman, and T. Hussey, "The Effect on Ambulatory Blood Pressure of Working Under Favourably and Unfavourably Perceived Supervisors," *Occupational and Environmental Medicine* 60 (2003): 468–74.

26. S.C. Segerstrom and G.E. Miller, "Psychological Stress and the Human Immune System: A Meta-Analytic Study of 30 Years of Inquiry," *Psychological Bulletin* 130 (2004): 601–30.

27. C.L. Mohren, G.M.H. Swaen, P.J.A. Borm, A. Bast, and J.M.D. Galama, "Psychological Job Demands as a Risk Factor for Common Cold in a Dutch Working Population," *Journal of Psychosomatic Research* 50 (2001): 21–27.

28. M.R. Frone, M.L. Cooper, and M. Russell, "Stressful Life Events, Gender, and Substance Use: An Application of Tobit Regression," *Psychology of Addictive Behaviors* 8 (1984): 59–69; and S. Liu, M. Wang, Y. Zhan, and J. Shi, "Daily Work Stress and Alcohol Use: Testing the Cross-Level Moderation Effects of Neuroticism and Job Involvement," *Personnel Psychology* 62 (2009): 575–97.

29. W. Darr and G. Johns, "Work Strain, Health, and Absenteeism: A Meta-Analysis," *Journal of Occupational Health Psychology* 13 (2008): 293–318; and S. Sonnentag and M. Frese, "Stress in Organizations," in W.C. Borman, D.R. Ilgen, and R.J. Klimoski, eds., *Handbook of Psychology, vol. 12: Industrial Organizational Psychology* (New York: Wiley, 2003), 453–91.

30. J.C. Cullen and L.B. Hammer, "Developing and Testing a Theoretical Model Linking Work–Family Conflict to Employee Safety," *Journal of Occupational Health Psychology* 12 (2007): 266–78; and T.M. Probst, "Layoffs and Tradeoffs: Production, Quality, and Safety Demands Under the Threat of Job Loss," *Journal of Occupational Health Psychology* 7 (2002): 211–20.

31. J.C. Quick, J.D. Quick, D.L. Nelson, and J.J. Hurrell, Jr., *Preventive Stress Management in Organizations* (Washington: APA, 1997).

32. CSA Group. "CAN/CSA-Z1003-13 Psychological Health and Safety in the Workplace—Prevention, Promotion, and Guidance to Staged Implementation," January 2013.

33. R.J. Burke, "Organizational-Level Interventions to Reduce Occupational Stressors," *Work and Stress* 7 (1993): 77–87; C.G. Hepburn, C.A. Loughlin, and J. Barling, "Coping with Chronic Work Stress," in B.H. Gottleib, ed., *Coping with Chronic Stress* (New York: Plenum, 1997).

34. C.G. Hepburn, C.A. Loughlin, and J. Barling, "Coping with Chronic Work Stress," in B.H. Gottleib, ed., *Coping with Chronic Stress* (New York: Plenum, 1997).

35. Ibid.

36. Ibid.

37. Quick et al., *Preventive Stress Management in Organizations*.

38. M. Elovainio, M. Kivimäki, and K. Helkama, "Organizational Justice Evaluations, Job Control, and Occupational Strain," *Journal of Applied Psychology* 86 (2001): 418–24; L. Francis and J. Barling, "Organizational Injustice and Psychological Strain," *Canadian Journal of Behavioural Science* 37 (2005): 250–61; B.J. Tepper, "Health Consequences of Organizational Injustice: Tests of Main and Interactive Effects," *Organizational Behavior and Human Decision Processes* 86 (2001): 197–215.

39. M. Elovainio, P. Leino-Arjas, J. Vahtera, and M. Kivimäki, "Justice at Work and Cardiovascular Mortality: A Prospective Cohort Study," *Journal of Psychosomatic Research* 61 (2006): 271–74; J. Greenberg, "Losing Sleep over Organizational Injustice: Attenuating Insomniac Reactions to Underpayment Inequity with Supervisory Training in Interactional Justice," *Journal of Applied Psychology* 91 (2006): 58–69.

40. R. Cropanzano and J. Greenberg, "Progress in Organizational Justice: Tunneling Through the Maze," in C.L. Cooper and I.T. Robertson, eds., *International Review of Industrial and Organizational Psychology*, vol. 12 (London: Wiley, 1997), 317–72.

41. J.E. Ferrie, J. Head, M.J. Shipley, J. Vahtera, M.G. Marmot, and M. Kivimäki, "Injustice at Work and Incidence of Psychiatric Morbidity: The Whitehall II Study," *Occupational and Environmental Medicine* 63 (2006): 443–50; M. Kivimäki, M. Elovainio, J. Vahtera, and J.E. Ferrie, "Organizational Justice and the Health of Employees: Prospective Cohort Study," *Occupational and Environmental Medicine* 60 (2003): 27–34; N. Wager, G. Fieldman, and T. Hussey, "The Effect on Ambulatory Blood Pressure of Working Under Favourably and Unfavourably Perceived Supervisors," *Occupational and Environmental Medicine* 60 (2003): 468–74.

42. G.S. Leventhal, J. Karuza, and W.R. Fry, "Beyond Fairness: A Theory of Allocation Preferences," in G. Mikula, ed., *Justice and Social Interaction* (New York: Springer, 1980), 167–218; J. Thibaut and L. Walker, *Procedural Justice: A Psychological Analysis* (Hillsdale: Erlbaum, 1975).

43. M.D. Coovert and L.F. Thompson, "Technology and Workplace Health," in Quick and Tetrick, *Handbook of Occupational Health Psychology*, 221–41.

44. Ibid.

45. H. Brenner and W. Ahern, "Sickness Absence and Early Retirement on Health Grounds in the Construction Industry in Ireland," *Occupational and Environmental Medicine* 57 (2000): 615–20.

46. L. Duxbury and C. Higgins, *Work–Life Conflict in Canada in the New Millennium: A Status Report (Final Report)*, Public Health Agency of Canada, 2003, http://www.phac-aspc.gc.ca/-publicat/work-travail/index.html, February 16, 2007.

47. Kelloway and Francis, *Stress and Strain*.

48. M.R. Frone, "Work–Family Balance," in Quick and Tetrick, *Handbook of Occupational Health Psychology*, 143–62.

49. M.R. Frone, J.K. Yardley, and K. Markel, "Developing and Testing an Integrative Model of Work–Family Interface," *Journal of Vocational Behavior* 54 (1997): 145–67.

50. Duxbury and Higgins, *Work–Life Conflict in Canada*.

51. Frone, "Work–Family Balance."

52. Frone et al., "Developing and Testing an Integrative Model of Work–Family Interface."

53. Frone, "Work–Family Balance."

Workplace Violence

CHAPTER LEARNING OBJECTIVES

After reading this chapter, you should be able to:

- define and distinguish among violence, aggression, and harassment
- identify the risk factors for workplace violence
- explain the idea of imminent risk
- describe ways to reduce the risk of workplace violence
- define sexual harassment
- describe what organizations should do to reduce the incidence of workplace sexual harassment

GRANT'S LAW

Like many other young people, 24-year-old Grant De Patie worked at a service station. Rising gas prices resulted in a dramatic increase in "gas and dash" incidents, in which drivers filled the tank of their car and drove away without paying. In trying to stop a driver from "dashing" with $12 worth of gas, Grant was dragged for 7.5 km and died as a result of the incident.

In terms of health and safety legislation, Grant De Patie's death resulted in the enactment of "Grant's Law" in British Columbia. The law requires service stations to require prepayment after 11 p.m.

and also requires employers to provide workers with occupation-specific health and safety training.

More broadly, Grant's death, and similar incidents across the country in which employees were attacked or killed in the course of their job, has focused attention on the issue of workplace violence in Canada. Many jurisdictions have now passed specific regulations dealing with the issue of workplace violence, and employers have assumed new responsibilities for risk assessment, training, and risk mitigation around the issue of workplace violence.

Source: Ministry of Labour and Citizens' Services, News Release: *"Grant's Law" to Protect Late-Night Workers*. Found at: http://www2.news.gov.bc.ca/news_releases_2005-2009/2007LCS0020-001251.htm (Accessed Apr. 5, 2010).

The postal shootings of the mid-1990s[1] and the resulting popularization of the phrase "going postal" to describe an enraged state were, arguably, the defining moments that focused organizational and research attention on the notion of workplace violence and aggression. The postal shootings were also certainly not the last highly publicized incidents of workplace violence. In Canada, tragic incidents such as the OCTranspo shootings (in which an employee of OCTranspo killed four coworkers and injured two others), the murders at Concordia (in which a faculty member killed four colleagues), and the shootings at the L'École Polytechnique (in which 28 people were shot and 14 women died) served to focus public and media attention on the phenomenon of workplace violence.

Though such acts are extremely serious and call for action to understand their causes and prevent their occurrence, the available evidence suggests that they are actually quite rare and represent only the "tip of the iceberg" of workplace violence and aggression. While there are approximately 14 workplace homicides each year in Canada,[2] other acts of physical violence and workplace aggression are considerably more prevalent. Not surprisingly, many jurisdictions have enacted health and safety legislation requiring employers to deal with issues of workplace violence and aggression.

violence

an actual physical assault or threat of an assault

aggression

behaviour by an individual or individuals within or outside an organization that is intended to physically or psychologically harm a worker or workers and that occurs in a work-related context

DEFINING WORKPLACE AGGRESSION AND VIOLENCE

Legislative approaches differ in how broadly they define workplace **violence** and **aggression**. Nova Scotia, for example, has adopted a very narrow definition that focuses solely on acts or threats of physical assault. Thus Nova Scotia's legislation focuses solely on workplace violence.[3] Other jurisdictions, such as Quebec and Ontario, focus more broadly on acts of workplace aggression. Schat and Kelloway[4] have defined workplace aggression as "behaviour by an individual or individuals within or outside an organization that is intended to physically or psychologically harm a worker or workers and occurs in a work-related context" (p. 191). Accordingly, all violent behaviours are, by definition, aggressive, whereas not all aggressive behaviours are violent. In Canada, legislation such as enacted in Quebec, Ontario, and the federal jurisdiction uses the term **harassment**, which is another term for aggression. In Ontario, for example, harassment is defined as vexatious (i.e., annoying or embarrassing) conduct that is unwelcome.

A host of other terms are commonly used to describe some aspects of workplace aggression.[5] For example, articles in the popular press often refer to workplace bullying and the similar constructs of workplace abuse, **emotional abuse**, mistreatment, victimization, and **mobbing** (a term used in Europe to describe bullying). Though there are slight variations in the definitions of these terms, Keashly[6] suggests that they generally refer to "interactions between organizational members that are characterized by repeated hostile verbal and nonverbal, often non-physical behaviours directed at a person(s) such that the target's sense of him/herself as a competent worker and person is negatively affected" (p. 234). Thus, **bullying** and these other constructs are defined as repeated behaviours that are explicitly nonphysical, are perpetrated solely by organizational members, and occur over a prolonged period of time (e.g., six months).[7]

Workplace **incivility**[8] is another construct that is conceptually related to workplace aggression. It is defined as "low-intensity deviant behaviour with ambiguous intent to harm the target, in violation of workplace norms for mutual respect. Uncivil behaviours are characteristically rude and discourteous, displaying a lack of regard for others" (p. 457). Incivility can be a precursor to more serious forms of aggression.[9] This suggests that if aggressive behaviour is classified along a continuum of severity or intensity, incivility would represent the low end of this continuum.

Recently, a number of researchers have included sexual harassment behaviours in their definitions and operationalizations of workplace violence and aggression.[10, 11] Workplace **sexual harassment**—which consists of **gender harassment**, **unwanted sexual attention**, and **sexual coercion**,[12] is a unique form of workplace aggression characterized by sexualized or sex-related behaviour. Though we include workplace sexual harassment in this chapter, much of the existing literature and legislation has emerged separately from that on workplace aggression. Therefore we consider harassment on its own at the end of this chapter.

THE PREVALENCE OF WORKPLACE AGGRESSION

Until recently, estimates of the prevalence of workplace aggression varied widely and were of dubious credibility. Accurate surveillance of the forms and frequency of workplace violence requires representative sampling procedures and standardized definitions, measures, and reporting mechanisms.[13] The most accurate estimates of the prevalence of workplace violence will be derived from large samples constructed so as to represent a known population. In the past three years, data from three such surveys (one American and two Canadian) have become available.

U.S. Prevalence Data

Schat, Frone, and Kelloway[14] reported a detailed analysis of a large, nationally representative sample of workers in the United States. They asked a series

harassment
engaging in annoying or embarrassing conduct against a worker in a workplace—conduct that is known or ought reasonably to be known to be unwelcome

emotional abuse
another term for bullying

mobbing
a term used mainly in Europe to refer to bullying

bullying
aggressive, nonphysical behaviours perpetrated by organizational members over a prolonged period of time

incivility
rude or discourteous behaviour

sexual harassment
intentional, persistent, and unwelcome sexual conduct or remarks that occur despite resistance from the victim

gender harassment
comments or actions seen as creating a hostile environment based on gender

unwanted sexual attention
persistent and unwelcome sexual comments or attention

sexual coercion
the attempt to extort sexual cooperation; can take the form of subtle or explicit job-related threats

of questions about the experience of both workplace violence and workplace aggression. Their operational definition of workplace violence focused solely on physical assaults (i.e., excluding threats). Respondents were asked to indicate how frequently somebody at work had: "(a) Pushed you, grabbed you, or slapped you in anger; (b) Kicked you, bit you, or hit you with a fist; (c) Hit you with an object, tried to hit you with an object, or threw an object at you in anger; and (d) Attacked you with a knife, gun, or another weapon."

Overall, they[15] reported that 6% of the sample—corresponding to just under 7 million American workers—experienced these forms of workplace violence in the course of year. Turning to the four specific physically aggressive behaviours examined in the survey, assault with an object was the most common, being reported by 4.2% of respondents. Being pushed, grabbed, or slapped in anger was reported by 3.9% of respondents; being kicked, hit, or bitten was reported by 3%; and being attacked with a knife, gun, or other weapon was reported by 0.7%.

Schat and colleagues[16] also reported on workplace aggression, which they termed "psychological abuse." Their measure included items such as "Shouted obscenities at you or screamed at you in anger; Insulted you or called you names in front of other people; Made an indirect or hidden threat, such as saying that 'something bad' would happen to you; Threatened to hit you or throw something at you; and Threatened you with a knife, gun, or another weapon." They found that 41% of their sample (representing 47 million workers) reported experiencing workplace aggression as measured by these items. About 35% reported being screamed at, and 24.4% being insulted. Fewer respondents reported being the victim of a hidden threat (12.2%), a threat of violence (7.6%), or a threat of an attack with a weapon (1.9%).

Canadian Data

Though there are no comparable national studies of workplace violence in Canada, Francis and Kelloway[17] conducted a large (N = 1400) study of Nova Scotian workers.* The sample was drawn to match population parameters in terms of gender and geographic distribution within the province. They defined violence in accordance with Nova Scotian legislation, which includes both physical assault and the threat of physical assault. Just under 21% of the respondents reported experiencing some form of physical violence:

- 9% reported being hit, kicked, punched, or shoved

- 12% had objects thrown at them

- 12.6% had been threatened with physical assault

- 2.7% had been threatened with a weapon

Francis and Kelloway[18] also examined a wide variety of aggressive but nonviolent behaviours. The results were strikingly different from those for violence—79.2% of the sample reported experiencing some form of aggressive behaviour in the workplace. Among their participants, they found that:

- 60.7% reported being glared at

- 43.5% reported being given the silent treatment

---

*L. Francis and E.K. Kelloway, "The Nova Scotia Workplace Stress Survey," Saint Mary's University, Halifax, 2007.

- 36.4% reported being the target of false accusations
- 27.1% reported being the target of obscene gestures
- 26.8% reported being refused needed resources
- 27.6% reported being made fun of
- 56.3% reported having their sense of judgment questioned
- 25.2% reported being assigned meaningless tasks
- 51.6% reported having their opinions dismissed
- 37.5% reported having bad things said about them
- 15.0% reported being told they were incompetent
- 36.7% reported being teased
- 44.9% reported being treated with disrespect
- 30.9% reported someone taking credit for their ideas

Clearly, there appears to be more violence and aggression in Canadian workplaces than in American workplaces. Though the Nova Scotian results may not generalize to the rest of Canada, there are at least two sources of converging evidence. First, the study of criminal victimization in Canadian workplaces[19] also reported that 17% of all violent victimizations happened in workplaces. This represents approximately 356,000 incidents of workplace violence in a 12-month period in Canada. Of these, 71% were physical (i.e., nonsexual) assaults. Second, in a study of Canadian public sector employees, 69% responded that they had experienced some form of verbal workplace aggression.[20]

Sources of Workplace Violence

A common approach to categorizing workplace violence focuses on the relationship between the assailant and the victim (see Table 8.1).[21] Here, various "types" of violence are considered based on who the perpetrator is.

Type I violence is associated with criminal activity; an assault or homicide that occurs in the context of a robbery is an example of Type I violence. **Type II violence** is also committed by a nonorganizational member but is not typically

Type I violence
violence committed by someone with no legitimate relationship to the organization, often while committing another criminal act

Type II violence
violence committed by clients or customers of the organization

TABLE 8.1	
The CAL/OSHA Framework	
Type	**Relationship of Assailant to the Organization**
Type 1	Member of the public with no legitimate relationship to the organization, usually committing a criminal act
Type 2	Member of the public who receives legitimate service from the organization (e.g., client, patient)
Type 3	An employee or former employee of the organization
Type 4	The spouse or partner of an employee

Source: State of California, "Cal/OSHA Guidelines for Workplace Security," (1995). Found at: http://www.dir.ca.gov/dosh/dosh_publications/worksecurity.html.

OH&S Notebook 8.1

INTIMATE PARTNER VIOLENCE

For many individuals, work is a "social address." That is, partners or family members know where the person works and, often, his or her schedule. Lifetime prevalence rates of partner violence have been estimated at 25% for women and 8% for men.[22] Intimate partners are identified as the perpetrator in 1% to 3% of all workplace violence incidents.[23] Also, women are five times more likely than men to be attacked at work by a current or former intimate partner.[24]

There are several ways that intimate partner violence plays out in the workplace. First, because work is a social address, acts of intimate partner violence can occur in the workplace when one partner shows up there and assaults the other. Second, a partner may stalk the other person, including by sending numerous emails and text messages to the workplace and by waiting outside it for the partner. A third form of intimate partner violence is sabotaging the others' ability to get to, or do, work. Denying access to a home computer or hiding the car keys are frequently noted ways of sabotaging a partner. Fourth and finally, even when events do not occur in the workplace, individuals victimized by a partner are unlikely to be able to perform their work to their full potential as a result of the ongoing strain involved.

Type III violence
violence committed by coworkers (e.g., other employees of the organization)

Type IV violence
violence committed by the spouse or partner of the victim

associated with other forms of criminal activity. It is sometimes referred to as "client-perpetrated violence." An example would be a patient who assaults a health care worker. **Type III violence** is violence perpetrated by organizational "insiders"; examples include coworker assaults as well as tragedies such as the post office murders of the 1990s. Finally, **Type IV violence** is committed by the spouse or partner of the victim and is more properly seen as family/spousal or intimate partner violence that happens to occur in the workplace (see **OH&S Notebook 8.1**).

The CAL/OSHA framework excludes violence that occurs during a labour dispute, which is in several respects a unique form of workplace violence.[25] Picket line violence has been defined as the "non-privileged physical interference with the person or property of another, or the threat, express or implied of such interference" (p. 14).[26] Labour disputes tend to involve two broad categories of violent acts: confrontational and purposeful. Confrontational violence breaks out at the spur of the moment during a conflict. For instance, following a trade of verbal insults, a group of picketers may throw rocks at line crossers. In contrast, purposeful violence is planned and deliberate.[27] Both forms tend to result in interpersonal attacks. Picket line violence is thought to occur most often when individuals (e.g., management or replacement workers) are trying to cross a picket line during a strike. Violence during labour disputes seems to have diminished over time, with a sharp decrease since 1995.[28] However, violence remains a real possibility during a labour dispute. Indeed, there is some speculation that picket line violence is "legitimated" by labour legislation and/or court rulings that do not discipline the participants in violent confrontations.[29]

Prevalence by Source

Though researchers have tried to estimate the prevalence of workplace violence by source, the most common distinction is between violence perpetrated by coworkers (Type III) and violence perpetrated by members of the public (Types I and II). The results of these analyses uniformly suggest that workplace violence is overwhelmingly perpetrated by members of the public. Respondents to the Canadian Public Service Employment Survey reported that violence was most likely from clients, residents, or other members of the public (approximately 71% of those reporting workplace violence) rather than from coworkers (approximately 34% of those reporting workplace violence).[30]

Analyses of American prevalence data suggest that an individual is four times more likely to be assaulted by a member of the public than by a coworker.[31] Results by source from the Nova Scotia Stress Survey[32] are shown in Figure 8.1. All four forms of physical violence were more likely to be experienced at the hands of members of the public.

RISK FACTORS FOR WORKPLACE AGGRESSION

Most workplace homicides in the United States are perpetrated by members of the public during the commission of a robbery or similar crime.[33] Employees in the retail (e.g., convenience stores), service (e.g., restaurants), security (protective agencies), and transportation (e.g., taxi) sectors are at highest risk.[34]

Robbery is the primary risk factor for occupational homicide. It is not, however, the primary risk factor for nonfatal assaults—providing service, care, advice, or education can place employees at increased risk for assault, especially if clients, customers, inmates, or patients are experiencing frustration, insecurity, or stress.[35] Industries reporting high rates of nonfatal assaults include health care, education, social services, and law enforcement.[36]

FIGURE 8.1

Prevalence of Workplace Violence by Source of Perpetrator

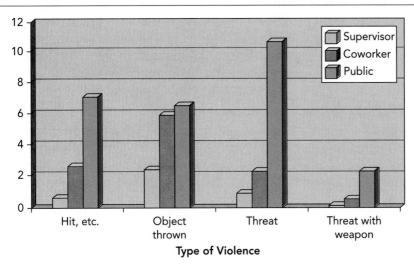

Source: L. Francis and E.K. Kelloway, "The Nova Scotia Workplace Stress Survey," Saint Mary's University, Halifax, 2007.

Occupational Risk Factors

Occupational analysis gives some insight into the risk factors for workplace violence. A more productive approach, though, might be to identify the specific tasks that increase the risk for workplace violence and aggression. Since violence and aggression tend to be perpetrated by members of the public, the first overall risk factor is working with the general public. There is a host of more specific risk factors[37] that can be subsumed under the acronym SAV-T[38] (i.e., Scheduling, Authority, Valuables, Taking Care of Others).

Scheduling

Individuals who work alone or at night and on weekends are at increased risk for violence. Taxi drivers, for example, often work at night and almost always work alone. They have long been identified as among those at greatest risk for workplace violence.

Authority

Individuals who have authority over others, who are in a position to deny services or requests, who supervise or discipline others, or who make decisions that influence others' lives are at increased risk for workplace violence. A social worker who decides whether a client gets benefits, an Emergency Room nurse who controls access to treatment, and wait staff at a bar who have to "cut off" a patron who has had too much to drink, are all at increased risk because of their authority.

Valuables

Individuals who work around valuable products or objects are at increased risk of violence largely because the risk of criminal activity is greater. Valuables include objects as diverse as prescription medications, cigarettes, alcohol, weapons, and, of course, money.

Taking Care of Others

Providing physical or emotional care for others, especially if such care is outside a traditional workplace (e.g., home-based health care), puts individuals at increased risk for workplace violence and aggression. For example, nurses who provide both physical and emotional care are at very high risk of violence.

Imminent Risk

It is useful to understand which tasks increase the risk of workplace aggression; even so, there are limits to this analytical approach. For example, a nurse who provides care for patients is at increased risk, *but* (a) most of the time these risks do not translate into workplace violence, and (b) the nurse cannot stop providing care in order to manage the risk. In occupations that are inherently risky (e.g., working in psychiatric or correctional facilities), the focus has turned to the prediction of "imminent risk."[39]

The assessment of **imminent risk** is conceptually grounded in the **assault cycle**,[40] (Figure 8.2) a model that identifies the escalation of violence from aggression to physical attack. Models based on the assault cycle typically point

imminent risk
the short-term risk of violence occurring in the current situation

assault cycle
a model suggesting that violence occurs only after a period of escalation

FIGURE 8.2

The Assault Cycle

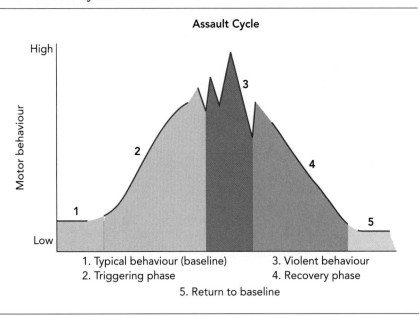

Assault Cycle

1. Typical behaviour (baseline)
2. Triggering phase
3. Violent behaviour
4. Recovery phase
5. Return to baseline

Source: Harold Hall, Pacific Institute for the Study of Conflict and Aggression, 2011.

to the escalation of violence interactions from a triggering event through an escalation phase to a crisis or assault. The assault cycle tells us (a) that aggression can escalate into violence, and (b) that violence does not "come out of nowhere"—rather, there are clear signs that individuals are increasingly likely to become violent. By recognizing these signs, employees may be alerted to the increased risk. Kelloway[41] proposed the SAV-T acronym (Swearing, Agitation, Volume, Threat) as a way of recognizing these signs. During the escalation phase of the assault cycle, individuals are more likely to use profane or obscene language, to show physical signs of agitation (e.g., getting red in the face, fidgeting or pacing, clenching fists, unable to keep still), and to begin shouting or talking loudly. Employees are advised to recognize these signs and to respond by establishing clear boundaries (e.g., pointing out that profane language or shouting is unacceptable, asking individuals to calm themselves), engaging in defusing, and alerting supervisors or coworkers to the situation. The more critical behaviours (swearing, agitation, shouting) present, the more employees should be concerned about the potential for violence.

Almost all acts of violence are preceded by a direct threat, and the articulation of that threat calls for the immediate cessation of the interaction. Employees should immediately escape from the situation and/or alert security personnel where appropriate. Employees should not try to defuse or reason with an individual who has uttered a threat—at this point, the time for managing the interaction has passed and employees should take immediate action to protect themselves. Though many threats may be uttered in the "heat

OH&S Notebook 8.2

MANAGING IMMINENT RISK

During the escalation phase of a conflict, individuals typically engage in swearing, are agitated, and increase the volume of their voice. As these behaviours occur, employees can respond with

- Empathic listening
  Avoid being judgmental
  Give your undivided attention
  Focus on feelings
  Use silence
  Use restatement
- Setting limits
  Explain which behaviour is inappropriate
  Explain why the behaviour is inappropriate
  Give reasonable choices and consequences
  Allow time to choose
  Enforce consequences

- Defusing
  Get them to say "yes"
  Remain calm
  Help them save face
  Use humour
  Use distraction/make requests
  Provide a nonviolent and productive course of action
  Go from "light" to "heavy" interventions

If the situation continues to escalate even when these responses have been tried, a supervisor and/or security personnel should be summoned. If the individual utters a threat or if at any time the employee feels threatened, the interaction should be brought to an immediate end.

of the moment" and not be serious, every threat should be interpreted as the onset of a violent interaction.

PREVENTION

Type I Violence

Because most workplace homicides occur during the commission of a robbery, actions aimed at preventing robberies will likely reduce the number of workplace homicides.[42] Robbery reduction strategies typically focus on increasing the risks, reducing the rewards, and increasing the effort associated with robbery.[43] Because risk factors for robbery differ among workplaces, no single strategy is appropriate for all organizations and prevention strategies must be customized to worksites. That being said, three principles—increasing visibility, reducing rewards, and hardening targets—underlie most robbery reduction strategies.[44]

Increasing Visibility

Increasing visibility is thought to increase the perceived risks for potential criminals, thereby deterring crime. For example, for taxi drivers, means of increasing visibility include external emergency lights; global positioning systems (GPSs) that allow the location of a driver in distress to be pinpointed; and in-car surveillance cameras that make it possible to identify perpetrators. Data from Australia and Canada confirm the effectiveness of surveillance cameras in taxis as a means of reducing assaults on taxi drivers. Crimes against taxi drivers have been reduced by more than 50% since the implementation of a bylaw in Toronto, Ontario, requiring taxi owners to install either security cameras or GPSs in their cars.[45]

In retail establishments, increasing visibility has meant increasing the chances of someone witnessing a crime. Most crimes occur late at night when there are few potential witnesses. Keeping windows clear of signs (e.g., advertisements) to allow passersby to see inside, and locating the cash register in a location that can be seen from the outside (e.g., in the centre of the store) are means of increasing visibility. Closed circuit televisions and video cameras may also deter criminal behaviour by increasing would-be robbers' perceptions of risk.[46] Clerk behaviour can also communicate visibility. Common recommendations are that clerks make eye contact with customers and greet them as they enter the store, thereby making would-be robbers feel conspicuous.[47]

A recommendation that remains contentious is that all retail outlets be required to employ two clerks during evening and night shifts to reduce the incidence of robberies. Industry associations and individual store owners resist this suggestion, pointing out (a) that there is limited empirical evidence supporting the utility of the two-clerk provision, (b) that hiring two clerks is expensive, and (c) that employing more than one clerk increases the number of workers exposed to robbery-related violence.[48] A more effective recommendation may be to ensure that commercial establishments have implemented work-alone procedures designed to ensure the safety of employees. For example, under regulations being implemented in British Columbia, late-night retail establishments are required to (a) have two employees working in the store at night, *or* (b) have the employee separated from the public by a locked barrier or door.

Target Hardening

Target hardening strategies focus on physical designs that make it difficult to assault employees. For example, protective screens have been found to reduce the number of assaults experienced by taxi drivers. Opinions on screens remain mixed, however.[49] Many taxi drivers and customers do not like them because they can restrict air circulation, leave little leg room, and limit communication between drivers and passengers.

In retail environments, strategies that make flight difficult may deter robbers.[50] Potential strategies to make retail stores less attractive targets include blocking off laneways and using speed bumps in parking lots. Revolving doors and longer rather than shorter distances between the cash register and the exit may also help deter crime.

Besides preventing robberies, some target hardening strategies may reduce the likelihood that employees will be hurt during the commission of a robbery. Installing high and wide counters, with raised floors on the employee side, to prevent robbers from jumping over counters to assault employees, is an effective means of protecting workers. So is installing a bullet-resistant barrier.

Employee training is another form of target hardening. Such training typically focuses on general safety precautions and on behaviour during a robbery or threatened assault. Having instructions on how to behave may give employees a sense of control of the situation and lessen the possibility that they will be injured. Employee training should stress cooperation with robbers, since there is ample evidence that employees who do cooperate sustain fewer injuries.[51] Workers should also be told not to make any sudden moves during a robbery, to keep their hands in plain sight at all times, and to inform the robbers of what they are doing when they are doing it. Staff should also be told to activate the silent alarm only when it is safe to do so. Employees should also be aware that it is not constructive to confront shoplifters.

Type II Violence

Service providers—health care workers, teachers, social service workers, prison guards, and police officers—are among the most common victims of nonfatal workplace violence. In the United States in 2000, 48% of all nonfatal assaults occurred in the health care and social service industries.[52]

There are three general approaches to preventing or dealing with Type II violence: environmental, organizational and administrative, and behavioural. Several factors increase risk for care or service providers. For example, staff may be at risk when they attempt to set limits on behaviour (e.g., tobacco use), especially if the employee's actions are perceived as unfair or unreasonable. Violence can also occur when a client is involuntarily admitted to the hospital, or confined. Long waits for service may result in frustration and increase the propensity for patients and visitors to become aggressive.

Environmental Strategies

Security devices that may reduce employee risk include metal detectors, surveillance cameras, and bullet-resistant glass surrounding reception areas and nursing stations. Other suggestions include effective lighting both inside and outside hospitals, and curved mirrors at hallway intersections. The presence of security personnel may be effective at preventing assaults. Card-controlled entrances and security checks for identification can be used to limit public access to restricted areas.[53]

Given long waiting times, hospitals should provide patients and their families with comfortable waiting rooms designed to minimize stress (e.g., soothing colours on walls; toys for children to play with; reading materials). Waiting areas and patient care rooms should be designed with safety in mind: furniture should be lightweight, have few sharp edges, and be laid out to ensure that staff can not be trapped in rooms. Rooms and waiting areas should be sparsely decorated (e.g., few pictures on the walls or vases on the tables) to limit the number of possible weapons that can be used against staff. Patient care rooms should have two exits and be equipped with phones and panic buttons.[54]

Organizational/Administrative Strategies

Organizations should establish policies and practices to prevent aggression. A written policy should outline what constitutes unacceptable behaviour in the workplace, and patients, visitors, and employees should be aware of the document. Policies that encourage the reporting of violence are also necessary, and management should stress to employees the importance of reporting acts of aggression. Management should take all reports of aggression seriously and ensure that employees are aware of the organization's commitment to safety. It is not uncommon for employees to express concerns about reporting incidents of violence, because they fear their employers will assume that they provoked the incident. Organizations also need to have detailed plans for dealing with violent

OH&S Notebook 8.3

BEST PRACTICES IN MANAGING WORKPLACE VIOLENCE

As a result of both legislative changes and concern for employee well-being, many Canadian organizations have implemented some form of policy for dealing with workplace violence and aggression. Organizations are required to comply with legislative requirements. Beyond that, an effective approach to dealing with workplace violence and aggression would include the following:

- A **Policy Statement** that clearly identifies violent and aggressive behaviour as unacceptable in the workplace. The statement should be clearly posted in the workplace and should apply both to employees and to members of the public.
- A **Risk Assessment** that considers the organization's history of violence and aggression, the nature of tasks performed in the workplace, and any special circumstances that may temporarily or permanently change these risks.

- **Risk Mitigation** strategies specifically designed to reduce or mitigate the risks identified in the risk assessment.
- **Training for Both Employees and Managers** in recognizing and managing risks and in applying the policy.
- An **Emergency Response Plan** that deals with violent incidents in progress and also their aftermath. The plan should include provisions for escape/evacuation, for calling security/police forces, for treating physical injuries, and so on.
- **Follow-Up Procedures** to ensure that victims receive appropriate physical and psychological treatment, that risks are reassessed following an incident, that all incidents are documented and reported to appropriate authorities, and that all aspects of the workplace violence management plan are current and effective.

attacks when they occur and should develop procedures to ensure the sharing of information about violent or potentially violent clients (see **OH&S Notebook 8.3**).

When service providers, such as health care workers, work inside patients' homes, access to protections of the sort available to employees who work in traditional organizational settings is delayed or limited at best.[55] Therefore organizations need to establish policies and procedures for home health care providers. For example, home care workers could be required to keep a designated colleague informed of their whereabouts throughout their work shift. Workers should be accompanied to a patient's home by a coworker or a police escort if their personal safety may be threatened. In a similar vein, employees should be prohibited from working alone in emergency areas or walk-in clinics, especially during late night and early morning shifts. Policies and practices should be in place to restrict public (e.g., patients, visitors) movement in hospitals.[56]

Behavioural/Interpersonal Strategies

Besides providing staff with necessary knowledge and skills, training may give employees the confidence to deal with potentially dangerous situations. One study found that hospital workers who received training targeting workplace violence reported higher levels of perceived control compared to workers who did not receive training. In that study, perceptions of control were positively correlated with employee emotional well-being and negatively associated with employee fear of future violence.[57]

Staff should be taught customer service skills, how to resolve conflicts, how to recognize escalating agitation, and how to manage and respond to aggressive behaviour.[58] Since violence is related to wait times, staff should provide patients and their families with sufficient information when there are going to be long delays for service (e.g., explain how long the delay will be and why there is a long delay). Employees who have direct patient contact (e.g., security guards, nurses, orderlies) should also be trained on how and when to physically restrain patients.

Type III Violence

Though violence and aggression committed by coworkers is uncommon compared to that committed by organizational outsiders, it *can* happen, so a comprehensive workplace violence program needs to address the potential for coworker aggression and violence. Reviews[59] generally point to the fact that coworkers do not *act* aggressively; rather, they *react* to certain situations in an aggressive way. Triggers for workplace aggression include unfair treatment, abusive supervision, role stress, and job insecurity. Efforts at prevention focus on eliminating or managing these triggering events. This can be accomplished by eliminating triggering events, by creating a transparent and nonthreatening environment, and by preventing aggressive acts.[60]

A focus on improving interpersonal relationships in the workplace often eliminates some of the triggers to workplace violence and aggression. For example, organizational justice (see Chapter 7) should be explicitly considered when decisions are being made; this can greatly reduce employees' perceptions of unfair treatment. Leadership training activities may result in a decrease in abusive supervision and an increase in organizational justice. Similarly, explicit attempts to reduce role (and other) stress may help control those events with the potential to trigger workplace violence and aggression.

Creating an open and transparent environment includes developing specific procedures for employees to resolve conflicts and discuss grievances. Training in conflict resolution and the creation of confidential and effective complaint procedures ensures that inappropriate behaviour is identified and dealt with before it leads to workplace violence and aggression.

Finally, an organizational policy that clearly labels violent and aggressive acts as inappropriate is key to violence prevention programs. Indeed, some organizations have gone beyond these prohibitions to implement "respectful workplace" policies. Such policies go beyond simply banning violent or aggressive behaviour—they establish the expectation that all organizational members are to be treated with respect and courtesy at all times. In their broadest sense, respectful workplace policies try to limit or exclude rude behaviours that can trigger more serious aggression or violence.

Type IV Violence

Intimate partner violence almost always is perpetrated by someone (e.g., a spouse) who is not a member of the organization. Some forms of this behaviour are not overtly violent (e.g., waiting outside the workplace) and fall into a "grey area" where it is unclear whether the authorities should be called. Preventing or managing intimate partner violence requires a comprehensive and open approach.

First, managers and organizational decision makers need to be educated about the forms that intimate partner violence can take. Second, organizations should be aware of the resources that are available (e.g., through the Employee Assistance Program) to employees experiencing intimate partner violence. Third, organizational policies should allow for temporary accommodation during times of crisis. For example, some organizations have provided additional security or escorts to/from the parking lot for employees experiencing intimate partner violence (these often turn out to be services that other employees value as well). Others have allowed employees to work offsite or to take a period of leave until the situation is resolved. Perhaps most important, organizations need to recognize the potential for intimate partner violence to be expressed in the workplace and to take action to protect employees.

Organizational Policies and Programs

There are a variety of guidelines and tools available to help organizations manage the risks of workplace violence. One of the most comprehensive that is tailored to a Canadian environment is the *Developing Workplace Violence and Harassment Policies and Programs* manual available through the Occupational Health and Safety Council of Ontario (OHSCO; available at http://www.labour.gov.on.ca/english/hs/pdf/wvps_guide.pdf). As with the management of other forms of occupational hazards, the management of workplace violence follows the sequence of recognition, assessment and control of hazards.

Recognition

In the OHSCO framework, organizations should conduct regular assessments of the risks for workplace violence. These assessments should occur at three levels: assessment of the general physical environment, identification of risk factors, and assessments for specific risks. OHSCO provides tools for each of these assessments.

In assessing the general physical environment, one would want to consider aspects of the environment that might affect the risks for workplace violence. OHSCO suggests specifically reviewing the outside and parking lot, entry systems to the buildings, reception and waiting areas, public counters, elevators and washrooms, the location of cash and other valuables, and many other areas—in short the idea is to do a comprehensive security review of the physical environment.

Beyond the general environment, OHSCO recommends identifying the specific risk factors applicable to the organization or occupation. Specific assessments are provided for (a) direct contact with clients, (b) handling cash, (c) working with unstable or volatile clients, (d) working alone, (e) working in a community-based setting, (f) the mobile workforce, (g) working in high crime areas, (h) securing or protecting valuable goods, and (i) transporting people or goods.   While not all of these risk factors are applicable in each organization, the idea is that you would identify the ones applicable to your context and conduct the appropriate assessment.

Assessment

Based on these risk assessments, one can rank the level of risk applicable to specific jobs. Although this a subjective process, OHSCO suggests that high risk would be when one or more risk factors regularly (i.e., as part of the normal routine) places an employee at severe risk. Severe in this context means that there is a potential for fatal or critical injury. Moderate risk is when the risk factors occasionally (i.e., a recognized part of work that occurs on an infrequent basis) place employees at moderately severe (i.e., potential for lost time injury or injury requiring medical aid). Finally, low risk occurs when risk factors occur rarely and the risk is minimal (potential for first aid). Based on this analysis, organizations can choose to prioritize the most severe risk factors to develop solutions. Of course, a comprehensive approach to dealing with workplace violence would deal with all of the risk factors, not just the high priority ones.

Control

OHSCO also provides guidelines and audit tools for the creation and monitoring of workplace violence programs and policies. Although this detail will not be repeated here, in general the formulation of a comprehensive workplace violence program would include:

1. Creation of workplace violence policy that conforms to the relevant legislation (not that these requirements vary by jurisdiction)
2. Creation of a violence prevention program that includes

    a. Mechanisms for assessment
    b. Procedures for obtaining immediate assistance for victims
    c. Procedures for reporting actual and potential violence
    d. Procedures for investigating such reports
    e. Procedures for dealing with incidents, complaints, and threats

3. Creation of an emergency response plan
4. Including workplace violence in work refusal policies
5. Procedures for recognizing and dealing with incidents of domestic violence that may occur in the workplace
6. Training procedures to ensure that all employees are aware of the policies, procedures, and risks related to workplace violence

After establishing the program, employers also need to institute ongoing monitoring and compliance to ensure that the program is operating as it should. The entire program should be reviewed on a regular basis to ensure that policies and procedures are current.

SEXUAL HARASSMENT

Several studies have identified sexual harassment as a workplace stressor of increasing importance. Most forms of sexual harassment involve unwelcome, intrusive sexual attention and verbal comments. A recent estimate, based on numerous research studies, is that 58% of women have experienced behaviours that are potentially harassing and that 24% of American women agree that they have experienced sexual harassment in the workplace.[61] Data collected in Canada suggest similar exposure rates: 56% of working women who responded to a large survey on sexual harassment indicated that they had experienced sexually harassing behaviour in the previous year.[62] The most commonly reported behaviours in the Canadian survey were insulting jokes and staring. Physically violent actions such as rape do occur in the workplace, but only rarely.[63]

Section 247.1 of the Canada Labour Code prohibits sexual harassment and defines sexual harassment as any conduct, comment, gesture, or contact of a sexual nature

(a) that is likely to cause offence or humiliation to any employee; or

(b) that might, on reasonable grounds, be perceived by the employee as placing a condition of a sexual nature on employment or on any opportunity for training or promotion.[64]

Sexual harassment, then, is any intentional, persistent (i.e., repeated), and unwelcome sexual conduct or remark that occurs despite resistance from the victim (see **OH&S Today 8.1**). Note that in cases of severe misconduct (e.g., sexual assault), a single incident meets the definition and constitutes sexual harassment. The act or conduct must be deliberate and intentional. In other words, the offender must be aware that the behaviour is offensive. To alleviate the potential loophole of offenders claiming during a sexual harassment hearing that they were unaware their behaviour was offensive, tribunals use what they call the "reasonable person" test. Basically, this test determines whether a reasonable person would be aware that the behaviour is offensive.

The Labour Code definition seems to point to two different types of sexual harassment:[65]

1. *Sexual coercion* (or "quid pro quo" harassment) is an attempt to extort sexual cooperation. This extortion can take the form of subtle or explicit job-related threats (e.g., job loss, loss of promotion), or the promise of job-related rewards (e.g., promotions, raises). The Ontario Human Rights Code

OH&S Today 8.1

Prototypical Cases of Sexual Harassment: Not What You Expect?

You'd likely agree that prototypical stories of workplace sexual harassment call to mind an attractive young woman being pursued by an older man in a relative position of power. In the face of persistent, unwanted advances from the man, the woman ultimately makes an accusation of sexual harassment.

Recent research conducted by Dr. Jennifer Berdahl from the Rotman School of Business at the University of Toronto has found that such assumptions about sexual harassment are in fact wrong. The most frequent targets of sexual harassment are not meek, young, attractive women dealing with sexually coercive actions from men. Dr. Berdahl found that outspoken women who do not comply with gender stereotypes and who work in male-dominated jobs are the most frequent victims of sexual harassment. In essence, these women are more likely to experience hostile work environments in which they are the recipients of rude remarks, are made fun of, and face obstacles to their career progression.

Dr. Berdahl suggests that her research has implications for organizational interventions relating to sexual harassment. Policies that rely on such things as dress codes and rules about dating do not address the realities of sexual harassment in today's workplaces. She suggests that workplaces should instead focus on achieving a work environment where skilled men and women are viewed as equals.

Sources: J. Berdahl, "The Evolution of Harassment in the Workplace," *Rotman Magazine* (Winter 2007) Pg. 48–51; C. Goar, "True Face of Sexual Harassment," *Toronto Star*, Jan. 24, 2007. Found at: http://www.thestar.com/article/174064 (Accessed Feb. 10, 2007).

specifically prohibits job-related rewards in exchange for sexual favours by a person in authority, as well as job-related punishment for not providing those favours.

2. *Hostile environment* is sexual harassment that occurs without any coercion or extortion; it does, however, create a hostile, intimidating, and discriminating environment. Sexually harassing behaviours of this nature can range from insulting, misplaced comments, through pervasive sex-related verbal or physical conduct, to life threats or physical attacks. According to most research on sexual harassment, "hostile environment" sexual harassment is the most prevalent type.

Sexual Harassment as a Health and Safety Issue

Sexual harassment becomes a health and safety issue for two primary reasons. First, studies show that being the victim of sexual harassment is associated with several organizational strains, including increased job dissatisfaction, decreased loyalty to the organization, and increased intent to leave the organization. Some women who have reported being a victim of sexual harassment to their organization have experienced the formal process as unjust—indeed, some report that they have been fired after making a sexual harassment claim. There are also personal consequences of sexual harassment, with victims significantly more likely to experience dissatisfaction with life in general and to experience psychosomatic disorders (e.g., respiratory, stomach, and sleep problems; headaches and migraines; weight loss or gain). Thus, exposure to sexual harassment is associated with impaired employee well-being and becomes a health and safety issue.

Second, the courts have increasingly viewed workplace sexual harassment as the responsibility of the employer. Before 1981, sexual harassment on the job was not prohibited by any human rights statute in Canada. A groundbreaking step occurred in 1989, when the Supreme Court of Canada concluded that sexual harassment is a form of sex discrimination and is therefore prohibited in employment. Sex discrimination had been prohibited by human rights statutes for some time in Canada, but sexual harassment was not initially recognized in those statutes.[66] This was an important progression from simply acknowledging that sexual harassment was a serious problem to taking steps to prevent it.

Another major change occurred when the Supreme Court of Canada stated that an employer is liable for the discriminatory acts of its employees. This decision had great implications, for employers now had a legal motive to prohibit sexual harassment in their companies. Legal liability translates into a strong financial incentive to prevent illegal acts from occurring. For example, in one of the largest lawsuits of its type, Mitsubishi Motors in the United States paid $34 million to settle allegations of sexual harassment filed by the Equal Employment Opportunities Commission on behalf of 300 female employees. Essentially, the allegations were that the women had been subjected to sexual comments, innuendo, and unwanted groping, and that plant managers knew of these problems but did nothing to correct them.

The ruling that employers are liable for discriminatory acts, including harassment, has a number of implications for organizations:[67]

1. Employers are responsible for the due care and protection of their employees' human rights in the workplace.
2. Employers are liable for the discriminatory conduct of and sexual harassment by their agents and supervisory personnel.
3. Sexual harassment by a supervisor is automatically attributed to the employer when such harassment results in a tangible job-related disadvantage to the employee.
4. Explicit company policy forbidding sexual harassment and the presence of procedures for reporting misconduct may or may not be sufficient to offset liability.
5. Employers will be pressured to take a more active role in maintaining a harassment-free work environment.
6. Employers will feel greater discomfort with intimate relationships that develop between supervisors and their subordinates because of the legal implications, and this may motivate employers to discourage such office relationships.
7. Employers' intentions to have effective sexual harassment policies are insufficient. To avoid liability, the policies must be functional and must work as well in practice as they do in theory.*

Clearly, the Supreme Court has made employers responsible for *any* sexual harassment in the organization. As a result, employers are more likely to launch interventions to eliminate or at least reduce the occurrence of sexual harassment in their workplaces.

SUMMARY

The scope of OH&S practice continues to expand and now incorporates the need for organizations to deal with issues of workplace violence, aggression, and harassment. Understanding these terms and how they occur in the workplace was a primary goal of this chapter. Addressing these issues requires understanding the situational *and* imminent risk factors in the workplace and devising ways of addressing these risks.

Key Terms

assault cycle 202	sexual coercion 197
aggression 196	sexual harassment 197
bullying 197	Type I violence 199
emotional abuse 197	Type II violence 199
gender harassment 197	Type III violence 200
harassment 197	Type IV violence 200
imminent risk 202	unwanted sexual attention 197
incivility 197	violence 196
mobbing 197	

*A.P. Aggarwal, *Sexual Harassment in the Workplace* (Toronto: Butterworths Canada) 1992.

Weblinks

Canadian Centre for Occupational Health and Safety
http://www.ccohs.ca/products/courses/violence_awareness

Ontario Ministry of Labour, "Workplace Violence and Workplace Harassment"
http://www.labour.gov.on.ca/english/hs/pubs/workplaceviolence.php

Workplace Bullying Institute
http://www.workplacebullying.org

Required Professional Capabilities (RPCs)

The following RPCs, listed by their CCHRA number, are relevant to the material covered in this chapter. All RPCs can be found at http://www.chrp.ca/rpc/body-of-knowledge.

RPC:170 Develops, implements, and ensures the application of policies, regulations, and standards relating to occupational health and safety.*

RPC:171 Ensures compliance with legislated reporting requirements.

RPC:172 Ensures due diligence and liability requirements are met.

RPC:173 Ensures that policies for required medical testing fall within the limits of statute & contract.

RPC:174 Develops and implements policies on the workplace environment.

RPC:175 Ensures adequate accommodation, modified work and graduated return to work programs are in place.

RPC:176 Ensures that modifications to the work environment are consistent with worker limitations.

RPC:177 Develops or provides for wellness and employee assistance programs to support organizational effectiveness.

RPC:178 Provides information to employees and managers on available programs.

RPC:179 Ensures that mechanisms are in place for responding to crises in the workplace, including critical incident stress management.*

RPC:180 Establishes a joint Health & Safety Committee as required by law.

RPC:181 Responds to any refusals to perform work believed to be unsafe.

RPC:182 Responds to serious injury or fatality in the workplace.

RPC:183 Analyzes risks to employee health & safety and develops preventive programs.*

RPC:184 Establishes an investigation process for incidents and accidents in the workplace.

RPC:185 Ensures that security programs and policies minimize risks while considering the obligation of the employer and the rights of employees, union, and third parties.

*Canadian Council of Human Resources Associations, Human Resources Professionals in Canada: Revised Body of Knowledge and Required Professional Capabilities (RPCs ®), 2007.

RPC:186 Establishes and implements strategies to minimize workers' compensation costs.

RPC:187 Prepares Organizational Health & Safety files for investigation and/or for litigation.

Discussion Questions

1. How far can legislation go? Workplace violence legislation can focus very narrowly on physical assaults or more broadly on behaviours that make employees feel uncomfortable. Can we realistically enforce legislation that prohibits rudeness or teasing? At what point can legislation be effective?
2. Many of the behaviours reviewed in this chapter are illegal (e.g., sexual assault, physical assault). Do we need special workplace legislation to address these issues? What is the value of specific legislation around issues of violence and harassment?
3. Some legislation defines harassment or aggression, in part, by focusing on either the intent of the perpetrator (e.g., behaviour that is intended to annoy or embarrass) or the reaction of the victim (e.g., behaviour that is unwelcome). Does this pose a problem for regulation? How can we know the intent of the perpetrator or the anticipated reaction of the victim?
4. Managers often do not know when to get involved in workplace conflicts. How does one distinguish between a situation that constitutes "violence" or "aggression" and one that is just "normal" workplace violence? When does a manager need to intervene in a situation between coworkers or between a coworker and a customer?
5. We've all heard the expression "the customer is always right." Does this have any implications for the management of workplace violence and aggression?

Using the Internet

1. Choose an occupation you know well and conduct a violence risk assessment for that job (*Hint:* Many provinces make sample risk assessments available online.)
2. Many people who experience workplace bullying simply don't know what to do about it. Using resources found on the Web, prepare a short (one-page) guide for victims of workplace bullying.
3. Research an organization in which employees may experience work-related threats or assaults. Conduct a risk assessment to determine whether there is a risk of violence. Describe the measures that a human resources manager can take to develop and implement a workplace violence prevention program. Numerous websites will be helpful in this exercise. The Workers' Compensation Board of British Columbia's publication "Take Care: How to Develop and Implement a Workplace Violence Prevention Program" may be particularly useful. It can be downloaded from http://www.worksafebc.com/publications/health_and_safety/by_topic/assets/pdf/take_care.pdf. (Based on an exercise by Catherine Fitzgerald.)

Exercises

1. Many students work, or have worked in retail environments. Find at least 10 students with this experience. Using the definitions in this chapter, ask them if they have ever experienced an act of workplace violence (i.e., a physical assault or threat of physical assault). What were the circumstances? What led up to the confrontation? Who was the perpetrator?
2. Over a period of time, collect articles from your local paper that report on incidents of workplace violence. What types of violence are reported? Does the reporting reflect research data suggesting that workplace violence is almost always perpetrated by people who are not members of the organization? Why might there be a difference between media reports and research findings?

Case 1 HARASSMENT OR NOT?

Vic Waggar is stumped. After 10 years working in various human resources positions he thought he had dealt with every possible problem, but this is a new one. One of the employees who works on the loading dock has come to Vic's office complaining that his coworkers are "picking on him." "They never tell me when they are going to lunch," says the employee, "and they make jokes at my expense." At a recent meeting, the coworkers "just ignored my suggestions and talked right over me. I can't take it any more and want to transfer to a different department." Vic knows there are laws and organizational policies that deal with violence and harassment, but he isn't sure whether either is going on in this case. "I know it sounds like something from grade school," says Vic, "but I really need the advice of an OH&S expert." What do you tell Vic Waggar? What, if anything, does he need to do about the situation described?

Case 2 HEALTH CARE RISKS

Jennifer Wong is a home care worker with Westwood Incorporated, a company that provides home-based medical services for a variety of clients. As part of her job, Jennifer goes to the homes of clients to provide basic medical and personal care. She has come to you as the Human Resources Manager for Westwood to complain that she just doesn't feel safe doing her job anymore. "You wouldn't believe the things I've seen," says Jennifer. "Between the client who exposes himself to me and the clients who swear at me, I just don't feel safe anymore." "My supervisor and coworkers say that this is all just part of the job—but that doesn't seem right to me. Isn't there something we can do to address these issues and make the job safer? I asked for someone to come with me on my calls so there would be some safety in numbers but my supervisor said that would be too expensive."

What do you tell Jennifer? What should be the response of the HR department? What are the legal requirements in your jurisdiction, and what steps do you need to take to address the issues that Jennifer raises?

NOTES

1. United States Postal Service Commission on a Safe and Secure Workplace, *Report* (New York: National Center on Addiction and Substance Abuse at Columbia University, 2000).
2. S. deLesulec, "Criminal Victimization in the Workplace 2004," Cat. no. 85F0033MIE–013, Canadian Centre for Justice Statistics, Ottawa, 2007.
3. A.C.H. Schat and E.K. Kelloway, "Workplace Aggression," in J. Barling, E.K. Kelloway, and M.R. Frone, eds., *Handbook of Work Stress* (Thousand Oaks: Sage, 2005), 189–218.
4. Ibid.
5. J. Barling, K. Dupre, and E.K. Kelloway, "Predicting Workplace Violence and Aggression," *Annual Review of Psychology* 60 (2009): 671–92.
6. L. Keashly, "Interpersonal and Systemic Aspects of Emotional Abuse at Work: The Target's Perspective," *Violence and Victims* 16 (2001): 233–68.
7. H. Hoel, C. Rayner, and C.L. Cooper, "Workplace Bullying," in C.L. Cooper and I.T. Robertson, eds., *International Review of Industrial and Organizational Psychology,* vol. 14 (Chichester: Wiley, 1999), 195–230.
8. L.M. Andersson and C.M. Pearson, "Tit-for-Tat? The Spiralling Effect of Incivility in the Workplace," *Academy of Management Review* 24 (1999): 452–71.
9. Ibid.
10. J. Barling, G. Rogers, and E.K. Kelloway, "Behind Closed Doors: In-Home Workers' Experience of Sexual Harassment and Workplace Violence," *Journal of Occupational Health Psychology* 6 (2001): 255–69.
11. M. Fendrich, P. Woodward, and J.A. Richman, "The Structure of Harassment and Abuse in the Workplace: A Factorial Comparison of Two Measures," *Violence and Victims* 17 (2002): 491–505.
12. M.J. Gelfand, L.F. Fitzgerald, and F. Drasgow, "The Structure of Sexual Harassment: A Confirmatory Analysis Across Cultures and Settings," *Journal of Vocational Behaviour* 47 (1995): 164–77.
13. A.C.H. Schat, M.R. Frone, and E.K. Kelloway, "Prevalence of Workplace Aggression in the U.S. Workforce: Findings from a National Study," in E.K. Kelloway, J. Barling, and J.J. Hurrell, eds., *Handbook of Workplace Violence* (Thousand Oaks: Sage, 2006), 47–89.
14. Ibid.
15. Ibid.
16. Ibid.
17. L. Francis and E.K. Kelloway, "The Nova Scotia Workplace Stress Survey," Saint Mary's University, Halifax, 2007.
18. Ibid.
19. deLesulec, *Criminal Victimization in the Workplace 2004.*
20. A. Pizzino, "Dealing with Violence in the Workplace: The Experience of Canada Unions," in M. Gill, B. Fisher, and V. Bowie, eds., *Violence at Work: Causes, Patterns, and Prevention* (Cullompton: Willan, 2002), 165–79.
21. State of California, "Cal/OSHA Guidelines for Workplace Security" (1995), http://www.dir.ca.gov/dosh/dosh_publications/worksecurity.html, November 7, 2007.
22. P. Tjaden and N. Thoennes, *Extent, Nature, and Consequences of Intimate Partner Violence* (Washington: U.S. Department of Justice, National Institute of Justice, 2000).
23. Ibid.
24. Ibid.
25. L. Francis, J.E. Cameron, and E.K. Kelloway, "Crossing the Line: Violence on the Picket Line," in E.K. Kelloway, J. Barling, and J.J. Hurrell, eds., *Handbook of Workplace Violence* (Thousand Oaks: Sage, 2006).

26. A.J. Thieblot and T.R. Haggard, "Union Violence: The Record and the Response by the Courts, Legislatures, and the NLRB," Industrial Research Unit, Wharton School, University of Pennsylvania, Philadelphia, 1983.

27. A.J. Thieblot, T.R. Haggard, and H.R. Northrup, "Union Violence: The Record and the Response by the Courts, Legislatures, and the NLRB," rev. ed., John M. Olin Institute of Employment Practice and Policy, George Mason University, Fairfax, 1999.

28. Francis et al., "Crossing the Line."

29. Ibid.

30. M. Teed, E.K. Kelloway, and J. Barling, "Incidents and Predictors of Workplace Violence and Aggression," paper presented at the biannual conference of the European Academy for Occupational Health Psychology, Valencia, 2008.

31. Schat et al., "Prevalence of Workplace Aggression in the U.S. Workforce."

32. Francis and Kelloway, *The Nova Scotia Workplace Stress Survey*.

33. Bureau of Labour Statistics, "National Census of Fatal Occupational Injuries 1997," USDL 98-336, Department of Labour, Washington, 1998.

34. C. Casteel, and C. Peek-Asa, "Effectiveness of Crime Prevention Through Environmental Design (CPTED) in Reducing Robberies," *American Journal of Preventive Medicine* 18 (2000): 99–115.

35. D.N. Castillo and E.L. Jenkins, "Industries and Occupations at High Risk for Work-Related Homicide," *Journal of Occupational Medicine* 36 (1994): 125–32.

36. C. Peek-Asa, C.W. Runyan, and C. Zwerling, "The Role of Surveillance and Evaluation Research in the Reduction of Violence Against Workers," *American Journal of Preventive Medicine* 20 (2001): 141–48.

37. M.M. LeBlanc and E.K. Kelloway, "Predictors and Outcomes of Workplace Violence," *Journal of Applied Psychology* 87 (2002): 444–53.

38. E.K. Kelloway, "Managing Workplace Violence: A Comprehensive Guide" (in progress).

39. R. Almvik, P. Woods, and K. Rasmussen, "Assessing Risk for Imminent Violence in the Elderly: The Broset Violence Checklist," *International Journal of Geriatric Psychology* 22 (2007): 862–67.

40. G.M. Breakwell, *Coping with Aggressive Behaviour: Personal and Professional Development* (Leceister: British Psychological Society, 1997).

41. Kelloway, "Managing Workplace Violence."

42. H.E. Amandus, D. Zahm, R. Friedmann, R.B. Ruback, C. Block, J. Weiss, D. Rogan, W. Holmes, T. Bynum, D. Hoffman, R. McManus, J. Malcan, C. Wellford, and D. Kessler, "Employee Injuries and Convenience Store Robberies in Selected Metropolitan Areas," *Journal of Occupational and Environmental Medicine* 38 (1996): 714–20.

43. Occupational Safety and Health Administration, "Recommendations for Workplace Violence Prevention Programs in Late-Night Retail Establishments" (1998), http://www.osha.gov/Publications/osha3153.pdf, March 5, 2004.

44. C. Mayhew, *Violence in the Workplace—Preventing Armed Robbery: A Practical Handbook*, Research and Public Policy series no. 33 (Canberra: Australian Institute of Criminology, 2000).

45. F. Calleja, "Cab Hold-Ups on Web" (2002), http://www.taxi-library.org/camera04.htm, May 29, 2010.

46. P.P. Purpura, *Retail Security and Shrinkage Protection* (Stoneham: Butterworth-Heinemann, 1993).

47. F.J. Desroches, *Force and Fear: Robbery in Canada* (Toronto: Nelson, 1995).

48. T. Gabor and A. Normandeau, "Preventing Armed Robbery Through Opportunity Reduction: A Critical Analysis," *Journal of Security Administration* 12 (1989): 3–18.

49. Idem, "Preventing Assaults on Taxi Drivers in Australia," *Trends and Issues in Crime and Criminal Justice* 179 (2000): 1–6.

50. M. Gill, *Commercial Robbery* (London: Blackstone, 2000).

51. K.A. Faulkner, D.P. Landsittel, and S.A. Hendricks, "Robbery Characteristics and Employee Injuries in Convenience Stores," *American Journal of Industrial Medicine* 40 (2000): 703–09.

52. Occupational Safety and Health Administration, "Guidelines for Preventing Workplace Violence for Health Care and Social Service Workers," http://www.osha.gov/Publications/osha3148.pdf, March 5, 2004.

53. National Institute for Occupational Safety and Health, *Violence: Occupational Hazards in Hospitals*, DHHS Publication no. 2002–101, http://www.cdc.gov/niosh/2002-101, March 5, 2004.

54. P.F. Levin, J. Hewitt, and T.S. Misner, "Insights of Nurses About Assault in Hospital-Based Emergency Departments," *Image—The Journal of Nursing Scholarship* 30 (1998): 249–54.

55. Barling et al., "Behind Closed Doors."

56. NIOSH, *Violence: Occupational Hazards in Hospitals*.

57. A. Schat and E.K. Kelloway, "Reducing the Adverse Consequences of Workplace Aggression and Violence: The Buffering Effects of Organizational Support," *Journal of Occupational Health Psychology* 8 (2003): 110–22.

58. J.C. DelBel, "De-escalating Workplace Aggression," *Nursing Management* 34 (2003): 30–34.

59. S.M. Herschovis and J. Barling, "Preventing Insider-Initiated Violence," in E.K. Kelloway, J. Barling, and J.J. Hurrell, Jr., eds., *Handbook of Workplace Violence* (Thousand Oaks: Sage, 2006).

60. K. Painter, "'It's Part of the Job': Violence at Work," *Employee Relations* 9 (1987): 30–40.

61. R. Ilies, N. Hauserman, S. Schwaohau, and J. Stibal, "Reported Incidence Rates of Work-Related Sexual Harassment in the United States: Using Meta-Analysis to Explain Reported Rate Disparities," *Personnel Psychology* 56 (2003): 607–31.

62. D. Crocker and V. Kalemba, "The Incidence and Impact of Women's Experiences of Sexual Harassment in Canadian Workplaces," *Canadian Review of Sociology and Anthropology* 46 (1999): 541–58.

63. L.F. Fitzgerald, "Sexual Harassment: Violence Against Women in the Workplace," *American Psychologist* 48 (1993): 1070–76.

64. A.P. Aggarwal, *Sexual Harassment in the Workplace* (Toronto: Butterworths Canada, 1992).

65. Ibid.; M.S. Hesson-McInnis and L.F. Fitzgerald, "Sexual Harassment: A Preliminary Test of an Integrative Model," *Journal of Applied Social Psychology* 27 (1997): 877–901.

66. Aggarwal, *Sexual Harassment in the Workplace*.

67. Ibid.

Interventions

Training

CHAPTER LEARNING OBJECTIVES

After reading this chapter, you should be able to:

- discuss the importance of occupational health and safety training
- identify the components of a training program
- explain the role of a needs analysis when designing a training program
- discuss issues that arise in training design and delivery
- describe various options for the delivery of health and safety training programs
- discuss the role of evaluation in any training program
- evaluate the measurement concerns surrounding organizational measures of occupational safety training effectiveness
- describe some common health and safety training initiatives including safety orientation, first-aid training, and WHMIS

THE CASE OF THE ENGLISHTOWN FERRY

On February 8, 2003, Donald LeBlanc died on the job. The 38-year-old drowned when the tractor he was operating to clear snow and ice from the ramp to the small cable ferry in Englishtown, Nova Scotia, slid into St. Ann's Bay. His body was not discovered until August 2003.

The employees at the Englishtown Ferry operation were responsible for clearing the dock and had received training on driving the tractor. However, the trainer had not provided any training on operating the tractor on the ramp itself or under poor weather conditions, having determined that such conditions were too dangerous for individuals who were learning this skill. Mr. LeBlanc had struggled in the training, failing his first test and barely passing on a second attempt.

Following the incident, investigations determined that chains that should have been on the tractor's tires were in fact sitting on the dock.

Also, there was no life preserver or survival gear in the tractor. The Nova Scotia provincial government ultimately launched a public inquiry into this incident, which started in October 2005. Provincial Court Judge A. Peter Ross filed the fatality investigation report in April 2007. The report outlined 27 recommendations, which focused on such things as improved emergency procedures, improved performance evaluation, and extensive improvements to the training provided to employees, including the addition of hazard assessment and emergency response to the training domain.

The circumstances surrounding this tragic incident illustrate the importance of OH&S training in organizations. Failing to provide training or offering inadequate training content and evaluation can place workers in hazardous situations, with catastrophic results.

Sources: CBC News, "Dying for a Job: The Englishtown Ferry Accident," April 25, 2006. Found at: http://www.cbc.ca/news/background/workplace-safety/ferry-accident.html, (Accessed Jan. 4, 2013); A.P. Ross, "In the Matter of a Fatality Inquiry Regarding the Death of Captain Donald LeBlanc, Englishtown, Nova Scotia," Report, Pursuant to the Fatality Investigations Act, (Halifax: April 5, 2007).

The tragedy at the Englishtown Ferry illustrates the disastrous events that can unfold when appropriate health and safety training is not delivered in a workplace. Workplace dangers are a reality for *all* workers. Workers of all ages, experience levels, and job types can and do experience safety incidents at work. A recent review of the occupational health and safety training research literature demonstrates that training in OH&S has a positive effect on worker practices and behaviour.[1] However, many workers in Canada have not received adequate safety training. A recent study of nearly 60,000 Canadian workers reported that only 12% of women and 16% of men had received workplace safety training in the previous year.[2] Though employees who were new to their jobs were more likely to receive training, the proportion who did remains disappointingly low, at only 20%.[3] Even though young workers and those in physically demanding jobs are at higher risk for injury, neither group was more likely to receive training.

In this chapter we explore the topic of health and safety training. Recent Canadian statistics on access to all types of employer-supported training suggest that vulnerable workers—who include the less educated, low-wage earners, and non-union members—face greater barriers to training access in the workplace than other groups. This discrepancy is particularly notable if the worker who falls into one of these groups is a woman.[4] Though these trends are not specific to health and safety training, they do raise a possible red flag about access to safety training for vulnerable workers.

In this chapter we apply a basic model of training in organizations to the specific concern of training workers in occupational health and safety. In particular, we consider the processes of designing, implementing, and evaluating health and safety training programs in organizations.

THE ROLE OF OCCUPATIONAL HEALTH AND SAFETY TRAINING

All workers have several rights pertaining to their health and safety while at work. Three basic rights apply to all Canadian employees:

1. *The right to know.* Workers have a right to be informed about dangerous or unsafe materials and machinery in the workplace.
2. *The right to participate.* Workers have a right to take part actively in the protection of their own health and safety. This participation generally involves reporting unsafe work practices and conditions.
3. *The right to refuse unsafe work.* Workers have a right to withhold their services if they are asked to perform a task that they deem to be unsafe or are asked to use equipment that is not in good repair.

OH&S Today (9.1

Passport to Safety

Passport to Safety is a Canadian not-for-profit enterprise that describes itself as a "catalyst for change." Its vision is "a country where workplace safety is assured and Canadians return home healthy at the end of each day." Passport of Safety focuses much of its activity on young workers, whom they believe have the ability to "influence the evolution of safe workplace cultures." Many youth who are injured at work report they were not aware of the life-threatening hazards in the workplace or basic safety rules that would have helped them avoid injury. Passport to Safety strives to increase risk awareness. The program is a creative one that focuses on a series of tests that young workers, or others soon to enter the workforce, can take to challenge their understanding of workplace safety. Following successful completion of a test, members receive transcripts to attach to their résumés.

Passport to Safety also partners with Workers' Compensation Boards, teachers, and employers to promote workplace safety. The website contains numerous educational resources, such as videos. In provinces such as Ontario, New Brunswick, Newfoundland and Labrador, and Nova Scotia, some students and teachers can access the passport testing program for free. For employers, the passport program is designed to supplement rather than replace job- and organization-specific training. For example, supervisors can use a provided assessment test to gauge employees' knowledge.

Source: Passport to Safety. Found at: http://passporttosafety.com (Accessed Jan. 14, 2013).

It is easy to see the vital role of training for the fulfillment of these basic rights. First, employees—especially new employees—must be advised of these rights. The communication of these basic rights can take place in a safety orientation when a person starts a new job.

Once employees are aware of their basic rights regarding health and safety at work, safety-related training is needed to help individuals ensure that these rights are being upheld. For instance, with respect to the right to know, employees must receive training on their workplace's potential dangers. Similarly, regarding the right to refuse unsafe work, effective health and safety training will help individuals judge accurately which tasks are indeed unsafe. As such, health and safety training plays a vital role in the protection of an employee's basic rights, and its provision is mandated in OH&S acts across the country. The importance of health and safety training is recognized internationally as well. For example, in the United States, training is prominently placed as one of five essential elements of OH&S programs, along with employer commitment, hazard surveillance, hazard control and prevention, and program evaluation.[5]

Of course, it is also important to ask the question of when organizations should not use training as an OH&S intervention. As you'll see in the following sections, training interventions are helpful when they address knowledge or skills 'needs' or gaps. If a skill or knowledge gap is not identified, training is likely not the appropriate intervention.

That said, there are also cases where even though employees may not have a certain skill set, training would still not be the best answer. Throughout this book, we have stressed that *engineering* interventions, which focus on changing the physical environment to reduce hazard exposure and risk should be the first line of intervention and defence when it comes to worker safety. Generally speaking, if an engineering-based solution is available, it should be used before administrative or behavioural interventions. For instance, one would not recommend training workers to use a machine with a broken guard. Similarly, there are safety-related tasks for which highly specialized skills and equipment are required. In these cases, one would not train in-house workers to perform these jobs. For instance, carpenters who work for a contractor specializing in home renovations would likely not be trained for a task like asbestos abatement. In that case, an external company, specializing in hazardous substance removal would be contracted to perform that kind of work.

Given the importance of effectively communicating health and safety information in today's workplaces, the question of how to develop and implement effective health and safety training programs is vital. In the remainder of this chapter, we examine the process of implementing a health and safety training program.

instructional systems design (ISD) model of training

a general model of the training process that incorporates needs analysis, training design and delivery, and training evaluation and that notes the interdependencies among the three major components of the training process

HEALTH AND SAFETY TRAINING PROGRAMS

As our starting point we take the **instructional systems design (ISD) model of training**[6] and apply it specifically to occupational health and safety. The ISD model of training has three parts: (1) needs analysis, (2) training design and delivery, and (3) training evaluation. The model is depicted in Figure 9.1. Each stage of this model is described and discussed in the sections that follow.

Needs Analysis

The training and development process begins when a need or concern arises. With respect to health and safety, that concern might be the occurrence of a number of safety incidents or injuries in the workplace. Following such incidents, company officials may opt to develop a training program to improve workplace safety. Also, a large number of workplace safety incidents in a particular company may draw attention from various OH&S governing bodies. These groups may determine that safety training is required and mandate training within a particular organization. Alternatively, the move toward safety training could be prompted by new legislation requiring that a particular type of health and safety training be offered to workers in a particular industry. Whatever the case, a health and safety training process begins with a **needs analysis**.

Needs analysis is the recommended starting point in many models of organizational training because it helps determine the nature of the problems at hand. Needs analysis is a way to determine whether there is a gap between current and desired reality.[7] Needs analysis can also be used to identify potential obstacles to the effectiveness of a training program so that they can be dealt with early in the training and development process. Such an analysis ideally includes assessing the organization, the task or job at hand, and the employee(s) in question. The inclusion of all three levels in the initial analysis will help answer questions about what groundwork must be done before training begins, what

needs analysis
the initial stage of the training development process, intended to identify employee and organizational deficiencies that can be addressed with training and to recognize potential obstacles to the success of a training program

OH&S Today 9.2

Safety Training Receiving Increased Attention in Incident Prevention and Investigation

If you read recent articles about organizations aiming to reduce their OH&S incident rates or increase worker safety, or reports from OH&S investigations, you'll see an increased focus on safety training. For example, the Workplace Safety and Prevention Services (WSPS) in Ontario offers a series of industry-specific safety opportunities. Some of the training sessions are classroom-based, others involve self-guided study, and still others are offered online. Topics covered include ladder safety, incident investigation, ergonomic assessments, and confined-space safety.

With respect to incident investigations, the Iron Ore Company of Canada pled guilty on three charges relating to a March 2010 incident when two employees fell off a scaffold at a mine in Labrador. One of the employees, Eldon Perry, died and the other, Joshua Hayse, was injured. The charges pertained to failing to make workers aware of workplace hazards. In December 2012, the company was fined in excess of $350,000. A lack of training was cited in the Transportation Safety Board's investigation of a March 2011 helicopter crash in Quebec. The wrong fuel was used in an unplanned refueling stop. The lone employee working at the time had only been in the position for four months and his training had not included information on different fuel requirements.

Sources: Workplace Safety and Prevention Services. Found at: http://www.healthandsafetyontario.ca/WSPS/Home.aspx, (Accessed Jan. 16, 2013); *OHS Insider*, "Largest Fine in Province's History Imposed on Mine for Worker's Death." Found at: http://ohsinsider.com/search-by-index/accidentsincidents/largest-fine-in-provinces-history-imposed-on-mine-for-workers-death (Accessed Jan. 16, 2013); *OHS Canada*, "Iron Ore Company pleads guilty in mine scaffold collapse." Found at: http://www.ohscanada.com/news/iron-ore-company-pleads-guilty-in-mine-scaffold-collapse/1001916775/ (Accessed Jan. 16, 2013); *OHS Canada*, "First fatal accidents of the year." Found at: http://www.ohscanada.com/news/first-fatal-accidents-of-year/1000373196/ (Accessed Jan. 16, 2013); *OHS Canada*, "Lack of training cited in fuel mix-up that brought down helicopter." Found at: http://www.ohscanada.com/news/lack-of-training-cited-in-fuel-mix-up-that-brought-down-helicopter/1001937587/ (Accessed Jan. 16, 2013.)

FIGURE 9.1

The Instructional Systems Design Model of Training

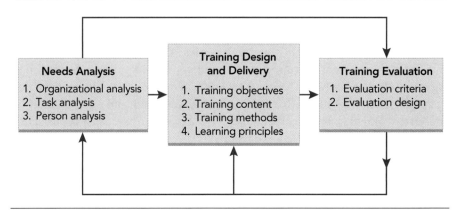

Source: From SAKS/HACCOUN. *Managing Performance Through Training and Development.*
© 2004 Nelson Education Ltd. Reproduced by permission. www.cengage.com/permissions.

the content of the training program should be, who should receive training, and how the program should be delivered. Let's consider the pertinent issues when assessing the needs of the organization, the task or job, and the employee.

Organizational Analysis

organizational analysis
an analysis of the entire organization designed to examine its resources, strategy, and environment in order to assess the organization's support for training

A needs analysis at the organizational level should be the starting point in any training intervention.[8] An **organizational analysis** should involve a study of the whole organization, considering such areas as the resources and strategy of the organization and the industry in which it operates. Organizational analysis can identify the health and safety areas that need knowledge and skills improvement and that may be targets for a training program. This analysis should also highlight any constraints that may limit the success of a training program before training is designed and delivered.

Successful training initiatives tend to be in line with the organization's overall strategy. Similarly, it is important to consider the resources the organization can dedicate to the training process, as the extent of the available resources can influence the nature of the training program. For example, if the organization has training facilities on-site, this may influence decisions about how the training is delivered. The budget available for training should also be considered, as financial constraints will influence decisions later in the training development process. Similarly, it is important to consider the industry and environmental factors that may affect the training program. For instance, if the organization is unionized, one must consider the role of the union in training program development.

Another major goal of the organizational analysis should be to establish organizational support for a training intervention. This can be done by developing a relationship with management. Support from the organization is vital to the success of any training program. An organization that truly values training will provide the necessary resources to make the program a success and get behind the training effort by encouraging employees to take part actively.

With respect to health and safety training, it is important that the individual conducting the organizational needs analysis determine not only the degree of organizational support for training and learning, but also the support for health and safety initiatives in general. The effectiveness of any health and safety efforts "will be a function of the organization's overall commitment to providing a safe work environment and the employee's perception and recognition of that commitment."[9] Certainly, studies show that organizational support plays a vital role in the success of health and safety training initiatives. In one examination of the effectiveness of hazard awareness training among individuals in construction trades, improvements in attitudes toward fall safety were associated with the organization's support for safety.[10] Investigations of the impact of management attitudes toward health and safety training generally illustrate the importance of managerial support for sustaining the positive outcomes associated with such training.

Examination of the organization's **safety climate** is one way to determine the extent of organizational support for a health and safety training program. That term relates to perceptions about safety-related policies, procedures, and practices that are shared by *all* stakeholders in the organization.[11] An organization that has explicitly enacted policies on safety, that encourages safety-related training, and that promotes safety may be said to have a strong safety climate. A company that has a strong safety climate is likely to enable and support initiatives relating to health and safety training. These organizations will invest the necessary money and time to make the training program a success, and employees are likely to be responsive to the effort.

> **safety climate**
> employees' shared perceptions of the importance of safety in the workplace

In this regard, consider an organization that does not place a high value on safety—that is, a company that does not have a strong safety climate. This type of operation may be hesitant to provide the support necessary to make health and safety training a successful endeavour. Similarly, employees of such an organization may be suspicious of the training program, wondering why the company suddenly seems concerned about their health and well-being. If analysis reveals that the organization's safety climate is not currently conducive to safety training, the next logical step may be to emphasize to organizational management the need for increased organizational attention to safety as well as the need to communicate to employees the intended move toward a health and safety focus. These efforts, if launched early in training development, will lay important groundwork for a health and safety training effort and ultimately contribute to the success of the training program.

One situation that may arise when conducting an organizational analysis regarding health and safety training needs involves an organization that does not generally focus on employee health and safety and that does not have a strong safety climate, but that is required by law to offer safety training. There is no easy answer for how to deal with such a situation. However, we suggest that individuals involved in a training needs analysis with such an organization emphasize the importance of a supportive organizational environment for successful training. Managers in this type of organization may respond to a bottom-line approach—an argument based on the return on investment of training dollars. If management can be convinced that its support will result in increased training effectiveness and tangible long-term benefits, they will be more likely to provide a supportive training environment.

Job/Task Analysis

job/task analysis

a component of the training needs analysis process during which the jobs and specific job tasks that are in need of training are identified and studied

The second step is to conduct a **job/task analysis**. The starting point here involves identifying the jobs to be targeted for training. Some forms of training, such as a basic safety orientation or a seminar on the role of health and safety committees, will apply to employees in many positions within the organization. Other types of training will be far more specific in terms of jobs being targeted. For example, training on the safe operation of a particular piece of machinery will apply only to those individuals whose jobs bring them into contact with that machinery.

Once the target job has been identified, one should obtain a detailed job description that outlines the tasks, duties, and responsibilities of individuals who hold that position. By working with a group of job incumbents and subject matter experts, one can rate the required tasks for their importance and frequency in the job. With respect to health and safety–related training, incumbents and subject matter experts should be surveyed on the health and safety risks involved in each task and their perceived competence to perform those tasks in a safe manner. The person developing the training program may want to observe several people performing the tasks in question to identify potential health and safety concerns that were not mentioned by the subject matter experts. The information can then be analyzed and interpreted.

The evaluation of the job in question and the inclusion of people with experience performing the job can greatly inform the training program that will ultimately be offered. The task analysis can help determine the exact nature of the problem to be solved. To consider a health and safety example, the survey component of the task analysis might reveal that though employees are vigilant about wearing their protective equipment, they tend to use it incorrectly. In that case, the training program should focus more on the proper use of the equipment rather than on convincing people to wear it. This point might have been missed were it not for the completion of a task analysis.

Person Analysis

person analysis

a component of the training needs analysis process during which individual employees' behaviour is studied to identify gaps in performance

Finally, the assessment needs to investigate the training needs of individual employees. Individual employees' behaviour is considered to see whether performance meets desired standards. The ultimate goal in the **person analysis** is to determine who needs training. Such a decision can be made by comparing a person's current performance with a desired standard or level of performance. Which individuals will be included at this stage of the analysis will be largely determined by the organization's needs. In some cases the consultant or training director may be asked to assess those individuals who have demonstrated poor or unsafe performance in the past. In other organizations, employees included in the person analysis may be chosen randomly.

The next step in the individual assessment is to identify the method of assessment. Common needs assessment techniques include observation, work samples, and tests.[12] From here, the relationship between the desired standard for performance and the actual performance can be measured and the potential reason for performance gaps can be determined. The data gathered during this stage of the process inform the next steps in developing a training program.

In some cases the person analysis may reveal that training will not be able to address the barriers to effective performance. For instance, one might discover that certain safety concerns are the result of worn equipment that is continually in a state of ill repair. In this case, the maintenance or replacement of equipment, rather than a training program, would be the next logical step. In other situations, training will be a viable or preferred option for addressing the problems uncovered in the needs analysis.

The type of training offered will depend on the nature of the problem. For example, if the person analysis reveals that safety concerns stem from the fact that individuals are not well versed in the operation of dangerous equipment, the training program to follow should focus on delivering knowledge about the proper operation of the machinery. Again, consider a case where the person analysis reveals that though individuals are aware of safety regulations in the operation of equipment and are capable of complying with those protocols, they choose to ignore them. In this situation, the training would best focus on safety-related attitudes in the workplace.

Training Design and Delivery

Following the needs analysis, an informed decision can be made about the potential effectiveness of training as an option for addressing health and safety concerns. If training has a role to play in the solution to a health and safety problem, several decisions must now be made. These decisions involve translating what was learned from the needs assessment into the actual training initiative. Some of the pertinent decisions include the following:

1. What are the objectives for training?
2. Will the training program be designed or purchased?
3. What is the appropriate content for the training?
4. Who will receive the training?
5. Who will deliver the training?
6. Where will the training take place?

Let's consider some of these questions as they apply to OH&S training. The first pressing question involves the objectives for training. In other words, what do you hope the trainees will take away from the program? Generally speaking, the **training objectives** will touch on the knowledge, skills, and behavioural changes that will be acquired through training. Objectives serve a number of important functions; for example, they set the groundwork for the needed training content, and they provide a starting point for tools for evaluating the effectiveness of the training program.

A second question is whether to purchase an existing training package or design an original program. In many cases, the purchase of an existing prepackaged program is more economical and fully meets the organization's needs. When it comes to health and safety, many training programs are readily available for purchase. For instance, St. John Ambulance "sells" first aid and CPR programs, both generic and custom. For an organization that wants to institute a first aid training program for individuals in particular high-risk jobs, it would make financial sense to choose a proven, prepackaged program from a reputable provider.

training objectives statements regarding the knowledge, skills, and behavioural changes that trainees should acquire in the training program

OH&S Notebook 9.1

TRAINING DELIVERY METHODS

Another decision in the design of a training program is what training delivery methods will be used. There are numerous training methods to choose from. Of course, training can be delivered on-the-job or off-the-job. In either case, the training may or may not involve technology. The training method one chooses might depend on where the training is being offered, the content of the training, or the people being trained. Here are some training delivery options to consider.

On-the-Job Training

Job Instruction: A structured approach to training job skills that involves a trainer developing a training plan and demonstrating tasks to a trainee, which the trainee then performs with the trainer's guidance and receives feedback on.

Performance Aid: Devices such as visual aids are used to help trainees perform tasks. For example, a sign with visual cues that help employees follow the lockout procedure on a piece of equipment.

Job Rotation: Trainees learn various tasks by completing different jobs/tasks within the organization.

Apprenticeships: Trainees receive on-the-job experience combined with classroom instruction.

Coaching: An experienced employee works closely with a new employee to help develop skills and provide feedback.

Mentoring: A senior employee is personally invested in helping a junior employee's development.

Off-the-Job Training

Lecture: The trainer presents the content orally to the trainees.

Discussion: The trainer and trainees have a verbal exchange about the material.

Audio-Visual Methods: Media are used to illustrate points and ideas.

Case Incident or Study: Trainees analyze a real life problem or situation.

Behaviour Modelling: Trainees attempt to imitate the actions of a model who is performing a task.

Role Play: Trainees practise skills within the training environment.

Games: Competition-based activities are employed to help develop skills.

Simulations: Trainees engage in physical or social events that are designed to recreate real situations. These may involve technology in terms of simulating devices or equipment.

Technology-Based Training

Web-based: Trainees engage in training materials that are provided via the Internet. One example would be a webinar in which a presentation is delivered via the Web.

Video/Television: Trainees watch video-based or televised material relevant to the topic on which they are being trained.

CD/DVD: Training materials are provided to trainees via a CD or DVD.

Teleconference: Trainees at various locations take part in audio or audio-visual exchange of information with a trainer using technology such as conference calls or Skype.

Source: From SAKS/HACCOUN. *Managing Performance Through Training and Development.* © 2004 Nelson Education Ltd.

In other cases the organization will decide to design a custom health and safety training program, either in-house or with the help of a consultant. When the program's content is highly specific to the organization, custom program design may be necessary. For instance, a company wanting to offer a health and safety orientation for new hires would need to incorporate information that is unique to itself; such a program would be difficult to purchase in a prepackaged form. Also, training in the safe use of particular equipment or in the performance of particular tasks may require a training program that is not readily available for purchase, and as such a customized program may be the only option.

With respect to training content, it is important for the program to match the needs identified in the needs analysis and that it allow trainees to achieve the training objectives. Even when the training program is purchased, there is likely some flexibility in the material that will be presented. One way to ensure that the training content is appropriate is to consult subject matter experts in the area in question. For instance, in a training program on the safe handling of hazardous materials, individuals with expertise in industrial hygiene may be consulted and asked for their input on the needed components of the training program.

Who will receive the training is another important question during this phase of curriculum development. In some cases the answer will be obvious. If the law requires that all operators of a particular type of machinery have training in the operation of that machinery, the job of selecting who receives training is as simple as identifying the operators. Similarly, if the training program is a health and safety orientation for all new employees, each employee will complete the program on joining the organization. In other cases, decisions about who receives training will not be as obvious. For instance, provincial and territorial legislation requires that organizations have a certain number of trained first aid providers on-site. Only a small number of employees will need to complete this training. The decision of who enters the program is one that will have to be dealt with case by case.

A related issue is *how many* people will be trained at the same time. The accumulated research on training in general and on health and safety training in particular reveals that smaller groups make for more effective learning.[13] Also, individuals in the same training group should have similar jobs characterized by common risk exposure.[14] This contributes to the success of health and safety training initiatives.

Yet another issue is who will *deliver* the training. An effective trainer is vital to a successful training program. The trainer should be knowledgeable about the material as well as an effective communicator. For instance, a recent study showed the effectiveness of occupational therapists providing workplace training on musculoskeletal disorders.[15] In some cases the trainer will require certification in a particular area—for instance, the person who delivers first aid training will need certification as an instructor.

Another effective approach is a **train the trainer** program. In these initiatives, a subject matter expert with the appropriate content skills is provided with coaching in areas such as program delivery and communication. For example, an individual who is a member of an organization's health and safety committee may be trained to deliver the health and safety orientation for new employees. Worker-trainers may also contribute to the evaluation of training effectiveness, further increasing a sense of worker empowerment and ownership over the training process.[16]

train the trainer
programs designed to offer subject matter experts in various content areas skills in program delivery and communication

OH&S Notebook 9.2

HOW TO SELECT A GOOD TRAINING PROVIDER

Once a decision has been made that health and safety training is an appropriate intervention, organizations are in a position to decide who will deliver that training program. If skilled trainers are not available in-house, the organization will turn to an external, professional trainer. What steps can the organization take to ensure that it hires a good training provider? The following are some qualities that organizations will want to ensure their training provider possesses:

- Knowledge of training models
- Experience in training
- OH&S expertise and experience
- Industry experience
- Willingness to customize the training to meet organizational needs
- Good references

Source: B. Broadbent, "Training Providers: How to Pick a Winner," *OHS Canada*. Found at: http://www.ohscanada.com/training/howtopickawinner.aspx (Accessed Jan. 5, 2013).

The research literature has examined the effectiveness of subject matter experts who have undergone train the trainer programs. Generally, it appears that trainees respond well to subject matter experts as OH&S trainers and that such an approach can result in improved safety performance in the workplace.[17]

The final question we consider here is *where* the training takes place. This has long been a question of on-the-job versus off-the-job training. On-the-job training takes place while individuals are at work performing their regular job tasks. In other words, the training is incorporated into the performance of the task. For example, on-the-job training in the safe operation of a particular tool may have subject matter experts demonstrate the safe use of the tool while a new hire observes the process. The new hire can then use the tool under the guidance of the subject matter expert.

Off-the-job training takes place away from the area where the work is conducted. It may be in a room on-site or in a different facility. The nature of the room will depend on the nature of the training. Some forms of training require little more than a boardroom and PowerPoint slides. Other forms may require simulators or particular equipment. **OH&S Notebook 9.1** reviews the training delivery method options for on- and off-the-job training.

More recently, a third dimension has been added to the question of where health and safety training will be conducted. Some health and safety training programs are now being offered on the Web. For example, courses in the **Workplace Hazardous Materials Information System (WHMIS)**, a legislated program in the safe handling of hazardous materials, are now being offered online. For more information on this program, see **OH&S Today 9.3**. Web-based training in programs such as WHMIS may prove useful to a company that often has new hires who are computer savvy. However, it may not be as appealing or effective when the individuals who require training do not have access to or a high degree of comfort with computers and the Internet. That said, some studies

WHMIS

Workplace Hazardous Materials Information System; a legislated training program in the handling of potentially hazardous chemicals in the workplace that ensures Canadian workers recognize hazardous materials and are knowledgeable in emergency procedures following a chemical spill

have found that computer-based instruction can be effective for some types of health and safety training. For example, in a study of agricultural workers with low levels of education and little computer experience, a computer-delivered training program on ladder safety saw an increase in safe ladder practices up to two months post training.[18] An online computer-based simulation emphasizing situation awareness proved effective among licensed pilots.[19] Ultimately, the program delivery choice will depend on the unique needs of the organization and employees.

Regardless of the location, research on the effectiveness of various health and safety training initiatives emphasizes the importance of active approaches to learning.[20] As you might conclude from a review of the training delivery options outlined in **OH&S Notebook 9.1**, training delivery methods vary substantially in their potential to engage trainees. For instance, a lecture is a passive and typically less engaging training method. On the other hand, training methods that use simulations of real events are an active and typically more engaging approach to training. Training efforts predominantly relying on less engaging methods such as posters or videos can result in initial improvements in safety behaviour, but the results may be short-lived. More active forms of training—such as hands-on or interactive—seem to have a stronger and more durable effect on behaviour. Training efforts that involve behavioural modelling (such as simulations) and multiway feedback are recognized as particularly engaging for trainees.[21] Dialogue and storytelling have also been identified as training tools that engage trainees' attention and encourage them to think about the material being presented.[22]

A recent meta-analytic review of the safety training literature noted that highly engaging training methods are particularly important when the risk associated with the hazards in question is high.[23] When hazard severity was high, highly engaging training methods were associated with better safety knowledge and safety performance than were less engaging methods. The training method did not appear to influence safety knowledge or performance gained in training when hazard severity was low. The authors of the study proposed that this effect is due to 'the dread factor.' When OH&S training involves a high-risk hazard, for instance use of explosives, active and engaging training helps trainees to realize the true degree of severity and experience dread for the outcomes associated with exposure. This dread is a motivating factor to prompt the trainees to learn how to avoid the risks associated with the hazard in question.

Even when safety training programs have demonstrated a positive impact on safety-related actions in the workplace, continual upgrading of skills may be important if employees are to maintain the knowledge and skills they gained in training. Consider the case of employees who are designated first aid providers in their workplaces. These individuals may well experience long periods during which they are not called on to use their first aid skills. Yet in the event of an emergency, it is imperative that they correctly recall what they learned in training. Periodic refresher courses that reinforce what employees learned in their initial training program will go a long way toward ensuring that first aid providers correctly and quickly recall their treatment skills when called on to do so.[24] In fact, retraining, upgrading, and refresher courses are valuable in *all* areas of safety training. The more often employees are reminded of safety-related issues in the workplace, the more likely they are to properly enact safety behaviour.

OH&S Notebook 9.3

LEARNING THEORY AND TRAINING DELIVERY

Training in occupational health and safety can be associated with positive safety outcomes, such as safer worker behaviour and a reduction in safety incidents. However, training experts sometimes point out that potential contributions from general theories of learning are not reflected in health and safety training programs. Thus, the training programs may not be maximally effective.[a]

The ultimate goal of OH&S training programs is that the knowledge and skills gained in the training environment be transferred effectively to the workplace. Principles determined from extensive psychological research on learning can help create such a training environment. Three major approaches to the study of learning are the behaviourist perspective, social learning, and experiential learning. How might these learning approaches influence the design of health and safety training programs?

Behaviourist Perspective

The behaviourist approach characterizes learning in terms of observable stimuli and responses, without reference to any activity that occurs inside the individual.[b] Behaviourists state that learning results when a person associates particular behaviours with certain immediate consequences or rewards. Certainly, this notion applies to the training context; the experience gained during training should influence later job performance. Thus, according to behaviourists, training can increase the performance of desired behaviours by following those actions with rewards. The behaviourist approach suggests that health and safety training should target specific actions.[c]

Several basic learning principles may be effective in helping increase the transfer of the knowledge,

skills, and abilities acquired during training to the jobsite.[d] These include using *identical elements*, such that the stimuli in the training environment are identical to those in the transfer environment. For instance, in a safety training program on the proper use of protective equipment, the very same brand and type of safety gear used at the jobsite should also be used in the training program. Furthermore, transfer of training may be improved when trainees are taught not only applicable skills, but also *general principles* that underlie the training content. For example, a training program on the safe operation of a piece of heavy equipment should also stress underlying principles regarding the widespread importance of safe behaviour in the workplace and the basic workings of the machinery itself. Also, multiple examples of a concept will provide the *stimulus variability* necessary to promote transfer of training to the worksite. For instance, in an emergency preparedness training program the trainers should provide examples from several types of emergency scenarios.

Social Learning

Social learning theory reflects a cognitive approach to learning. Its premise is that people learn by observing others. Observing others can help us learn various motor skills or styles of behaving. For instance, observing more experienced people can help a new employee learn how to use safety equipment at work. The people we observe during social learning are called *models*. The influential proponent of the social learning approach is Canadian Albert Bandura, who proposed that four mental processes facilitate social learning:[e]

---

training evaluation

a component of the ISD training model designed to assess the value added for individuals and organizations following the implementation of a training program

Training Evaluation

Evaluation efforts following training programs consider the extent to which the training program has added value to the organization and the individual employees. Information gathered during **training evaluation** can be useful for identifying strengths and weaknesses in the training program and thus guide

1. *Attention.* Learners must notice the behavioural models and find them interesting. For instance, new employees who are looking for models will likely look to experienced employees who attract their attention and seem willing to help.

2. *Memory.* Learners must remember what they have observed. New employees who are observing senior employees operate a particular piece of machinery must remember all the actions taken by the senior employees as they complete the task.

3. *Motor control.* Learners must use their observations to guide their own actions. For instance, if new employees are modelling a work task that involves heavy lifting, they must be capable of lifting that weight.

4. *Motivation.* The learner must have some reason to perform the modelled actions. For instance, OH&S trainees must be motivated to perform the job in a safe manner.

In the training environment, the trainer is the model, who must capture the attention of the trainee and appear interesting. This person should be perceived as an expert in the relevant field and be credible and appealing to the trainees. The information should be presented in such a manner that the trainees store it in memory and draw from this information to guide their future performance (i.e., when they are back on the job).

Experiential Learning

Experiential learning is a process aimed at developing knowledge and skills. Proponents of experiential learning contend that learning is maximized when knowledge is acquired via direct participation, when new insights are applied to realistic situations, and when trainees reflect on prior and new experiences.[f] This type of learning can be accomplished by numerous methods, including problem-based learning, role playing, and simulations. From a health and safety perspective, experiential learning approaches mean that trainees should engage in active learning environments that incorporate the training content into their experiences. Also, trainees should be encouraged to reflect on what they are learning and how it relates to their work setting.[9] For example, a stress management program that follows an experiential learning approach might explore how individuals currently manage stress, have them actively incorporate new coping techniques in role plays and their daily lives, and ask trainees to keep a diary in which they reflect on how the new techniques are working and help them manage their stress responses.

Sources: (a) M. Burke, D. Holman, and K. Birdi, "A Walk on the Safe Side: The Implications of Learning Theory for Developing Effective Safety and Health Training," *The International Review of Industrial and Organizational Psychology*, Vol. 21, Pg. 1–44, 2006; M. Colligan & A. Cohen, "The Role of Training in Promoting Workplace Safety and Health," in J. Barling and M. Frone, eds., *Handbook of Workplace Safety* (Washington: APA, 2004), Pg. 223–48; (b) M.S. Gazzaniga & T.F. Heatherton, *Psychological Science: Mind, Brain, and Behavior*, 2nd ed. (New York: Norton, 2006); (c) M. Burke, D. Holman, and K. Birdi, "A Walk on the Safe Side: The Implications of Learning Theory for Developing Effective Safety and Health Training," *The International Review of Industrial and Organizational Psychology*, Vol. 21, Pg. 1-44, 2006 (d) T. T. Baldwin, J.K. Ford, & B.D. Blume, "Transfer of Training 1988–2008: An Updated Review and Agenda for Future Research," *International Review of Industrial and Organizational Psychology*, Vol. 24, Pg. 41–70, 1990; (e) A. Bandura, *Social Functions of Thought and Action: A Social Cognitive Theory* (Englewood Cliffs: Prentice Hall) 1986; (f and g) M. Burke, D. Holman, and K. Birdi, "A Walk on the Safe Side: The Implications of Learning Theory for Developing Effective Safety and Health Training," *The International Review of Industrial and Organizational Psychology*, Vol. 21, Pg. 1-44, 2006.

further curriculum development. Evaluation results can also be used to estimate the economic value of a training program. In a safety training endeavour, an economic factor that can be measured is the number of safety incidents or injuries. A training program that reduces injury rates will save the company money in days lost and compensation claims.

OH&S Today   9.3

Online WHMIS Courses

A quick Internet search will reveal any number of providers offering online training programs in WHMIS. Most of these websites point to the speed, ease, and convenience of using Internet-based training for this often required health and safety training program. One such provider, WHMIS-in-Minutes, provides training programs in both English and French and promotes its online course as suitable for individuals who are interested in a refresher course and for those who are learning about hazardous materials for the first time. This program features a certificate of completion and does not require the organization to pay start-up fees. Rather, the fee is on a per user basis. WHMIS-in-Minutes has a number of well-known clients, including Tim Hortons, Dupont, and Shell. An administrative feature enables the system to track for organizations which of their employees have completed the training program. Another basis on which the online service is promoted is the possibility of customization. Additional questions, customized to the organization's needs, can be added to the standard WHMIS program.

Source: WHMIS-in-Minutes. Found at: http://www.whmis.net (Accessed Jan. 5, 2013).

What type of information should be considered when a health and safety training program is being evaluated? Kirkpatrick's hierarchical model—a frequently used training evaluation model—suggests that there are four important measures that provide insight into the effectiveness of a training program, as follow:[25]

1. Did the trainees have positive *reactions* to the training?
2. Did the trainees *learn* the material covered in the training?
3. Did the trainees apply what they learned in training and realize a change in their work *behaviour*?
4. Did the organization see positive *organizational results* following training?

According to Kirkpatrick, these four form a hierarchy, with succeeding levels providing increasingly important information regarding the value of the training program. Training programs in which trainees report positive reactions, learn the material, apply that learning to their workplace behaviour, and contribute to positive organizational outcomes (e.g., increased productivity, fewer lost-time injuries) are considered effective.

How might a training evaluator go about gathering information on these four levels of training outcomes? The HR manager or training consultant has several measurement options open to him or her. Individual reactions to the training program might be assessed using such tools as surveys, interviews, or focus groups. Questions should be designed to assess all aspects of the program—including overall reactions as well as attitudes toward particular aspects of the training schedule. For instance, a training evaluation questionnaire for a workplace safety orientation might ask trainees to share their perceptions of the presentation by the health and safety committee chairperson; to indicate whether they thought the safety walkabout—where the trainees tour various parts of the building to discuss the safety issues at each site—was informative;

to report their degree of satisfaction with the overall curriculum; and to rate the effectiveness of the orientation facilitator. Clearly, both affective reactions and utility-based reactions can be garnered at this stage of the evaluation. Affective reactions involve whether the trainees enjoyed the program; utility reactions incorporate the trainees' perceptions of the usefulness of the program.[26] Positive affective and utility reactions are important in training programs. If employees do not enjoy the training program or do not feel it is useful, they may be less likely to give it their full attention and will be less likely to take away the important messages delivered by the program. Some frameworks for training evaluation suggest that it is also important to assess the strength of the trainee's attitudes about training.[27] For instance, did the trainees have intense or extreme affective responses to a particular aspect of the training program?

Efforts to measure learning must assess trainees' mastery of the information presented. Evaluators may be interested in how well the trainees recall the information and in the extent to which they are able to incorporate the information into actions. For instance, in a health and safety training program designed to teach safe operating procedures for heavy machinery, the evaluator would be interested in the trainee's ability to recall the points on the safety inspection checklist for a particular piece of equipment. There are a number of ways to assess this knowledge. An evaluation could measure a trainee's ability to recognize the material covered in training using multiple-choice tests. The mastery of skills introduced in the training program could also be assessed using longer, written tests. To continue the example given above, a trainee might be asked to list all the steps included in the safety inspection for a particular piece of equipment. Obviously, a successful training program is one that results in considerable knowledge and skill acquisition on the part of trainees.

Recently there has been a shift in the types of cognitive outcomes that training evaluators hope to capture. The traditional focus on straight recall of verbal knowledge is increasingly shifting toward a focus on "procedural understanding" of the material presented, including questions about *why* things work in particular ways.[28] Keeping with our example of safe operating procedures for heavy machinery, procedural knowledge would involve *why* the safety practices are important and *why* they follow in a particular order.

Behavioural outcomes can be assessed *during* the training or *after* training back in the workplace. When task simulation is incorporated into training, evaluators can assess trainees' performance during the training program. Similarly, evaluators can assess trainees' motivation to incorporate new skills or knowledge by asking questions about their performance goals and their confidence in their ability.[29]

On-the-job behaviour can be assessed using self-report inventories in which trainees rate their own behaviour or by having supervisors complete a report on trainees' actions when performing the task in question. Similarly, the training evaluator may observe the employees' on-the-job performance. For example, following the training program on the safe operation of heavy machinery introduced above, a supervisor might observe an employee performing a safety inspection on the piece of equipment and rate his or her performance. The evaluator might then use objective indices of performance to assess behavioural change. For instance, after a training program on the importance and use of safety equipment such as earplugs for loud environments, a behavioural assessment might include observing employees at work to see whether they have a high rate of compliance in using their earplugs and other safety equipment.

Organizational results following training initiatives can also be assessed. Usually, the assessment of organizational outcomes involves analyzing organizational records. With respect to health and safety training initiatives, a number of organizational outcomes may be especially relevant:

1. *Incident, injury, and fatality rates.* Safety training programs designed to increase safe behaviour should contribute to reduced incident rates and, ultimately, reduced injury and death rates.
2. *Incidence of close calls.* **Close calls** or near misses occur when incidents or injuries are narrowly avoided. Effective safety training programs should reduce the number of near misses.
3. *Incidence of lost-time injuries.* **Lost-time injuries** are those in which the employee involved misses some work time because of the injury in the days following the incident. Successful safety training programs should see a reduction in lost-time injuries.
4. *Absenteeism.* This objective factor may be of particular importance in evaluating health-related training programs designed to reduce stress.
5. *Workers' Compensation claims and costs.* Ultimately, health and safety training programs should result in decreased resort to Workers' Compensation programs, as successful training programs should decrease incident and injury rates.
6. *Employee benefit costs.* Effective safety training can contribute to reduced use of programs such as physiotherapy and occupational therapy.
7. *Safety inspection reports.* If an organization is subject to internal or external safety inspections, improved performance on these inspections should be seen in areas that have been the subject of health and safety training.

The training evaluator will want to compare the organization's performance *after* the training program with its performance *before* training. Access to pre-training *and* post-training information will allow the evaluator to reach conclusions about improvements in organizational outcomes that are a result of training.

However, training evaluators will want to take great care to ensure that their measurements of pre-training and post-training variables are accurate. The training evaluator must consider a number of factors when assessing organizational indices of health and safety. As noted earlier, incident, injury, and fatality rates are indicators of safe or unsafe behaviour in the workplace. Most discussions about occupational safety, whether in the academic literature or in workplaces themselves, focus on actual safety incidents or fatalities. As a result, the focus is often on the number of incidents, the amount of lost time, whether the incident resulted in a claim for Workers' Compensation, and occasionally the number of workplace fatalities. The focus on such variables is understandable, given their visibility and the social and economic interest they attract.

Several factors, however, limit the reliability and utility of incident and fatality measures for organizational research and practice. First, major

close call

a series of events that could have led to a safety incident but did not

lost-time injuries

a workplace injury that results in the employee missing time from work

incidents with injuries and especially fatalities are relatively rare. As such, the distribution of major incidents and fatalities is skewed, rather than normally distributed, and this introduces challenges for statistical analyses of such data. Second, there is no clear agreement across jurisdictions as to what constitutes an occupational injury. For example, what one province or territory accepts as evidence of a back injury requiring time off work, another might refuse, which renders any comparisons of injury rates across jurisdictions limited at best. Third, there is considerable concern that organizations' databases on incidents and fatalities may misrepresent the actual prevalence of problems.

Logs of lost-time injuries maintained by government agencies actually underrepresent the magnitude of these incidents.[30] In particular, initial episodes of lost-time injury may be accurately reported, but lost time due to reinjury or the persistence of problems following return to work are underreported. Organizations' in-house recordkeeping processes may contribute to this problem.[31] To offset the statistical imbalance, researchers have begun to ask how incident reports can be improved. For example, the inclusion of close calls may provide a useful supplement to incident reports, because they occur with greater frequency than do safety incidents. Also, the difference between a close call and an incident may be no more than luck. Therefore, including close calls in incident reporting is important for a more complete picture of safety-related events.

Self-reported measures of occupational events and injuries may provide a more valid indication than compulsory reports by the organization to government agencies, as there appears to be little incentive for workers to misreport safety incidents and injury experiences in a deliberate way.[32] Though there could be legitimate errors as a result of memory lapses, these would occur randomly across people and organizations and therefore would not bias the reporting of injuries or safety incidents in any way. A potential solution is to use multiple sources or records in identifying the "real" rates of incidents and injuries.[33]

COMMON SAFETY TRAINING INITIATIVES

The health and safety training needs of any particular organization will be largely determined by factors unique to that organization—its size and the industry in question being two factors that contribute heavily to safety training needs. That said, several common safety training initiatives are applicable to organizations of all sizes and sectors. Next we review three of these: safety orientation, first aid training, and WHMIS training.

Safety Orientation

Organizations with successful safety programs and safety records often begin to emphasize health and safety through an orientation program at the time employees are first hired. Integrating health and safety into the employee orientation program ensures that all employees are provided with a base level of health and safety training; it also reinforces the development of a safety climate in the workplace. Though the details will vary with the needs of specific workplaces, a general orientation to health and safety should include a review and introduction to:

- fire and emergency safety procedures
- incident policies (e.g., reporting, procedures for obtaining first aid)
- hazards unique to the workplace (e.g., material hazards, chemical hazards, physical hazards)
- protective personal equipment (e.g., how to obtain, how to use)
- WHMIS training
- the role of the Joint Occupational Health and Safety Committee
- the roles and responsibilities of individual employees
- job-specific safety procedures (e.g., proper lifting technique, decontamination, lockout procedures); *and*
- housekeeping and safety awareness

First Aid Training

Many Canadian employers are required under OH&S acts to provide first aid training to employees. The number of employees requiring certification in first aid in any given organization depends on several factors. Provincial or territorial health and safety laws determine first aid requirements based on factors such as the number of workers per shift, the distance away from fixed medical services, and the hazard level of the workplace. Larger, isolated, higher hazard worksites require more trained first aid providers. The exact number of first aid certificates and the level of certification required vary among the provinces and territories.

Organizations such as St. John Ambulance provide first aid training programs that help employers meet or exceed the requirements set forth in provincial and territorial OH&S acts. In fact, St. John Ambulance provides full services in the provision and management of workplace first aid training programs. For instance, via its key account program, St. John Ambulance tracks the training and certificates of employees in an organization and notifies the organization when recertification is required.

WHMIS Training

WHMIS has been discussed throughout this book. It is the standard for communicating information about hazards in Canada. Under WHMIS, hazardous or controlled products are labelled in a standardized manner and information regarding the safe handling of these products is provided via material safety data sheets (MSDSs) and worker training programs. The federal, provincial, and territorial health and safety jurisdictions all incorporate WHMIS. Employers are required to properly store and dispose of hazardous materials and to ensure that workers receive training in handling and using controlled products. **OH&S Today 9.3** discusses Web-based WHMIS training.

SUMMARY

Canadian employees have the right to be informed about the hazards they may encounter in the workplace, and OH&S acts require the provision of health and safety training. Even so, many Canadians report that they have never received any safety training at work. Recent legislation means that employers who fail to provide a safe workplace may face charges of criminal negligence.

OH&S training can be described under a general training model. The ISD model, applied to the issue of health and safety, emphasizes the importance of a complete needs analysis before training is designed and offered. Needs analysis includes a consideration of the organization, the job, and the person. Key to health and safety training is ensuring that the organization is supportive of the initiative. If a company is not supportive of health and safety issues in general, the training effort is likely to encounter roadblocks.

Several factors must be considered in the design and delivery of OH&S training, including the content of the training, who will receive training, and who will do the training. Organizations must make certain that the training programs they offer comply with the standards set out in their jurisdiction's occupational health and safety act.

Health and safety training efforts should be evaluated to consider whether the trainees had positive reactions to them and learned the material. Evaluations should also consider the extent to which employee behaviours and organizational outcomes were influenced by the training. Health and safety training programs should be evaluated for their impact on safety-related outcomes in the workplace, such as incident, injury, and fatality rates and the incidence of close calls. Safety training programs designed to increase safe behaviour should reduce incident rates and ultimately reduce injury and death rates, besides reducing the number of near misses and lost-time injuries.

Key Terms

close call 240
instructional systems design (ISD)
   model of training 226
job/task analysis 230
lost-time injuries 240
needs analysis 227
organizational analysis 228

person analysis 230
safety climate 229
train the trainer 233
training evaluation 236
training objectives 231
WHMIS 234

Weblinks

Association of Workers' Compensation Boards of Canada, "Links to Young Worker Resources"
http://www.awcbc.org/en/linkstoyoungworkerresources.asp

Canada's National Occupational Health and Safety
http://www.canoshweb.org

Canadian Centre for Occupational Health and Safety
http://www.ccohs.ca

Canadian Centre for Occupational Health and Safety, "Young Workers Zone"
http://www.ccohs.ca/youngworkers

CBC Indepth, "Workplace Safety Inspections"
http://www.cbc.ca/news/background/workplace-safety

Institute for Work and Health
http://www.iwh.on.ca

Life Quilt: Protect the Future of Young Workers
http://www.youngworkerquilt.ca

OHS Canada
http://www.ohscanada.com

Passport to Safety
http://passporttosafety.com

St. John Ambulance
http://www.sja.ca

WHMIS
http://whmis.net

Workplace Safety and Prevention Services
http://www.healthandsafetyontario.ca/WSPS/Home.aspx

WorkSafeBC
http://www.worksafebc.com

Required Professional Capabilities (RPCs)

The following RPCs, listed by their CCHRA number, are relevant to the material covered in this chapter. All RPCs can be found at http://www.chrp.ca/rpc/body-of-knowledge/.

RPC:145 Determines the most effective learning and development initiatives required for organizational success.*

RPC:147 Monitors and reports on the impact of development activities on organizational performance.

RPC:159 Ensures compliance with legislated training obligations.*

RPC:160 Conducts training needs assessments.*

RPC:161 Recommends the most appropriate way to meet identified learning needs.*

RPC:162 Establishes training priorities based on needs analysis.

RPC:167 Recommends the selection of external training providers.

RPC:168 Participates in course design and selection and delivery of learning materials.

RPC:171 Ensures compliance with legislated reporting requirements.

RPC:172 Ensures due diligence and liability requirements are met.*

*Canadian Council of Human Resources Associations, Human Resources Professionals in Canada: Revised Body of Knowledge and Required Professional Capabilities (RPCs ®), 2007.

RPC:178 Provides information to employees and managers on available programs.*

RPC:183 Analyzes risks to employee health & safety and develops preventive programs.*

Discussion Questions

1. Canadian statistics suggest that many Canadians are not receiving appropriate safety training in the workplace. What are some of the reasons organizational managers might give for not providing safety training for their employees? Imagine that you are a health and safety consultant trying to convince the top management of a negligent organization to provide a health and safety orientation for new employees. What are some arguments you might use to convince the organization to support the training program?
2. Why is organizational support for a health and safety training initiative so important for the success of the training program?
3. What are some important organizational outcomes that can be used to evaluate the value that a training program has added to an organization?
4. What are some of the advantages and disadvantages associated with the use of Web-based health and safety training programs for individual employees? for organizations?

Using the Internet

1. Each provincial and territorial government has its own health and safety legislation. Each refers to the importance and role of health and safety training. Using the Internet, look up the health and safety legislation in your province or territory. Note the ways in which training can help organizations and employees adhere to the law.
2. Using various Web resources, find out more about young workers' safety. Along with your classmates, brainstorm ways to build health and safety knowledge among young Canadians entering the workforce. How might we educate parents and employers about the health and safety risks associated with young workers?
3. Visit the websites of some large organizations in various industries, and look for information about their health and safety policies. What portion of the sites you visited contained information about health and safety training? Did the attention given to training or the type of training described vary by industry or organizational size?
4. Search your school's website to investigate the health and safety training programs offered in your institution.

---

*Canadian Council of Human Resources Associations, Human Resources Professionals in Canada: Revised Body of Knowledge and Required Professional Capabilities (RPCs ®), 2007.

Exercises

1. Young workers are at considerable risk for safety incidents and injury in the workplace. Perform a person analysis by interviewing a young person who has recently entered the workforce. Based on what you have learned about occupational health and safety in this course, try to get an idea of that individual's awareness of health and safety in the workplace and the extent to which he or she is worried about his or her own safety at work. If you are unable to interview a new worker, have a classmate think back to his or her very first job and try to recall his or her health and safety–related attitudes upon entering the workforce. You will want to find out some information about the tasks this person performed at work and identify some of the potential hazards that were associated with the job.

2. Think back to various jobs that you have held. What types of health and safety training did you receive? Were the training programs effective? Compare your experiences with those of your classmates.

3. To find out more about health and safety training, contact a human resource professional and ask about health and safety training programs in his or her organization. You might use some of the following questions to guide your discussion.

   a. Does your organization have a health and safety orientation program? If so, what types of information does it cover?

   b. How many trained first aid providers are required per shift in your organization?

   c. What are some of the safety hazards and concerns employees in your organization encounter? Do you think that training is a useful option to help employees manage their exposure to these risks? Why or why not?

   d. Under what conditions does your organization rely on purchased, pre-existing health and safety programs? When might the company opt for custom-designed health and safety training programs? What factors influence this decision?

   e. What is the general attitude toward occupational health and safety training among employees in your organization? among management?

4. Bill C-45, the "Westray Bill," went into effect on March 31, 2004. Research this legislation. How many charges could you find? How many convictions? What impact do you think this legislation will have on Canadian employees' access to health and safety training? Do you think it will influence Canadian employers' attitudes toward health and safety training? Debate these issues with your classmates.

5. Imagine that you are a health and safety training consultant who has been working with an international courier company to offer training for their on-the-ground delivery staff regarding proper lifting procedures and safe driving. When thinking about how to evaluate the effectiveness of the training programs, what specific measures would you include?

Case 1 THE NEW HR MANAGER AT A1 MANUFACTURING

Sabine is the new HR manager at A1 Manufacturing. When she began her new position, she quickly realized that A1 did not pay much attention to issues of occupational health and safety. In fact, she determined that this company was in violation of a number of legislated health and safety requirements. She approached members of upper management with her concerns. At first they seemed unruffled by her warnings about health and safety violations throughout the company. Only when she reminded the upper management that the organization could face fines and that some executive-level individuals could face criminal charges if there was a safety-related incident did they sit up and listen. Sabine was given the job of fixing the problem.

She has determined that the organization needs to provide more health and safety training programs. She has contacted you, a training consultant, to help her design and implement new programs. What steps do you take in helping Sabine determine her training needs and implement training programs? Is there anything about the organization or Sabine's conclusion that training is the answer that concerns you? What are some potential obstacles to a potential training effort?

Case 2 A YOUNG WORKER'S QUANDARY

Eighteen-year-old Gurjit has just started his very first job, working at a lumber yard. On his first day, Gurjit was given a hardhat and told he should purchase steel-toed boots. A more senior employee gave him some basic instruction about how to operate the forklift and told him to be careful. After his first shift, Gurjit has a feeling he can't shake. His new job feels dangerous, yet the company managers and his fellow employees do not appear particularly concerned about training him on safe work procedures. He doesn't want to let down the boss, who has given him his first job, by complaining. He doesn't want to disappoint his family, who are proud that he is working, by quitting—and besides, he needs the money. What options does Gurjit have? Whom can he contact about his health and safety concerns?

NOTES

1. L.S. Robson, C.M. Stephenson, P.A. Schulte, B.C. Amick III, E.L. Irvin, D.E. Eggerth, S. Chan, A.R. Bielecky A.M. Wang, T.L. Heidotting, R.H., Peters, J.A. Clarke, K. Cullen, C.J. Rotunda, P.L. Grubb. "A Systematic Review of the Effectiveness of Occupational Health and Safety Training," *Scandinavian Journal of Work, Environment, and Health* 38 (2012): 193–208.

2. P. Smith and C. Mustard, "How Many Employees Receive Safety Training During Their First Year of a New Job?" *Injury Prevention* 13 (2007): 37–41.

3. Ibid.

4. G.B. Cooke, I.U. Zeytinoglu, and J. Chowhan, "Barriers to Training Access," *Perspectives*, July 2009: 14–25, Cat. No. 75-001-X, http://www.statcan.gc.ca/pub/75-001-x/2009107/pdf/10907-eng.pdf, March 30, 2010.

5. M.J. Colligan and A. Cohen, "The Role of Training in Promoting Workplace Safety and Health," in J. Barling and M. Frone, eds., *Handbook of Workplace Safety* (Washington: APA, 2004), 223–48.

6. A.M. Saks and R.R. Haccoun, *Managing Performance Through Training and Development*, 5th ed. (Toronto: Nelson Canada, 2010).

7. I.L. Goldstein and J.K. Ford, *Training in Organizations: Needs Assessment, Development, and Evaluation*, 4th ed. (Belmont: Wadsworth, 2002); Saks and Haccoun, *Managing Performance*.

8. Goldstein and Ford, *Training in Organizations*; Saks and Haccoun, *Managing Performance*.

9. M.J. Colligan and A. Cohen, "The Role of Training in Promoting Workplace Safety and Health," in J. Barling and M. Frone, eds., *Handbook of Workplace Safety* (Washington: American Psychological Association, 2004), 223–48.

10. R.K. Sokas, E. Jorgensen, L. Nickels, W. Gao, and J.L. Gittleman, "An Intervention Effectiveness Study of Hazard Awareness Training in the Construction Building Trades," *Public Health Reports* 124 (2009): 161–68.

11. D. Zohar, "Safety Climate in Industrial Organizations: Theoretical and Applied Implications," *Journal of Applied Psychology* 65 (198): 96–102; D. Zohar and G.A. Luria, "A Multilevel Model of Safety Climate: Cross-Level Relationships Between Organization and Group-Level Climates," *Journal of Applied Psychology* 90 (2005): 616–28.

12. Goldstein and Ford, *Training in Organizations*.

13. Colligan and A. Cohen, "The Role of Training"; K.R. Saarela, "An Intervention Program Utilizing Small Groups: A Comparative Study," *Journal of Safety Research* 21 (1990): 149–56.

14. Colligan and A. Cohen, "The Role of Training."

15. T.F. Fisher, B. Brodzinski-Andriae, and S. Zook. "Effectiveness of Work Injury Prevention Education and Safety Training by an Occupational Therapist," The British Journal of Occupational Therapy 72 (2009): 450–57.

16. J.A. Daltuva, V. Williams, L. Vazquez, T.G. Robins, and J.A. Fernandez, "Worker-Trainers as Evaluators: A Case Study of a Union-Based Health and Safety Program," *Health Promotion Practice* 5 (2004): 191–98.

17. Colligan and A. Cohen, "The Role of Training." For a specific example of a successful program see Q. Williams, Jr., M. Ochsner, E. Marshall, L. Kimmel, and C. Martino. "The Impact of a Peer-Led Participatory Health and Safety Training for Latino Day Labourers in Construction," *Journal of Safety Research* 41 (2010): 253–61.

18. W.K. Anger, J. Stupel, T. Ammerman, A. Tamulinas, T. Bodner, and D.S. Rohlman, "The Suitability of Computer-Based Training for Workers with Limited Formal Education: A Case Study from the US Agricultural Sector," *International Journal of Training and Development* 10 (2006): 269–84.

19. S. Kearns, "Online Single-Pilot Resource Management: Assessing the Feasibility of Computer-Based Safety Training," *The International Journal of Aviation Psychology* 21 (2011): 175–90.

20. Colligan and A. Cohen, "The Role of Training."

21. M.J. Burke, S.A. Sarpy, K. Smith-Crowe, S. Chan-Serafin, O.S. Rommel, and G. Islam, "Relative Effectiveness of Worker Safety and Health and Training Methods," *American Journal of Public Health* 96 (2006): 315–24.

22. M.J. Burke, M.L. Scheuer, and R.J. Meredith, "A Dialogical Approach to Skill Development: The Case of Safety Skills," *Human Resource Management Review* 17 (2007): 235–50; E.T. Cullen, "Tell Me a Story," *Professional Safety*, July 2008, 20–27.

23. M.J. Burke, R.O. Salvador, K. Smith-Crowe, S. Chan-Serafin, A. Smith, and S. Sonesh. "The Dread Factor: How Hazards and Safety Training Influence Learning and Performance, *Journal of Applied Psychology* 96 (2011): 46–70.

24. D. Arnold, "A Matter of Life and Death," *Occupational Health* 55 (2003): 21–23.

25. D.L. Kirkpatrick, "Evaluating Training Programs: The Four Levels (San Francisco: Berrett-Koehler, 1994); Saks and Haccoun, *Managing Performance*.

26. Saks and Haccoun, *Managing Performance*.

27. J.K. Ford, K. Kraiger, and S.M. Merritt, "An Updated Review of the Multidimensionality of Training Outcomes: New Directions for Training Evaluation Research," in S.W.J. Kozlowski and E. Salas, eds., *Learning, Training, and Development in Organizations* (New York: Routledge/Taylor and Francis Group, 2010).

28. Ibid.

29. Ibid.

30. B. Evanoff, S. Abedin, D. Grayson, A.M. Dale, L. Wolfe, and P. Bohr, "Is Disability Underreported Following Work Injury?" *Journal of Occupational Rehabilitation* 12 (2002): 139–50.

31. H. Conway and J. Svenson, "Occupational Injury and Illness Rates, 1992–1996: Why They Fell," *Monthly Labor Review* 121, no. 11 (1998): 36–58.

32. L. Grunberg, S. Moore, and E. Greenberg, "The Relationship of Employee Ownership and Participation to Workplace Safety," *Economic and Industrial Democracy* 17 (1996): 221–41.

33. Conway and Svenson, "Occupational Injury and Illness Rates."

CHAPTER 10

Motivation

CHAPTER LEARNING OBJECTIVES

After reading this chapter, you should be able to:

- discuss the importance of safety behaviour in the workplace
- identify the categories of safety behaviour
- explain the importance of individual motivation in safety behaviour
- describe behaviour modification approaches to motivating safety
- recognize the importance of goal setting and feedback in safety behaviour in the workplace
- understand the facets of self-determination theory of motivation and its potential in helping to understand safety motivation
- evaluate the role of organizational support for safety in contributing to safety behaviour
- discuss the role of the safety climate in the performance of safety behaviours
- understand the role that safety leadership plays in creating a safe work environment
- describe OH&S management systems, such as CSA-Z1000-06, and appreciate how they help organizations promote workplace safety

ONTARIO POWER GENERATION

Ontario Power Generation (OPG) is an Ontario-based corporation that both generates and sells electricity. Aiming to be the premier producer of electricity in North America, OPG is working toward this goal by focusing on safety and environmental sustainability. Its efforts have been acknowledged. In 2010, OPG was the first employer in the province of Ontario to win the Infrastructure Health and Safety Association's ZeroQuest Platinum award. This award recognized OPG's efforts relating to safety performance, effective safety management programs, and safety culture.

This corporation has several systems in place to support its focus on safety behaviour at work. With the slogan "Zero Injuries: Believe It. Achieve It," OPG has a multifaceted safety management system that includes organizational resources, organizational culture, and the structure of work. A visit to the OPG website illustrates the focus on continuous improvement to achieve the goal of zero injuries. OPG also recognizes the risks to young workers and has made an explicit commitment to young workers' safety. OPG's safety efforts are guided by the use of safety management systems that are consistent with internationally recognized standards (e.g., the British Standards Institute's OHSAS 18001).

The OPG employee health and safety policy is available to download and is an excellent example of corporate responsibility for safety. OPG believes that "healthy employees working safely in an injury-free and healthy workplace is good business." The policy notes how continual improvement will contribute to the physical, psychological, and social health of its employees. The safety policy also clearly lays out the safety-related responsibilities of employees and management. For instance, the policy outlines that employees are responsible for identifying and communicating workplace hazards. Similarly, management is accountable for such things as "providing employees with the information, training, tools, procedures and support required to do their job safely."

This policy is a good example of corporate responsibility in health and safety. It illustrates the importance of employees' involvement in their own safety at work and the vital role of organizational support for health and safety initiatives. The policy also states that health and safety performance will be assessed and recognized in the workplace. OPG's approach to safety management highlights several topics that we will cover in this chapter—most notably safety behaviour and the roles of individual and organizational responsibility in achieving a safe workplace.

Source: Ontario Power Generation, "Safety at OPG: Corporate Safety." Found at: http://www.opg.com/safety/nsafe/corpsafe.asp (Accessed Dec. 30, 2012).

In the previous chapter we considered the importance of health and safety training in the workplace. In this chapter we consider the equally important issue of how employees are motivated to utilize their knowledge and skills, perhaps those gained during training, to consistently perform their work duties in a safe manner. We explore this issue by considering safety behaviour, theories of motivation, and organizational factors (e.g., safety leadership and climate and management systems and policies) that support employee safety efforts. The issues we consider here focus on preventing incidents and injuries at work rather than simply responding to workplace incidents.

Psychological research in the area of motivation provides a useful starting point for considering how to motivate the safe performance of work tasks. Other psychological factors, including organizational safety culture and safety leadership, are useful in establishing the value an organization places on safety and how those values in turn influence employees' safety attitudes and behaviour. Before we turn our attention to these psychological variables, we first consider the issue of safety behaviour to illustrate the value of employee behaviour in incident and injury prevention in the workplace.

SAFETY BEHAVIOUR

There are several ways to categorize health and safety programs. One is in terms of *engineering* interventions, *administrative* interventions, and *behavioural* interventions.[1] Engineering interventions typically focus on changing the physical environment to reduce exposure to hazards, either by providing personal protective equipment or by redesigning the physical workplace. Administrative interventions modify procedures and exposure in the work environment. Techniques such as job rotation, the scheduling of work breaks, the use of safety officers, and the use of standard operating procedures all count as administrative interventions. Finally, behavioural interventions focus on changing employee attitudes, knowledge, or behaviour regarding occupational health and safety. Information campaigns, risk awareness, skills training, and behaviour modification techniques are all behavioural interventions. All three types of intervention have been at least somewhat successful in improving health and safety at work. A recent review of the empirical research on comprehensive OH&S management systems—those encompassing multiple intervention categories—reports mostly favourable results for these programs on such outcomes as safety climate, injury rates, and economic factors like insurance rates.[2] However, the authors of that review warn that the number of available studies is small and that many that do exist have methodological limitations such as small samples and lack of comparison groups.

All things being equal, it is preferable to remove or eliminate the hazard via an engineering solution than to rely on other types of health and safety programming. However, such engineering controls are not always possible.[3] Therefore, much of the psychological research in the area of occupational safety has focused on behavioural interventions, in particular those designed to increase safety-related behaviours. There is a relationship between **safety behaviours** and injury rates.[4] Reviews of the research illustrate that targeting employee behaviour is an effective injury prevention strategy.[5] Generally, as behaviourally based safety programs are introduced, the number of safety-related events, including incidents and injuries, is decreased.

At least eight general categories of behaviour contribute to safe working performance:[6]

- Proper use of hazard control systems in the workplace
- Development of safe work habits
- Increased awareness and recognition of workplace hazards
- Acceptance and use of personal protective equipment
- Maintenance of housekeeping and maintenance standards
- Maintenance of accepted hygiene practices
- Proper responses to emergency situations
- Self-monitoring and recognition of symptoms of hazardous exposure

safety behaviours
behaviours leading to safe performance of a particular job

Health and safety programs have been aimed largely at encouraging one or more of these general classes of behaviour. Some of these categories will be familiar to you as the targets of the health and safety training efforts we described in Chapter 9. For example, training programs might teach proper lifting techniques (i.e., develop safe work habits), and WHMIS training is designed to enhance the worker's ability to recognize chemical hazards in the workplace. However, workplace safety promotion encompasses more than ability-based training.

When considering safety behaviour a distinction is often made between safety compliance and safety participation.[7] **Safety compliance** is achieved when employees follow core safety-related rules and generally work in a safe manner. Certainly, safety compliance helps reduce injuries and safety incidents.[8] **Safety participation** refers to employee behaviours that go beyond simply working within safety standards and safety compliance. It involves employees behaving proactively and voluntarily to improve safety levels in the working environment.[9] For example, proactive employees engage in such behaviours as volunteering to participate in safety audits, attending safety meetings and encouraging their supervisor to take actions to improve safety. Both safety compliance and safety participation are components of safety behaviour.

Generally, for individuals to work safely at least three conditions are necessary. First, workers must have the *ability* to work safely—that is, they must possess the knowledge and skills to perform their jobs in a safe manner. This requirement is generally addressed through the provision of OH&S training. Second, workers must be *motivated* to work safely—that is, they must intend to use their knowledge and skills to enhance safe working performance. Finally, workers must have the *opportunity* to work safely—that is, the environment or organization must support and encourage safe work.

These three factors combine in a multiplicative rather than an additive fashion (see Figure 10.1). Thus,

Safety performance = Ability × Motivation × Opportunity

safety compliance
the extent to which employees follow safety rules and procedures

safety participation
the extent to which employees go beyond compliance and engage proactively and voluntarily to actively improve safety

FIGURE (10.1)

Ability, Motivation, Opportunity

Safety performance relies on ability, motivation, and opportunity. This figure presents safety behaviour as a full circle. You can see that if any one of these important components is missing, the full circle of safety behaviour will not be achieved and thus safety performance in the workplace will not be realized.

OH&S Notebook 10.1

ELEMENTS OF A BEHAVIOUR-BASED SAFETY PROGRAM

The content of a behaviour-based safety initiative will vary with the context in which it is offered (e.g., organization, type of job), but several basic elements are common across behaviour-based safety programs:

1. Identifying observable behaviours that affect safety-related outcomes
2. Outlining precise measurement of the identified behaviours
3. Providing feedback on how to perform the behaviour more safely
4. Highlighting the consequences of the behaviour to motivate employees
5. Rewarding safe performance of the targeted behaviour

Sources: Adapted from: E.S. Geller, "Behavior-Based Safety in Industry: Realizing the Large-Scale Potential of Psychology to Promote Human Welfare," *Applied and Preventive Psychology*, Vol. 10, Pg. 87–105, 2010; B. Sulzer-Azaroff & J. Austin, "Does BBS Work? Behavior-Based Safety and Injury Reduction: A Survey of the Evidence," *Professional Safety*, July, 2010, Pg. 19–24.

An important implication of this multiplicative equation is that the model of safety performance is noncompensatory. A high level of motivation and many opportunities do not compensate for a lack of ability. Similarly, a high level of ability and motivation cannot make up for a work environment that does not provide opportunities and support for safe working. Safety performance relies on ability, motivation, and opportunity. If any one of these components is missing, safety performance in the workplace will not be realized. The question for health and safety programs is, How do we use this model to increase safe work behaviours?

The basic premise of the multiplicative model of safety performance is that safety can be enhanced by increasing an employee's abilities, motivation, and opportunities to work safely. Having said this, it is important to note that all three components of the model must be implemented for safety performance to be enhanced. For example, training (i.e., increasing ability) alone is insufficient to change safety behaviours over the long term.[10] However, safety training coupled with motivational programs appears to be an effective combination in changing safety behaviours. Given the great deal of attention paid in Chapter 9 to increasing employees' ability to perform safety behaviours, this chapter focuses on motivation and opportunity. We will consider these facets of safety performance in turn.

MOTIVATING SAFETY BEHAVIOUR

The word *motivation* comes from the Latin *movere*, "to move." Generally speaking, **motivation** is the process that initiates, directs, and sustains behaviour.[11] Some psychological researchers consider the motivation process as it applies to very basic biological functions such as eating and sleeping. Others focus on motivation as it applies to goal-directed behaviour. In this section we consider the role of motivation in safety behaviour at work. Specific to the safety domain, **safety motivation** has been defined as an individual's willingness to exert effort to enact

motivation
the process that initiates, directs, and sustains behaviour

safety motivation
an individual's willingness to exert effort to enact safety behaviour and the valence associated with those behaviours

safety behaviour and the valence associated with those behaviours."[12] Meta-analytic research evidence shows that safety behaviour is positively influenced by one's motivation to work safely.[13] Our analysis focuses on three major theoretical explanations of motivation: reinforcement theory (or behaviour modification), goal-setting theory, and self-determination theory.

Reinforcement Theory

Reinforcement theory focuses on the power of external rewards and punishments in the motivation of behaviour. Reinforcement theory, forwarded by learning theorists who adhere to the school of psychology called behaviourism, posits that the likelihood of an action being performed in the future is determined by its current consequences. Generally, the chances of a behaviour being performed again increase when a current performance of that behaviour is followed by reinforcement (i.e., a reward) and decrease when it is followed by punishment. Rewards can be things such as a prize, money, or praise. Reinforcement theory has been used in organizations in the form of incentive systems. Employees are promised a reward if they meet some behavioural expectation—for example, improved sales, increased productivity, or—of particular importance for the current discussion—improved safety behaviour. The application of reinforcement theory in this way is sometimes called behaviour modification.

The use of behaviour modification principles to increase safety behaviours in the workplace has been largely successful.[14] Evidence suggests that behavioural programs are effective in promoting safe working behaviours and are associated with substantial reductions in incident and injury rates.[15] Moreover, behavioural interventions appear to be effective in promoting safety behaviours in a wide range of work environments, including mining,[16] bus driving,[17] and construction.[18] In short, behavioural approaches to occupational safety have been shown to be effective, cost efficient, and adaptable to a wide range of industrial environments.

The basic model underlying most applications of behavioural programming in the workplace is the ABC model of behaviour.[19] Simply stated, the ABC model holds that any behaviour occurs because of events that trigger the behaviour (the antecedents) and the results that follow the behaviour (the consequences). Thus, any behaviour can be represented as

$$\textbf{Antecedent} \rightarrow \textbf{Behaviour} \rightarrow \textbf{Consequence}$$

To change a specific behaviour, we have to change either the antecedent or the consequence of the behaviour. Most applications of behavioural programming focus on changing the consequences of behaviour. If we want to understand why workers perform unsafe acts or fail to engage in safe practices, a good place to begin is by considering the consequences of both safe and unsafe behaviours.[20] Such consequences can be characterized along three dimensions: positive or negative, immediate or delayed, and contingent or noncontingent. Generally, behaviour that is followed by immediate, positive, and contingent consequences is more likely to occur again. Conversely, consequences that are delayed, negative, or noncontingent have either a minimal or an adverse effect on safety behaviour.

Even a brief consideration of most safety behaviours suggests that the consequences of safe behaviour are typically delayed, negative, or noncontingent.

It is rare for coworkers to praise or even recognize an individual for proper lifting techniques or for wearing safety goggles. Indeed the most likely consequence of engaging in such practices is the lack of notice from either supervisors or coworkers. Some safe actions such as mopping up spills or putting on safety goggles require extra time, thereby slowing down the work. This may be a negative consequence, especially if working more slowly is associated with disciplinary warnings. Some forms of personal protective equipment may also be uncomfortable, again a negative consequence. Even when there are positive

OH&S Today 10.1

A Risky Side of Behaviour-Based Safety Programs?

Behaviour-based safety programs appear to succeed in reducing workplace incidents. However, some stakeholders are wary of this approach, even questioning whether it revives the notion of "accident proneness" as an explanation for why some workers get injured. Some workers' groups note the downsides of safety programs that focus exclusively on behavioural interventions.

At some point safety incentives can be intimidating for employees. No one wants to be the person who costs coworkers a reward for achieving a reduction in injury rates. As such, some workers feel peer pressure not to report an actual injury and may even rely on their leave days rather than file a Workers' Compensation claim.

Other workers fear discipline if they are injured; thus, an employee who sustains an injury may fear reprisal from the organization and decide not to report the incident. Of course, the result in these cases is the underreporting of workplace injury and illness.

Others have pointed out that far too often the actions rewarded under behaviour-based programs are the avoidance of negatives that may be out of the individual's control (e.g., the reduction in lost-time injuries) rather than the achievement of positives that *are* under an individual's control (e.g., consistently wearing protective equipment, refusing unsafe work). Critics also note that a focus on employee behaviour as an avenue for injury reduction sometimes leaves real hazards unabated in the workplace, diverting attention from the core concern, which is to make the workplace safer. Additionally, they question whether such an approach is effective at reducing occupational illnesses.

How might an HR manager address these concerns about behaviour-based safety programs? Certainly, the use of engineering interventions whenever possible will reduce the burden placed on individual employees. Additionally, comprehensive safety programs incorporate administrative interventions in the health and safety management program. The organization should have a progressive health and safety policy, strive for a positive safety culture, and truly support employee safety initiatives. Employees need to have the opportunity to work as safely as possible. If value is truly placed on the well-being of every worker, rather than on the interpretation of injury or safety incident statistics alone, employees may feel less threatened by behavioural interventions at work.

When the decision is made to include incentives as part of a behaviour-based safety program, keep the following in mind:

a. Feedback alone may be a sufficient incentive.

b. Incentives should be tied to behaviours under individual control (e.g., the proper use of a personal protective device) rather than to outcomes such as incidents or injuries that may be beyond control.

c. Incentive programs should not attempt to compensate for a lack of training, shoddy equipment, poor maintenance, or, more generally, other failures in the safety systems.

d. All employees should be eligible to receive incentives.

e. Incentives should be meaningful.

Sources: Workers' Health and Safety Centre, "Behaviour-Based Safety: The Blame Game." Found at: http://www.whsc.on.ca/pubs/res_lines2.cfm?resID=21 (Accessed Dec. 30, 2012); Canadian Auto Workers, "Behaviour-Based Safety Program." Found at: http://www.caw.ca/en/services-departments-health-safety-environment-behaviour-based-safety-systems-pdf.htm (Accessed Dec. 30, 2012).

consequences associated with behaviour, these consequences are often delayed or noncontingent. For example, a worker safety award may be given to an individual based on behaviours that occurred a year or more ago, irrespective of what behaviours the worker engaged in that day.

In contrast, there are often positive, immediate, and contingent rewards associated with unsafe behaviours. For example, the result of not wearing protective equipment may be increased comfort and speed of work. Negative consequences such as disciplinary warnings or injuries are typically rare and often delayed. Individuals may go months and even years not wearing safety goggles and never experience an injury as the result. Even this simplistic consideration suggests that wearing the protective clothing is unlikely to be based on the consequences associated with not wearing the clothing.

Given these observations, the goal of behavioural safety programs is to change the consequences associated with specific behaviours. Specifically, behavioural programs attempt to institute positive, immediate, and contingent consequences for safe working procedures. By far the most popular form of consequence is simple feedback; individuals are typically observed as they perform their job and given immediate feedback on the safety of their work practices. Second in popularity is the use of incentive-based programs in which employees are offered incentives such as free lunches or lottery tickets for their safe behaviour. Generally, the organizational behaviour-modification literature suggests that feedback alone, without the use of material rewards and incentives, is an effective means of behavioural change. For example, one experimental study in an industrial setting illustrated that increased feedback from supervisors regarding safety incidents and the use of personal protective equipment increased hearing protection use, reduced injury, and improved perceptions of safety climate.[21]

Goal Setting

Theories of motivation based on the notion of goal setting point out that behaviour is in fact motivated by our own internal intentions. These intentions might be described as the goals we want to achieve.[22] A large number of studies illustrate that setting goals can have desirable behavioural effects.[23] Goal setting has been extensively applied in organizations, and its effectiveness in influencing a wide array of behaviours is well documented in the research literature. Like behaviour modification, goal setting is a method for changing behaviour. However, unlike behaviour modification, goal setting does not focus on changing the consequences of behaviour; rather, it concerns itself with the antecedents of behaviour—that is, the "A" of the ABC model described above. One interesting study examined how changing the antecedents of a behaviour can influence attendance at a health and safety training program for university staff. In this study, researchers manipulated the type of mailing that the staff members received about the training program. Some received messages that stressed the importance of the content of the training program and invited them to take part in a session. Others received a mailing that asked them to commit to attending a particular session. Those who signed up for a session in advance had a higher rate of actual attendance at the training program than did those who received the message encouraging them to attend.[24]

Setting a specific goal (e.g., wearing personal protective equipment 95% of the time) provides an antecedent for the behaviour by reminding the individual of what he or she is expected to do. Goals serve as antecedents to behaviour in four main ways:

1. They direct attention and action to the desired behaviour.
2. They mobilize effort toward actions to achieve the goal.
3. They increase persistence.
4. They motivate the search for effective strategies to help obtain them.

Several investigators have demonstrated that goal-setting techniques provide a valuable adjunct to feedback systems in motivating desired behaviours. It appears that five factors augment the effectiveness of goal setting:[25]

1. Goals must be *difficult and challenging* to result in improved performance. If we set our goals too low, we often stop thinking about them. Goals should be a stretch for the individual, and those that are have more of an impact on performance than easy goals or the absence of goals.
2. Goals must be *achievable* to lead to better performance. Goals that are too hard can quickly become demotivating.
3. Goals must be *specific*. Goals have a more positive impact on behaviour when they are specific rather than vague. The goal must identify specific behaviours, specify how many times they must be performed, and specify the performance standard. Nonspecific goals that are too broad are more like wishes or desires—not goals.
4. Individuals must be *committed* to the goals. The person must accept the goal as being reasonable and achievable. Goals that aren't accepted aren't acted on. People tend to accept goals when they see the importance of the goal, when they participate in setting the goal, when they trust the coach, and when they see the behaviour as something they can control.
5. *Feedback* regarding the degree to which the goal is being met is also helpful in goal achievement.

Goal setting is one component of the classic management by objectives approach introduced by Peter Drucker.[26] Management by objectives is an approach to management that focuses efforts on goal setting, employee participation in decision making, and feedback on one's efforts and progress. Research suggests that management by objectives interventions can positively influence employee productivity.[27] Management by objectives has been applied specifically to occupational health and safety initiatives. For instance, the Norwegian Public Roads Administration has implemented a series of objectives designed to achieve the primary objective of an overall reduction of road fatalities and serious injuries by 2020.[28] As you'll see later in the chapter, Occupational Health and Safety Management Systems draw on elements of the management by objectives approach including goal setting and employee involvement to help organizations effectively integrate health and safety into their broad-based business operations.

Self-Determination Theory

The self-determination approach recognizes that people are motivated by a variety of things.[29] Perhaps a person engages in a behaviour to gain a reward or avoid punishment. Someone might pursue a course of action to develop a skill that is important to them or because it is enjoyable. Thus, self-determination theory incorporates several different categories of motivation reflecting people's varied reasons for acting in a particular way. Looking to various motivators for safety, we might presume that some people wear their personal protective equipment to avoid injury while others might wear it only to comply with their employer's behavioural safety program. People may volunteer for the JOHSC to garner favour with their boss or they may do so because they truly value safety.

An important feature of self-determination theory is that it distinguishes **amotivation** from motivation. Amotivation reflects a complete lack of motivation.[30] Self-determination theory describes motivation as multi-dimensional. At one level, self-determination theory differentiates between extrinsic and intrinsic motivation.[31] **Intrinsic motivation** or internal motivation happens when people engage in behaviour purely out of interest and because they find the experience satisfying. To use a broad example, Chung is taking a dance class because he feels that dancing is fun. **Extrinsic motivation** happens when people act for more instrumental reasons, such as gaining a reward or avoiding a negative outcome. To continue the above example, Chung's friend Mike is taking the same dance class because his girlfriend insisted and he wants to make her happy.

Applying the concepts of intrinsic and extrinsic motivation to safety, it is easy to articulate extrinsically motivated examples of safety behaviour.[32] For instance, Angie attends the safety meetings at work because they are required for all employees. Sadek wears his fall protection while working at heights because his supervisor strictly enforces safety rules. Examples of true, instrinsically motivated safety behaviour are perhaps less common. We can imagine cases of individuals who become very interested in aspects of workplace health and safety and engage in it because of true interest and enjoyment. For instance, an OH&S officer might nominate her employer for a health and safety award out of a true pleasure gained by presenting the good work they have accomplished at the company. That said, it is harder to imagine a person who wears their earplugs, eye protection, and so on because it is so much fun to wear![33] However, self-determination theory has a more nuanced view of extrinsic motivation that may have important implications in the realm of OH&S.

Self-determination theory further differentiates different types of extrinsic motivation that reflect the extent to which the person experiences the extrinsic motivation as controlling or as autonomous.[34] **Autonomous motivation** is self-directed and happens when people engage in an action of their own will and choice. **Controlled motivation** happens when people act because of various contingencies. In other words, their actions are in response to pressure, like Sadek wearing his fall protection or Angie attending the safety meetings.

In particular, self-determination theory identifies four types of extrinsic motivation that vary in the extent to which they reflect controlled or autonomous behaviour.[35] The most controlled form of motivation is external regulation, which occurs when pressures outside the individual, for example a boss, a law, or a reward, prompt a person to behave in a particular way. Consider an OH&S example. Evan, who works in a machine shop, consistently uses PPE on a particular day because he knows a safety inspector is on site and being caught without it may result in disciplinary action. Another type of controlled motivation, introjected regulation, happens when a person acts in a particular way because of pressure

amotivation
complete lack of motivation

intrinsic motivation
motivation based on one's interest and enjoyment

extrinsic motivation
motivation rooted in instrumental reasons for acting

autonomous motivation
self-directed motivation reflecting an individual's free will

controlled motivation
motivation based in response to pressure

originating within him or herself. For instance, Gretchen, Evan's colleague in the machine shop, uses PPE because she'd feel guilty if she didn't.

Extrinsic motivation can also stem from self-directed or autonomous reasons.[36] With identified regulation people choose to act in a manner that is in line with their own goals. Applied to safety, at the machine shop, Ricardo consistently performs all the appropriate lockout procedures before working on a machine because he wants to avoid injury and knows that the lockout procedures will help him achieve that goal. Finally, integrated regulation, the most autonomous form of extrinsic motivation, reflects individuals who engage in actions because the behaviour reflects their sense of self-identity. Harry, the supervisor in the machine shop, acts safely and encourages others to do so because he identifies himself as a safety conscience person, whether it be in wearing PPE, following the OH&S regulations, or driving the speed limit. Table 10.1 summarizes the relationships among the different types and levels of motivation incorporated in Self-Determination Theory.

Considering the ABC model described above, one can see that self-determination theory relates to both the antecedents and the consequences of behaviour. Like behavioural reinforcement models, controlled motivation focuses on the consequences of actions (e.g., reward, guilt). Alternatively, like goal-setting models, autonomous motivation focuses on the antecedents of behaviour (e.g., goals, self-identity).

In a recent paper, Scott, Fleming, and Kelloway described how self-determination theory offers several important implications for OH&S research and practice.[37] For instance, the distinction between controlled and autonomous motivation might help us better understand people's safety compliance efforts versus their safety participation efforts. As suggested above, it is easier to imagine a case where safety behaviour is extrinsically, as opposed to intrinsically, motivated, which might lead us to focus exclusively on behaviour-based safety interventions that focus on contingent rewards. However, as you'll see in the next sections on safety climate and safety leadership, other efforts that focus safety at the organizational level are also effective at promoting safety. Considering autonomous motivation might help to explain these findings.[38] Self-determination theory also offers researchers and practitioners guidance for developing autonomous motivation among workers. Certain social conditions, particularly those that promote people's sense of autonomy, sense of competence, and sense of relatedness promote self-directed, internalized motivation.[39] The development of interventions targeting workplace climate and leadership as organizational factors to foster these social conditions may be advantageous.

TABLE 10.1					
A Summary of Levels and Types of Motivation in Self-Determination Theory					
Self-Determination Theory					
No Motivation	**Extrinsic Motivation**				**Intrinsic Motivation**
Amotivation	External	Introjected	Identified	Integrated	Internal
	[__Controlled Motivation__]		[_____Autonomous Motivation_____]		

Source: Based on M. Gagné & E. L. Deci, "Self-determination theory and work motivation," *Journal of Organizational Behaviour*, Vol. 26, Pg. 331–362, 2005.

INCREASING OPPORTUNITY FOR SAFETY BEHAVIOUR

Even when workers are well trained and highly motivated, they may not perform safely on the job. The final component that must be in place to promote safety behaviour is the provision of resources and organizational support. The need for workers to have an opportunity to perform safely is evident in the following list of the factors that contribute to the use of personal protective equipment:[40]

- Workers must be aware of the hazard that surrounds them.

- The protective equipment must be easily and conveniently available and properly fitted.

- Workers must understand how the equipment works and how to use it properly.

- There must be no other factors present that would interfere with the workers' use of the equipment.

Even in this brief description, the role of management in promoting health and safety is apparent. Management must make equipment and training available. Perhaps more important, management must demonstrate a commitment to health and safety and communicate it throughout the organization.

Management Commitment to OH&S

Management commitment to health and safety has emerged in numerous studies as a key requirement for improved workplace health and safety. For instance, a review of the empirical literature on health and safety training initiatives shows that a high level of management support for safety increases the impact of health and safety–related training in workplaces.[41] Certainly managers who

OH&S Today 10.2

OH&S and Social Media

Facebook. YouTube. Twitter. What's the safety link to social media, you ask? Companies, employees, and OH&S agencies alike are recognizing the power of social media to share ideas and get important messages out to people. For example, the Canadian Centre for Occupational Health and Safety (CCOHS) hosts Workscape, an online discussion forum where individuals interested in OH&S can share ideas and experiences relating to particular health and safety issues. CCOHS also has a Facebook page where it posts information and updates on OH&S topics. WorkSafeBC has a YouTube channel where it posts health and safety videos. Other organizations are using blogs, Twitter, and wikis to communicate their health and safety messages, goals, and successes. Increasingly, individuals can access health and safety information from an array of sources and formats. Furthermore, given the interactive nature of social media, individuals have an increasing ability to communicate with OH&S experts, raise safety concerns, and get their questions answered.

Sources: CCOHS, "Online Discussion Board Enables Information Exchange Within Workplace Health and Safety Community." Found at: http://www.ccohs.ca/newsroom/news_releases/workscape_13nov08.html (Accessed Nov. 13, 2008); Work SafeBC Channel. Found at: http://www.youtube.com/user/WorkSafeBC (Accessed April 20, 2010); D. Birch, "A New Conversation," *OHS Canada*, March 2010.

are committed to health and safety can help create opportunities for employees to engage in safety behaviours. For instance, managers can encourage safety behaviours by not placing productivity-related goals ahead of employee safety.[42] Knowing that their safety comes first will allow employees the freedom to take the time to work safely, properly use protective equipment, and halt work operations if there is a risk to safety.

Though top management has an important role to play in the promotion of workplace health and safety, it is also apparent that management initiatives are delivered through frontline supervisors, which means that supervisors' attitudes play an important role in shaping risk perceptions. Coworker attitudes help shape individual perceptions of workplace hazards and encourage or inhibit self-protective behaviour. One study of manufacturing employees illustrated the impact of other employees' safety commitment on individual safety attitudes. That study found that workers' perceptions of risk were influenced mainly by their perceptions of management, supervisory, and coworker commitment to health and safety. Moreover, perceptions of others' commitment to health and safety had a much larger effect (approximately three times as large) on perceptions of risk than did workers' own experiences with incidents in the workplace.[43]

In short, management has a central role to play in improving safety performance. By sending a strong message about the importance of health and safety in the organization, by holding individuals responsible for their own and their subordinates' safety performance, and by taking safety concerns seriously, managers establish an orientation toward health and safety that allows individuals to perform their jobs safely. We suggest that there are two important vehicles by means of which management communicates the value they place on safety in their organization: the safety climate, and safety leadership. We will consider each of these in turn.

Safety Climate

You will recall from the previous chapter that an organization's **safety climate** reflects the shared perceptions among all employees and organizational stakeholders regarding the importance of safety in the workplace.[44] A positive safety climate is associated with a number of positive safety outcomes such as improved safety motivation, reduced injuries, and lower rates of underreporting for workplace injury.[45]

safety climate employees' shared perceptions of the importance of safety in the workplace

If employees are to have positive perceptions regarding the safety climate in their workplace, the organization itself must be committed to workplace safety. An organization can promote a positive safety climate in several ways. One approach is to have explicit and enacted policies on safety. If employees are aware of the organizational safety policy and believe the organization stands behind that policy, they should feel secure in making safety a priority in their own actions. In this way, the policy will contribute to safe conduct. As you'll see below, an Occupational Health and Safety Management System can help integrate OH&S concerns across a company's operations.

A second approach that organizations can take to promote a healthy awareness of safety in the workplace, and as such promote a positive safety climate, is to include safety-related information when communicating production-related goals. A managerial focus on achieving high productivity may inadvertently deter employee safety. To the extent that employees want to reach or exceed the organizational production expectations, they may become so focused on working quickly that they ignore safety protocols. Certainly, such a course of events is most likely in cases where following safety procedures slows the pace of work. Therefore, managers should be careful to stress that the achievement of production goals does not come before employee safety at work.

As we noted in Chapter 9, an organization can also foster a positive safety climate by ensuring that employees have the appropriate safety training and by encouraging the utilization on the worksite of knowledge gained in such training. Training ensures that employees have the needed ability to engage in safe behaviour at work. For instance, safety training has been associated with improved safety climate in university laboratories.[46]

Some organizations choose to promote safety, and influence the safety climate, by rewarding safe behaviour. In these organizations, individuals or groups with good safety records benefit from various bonuses or even job promotions. Other companies opt to withhold rewards from those who have a safety violation on their record. Still others promote their reputation as a safe organization by making their safety records—such as number of days without a lost-time injury—available to the public. The data are mixed as to the effectiveness of these approaches. As discussed in **OH&S Today 10.1**, there is potentially a risky side to behavioural-based programs.

Perceived safety climate is a strong predictor of employees' safety performance.[47] One study of restaurant employees nicely illustrates the impact of an organization's safety climate on safety-related outcomes. The study reported that positive safety climate perceptions were related to a reduction in safety-related events common in restaurants (e.g., knife slips, grease spatters, trips). This decrease in safety events in turn contributed to a reduction in occupational injuries (e.g., cuts, burns, fractured bones).[48] A study of drivers in a motor vehicle fleet found that safety climate perceptions were associated with the safety of current work-related driving behaviour and of future driving intentions.[49] Thus, linking back to our earlier consideration of safety behaviour, it seems that a positive safety climate encourages employees to engage in safety compliance and in safety participation.

Safety Leadership

safety leadership
organizational leadership that is actively focused on and promotes occupational health and safety

One effective way for organizations to create opportunities for safety behaviour and to achieve a positive safety climate is to promote **safety leadership**—that is, organizational leadership that focuses on and promotes safety. Substantial evidence suggests that when leaders actively promote safety, employees and organizations alike experience better safety records and more positive safety outcomes.[50] For instance, employees' perceptions of managers' and supervisors' commitments to safety are strongly related to safety-related outcomes.[51] Similarly, employees' perceptions of managerial receptiveness to safety issues predict individual willingness to raise work-related safety concerns.[52] Additionally, employees' perceptions of supervisors' safety-related leadership are positively associated with safety consciousness, perceptions of the safety climate, and, through these intervening variables, safety events and actual injuries.[53]

The accumulated research illustrates the importance of active safety-focused behaviour on the part of leaders to realize positive safety-related attitudes and safety behaviour in the workplace. In a recent study, the tendency for leaders to take a passive approach to safety rather than actively promote safe behaviour among employees was associated with negative health and safety–related outcomes.[54] Leaders who ignore safety concerns and who "turn a blind eye" to safety-related issues may think they are not doing any harm. However, it appears that such leaders are sending a message to their employees that safety issues are not important and in that way are discouraging safe performance of work-related tasks.

How can leaders actively promote safety? There are several styles of leadership that focus on active and engaged leaders. Two such styles that have received attention in the OH&S domain are active transactional leadership and transformational leadership. Let's consider each of these as they apply to workplace health and safety.

ACTIVE TRANSACTIONAL LEADERSHIP   Via transactional leadership, leaders articulate to workers the tasks that are required to meet leadership expectations.[55] Sometimes this is achieved in a passive manner, whereby leaders only intervene to correct problems that occur. More effectively, individuals can use **active types of transactional leadership**. One such active approach is **contingent reward**, in which leaders reward employees who meet their communicated expectations.[56] Sound familiar? Influencing safety behaviour by rewarding consequences is an aspect of behaviour-based safety programs. In the academic safety literature, safety-related contingent rewards have been associated with fewer injuries, as well as increased safety compliance and participation.[57] Certainly, one would imagine that being rewarded for adhering to articulated safety rules would lead to safety compliance behaviour.

Leaders might also invoke a type of active transactional leadership called **management by exception (active)**. Via this method, leaders monitor workers' actions and step in with corrective action when needed to prevent serious problems from occurring.[58] The influence of management by exception (active) on safety behaviour is not fully clear. Some research has treated this method as an intrusive and corrective form of leadership and found it has negative effects on safety.[59] However, in the broader sense, management by exception (active) has been associated with positive outcomes such as perceived leader effectiveness.[60] Certainly, in safety-critical occupations well-timed corrective actions can help avert disaster.[61] Such an approach may also draw attention to safety rules, thus promoting safety compliance.

A recent meta-analytic review of safety leadership found that active transactional leadership was directly associated with increased safety compliance, which in turn predicted reduced workplace injuries. Active transactional leadership also has a positive effect on safety climate. Safety climate was related to safety participation, which in turn predicted injuries.[62] The take home message? Active transactional leadership can exert a positive influence on safety in workplaces.

active transactional leadership

a form of leadership based on the foundation that leaders actively communicate to followers the tasks that are required to meet expectations.

contingent reward

a form of active transactional leadership in which leaders reward employees who meet their communicated expectations.

management by exception (active)

a form of active transactional leadership in which leaders monitor workers' actions and step in with corrective action when needed to prevent serious problems from occurring

transformational
leadership

highly effective approach
to leadership that
emphasizes employee well-
being and is characterized
by idealized influence,
inspirational motivation,
intellectual stimulation,
and individualized
consideration

TRANSFORMATIONAL LEADERSHIP   Another active approach to safety leadership is **transformational leadership**. Transformational leadership can help leaders become champions of safety.

Transformational leaders are highly effective leaders who also show a substantial degree of concern for the well-being of their employees.[63] Transformational leaders exhibit four characteristics in their interactions with their employees: idealized influence, inspirational motivation, intellectual stimulation, and individualized consideration.[64] Transformational leaders provide idealized influence in that they are admired and trusted role models. Via inspirational motivation, transformational leaders communicate high expectations to their subordinates and provide a sense of meaning and challenge for followers. Transformational leaders intellectually stimulate their followers in that they encourage creativity and questioning of the status quo. Finally, transformational leaders provide individualized consideration in that they pay attention to each employee as an individual and act as a mentor or coach.

When these characteristics are directed toward safety-related concerns, improved safety behaviours tend to follow.[65] Research evidence shows that transformational leadership is associated with increased safety compliance and participation.[66] For instance, a leader who communicates high expectations regarding the safe performance of work tasks, who motivates employees to behave safely and report safety concerns, who encourages employees to question the assumption that working safely is working slowly, and who individually discusses safety concerns with employees is engaging in safety-specific transformational leadership. Such a leader is likely to foster a highly safe work environment. A research example from the nuclear power industry shows that the promotion of open communication via empowering leadership is associated with improved safety participation.[67]

For an organization looking to improve its safety climate and provide an environment in which employees feel able to engage in safety behaviours, an increased focus on transformational leadership may be one option. Studies suggest that transformational leadership, including safety-specific transformational leadership, can be effectively trained.[68]

In the same review and meta-analysis referenced above, the accumulated evidence showed that transformational leadership had a direct and positive effect on safety participation behaviour and an indirect effect, via its influence on safety climate, on safety compliance. Contrast this to active transactional leadership, which had the opposite pattern directly affecting compliance, but only indirectly affecting participation.[69] What does this pattern mean? It might mean that different types of active leader behaviour differentially predict safety outcomes. That is, active transactional leadership on its own might promote and sustain safety compliance behaviour among employees, but promoting and sustaining safety participation may require the safety championing support of a transformational safety leader.

Academic research provides further support for the importance of leaders consistently engaging in active forms of safety leadership. A recent study showed that when leaders display inconsistent safety leadership, or leadership that varies between active and passive, it can reduce the positive effects of transformational safety leadership on safety outcomes.[70] Under such circumstances employees may feel that they are getting mixed messages about the true value that their leader and organization place on safety.

ORGANIZATIONAL HEALTH AND SAFETY MANAGEMENT SYSTEMS

Throughout this chapter and the previous chapter on training, we have considered how to promote safe behaviour in the workplace. We have concluded that the utilization of safety behaviour requires that employees have the needed skills, be motivated to act in a safe manner, and have the opportunity to engage in safe behaviour while at work. We now consider how all of these come together in workplaces. One vital tool for organizations is an **Occupational Health and Safety Management System (OHSMS)**. OHSMS interventions have become increasingly popular over the past two decades with organizations implementing systems and various agencies, for instance, the Canadian Standards Association and the International Labour Organization, developing standards and auditing practices for their development and implementation.

Occupational Health and Safety Management Systems range in scope. The Canadian Standards Association (CSA) defines OHSMS as "part of the overall management of the organization that addresses OH&S hazards and risks associated with its activities."[71] An effective OHSMS places OH&S as an integrated concern across all aspects of an organization's business operations. For instance, all departments, such as human resources, purchasing, maintenance, finance, and sales should consider OH&S as a core concern. What might this look like in practice? An OHSMS might dictate that the purchasing department should routinely consider safety as a decision factor before deciding on new equipment to buy and install. The finance department should consider OH&S in its budgeting processes, and maintenance should keep in mind all the recommended upkeep procedures to ensure that equipment functions safely.

What separates an OHSMS from more traditional OH&S programs? Typically, OHSMS feature OH&S concerns in a more integrated and proactive light.[72] Although OHSMS approaches may differ across organizations, there are some common features. First and foremost in many OHSMS is a focus on organizational and leadership commitment to safety. Similarly, employee participation, the assurance of adequate resources to support OH&S activities, and safety goals and objectives are core features in these systems.[73] For more on these and other common OHSMS features see **OH&S Notebook 10.2**.

There are several standards available internationally by which to measure OHSMS. These include the International Labour Organization's ILO-OSH 2001, The British Standards Institute's OHSAS 18001, and the American National Standards Institute's ANSI Z10. The Canadian Standards Association published its standard for Occupational Health and Safety Management Systems, CSA-Z1000-06, in 2006. The various standards have much in common in guiding organizations toward effective occupational health and safety management systems. Let's consider the CSA-Z1000-06 in more detail.

Like many other standards, the CSA-Z1000-06 is based on the Plan-Do-Check-Act continuous quality improvement model.[74] As illustrated in Figure 10.2, this cycle promotes OH&S in a strategic and continuous manner. Guided by OH&S policy, the Plan stage allows organizations to consider such issues as hazards and risk, legal requirements pertaining to safety, and the setting of OH&S goals and objectives. At the Do stage organizations are engaged in ongoing safety activities such as emergency preparedness, safety training, and preventive measures. The Check stage incorporates such activities as incident investigation, safety monitoring, and auditing. The Act stage involves managerial review and continuous improvement.

Occupational Health and Safety Management System (OHSMS)

part of the overall management of the organization that addresses OH&S hazards and risks associated with its activities

The Plan-Do-Check-Act model is cyclical. For instance, a concern raised via managerial review would influence later planning and acting with respect to OH&S.

CSA-Z1000-06 notes that commitment, leadership, and participation are "crucial to the success of an OHSMS."[75] Its proscribed activities for senior management include establishing the OHSMS, ensuring appropriate resources for OH&S, developing OH&S policy, and encouraging worker participation. To encourage worker participation, the CSA-Z1000-06 encourages organizations to do such things as remove barriers to participation, establish OH&S committees, and deliver appropriate health and safety training.

FIGURE 10.2

The CSA-Z1000-06 Plan-Do-Check-Act Model for Occupational Health and Safety Management Systems

Source: With the permission of the Canadian Standards Association (operating as CSA Group), material is reproduced from CSA Group standard, Z1000-06 entitled "Occupational Health and Safety Management" which is copyrighted by CSA Group, 5060 Spectrum Way, Suite 100, Mississauga ON, L4W 5N6. This material is not the complete and official position of CSA Group on the referenced subject, which is represented solely by the standard in its entirety. While use of the material has been authorized, CSA is not responsible for the manner in which the data is presented, nor for any interpretations thereof. For more information or to purchase standards from CSA Group, please visit http://shop.csa.ca/ or call 1-800-463-6727.

OH&S Notebook 10.2

PRIMARY ELEMENTS OF OCCUPATIONAL HEALTH AND SAFETY MANAGEMENT SYSTEMS

There are several standards for Occupational Health and Safety Management Systems available internationally. These various models have much in common with each other and provide frameworks by which organizations can become more proactive about safety and integrate OH&S across their business operations. What are the core elements of an OHSMS? One team of researchers who were developing a performance measurement tool for OHSMSs compared a range of models. Choosing four highly comprehensive models they identified 16 primary elements of OHSMSs to incorporate into their assessment tool. They are:

1. Management commitment and resources
2. Employee participation
3. OHS policy
4. Goals and objectives
5. Performance measures
6. System planning and development
7. OHSMS manual and procedures
8. Training system
9. Hazard control system
10. Prevention and corrective action system
11. Procurement and contracting
12. Communication system
13. Evaluation system
14. Continual improvement
15. Integration
16. Management review

Sources: C.F. Redinger & S.P. Levine, "Development and Evaluation of the Michigan Occupational Health and Safety Management System Assessment Instrument: A Universal OHSMS Performance Measurement Tool," *American Industrial Hygiene Association Journal*, Vol. 59, Pg. 578, 1998; L.S. Robson, J.A. Clarke, K. Cullen, A. Bielecky, C. Severin, P.L. Bigelow, E. Irvin, A. Culyer, & Q. Mahood, "The Effectiveness of Occupational Health and Safety Management System Interventions: A Systematic Review," Safety Science, Vol. 45, Pg. 332, 2007.

The CSA-Z1000-06 also recognizes the core role of an OH&S policy in the effective delivery of an OHSMS.[76] The policy should be developed in consultation with employee groups. Once adopted, it should be widely publicized by means of meetings, newsletters, pamphlets, and so forth. The policy should be posted in management offices to serve as a constant reminder of the commitment and responsibility of the executive branch. The corporate health and safety policy is the most visible sign of management commitment to health and safety, so this commitment should be expressed clearly and unambiguously.

Individuals must understand their role in enacting the health and safety policy. Accountability for OH&S elements assigned to various positions should be articulated. Employees should be held responsible for safe work practices, including the reporting of all observed unsafe practices, procedures, and hazards to the appropriate supervisor. All employees should be required to participate in OH&S training and development programs. As part of the OHSMS, a timetable for the review and evaluation of the policy and regulations by the chief executive officer, president, or board should be outlined.

For more information, see the tips for writing a health and safety policy outlined in **OH&S Notebook 10.3**.

OH&S Today (10.3

Setting a Goal for Safety: "Nobody Gets Hurt" at Imperial Oil

Imperial Oil is committed to a safe and productive workplace with the goal "Nobody Gets Hurt." The company is working toward this goal via the company-wide Operations Integrity Management System (OIMS), which is a comprehensive health and safety framework that focuses on 11 elements, with management leadership, commitment, and accountability viewed as a core driver of the system. Imperial Oil believes that its health and safety focus contributes to organizational performance and increases its competitive advantage.

Imperial Oil's commitment to health and safety is showing results. In 2009, the company was awarded the Steward of Excellence award for safety performance by the Canadian Association of Petroleum Producers for its program "Contractor Safety: Improving More than Statistics." This program realized substantial change in the challenging, high turnover business of well-servicing. Others aspects of Imperial's health and safety program includes safety leadership training, office safety, and driver safety. Imperial Oil also involves employees at all major sites and its contractors in discussions about health and safety priorities.

Source: Imperial Oil. Found at: http://www.imperialoil.ca/Canada-English/community_safety.aspx (Accessed Dec. 30, 2012).

Occupational Health and Safety Management Systems can be mandatory or voluntary, depending on your location. In some countries, it is mandatory for organizations to have an OHSMS in place. For example, Norway via its regulations requires an OHSMS. In Canada, an OHSMS and compliance with CSA-Z1000-06 is voluntary for organizations. However, despite its voluntary nature, implementing an OHSMS that meets the CSA-Z1000-06 standards carries numerous benefits. An effective OHSMS can help to improve an organization's OH&S performance. One study found that organizations that adopted an OHSMS had better safety performance on a variety of outcomes including employee safety training, articulation of safety goals, risk identification, and risk analysis.[77] Another study reported that improvements in existing OHSMSs were associated with improved safety outcomes including safety participation.[78]

Another benefit of adopting an OHSMS that complies with the CSA-Z1000-06 standard is that if a safety incident were to occur, compliance with the standard would help an organization establish due diligence. A common misconception exists that written programs, policies, and audits raise the liability of the corporation in terms of regulatory compliance or in the event of a safety incident. In fact, many courts are basing the severity of civil and criminal penalties in part on the employer's ability to prove that it was duly diligent in auditing and correcting deficiencies in its own operations. If the corporation does not have an OHSMS in place, how will it prove beyond a reasonable doubt that it has taken every reasonable precaution to ensure the health and safety of the workers and the environment? In Canada, what was once the maximum fine for OH&S violations—$25,000—is now routine. Corporations in some jurisdictions can be fined up to $500,000 for each offence. As of March 31, 2004, Bill C-45, the Westray Bill, became an enforceable law in Canada. Under this law, employers whose OH&S violations are deemed negligent can be criminally charged and face substantial jail time. Clearly, maintaining an OHSMS is increasingly important for Canadian employers.

OH&S Notebook 10.3

HEALTH AND SAFETY POLICY CHECKLIST

An organizational health and safety policy must be comprehensive and effective. The CCOHS provides useful information regarding policy development and evaluation on its website. Below is a list of example questions that a health and safety committee might ask when evaluating its own policy. Responses to the following checklist questions of this type will help guide further development and refining of the policy:

- Is a clear commitment to health and safety evident in the policy statement?
- Is the senior officer responsible for implementing and reviewing the policy identified?
- Is the policy signed by the president or CEO?
- Have the views of all stakeholders (e.g., employees, managers, supervisors, safety representatives, and safety committees) been incorporated?
- Was the safe performance of work tasks discussed with employees? Is there a clear statement of how their performance will be assessed?
- Is the role of employees in health and safety matters stated (e.g., the position on inspection teams and safety committees)?
- Are individual responsibilities for health and safety duties clearly allocated?
- Are the people responsible for such functions as safety incident reports, safety inspections, and first aid identified?

- Is health and safety given as great a priority as economic and marketing matters?
- Is the employer's duty to provide health and safety training to all employees stated in the policy?
- Does the policy ensure that health and safety issues will be considered when planning new methods or processes?
- Is the financing of health and safety programs detailed and ensured?
- Are all employees aware of the policy? Are copies of the policy available to all employees?
- Are there periodic revisions and updates of the safety policy? Are the procedures for and timing of such reviews clarified?
- Does the policy make clear that the ultimate responsibility for safety rests with senior management?
- Is safety and health performance included in employee performance reviews?
- Does the policy list arrangements for liaison with contractors?
- Does the policy help make individuals aware of their legal responsibilities?

For additional information on how to implement OH&S programs, visit the WorkSafeBC website, which has a useful publication on program development that can be downloaded (see **Weblinks**).

Source: CCOHS, "Guide to writing an OHS policy statement." Found at: http://www.ccohs.ca/oshanswers/hsprograms/osh_policy.html (Accessed Jan. 15, 2010).

SUMMARY

A comprehensive approach to increasing health and safety in the workplace should emphasize employees' ability to act in a safe manner, their motivation to do so, and the provision of opportunities to perform their tasks safely. A number of approaches can be taken to increase employees' safety motivation, including the use of behaviour modification, goal setting, and a focus on autonomous motivation via self-determination theory. Also, the organizational context in which the employee is asked to perform his or her work should emphasize safety. We stressed the importance of a positive safety climate and active safety leadership in setting the stage for safety behaviours. We also considered the importance of an Occupational Health and Safety Management System, particularly those that comply with standards such as the CSA-Z1000-06 to help integrate OH&S with other organizational functions, to improve an organization's safety performance and to demonstrate due diligence.

Key Terms

active transactional leadership 265
amotivation 260
autonomous motivation 260
contingent reward 265
controlled motivation 260
extrinsic motivation 260
intrinsic motivation 260
management by exception (active) 265
motivation 255

Occupational Health and Safety
    Management System (OHSMS) 267
safety behaviours 253
safety climate 263
safety compliance 254
safety leadership 264
safety motivation 255
safety participation 254
transformational leadership 266

Weblinks

Canadian Centre for Occupational Health and Safety, "OSH Answers"
http://www.ccohs.ca/oshanswers

Canadian Standards Association
http://www.csa.ca/cm/ca/en/home

Imperial Oil
http://www.imperialoil.ca

International Labour Organization
http://www.ilo.org/public/english/region/afpro/cairo/downloads/wcms_153930
.pdf

Ontario Power Generation
http://www.opg.com

Safety Leader of the Year
http://www.cos-mag.com/cos-safety-leader-of-the-year-award.html

Self-Determination Theory
http://www.selfdeterminationtheory.org/theory

Transport Canada, "Score Your Safety Culture (TP 13844)"
http://www.tc.gc.ca/eng/civilaviation/publications/tp13844-menu-275.htm

Workers' Health and Safety Centre
http://www.whsc.on.ca

Required Professional Capabilities (RPCs)

The following RPCs, listed by their CCHRA number, are relevant to the material covered in this chapter. All RPCs can be found at http://www.chrp.ca/rpc/body-of-knowledge.

RPC:170 Develops, implements, and ensures the application of policies, regulations, and standards relating to occupational health and safety.

RPC:172 Ensures due diligence and liability requirements are met.*

RPC:174 Develops and implements policies on the workplace environment.*

RPC:177 Develops or provides for wellness and employee assistance programs to support organizational effectiveness.*

RPC:178 Provides information to employees and managers on available programs.

RPC:179 Ensures that mechanisms are in place for responding to crises in the workplace, including critical incident stress management.*

RPC:183 Analyzes risks to employee health & safety and develops preventive programs.*

Discussion Questions

1. Though considerable empirical data support their effectiveness, debate continues about the use of behaviourally based safety programs in industry. Employees and unions have often rejected such programs. Why do you think this is so? What can be done to enhance the acceptance of such programs?
2. Explain how focusing on behaviours rather than on safety incidents might be a better approach to improving occupational health and safety.
3. Why do you think setting goals can influence an employee's safety-related actions in the workplace?
4. How might organizations help employees create autonomous motivation for safety-related behaviours?
5. Describe the role of an organization's safety climate in the promotion of safety behaviours at work.
6. What role must organizational leaders play in creating a safety-focused workforce?
7. What are the main characteristics of Occupational Health and Safety Management Systems?
8. What are the main benefits of OH&S management systems, like CSA-Z1000-06? What types of challenges might an organization face when trying to implement such a program?

Using the Internet

1. Many organizations have their health and safety policies posted on their websites. With a group of classmates, examine these policies. Each of you should choose a different organization in a different market sector. How long are the policies? What information do they cover? Do they establish the unique responsibilities of management and employees? Do they refer to the organization's safety leadership? Compare your findings with those of your classmates.

* Canadian Council of Human Resources Associations, Human Resources Professionals in Canada: Revised Body of Knowledge and Required Professional Capabilities (RPCs ®), 2007.

2. Assess the safety climate of your school or workplace. The following Weblink may give you some ideas about questions that assess factors related to safety climate: http://www.tc.gc.ca/eng/civilaviation/publications/tp13844-menu-275.htm.

3. Search social media sites such as Facebook and Twitter for organizations that are using these sites to promote occupational health and safety. What are some of the messages they are getting out? Who are they likely to reach? To what extent are they interactive? Do you think that social media are effective tools in communicating OH&S messages?

4. Organizations are increasingly adopting comprehensive OH&S management systems that aim to comply with the standards articulated by various agencies (e.g., CSA, ILO). Search the Internet for examples of the types of management systems companies are using. Compare the programs to the frameworks suggested by the standards' associations. Do you think they comply?

Exercises

1. In discussing health and safety management systems, we have emphasized the responsibilities and roles of management in establishing and enforcing safety standards. What is the role of employees in these programs? To what extent should employees be responsible for taking the initiative to enhance health and safety in the workplace?

2. Imagine you are on a newly formed national committee that will be awarding safety awards to Canadian organizations. The mandate of this committee is to recognize excellence in the promotion of safety at work. What criteria do you think should be used to assess organizations' performance in this area? Create a draft of a rating form that the committee might use to evaluate nominated organizations.

3. Throughout this chapter we have emphasized the importance of managerial support for health and safety initiatives. In particular, we have noted the importance of a positive safety climate in the realization of safety-related goals. Imagine you are the newly hired human resource director in a manufacturing organization that currently does not place a high degree of value on health and safety—in other words, an organization with a negative safety climate. Top executives have indicated that they would like this situation to change, and they tell you that part of your job will be to improve safety performance in the organization. What are the first three initiatives you would launch to improve the safety climate of this organization?

4. With a small group of classmates, create a proposal for developing an effective OH&S management system for an organization that one of the team members has worked in (or is knowledgeable about). You will need to identify the health and safety concerns in that organization, suggest ways that

these concerns could be addressed, and describe how you (as an HRM consulting team) would go about solving these problems. Here are some questions you will need to consider:

a. What do you think the critical issues and real problems are, and why?
b. What OH&S knowledge that you have gained in this course can be applied to the problems you have identified?
c. What solutions do you propose, and why?
d. How would you implement your plan? Why?

Prepare a written proposal (eight to 10 doubled-spaced pages) detailing the proposed system. Your proposal must include an executive summary of no more than one page. Then develop an audio-visual presentation based on that proposal and deliver it to the class. (Based on an exercise by Catherine Fitzgerald.)

Case 1 NONCOMPLIANCE WITH SAFETY STANDARDS

Pat Singh is confused. As plant manager at a manufacturing plant, he has tried to comply with all applicable legislation. Based on his experiences as a line employee, Pat is particularly keen on health and safety initiatives, and he has spent a considerable sum of money to purchase the best available protective gear (e.g., hearing protectors, safety glasses, hardhats). Yet today when he walked through the plant, he saw many employees with the hearing protectors draped around their necks, the safety glasses tucked into their shirt pockets, and the hardhats hung on convenient pegs. Pat does not understand why workers won't wear the equipment bought for their protection. Pat has turned to you as a recognized expert in health and safety programming to improve conditions at the plant. What should Pat do?

Case 2 SAFETY IN THE BAKERY

Su Mei Lawrence manages the bakery department in a large supermarket. She oversees 20 employees working three shifts (the store is open 24 hours a day). Most employees are part-time, working 20 hours a week or less. Many are high school and university students working their way through school. In the past three weeks, Su Mei has noticed a marked increase in the number of safety-related incidents in the department. Several employees have injured their backs lifting racks of bread into position, and product has been crushed by the careless use of a forklift in the rear storage area. Today, one employee was knocked to the floor when a stack of 15 trays of bread fell on him. Su Mei is convinced it is time to take action to improve the safety of working conditions in the department, but she needs your help in deciding exactly what to do.

Case 3 WORKING TO CHANGE SAFETY

Ali Al-Farsi has recently purchased a medium-sized sawmill. He recognizes that health and safety has been a problem at the mill in the past—just last year, one worker lost a limb in a safety incident. Ali and his new management team are serious about safety and want to improve the mill's safety performance. You are the health and safety consultant who has been contracted to help Ali and his team engineer a safety turnaround at the mill. Your primary task is to help design and implement an occupational health and safety management system. What are the vital components of a successful health and safety management system? What steps would you work through with the team? How might Ali convince skeptical employees that a safer workplace is truly a priority?

NOTES

1. L.M. Goldenhar and P.A. Schulte, "Intervention Research in Occupational Health and Safety," *Journal of Occupational Medicine* 36 (1994): 763–75.
2. L.S. Robson, J.A. Clarke, K. Cullen, A. Bielecky, C. Severin, P.L. Bigelow, E. Irvin, A. Culyer, and Q. Mahood, "The Effectiveness of Occupational Health and Safety Management System Interventions: A Systematic Review," *Safety Science* 45 (2007): 329–53.
3. M.J. Colligan and A. Cohen, "The Role of Training in Promoting Workplace Safety and Health," in J. Barling and M. Frone, eds., *Handbook of Workplace Safety* (Washington: APA, 2004), 223–48.
4. S.E. Johnson, "Behavioral Safety Theory: Understanding the Theoretical Foundation," *Professional Safety*, October 2003, 39–44; B. Sulzer-Azaroff and A. Austin, "Does BBS Work? Behavior-Based Safety and Injury Reduction: A Survey of the Evidence," *Professional Safety*, July 2007, 19–24.
5. E.S. Geller, "Behavior-Based Safety in Industry: Realizing the Large-Scale Potential of Psychology to Promote Human Welfare," *Applied and Preventive Psychology* 10 (2001): 87–105; Sulzer-Azaroff and Austin, "Does BBS Work?"
6. A. Cohen and M.J. Colligan, "Accepting Occupational Health and Safety Regimens," in D.S. Gochman, ed., *Handbook of Health Behaviour Research II: Provider Determinants* (New York: Plenum, 1997), 379–94.
7. M.A. Griffin and A. Neal, "Perception of Safety at Work: A Framework for Linking Safety Climate to Safety Performance, Knowledge, and Motivation," *Journal of Occupational Health Psychology* 17 (2000): 347–58.
8. Ibid.
9. Ibid.
10. B. Sulzer-Azaroff, T.C. Harris, and K.B. McCann, "Beyond Training: Organizational Performance Management Techniques," in M.J. Colligan, ed., *Occupational Safety and Health Training* (Philadelphia: Hanley and Befus, 1994), 321–40.
11. M.S. Gazzaniga and T.F. Heatherton, *Psychological Science* (New York: Norton, 2006).
12. A. Neal and M.A. Griffin," A Study of the Lagged Relationships Among Safety Climate, Safety Motivation, Safety Behaviour, and Accidents at the Individual and Group Levels," *Journal of Applied Psychology* 91(2006): 946–53.
13. M.S. Christian, J.C. Bradley, J.C. Wallace, and M.J. Burke, "Workplace Safety: A Meta-analysis of the Roles of Person and Situation Factors," *Journal of Applied Psychology* 94 (2009):1103–27.

14. Geller, "Behavior-Based Safety in Industry"; J. Saari, "When Does Behaviour Modification Prevent Accidents?" *Leadership and Organizational Development Journal* 15 (1994): 11–15.

15. T. Setenay, H. Lotlikar, S. Salen, and N. Daraiseh, "Effectiveness of Behaviour Based Safety Interventions to Reduce Accidents and Injuries in Workplaces: Critical Appraisal and Meta-analysis," *Theoretical Issues in Ergonomics Science* 7 (2006): 191–209.

16. J.S. Hickman and E.S. Geller, "A Safety Self-Management Intervention for Mining Operations," *Journal of Safety Research* 34 (2003): 299–308.

17. K.A. Hutton, C.G. Sibley, D.N. Harper, and M. Hunt, "Modifying Driver Behaviour with Passenger Feedback," *Transportation Research Part F: Traffic Psychology and Behaviour* 4 (2001): 257–69.

18. M.D. Cooper, R.A. Phillips, and I.T. Robertson, "Improving Safety on Construction Sites by Psychologically Based Techniques: Alternative Approaches to the Measurement of Safety Behaviour," *European Review of Applied Psychology* 43 (1993): 33–37.

19. L.M. Frederiksen, ed., *Handbook of Organizational Behaviour Management* (New York: Wiley, 1982); Geller, "Behavior-Based Safety in Industry."

20. J. Komaki, "Promoting Job Safety and Accident Prevention," in M.F. Cataldo and J. Coates, eds., *Health and Industry: A Behavioural Medicine Perspective* (New York: Wiley, 1986), 301–19.

21. D. Zohar, "Modifying Supervisory Practices to Improve Subunit Safety: A Leadership-Based Intervention Model," *Journal of Applied Psychology* 87 (2002): 156–63.

22. M.L. Ambrose and C.T. Kulik, "Old Friends, New Faces: Motivation Research in the 1990s," *Journal of Management* 25 (1999): 231–92; E.A. Locke and G.P. Latham, "Building a Practically Useful Theory of Goal Setting and Task Motivation: A 35-Year Odyssey," *American Psychologist* 57 (2002): 705–17.

23. Locke and Latham, "Building a Practically Useful Theory."

24. P. Sheeran and M. Silverman, "Evaluation of Three Interventions to Promote Workplace Health and Safety: Evidence for the Utility of Implementation Intentions," *Social Science and Medicine* 56, no. 10 (2003): 2153–63.

25. Locke and Latham, "Building a Practically Useful Theory."

26. P.F. Drucker, "What Results Should You Expect: A User's Guide to MBO," *Public Administration Review* 36 (1976): 12–19.

27. R. Rodgers and J.E. Hunter, "Impact of Management by Objectives on Organizational Productivity," *Journal of Applied Psychology* 76 (1991): 322–36.

28. E. Rune, "Road Safety Management by Objectives: A Critical Analysis of the Norwegian Approach," *Accident Analysis and Prevention* 40(2008): 1115–22.

29. E.L. Deci and R.M. Ryan, *Handbook of Self-Determination Research* (Rochester, NY: The University of Rochester Press, 2002).

30. M. Gagné and E.L. Deci, "Self-determination Theory and Work Motivation," *Journal of Organizational Behaviour* 26 (2005): 331–62; and E.L. Deci and R.M. Ryan, *Handbook of Self-Determination Research.*

31. Ibid.

32. N. Scott, M. Fleming, and E.K. Kelloway, "Understanding Why Employees Behave Safely from a Self-Determination Theory Perspective," *The Oxford Handbook of Work Engagement, Motivation, and Self-Determination Theory.* Ed. M. Gagné, Oxford University Press, forthcoming.

33. Ibid.

34. M. Gagné and E.L. Deci, "Self-determination Theory and Work Motivation."

35. M. Gagné and E.L. Deci, "Self-determination Theory and Work Motivation"; and E.L. Deci and R.M. Ryan, "*Handbook of Self-Determination Research.*"

36. Ibid.

37. N. Scott, M. Fleming, and E.K. Kelloway, "Understanding Why Employees Behave Safely from a Self-Determination Theory Perspective," to appear in *The Oxford Handbook of Work Engagement, Motivation, and Self-Determination Theory.* Ed. M. Gagné, Oxford University Press.

38. Ibid.

39. M. Gagné and E.L. Deci, "Self-determination Theory and Work Motivation."

40. R.J. Feeney, "Why Is There Resistance to Wearing Protective Equipment at Work? Possible Strategies for Overcoming This," *Journal of Occupational Accidents* 8 (1986): 207–13.

41. Colligan and Cohen, "The Role of Training."

42. M.J. Smith, B.T. Karsh, P. Carayon, and F.T. Conway, "Controlling Occupational Safety and Health Hazards," in J.C. Quick and L.E. Tetrick, eds., *Handbook of Occupational Health Psychology* (Washington: APA, 2003), 35–68.

43. T. Cree and E.K. Kelloway, "Responses to Occupational Hazards: Exit and Participation," *Journal of Occupational Health Psychology* 2 (1997): 304–11.

44. D. Zohar, "Safety Climate in Industrial Organizations: Theoretical and Applied Implications," *Journal of Applied Psychology* 65 (1980): 96–102; idem, "The Effects of Leadership Dimensions, Safety Climate, and Assigned Priorities on Minor Injuries in Work Groups," *Journal of Organizational Behavior* 23 (2002): 75–92.

45. J. Barling, C. Loughlin, and E.K. Kelloway, "Development and Test of a Model Linking Safety-Specific Transformational Leadership and Occupational Safety," *Journal of Applied Psychology* 87 (2002): 488–96; A. Neal and M.A. Griffin, "A Study of the Lagged Relationships Among Safety Climate, Safety Motivation, Safety Behaviour, and Accidents at the Individual and Group Levels," *Journal of Applied Psychology* 91 (2006): 946–53; T.M. Probst, T.L. Brubaker, and A. Barsotti, "Organizational Injury Rate Underreporting: The Moderating Effect of Organizational Safety Climate," *Journal of Applied Psychology* 93 (2008): 1147–54.

46. T.-C. Wu, C.-W. Liu, and M.-C. Lu, "Safety Climate in University and College Laboratories: Impact of Organizational and Individual Factors," *Journal of Safety Research* 38 (2007): 91–102.

47. M. Hemingway and C.S. Smith, "Organizational Climate and Occupational Stressors as Predictors of Withdrawal Behaviours and Injuries in Nurses," *Journal of Occupational and Organizational Psychology* 72 (1999): 285–99; D.A. Hofmann and A. Stetzer, "A Cross-Level Investigation of Factors Influencing Unsafe Behaviours and Accidents," *Personnel Psychology* 49 (1996): 307–39.

48. Barling et al., "Development and Test of a Model."

49. A. Wills, B. Watson, and H. Biggs, "An Exploratory Investigation into Safety Climate and Work-Related Driving," *Work: Journal of Prevention, Assessment, and Rehabilitation* 32 (2009): 81–94.

50. Barling et al., "Development and Test of a Model"; C.-S. Lu and C.-S. Yang, "Safety Leadership and Safety Behaviour in Container Terminal Operations," *Safety Science* 48 (2010): 123–34; J. Mullen, "Testing a Model of Employee Willingness to Raise Safety Issues," *Canadian Journal of Behavioural Science* 37, no. 4 (2005): 273–82; H.S. Shannon, J. Mayr, and T. Haines, "Overview of the Relationship Between Organizational and Workplace Factors and Injury Rates," *Safety Science* 26 (1997): 201–17.

51. Cree and Kelloway, "Responses to Occupational Hazards."

52. J. Mullen, "Testing a Model of Employee Willingness to Raise Safety Issues," *Canadian Journal of Behavioural Science* 37, no. 4 (2005): 273–82.

53. Barling et al., "Development and Test of a Model."

54. E.K. Kelloway, J. Mullen, and L. Francis, "The Divergent Effects of Transformational and Passive Leadership on Employee Safety," *Journal of Occupational Health Psychology* 11 (2006): 76–86.

55. B.M. Bass, *Leadership and Performance Beyond Expectations* (New York: Free Press, 1985).

56. Ibid.

57. D. Zohar, "The Effects of Leadership Dimensions, Safety Climate, and Assigned Priorities on Minor Injuries in Work Groups," *Journal of Organizational Behavior* 23 (2002): 75–92; and E.A. Kapp, "The Influence of Supervisor Leadership Practices and Perceived Group Safety Climate on Employee Safety Performance," *Safety Science* 50 (2012): 1119–24.

58. B.M. Bass, *Leadership and Performance Beyond Expectations*.

59. D. Zohar, "The Effects of Leadership Dimensions, Safety Climate, and Assigned Priorities on Minor Injuries in Work Groups."

60. T.A. Judge and R.F Piccolo, "Transformational and Transactional Leadership: A Meta-analytic Test of Their Relative Validity," *Journal of Applied Psychology* 89 (2004): 755–68.

61. S. Clarke, "Safety Leadership: A Meta-analytic Review of Transformational and Transactional Leadership Styles as Antecedents of Safety Behaviour," *Journal of Occupational and Organizational Psychology*, early view published online 2012, DOI: 10.1111/j.2044-8325.2012.02064.x.

62. Ibid.

63. B.M. Bass, *Leadership and Performance Beyond Expectations*; T.A. Judge and J.E. Bono, "Five-Factor Model of Personality and Transformational Leadership," *Journal of Applied Psychology* 85 (2000): 751–65.

64. Idem, "From Transactional to Transformational Leadership: Learning to Share the Vision," *Organizational Dynamics* 18, no. 3 (1990): 19–31.

65. Barling et al., "Development and Test of a Model."

66. E.A. Kapp, "The Influence of Supervisor Leadership Practices and Perceived Group Safety Climate on Employee Safety Performance."

67. M. Martínez-Córcoles, M. Schöbel, F.J. Gracia, I. Tomás, and J.M. Peiró, "Linking Empowering Leadership to Safety Participation in Nuclear Power Plants: A Structural Equation Model," *Journal of Safety Research* 43 (2012): 215–21.

68. J. Barling, T. Weber, and E.K. Kelloway, "Effects of Transformational Leadership Training on Attitudinal and Financial Outcomes: A Field Experiment," *Journal of Applied Psychology* 81 (1996): 827–32; J.E. Mullen and E.K. Kelloway, "Safety Leadership: A Longitudinal Study of the Effects of Transformational Leadership on Safety Outcomes," *Journal of Occupational and Organizational Psychology* 82 (2009): 253–72.

69. S. Clarke, "Safety Leadership: A Meta-Analytic Review of Transformational and Transactional Leadership Styles as Antecedents of Safety Behaviour," *Journal of Occupational and Organizational Psychology*, early view published online 2012, DOI: 10.1111/j.2044-8325.2012.02064.x.

70. J. Mullen, E.K. Kelloway, and M. Teed, "Inconsistent Style of Leadership as a Predictor of Safety Behaviour," *Work and Stress* 25 (2011): 41–54.

71. Canadian Standards Association, CSA Standard Z1000-06: Occupational Health and Safety Management (Mississauga, Ontario: Canadian Standards Association, March 2006), p. 2.

72. L.S. Robson, J.A. Clarke, K. Cullen, A. Bielecky, C. Severin, P.L. Bigelow, E. Irvin, A. Culyer, and Q. Mahood, "The Effectiveness of Occupational Health and Safety Management System Interventions: A Systematic Review."

73. C.F. Redinger and S.P. Levine, "Development and Evaluation of the Michigan Occupational Health and Safety Management System Assessment Instrument: A Universal OHSMS Performance Measurement Tool," *American Industrial Hygiene Association Journal* 59 (1998): 572–81, p. 578.

74. L.S. Robson, J.A. Clarke, K. Cullen, A. Bielecky, C. Severin, P.L. Bigelow, E. Irvin, A. Culyer, and Q. Mahood, "The Effectiveness of Occupational Health and Safety Management System Interventions: A Systematic Review"; Canadian Standards Association, CSA Standard Z1000-06: Occupational Health and Safety Management and International

Labour Organization, OSH Management System: A Tool for Continual Improvement (ILO, 2011, ISBN for pdf 978-92-2-124740-1).

75. Canadian Standards Association, CSA Standard Z1000-06: Occupational Health and Safety Management.

76. Ibid.

77. E. Bottani, L. Monica, and G. Vignali, "Safety Management Systems: Performance Differences Between Adopters and Non-adopters," *Safety Science* 47 (2009), 155–62.

78. S. Torp and B.E. Moen, "The Effects of Occupational Health and Safety Management on Work Environment and Health: A Prospective Study, *Applied Ergonomics*, 37 (2006): 776–83.

Emergency Planning

CHAPTER LEARNING OBJECTIVES

After reading this chapter, you should be able to:

- define an emergency
- list the key elements in emergency preparedness
- describe the concept of an emergency plan
- explain the necessity of having emergency and evacuation plans
- describe the principles of fire prevention and suppression

DEEPWATER HORIZON

It was the largest offshore oil spill in North American history. On April 20, 2010, an explosion on the Deepwater Horizon oil rig—an offshore drilling platform in the Gulf of Mexico—killed 11 workers and caused a blowout that resulted in a massive oil spill in the Gulf. Although owned by Transocean, at the time of the explosion, the Deepwater Horizon was being operated by BP. At the time of this writing, the trial of BP has just commenced to determine whether, and to what extent, the company is liable. Early evidence suggests that although BP had a safety plan developed, it was not implemented on the Deepwater Horizon. If true, then one of the biggest environmental and OH&S tragedies might have been averted through better planning.

Source: M. Kunzelman, "BP didn't use rig safety plan, trial told," *Herald News*, Feb. 26, 2013. Found at: http://thechronicleherald.ca/world/790133-bp-didn-t-use-rig-safety-plan-trial-told (Accessed Mar. 4, 2013).

INTRODUCTION

The widespread impact of the 1998 ice storm in Ontario and Quebec, the events of September 11, 2001, the subsequent rash of anthrax-related scares, the outbreak of severe acute respiratory syndrome (SARS) in Canadian cities, the predicted H1N1 pandemic of 2009, the devastation of Hurricane Juan in Nova Scotia in 2003 and, of course, the Deepwater Horizon disaster, are all recent examples of emergencies. Some, such as the events of 9/11 and the SARS outbreak, happened in workplaces. The others were not specific to workplaces but required a response from both employers and employees.

In Canada, emergency response is largely up to individuals and each individual is responsible for knowing what to do in an emergency. As events overwhelm an individual's capacity to respond, governments take action in a progressive manner.

First, local emergency organizations (e.g., municipal emergency services, emergency measures organizations) respond. At the next level, each province and territory has an emergency measures organization (EMO) that is tasked with managing large-scale emergencies and with supporting local organizations as required. Finally, the federal government and its agencies may become involved in emergency response efforts, depending on the nature of the disaster. For example, during Hurricane Juan in Nova Scotia, the Canadian Forces were deployed to assist in the cleanup efforts.

Organizations must consider the possibility of a disaster, in which the potential for loss is very high. No safety program is complete without a planned response to the threat of a disaster.

Such plans comprise part of a company's due diligence on safety. In cases like the Deepwater Horizon, the company's liability for disasters may be increased by the failure to plan for emergencies that a reasonable person might anticipate. Many would suggest that there is also a moral responsibility (i.e., in addition to a legal responsibility) for companies to have emergency plans in place. This responsibility might be enhanced when companies' engage in activities that are thought to pose a special risk to the environment or to workers.

In this chapter we consider two central aspects of emergency planning in organizations. First, we consider issues related to emergency preparedness. Second, we address the organization's response to emergency. We finish the chapter with a specific consideration of fire and evacuation plans.

EMERGENCY PREPAREDNESS

An **emergency** is any sudden set of circumstances demanding immediate action. For the most part, we are concerned with emergencies that either cause or threaten to cause the loss of, or damage to, life or property. Being a victim of a computer virus or having your computer crash is also an emergency (and one that business needs to be concerned with), but we will limit our consideration to health and safety–related emergencies.

Emergencies can be naturally occurring or caused by humans. Naturally occurring emergencies include disease epidemics (animal, human, plant) and weather conditions (e.g., blizzards, hail, hurricanes, earthquakes, storm surges, torrential rain). Some natural emergencies may be deceptive, in that their severity may not be immediately apparent. For example, at the beginning of the SARS outbreak, nobody recognized the seriousness of the impending crisis—indeed, the initial diagnosis was atypical pneumonia. It was only a month after the initial reports from China that the World Health Organization issued a health alert.

Other emergencies are caused by humans. They can include explosions, accidents, fires, and chemical and oil spills. They can also include riots, civil disorder, terrorism, and acts of workplace violence. Riots and civil disorder have always been concerns of health and safety professionals; we now also recognize the need to anticipate and respond to terrorism and acts of violence.

The general probability of any of these emergencies actually happening may be low, but they *can* happen, and a company (or the home) is remiss if it does not institute an emergency plan. A disaster may be prevented or mitigated by an effective emergency plan.

Many organizations focus on how they will respond during an emergency; true emergency planning, though, begins long before the onset of any emergency and continues long afterwards. Emergency planning involves anticipating and planning for emergencies, putting those plans into action as needed, and then (1) getting back to work and (2) refining plans in light of new learning.

A recent study describes a five-stage crisis management process that generates specific strategies at each stage.[1] The first step, *signal detection*, is targeted at prevention and begins with the recognition that an emergency is possible or imminent. The next step, *preparation*, involves senior management in the adoption of a crisis management mindset, the creation of a response plan, and the introduction of response training. The third stage, *damage containment*, consumes most of an organization's crisis-management resources. The literature on organizational communication, organizational support, employee assistance programs (EAPs), and stress interventions focuses largely on activities at this stage. The fourth stage, *recovery*, involves developing short- and long-term plans to resume normal business.[2] The final stage is *learning*, where the focus is on

emergency
a sudden, generally unexpected occurrence or set of circumstances demanding immediate action

OH&S Notebook 11.1

EMERGENCY MEASURES ORGANIZATION

Each province and territory has its own emergency measures organization (EMO). EMOs specialize in emergency preparedness and emergency response and are often the best source of information on emergency-related topics. A contact list is provided below.

Alberta

Emergency Management Alberta
Phone: (780) 422-9000
Toll-free in Alberta: 310-0000
Fax: (780) 422-1549
http://www.municipalaffairs.gov.ab.ca/ ema_index.htm

British Columbia

Provincial Emergency Program (PEP)
Phone: (250) 952-4913
Fax: (250) 952-4888
http://www.pep.bc.ca

Manitoba

Emergency Measures Organization
Phone: (204) 945-4772
Toll-free: 1 (888) 267-8298
Fax: (204) 945-4620
http://www.manitobaemo.ca

New Brunswick

Emergency Measures Organization
Phone: (506) 453-2133
Toll-free: 1 (800) 561-4034
Fax: (506) 453-5513
http://www.gnb.ca/cnb/emo-omu/index-e.asp

Newfoundland and Labrador

Fire and Emergency Services
Fire Service Telephone: 1 (709) 729-1608
Fire Service Fax: 1 (709) 729-2524
Emergency Management Telephone: 1 (709) 729-3703
Emergency Management Fax: 1 (709) 729-3757
http://www.gov.nl.ca/fes/agency/index.html

Northwest Territories

Emergency Measures Organization
Phone: (867) 873-7083
http://www.maca.gov.nt.ca/emergency_management/index.htm

Nova Scotia

Emergency Measures Organization
Phone: (902) 424-5620
Fax: (902) 424-5376
http://emo.gov.ns.ca

assessing and reflecting on the incident with a view to improving operations and procedures.[3]

Though the benefits of a proactive response to emergencies are well known,[4] many organizations resist this and do not do any systematic preparation for emergencies.[5] Management commitment to preparedness seems to be a critical determinant of how organizations prepare for emergencies. Response strategies typically begin with organizational leaders.[6] Moreover, organizational leaders are responsible for both minimizing risk and responding to events in an effort to aid recovery and readjustment after the events have occurred.[7]

With respect to workplace violence, organizations make a huge mistake when they "focus on systems, operations, infrastructures and public relations and ignore the people ... [Employees] need to be assured of their safety and have their trust in leadership reinforced."[8] The importance of "people" issues was shown by a recent study in the aftermath of the Mount

Nunavut

Nunavut Emergency Management
Phone: (867) 975-5319
Fax: (867) 979-4221

Ontario

Ontario Emergency Management
Phone: (416) 314-3723
Fax: (416) 314-3758
http://www.mpss.jus.gov.on.ca/english/pub_security/
emo/about_emo.html

Prince Edward Island

Emergency Measures Organization
Phone: (902) 368-6361
Fax: (902) 368-6362
http://www.gov.pe.ca/jps/index.php3?number=
1030226&lang=E

Quebec

Sécurité Publique Quebec
Phone: (418) 644-6826
Fax: (418) 643-3194
Or one of the regional offices:
Gatineau: (819) 772-3737

Montreal: (514) 873-1300
Rimouski: (418) 727-3589
Sillery (Quebec): (418) 643-3244
Trois-Rivières: (819) 371-6703 or your municipality
http://www.msp.gouv.qc.ca/secivile/
secivile_en.asp?txtSection=oscq

Saskatchewan

Emergency Management Organization
Phone: (306) 787-9563
Fax: (306) 787-1694
http://www.cpsp.gov.sk.ca/SaskEMOYukon
Emergency Measures Organization
Phone: (867) 667-5220
Toll-free (in Yukon): 1 (800) 661-0408
Fax: (867) 393-6266
http://www.community.gov.yk.ca/emo/index.html

In addition, a federal department, Public Safety Canada, was formed in December 2003 to secure public safety in Canada. The department has several functions, of which emergency preparedness and response is one. The department of Public Safety and Emergency Preparedness can be found at http://www.publicsafety.gc.ca/index-eng.aspx.

Allison University Norwalk outbreak (see **OH&S Today 11.1**).[9] Students' perceptions of how well the university administration handled the crisis were a better predictor of their fear of future contamination and resulting stress than students' own experiences with the virus. Clearly, given the importance of these issues, HR has a major role to play in developing and implementing emergency plans.[10]

As was the case with other forms of hazard control (see Chapter 4), an emergency plan needs to consider issues at the precontact, contact, and postcontact stages of any emergency. Issues at the precontact stage include assessing hazards and planning potential responses. Issues at the contact stage include evacuation, caring for the injured, and ensuring emergency response. Issues at the postcontact stage include dealing with the emotional trauma of an emergency and issues regarding the orderly return to work.

OH&S Today 11.1

Norwalk Outbreak at Mount Allison

Mount Allison University, a small undergraduate university in Sackville, New Brunswick, reported an outbreak of the Norwalk virus on October 12, 2006. The outbreak had apparently begun five days earlier, and more than 300 students were thought to be affected. The university cancelled classes on Friday, October 13, and suspended all campus activities for the weekend. Hand-washing stations were established throughout the university, and all public areas of the university underwent decontamination procedures. These strategies were effective, and classes resumed on the Monday without further incident. However, students who were still recuperating from the illness were encouraged to not attend classes. On the advice of Public Health officials, the university resumed extracurricular activities and events on Wednesday, October 18.

Norwalk is actually a family of viruses that are spread primarily through fecal–oral contact. Contamination of food, water, or other vehicles as well as person-to-person transmission is possible. As such, Norwalk is highly contagious, and the Norwalk virus is the likely culprit behind many outbreaks of "stomach flu." Outbreaks are fairly frequent, especially in institutional settings (e.g., nursing homes, hospitals) and in close quarters (e.g., cruise ships). The virus results in a variety of gastro-intestinal symptoms and "is characterized by acute onset of nausea, vomiting, abdominal cramps, and diarrhea." The symptoms typically last one or two days.

Sources: CBC, "Mount Allison Virus Spread Through Bathrooms, Cafeteria: Officials." Found at: http://www.cbc.ca/canada/new-brunswick/story/2006/10/13/nb-fluoutbreak.html; Centers for Disease Control, "Norwalk-Like Viruses," Public Health Consequences and Outbreak Management (Atlanta: 2001).

Precontact

The necessary elements in managing emergencies include an emergency plan, an emergency manager, a fire plan, an evacuation plan, and a medical attention plan.

An Emergency Plan

The first thing required is a formal, workable, well-controlled, rapid-response emergency plan. Low levels of loss will depend on this plan. The JHSCs as well as the local government should be involved in developing the plan.

An organization requires the following: hazard evaluation, an emergency response plan, an evacuation plan, a means to notify the authorities, supplies, and drills.

HAZARD EVALUATION   HR and safety professionals (and managers) must evaluate the hazards that could cause an emergency (e.g., storage of flammable solvents near static electricity or ignition sources), as well as the hazards with the greatest risk and loss potential. They must also understand how emergency plans could be aborted or sidetracked if an emergency were to occur; the extent of possible damage and injuries or fatalities; and the possibility of the loss (including financial) of the total plant, its individual departments, and critical equipment or processes.

An emergency is a rare occurrence; knowledge of these hazards can be augmented by consulting Emergency Planning Canada, the Fire Commissioner of Canada, and Environment Canada, as well as fire departments and insurance companies. The likelihood of natural disasters varies by region. The federal government provides a Natural Hazards Map of Canada (see the Weblinks at the end of this chapter) and can assist in determining the risk for various disasters in your area based on historical precedent (see **OH&S Notebook 11.2**).

OH&S Notebook 11.2

FUTUREPROOFING

Writing for the Canadian Centre for Emergency Preparedness, Geary Sikich uses the term "futureproofing" to denote an integrated approach to emergency preparedness. Futureproofing is based on the notion that organizations have to anticipate and assess the potential risk and consequences of a wide range of emergencies in order to be protected from unexpected events. This approach is based on "graceful degradation" and "agile restoration"—that is, on the ability of the organization to identify an event, determine its consequences, establish a minimal functionality, and begin to direct efforts toward restoration in a timely fashion.

Source: G. Sikich, *Futureproofing—The Process of Active Analysis*. Found at: http://www.continuitycentral.com/ActiveAnalysisFutureproofing.pdf. (Accessed May 29, 2010).

EMERGENCY RESPONSE PLAN A response plan for different types of emergencies must be developed. These plans should be written, published, and posted. There must be good alarm facilities with emergency communication devices, and everyone in the plant must be familiar with their locations and use.

A list should be published of the people in charge of every aspect of any emergency activity. Accompanying the list should be information on the actual event, security and protection for the workers, protection of what is left, documentation of damage and injuries, and liaison with bureaucrats, insurance firms, and the media.

OH&S Today 11.2

Pandemic Planning

Health experts generally agree that there is a real risk of a pandemic flu outbreak in the near future. Indeed, many commentators maintain that the outbreak of Swine Flu, or H1N1 virus, in 2009 was the pandemic that had been predicted for the past 10 years or so. Possibly as a result of mass immunization and a large-scale public health response, the predicted pandemic did not occur. However, the possibility of such an outbreak is still very real. Any such outbreak is going to present substantial challenges to businesses. Imagine, for example, how businesses will cope with absenteeism rates in the neighbourhood of 35% to 50%, disruptions in key supplies, and the loss of key customers—conditions that may last for six weeks or more. Health care organizations will be particularly hard hit, as they are expected to experience the same staff and material shortages while at the same time being overwhelmed by the sudden increase in demand for their services. Staff will experience exceptionally high levels of stress from workloads—and the predicted mounting death rate will also extract a toll on health care workers. To begin preparing for the potential outbreak, the federal government has launched a coordinating website (http://www.influenza.gc.ca/index_e.html), as have provincial agencies (e.g., http://www.wsib.on.ca/wsib/wsibsite.nsf/Public/H1N1; http://www.health.gov.bc.ca/pandemic/planning.html) and larger municipalities (http://www.toronto.ca/health/pandemicflu/pandemicflu_plan.htm). As is the case for emergency planning in general, these plans attempt to forecast the likely effects of a pandemic and outline the necessary responses of various organizations.

EVACUATION PLAN   Plans for evacuating employees and clients in the event of a major emergency or disaster are a key element in emergency preparedness. Every worker in the plant must know exactly where to congregate when the need arises and be aware of at least two evacuation routes. There should be well-marked, unobstructed evacuation paths with well-lit exits. Notices about exit procedures should be posted, along with instructions about notifying appropriate personnel of the emergency. Designated assembly areas and assigned assistance should be part of the plan (see **OH&S Notebook 11.3**).

A roll call (head count) should be done at the assembly site, and a list of missing employees should be given to the command centre. No one should be allowed to re-enter a building until all personnel are accounted for and debriefed.

The following are some basic requirements of evacuation plans:

1. The site must be divided into small, related areas. The workers in each area must be identified and trained to recognize and remember workers who are not part of their section. This probably happens routinely during working hours, but the noted presence of these "outsiders" must become second nature. In case of a major emergency, all workers must be accounted for.

2. Outside the building and away from any roadways there should be assembly points that allow for the movement of emergency vehicles. The personnel from each work area noted above must be trained to quickly move to their respective assembly points and remain there until a head count is complete and missing workers are accounted for.

3. Once every employee has been accounted for and the extent of the emergency has been determined, employees can be instructed to return to work or to go home and report when called.

4. Any critical equipment or process that may increase the overall risk of the emergency should be addressed. For example, the supply sources of flammable materials such as gas must be shut off. These tasks should be undertaken only by maintenance personnel who are highly trained in emergency procedures.

5. The end of the emergency can be called only by the senior person responsible for the operation's emergency procedures.

6. A post-evacuation assessment must be done to identify problems in the evacuation plan. Remedial measures can then be taken.

OH&S Notebook 11.3
EVACUATION PLANS

Many types of organizations need well-developed evacuation plans that specify what should happen in case of an emergency such as a fire. Public institutions (e.g., schools, universities, hospitals, etc.) are examples of organizations that require specific evacuation plans. However, many workplaces are now located in high rise towers that require specific planning for emergencies. Human Resource Development Canada provides standards for such plans at http://www.hrsdc.gc.ca/eng/labour/fire_protection/policies_standards/guidelines/guide/high_rise.sht.

The Canadian Standards Association has developed a standard for emergency response plans (ERPs) that provides further information on evacuation requirements (CAN/CSA-Z731-03).Many organizations are now adopting two-stage alarm systems to alert building occupants to the possibility of an emergency and to provide instructions. In contrast to a one-stage alarm (e.g., in which a bell or horn sounds when the alarm is triggered and immediate evacuation is necessary), a two-stage alarm allows for different signals depending on the condition and locale. For example, at a university with many connected buildings a fire in the Science building may trigger an evacuation alarm. Additionally, however, connected buildings might receive an alert telling them to gather their belongings and be ready but not necessarily to evacuate. Two-stage alarms allow for the programmed evacuation of a building or buildings—when coupled with a voice system the alarms may also provide specific instructions to building occupants. If conditions worsen, then occupants of the second building can also be evacuated. The capacity to deliver announcements makes the alarm system more adaptable to a wide variety of emergency situations beyond fires.

NOTIFICATION OF AUTHORITIES Companies should be aware of any legislative requirements—such as the requirement to notify the Ministry of Labour, police, and so on—related to an emergency. In locations with the 911 emergency system, an industrial call for medical assistance will automatically bring police, ministry, and other associated specialists, along with medical assistance.

SUPPLIES   Emergency first-line equipment such as fire extinguishers must be in well-defined, easily accessible locations. Designated workers must be trained in their use.

DRILLS   Regular emergency drills, with the occasional unannounced drill to keep everyone current and knowledgeable, are a standard part of most plans. Rehearsals are an important part of training. Simulating disasters will help employees deal effectively with real emergencies. Fire drills are rehearsals that require employees to be aware of reporting requirements and the locations of exits and fire extinguishers. Drills test the response capability of the organization. The results (evacuation times, etc.) are monitored and reported to management. A full-scale dress rehearsal involves simulated injuries and provides a measure of an organization's ability to respond.

Emergency Manager

Any emergency plan must have a senior person—generally the plant manager— who will be in charge of all emergency activities. This individual should speak for the organization and must be committed to the plan. If the emergency manager works a regular day shift and the plant is on multiple shifts, there must be assistants on each of the other shifts with the authority and training to handle emergencies. The command centre, with a designated chain of command, is a critical component of the plan (see **OH&S Notebook 11.4**).

OH&S Notebook 11.4
EMERGENCY OPERATIONS CENTRES (EOCS)

Also called the command post or the command centre, an EOC is a geographic space dedicated to the strategic management of an emergency. An EOC is typically geographically separate from the actual emergency site. The role of the EOC is to designate the individual in charge of the emergency site, facilitate communications with the public, disseminate emergency public information, and initiate the recovery process.

The requirements for an EOC vary with circumstances but in general should include communications capabilities sufficient to allow coordination of efforts and space for briefings and decision making. Basic supplies (e.g., office supplies) should also be available along with connectivity through networks, radios, and so on.

Source: Province of New Brunswick, *Planning Guide for the Emergency Operations Centre*. Found at: http://www.gnb.ca/cnb/emo-omu/opscentre-e.pdf (Accessed May 29, 2010).

Contact

Fire Plan

The fire plan will have the same characteristics as the main emergency plan, though some of the requirements dealing with major damage and fatalities may not be followed if the fire gets out of control and a full-blown emergency results. A group of workers must be trained in firefighting techniques and be part of the plant's fire brigade. In small to mid-sized businesses in which an in-house fire brigade is not economically feasible, workers should receive fire extinguisher training and participate in ongoing practice sessions.

The local fire department is a good source of training for any in-house firefighting team that may be required. The fire department can also assist in fire hazard evaluations and regular inspections. Fire prevention and suppression is discussed next.

Fire Prevention and Suppression

fire
a chemical process in which fuel, oxygen, and heat are combined

A **fire** is a chemical process in which fuel, oxygen, and heat combine to create a disastrous condition. The products of fire are gases, flame, heat, and smoke.

The fire process can be graphically represented by means of the fire triangle (see Figure 11.1). The new model is the fire tetrahedron (see Figure 11.2). The triangular model shows that the three elements—fuel, oxygen, and heat—must come together for a fire to be sustained. The second model adds a fourth element: the chain reaction. Once a fire starts, it is perpetuated by the ongoing (or chain) reaction of the other three elements.

Fire has four stages:

incipient stage
a source of ignition and fuel come together

1. The **incipient stage**. At this stage, a source of ignition (a cigarette butt or a hot electrical wire connection) and fuel (papers or wood) come together. This stage can continue for hours until the resultant heat from the initial reaction becomes great enough to cause combustion. The air is filled with molecule-sized products of combustion. The airborne particulate can be

FIGURE 11.1

Fire Triangle

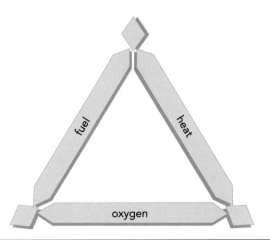

FIGURE 11.2

Fire Tetrahedron

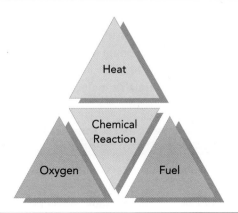

detected with an ionizing (smoke) detector. In the case of an explosion, this stage (and the next) is very short.

2. The **smouldering stage**. The three elements are present and are causing the heat to rise through limited chain reaction. The area begins to fill with smoke, which increases in amount as the process continues. With visible airborne particulate (smoke) now present, a photoelectric detector is effective. This stage is short and can be measured in minutes.

3. The **free-burning stage**. This is the stage at which flames first appear. The rate of energy release (heat) is increasing very rapidly, and the surrounding combustible materials are beginning to burn. The free-burning stage is very short and can be measured in minutes or less. A rate-of-rise detector can be effective at this stage because it senses the rapid temperature increase. This detector works well in conjunction with a sprinkler system.

smouldering stage
fuel, oxygen, and heat are present and are causing the heat to rise through limited chain reaction

free-burning stage
the stage at which flames first appear

uncontrolled fire stage

fire is out of control and major property damage is under way

4. The **uncontrolled fire stage**. The fire is out of control, and major property damage is under way. All personnel must be evacuated. This stage can be measured in seconds. The rate of reaction doubles every 10°C. No heat is lost during this reaction; rather, it becomes cumulative.

The fire triangle or tetrahedron (see Figures 11.1 and 11.2) can serve to illustrate the requirements for extinguishment. If any one of the parts of these models is removed, the fire cannot be sustained and will be put out. For instance, a carbon dioxide fire extinguisher blankets a fire with a gas that displaces the oxygen, thereby smothering the fire. Similarly, water sprayed on the fire reduces the heat, also resulting in extinguishment (see Table 11.1).

Hazardous byproducts of fires, besides heat and smoke, include carbon monoxide, carbon dioxide, hydrogen sulphide, sulphur dioxide, hydrogen cyanide, and hydrogen chloride. These toxic materials are produced when the burning materials (fuel) are broken down into their original chemicals under extreme heat and chain reactions.

When a fire prevention program is being developed, the following should be considered:

1. *Structural design.* Standards for the construction of buildings are detailed in the federal and provincial or territorial fire codes, as well as in fire marshal and building codes and regulations.
2. Barriers. Walls and floors can delay or prevent the spread of fire. Specially constructed fire barriers should be maintained.

reactive material

causes a violent, explosive reaction when it comes in contact with another material, such as acetylene with water, or bleach with chlorinated cleaner

3. *Detection and suppression.* Most buildings have a detection system that senses heat and smoke. When triggered, sprinklers are activated to suppress the fire.
4. *Storage.* Combustible materials should be rated and stored in separate or isolated areas. They should *not* be stored near exits, and **reactive materials** should not be stored near flammable materials.

TABLE (11.1)

Classes of Fire

Class	Group	Material	Symbol	Colour	Extinguisher
A	Combustible	Paper, wood	Triangle	Green	Water
B	Flammable liquid	Oil, grease, gas	Square	Red	CO_2, dry chemical
C	Electrical	Wiring	Circle	Blue	CO_2, halon
D	Metals	Flammable metals such as magnesium or titanium	Star	Yellow	Powder
K	Grease	Cooking oil, fat	Frying pan or K	Black	Wet grease chemical

Notes: Though comparatively rare, Class D fires require metal/sand extinguishers that work by smothering the fire. The most common extinguishing agent in this class is sodium chloride, but powdered copper metal (for lithium fires) and other materials are used. Class K is a more recent designation of fires. Extinguishers of this class are specially designed to supplement the fire suppression systems found in commercial kitchens. They use a wet chemical agent such as potassium acetate.

OH&S Notebook 11.5

RESCUES

As a result of some emergency conditions, individuals may be trapped in buildings that have been damaged. Rescue work requires highly specialized training and equipment. During the 1985 earthquake in Mexico City, some 130 untrained or ill-equipped volunteer rescuers died attempting to save others. A rescue proceeds in five stages:

1. Reconnaissance and dealing with surface casualties
2. Location and removal of lightly trapped casualties
3. Exploration of likely survival points
4. Further exploration and debris removal
5. Systematic debris removal

Source: Adapted from: *Keeping Canadians Safe: Basic Rescue Skills*, published by Public Safety Canada. Found at: http://www.ps-sp.gc.ca/prg/em/gds/brs-en.asp. Reproduced with the Permission of the Minister of Public Works and Government Services Canada, 2010.

OH&S Notebook 11.6

CHEMICAL SPILLS

A chemical spill is an uncontrolled release of gas, liquid, or solid chemical. Chemicals can, of course, be highly toxic, and emergency procedures must be oriented toward avoiding exposure to the chemical. Good procedures for a chemical spill include the following:

- Avoid coming into contact with the chemical and warn others in the area.
- Isolate the area around the spill.

- Assist those who are injured but do not risk exposing yourself to the chemical.
- Determine the level of response. If the spill is minor and trained personnel are available with the necessary protective gear and materials, the material should be cleaned up. Otherwise, the authorities should be contacted.

Source: University of Alberta, Environmental Health and Safety, "Chemical Spills." Found at: http://www.ehs.ualberta.ca/index.aspx?Pg=52#Spill, (Accessed Feb. 7, 2007).

Many fires are triggered by unsafe acts (e.g., a person tries to weld a container holding flammable liquid residue without cleaning it first) and unsafe conditions (e.g., faulty or improper equipment is installed near a potentially flammable material).

First Aid and Medical Attention

The various provincial and territorial regulations spell out in detail the requirements for first aid and medical aid facilities. Medical services run the gamut from a first aid kit in a small firm to a fully equipped hospital with doctors in very large firms. Degree of risk can be an additional factor in determining the extent of medical services. An insurance office with a staff of 4,000 would not likely need the same facilities as an automobile manufacturer with the same number of workers (see **OH&S Notebook 11.7**).

OH&S Notebook 11.7

LEGISLATED FIRST AID REQUIREMENTS

First aid training and supplies are mandated in OH&S legislation. The exact requirements vary by (1) jurisdiction, (2) the number of workers in the workplace, (3) the nature (and danger) of the work, and (4) the distance to the nearest medical facility. Regulations typically specify the number of trained first aiders, the level of training required, and the amount and type of first aid equipment that must be present. In remote workplaces, employers may also be required to provide emergency medical transportation.

Source: Saskatchewan Department of Labour, "First Aid in Saskatchewan Workplaces." Found at: http://www.labour.gov.sk.ca/safety/firstaid/index.htm (Accessed Feb. 7, 2007).

Beyond conforming to legal requirements, every company should arrange to have at least one trained first aid attendant present on each shift. All employees should be given the opportunity to take a cardiopulmonary resuscitation (CPR) course. A cost–benefit analysis may show that there would be advantages to contracting with a local occupational health clinic for medical aid services. These services might include pre-employment and post-employment medicals, exposure medical testing, and potential occupational illness identification. Complete first aid records must be kept and maintained.

Postcontact

Postcontact efforts focus on two areas: helping individuals deal with the stresses associated with experiencing or witnessing an emergency situation, and getting back to "normal" operations.

Stress

An emergency is an acute or catastrophic stressor (Chapter 7), and individuals may experience long-lasting consequences as a result. Acute stressors can be more psychologically devastating, and their effects more enduring, than chronic stressors, which suggests that their effects need to be understood. For example, individuals exposed to hurricanes and other traumatic stressors have reported ongoing impairments of psychological well-being, including symptoms of post-traumatic stress that endure for much longer than the actual precipitating event.[11] Studies of a variety of traumatic stressors suggest several dimensions that may be important to understanding the impact of stressors on individuals.

Studies have highlighted the role of control perceptions when individuals are exposed to stressful situations, including acute stressors.[12] Natural disasters such as hurricanes or blizzards may involve an almost total lack of control, suggesting that their effects may be pronounced.[13]

The multivariate risk/resilience model has been developed to explain individual reactions to disasters.[14] The model incorporates situational factors such as the extent to which the individual receives social support on an ongoing basis, targeted social support, or social support in direct response to the disaster, as well as the individual's exposure to the disaster.[15]

One approach to crisis response has been referred to as **critical incident stress debriefing (CISD)**. The characteristics of CISDs vary; generally, though, they involve psychologists (or other trained personnel) providing assistance immediately following a traumatic event in order to prevent the development of serious or lasting negative consequences. Elements of CISDs include ensuring confidentiality; providing individuals with the opportunity to talk about their perspective on, thoughts about, and emotional reactions to the incident; assessing psychological and physical symptoms; and providing information about stress responses and coping strategies.[16] CISD interventions are popular among individuals who are regularly exposed to traumatic stressors. For example, almost every police, fire, and ambulance service in the country has some form of CISD intervention for its employees. The Canadian Forces uses CISD to debrief returning peacekeepers.

One study of the effectiveness of CISD compared the coping strategies and levels of anger of two groups of police officers who had experienced a traumatic event.[17] One group of officers received CISD, the other did not. The results suggested that the CISD group exhibited more adaptive coping strategies and lower levels of anger than did those in the non-CISD group. The lack of random assignment to conditions casts some doubt on the validity of these findings, though they do provide preliminary evidence of the efficacy of CISD following exposure to traumatic work-related events. If these results are replicable, it would be unethical to withhold such debriefings from employees who experience traumatic events.

Unfortunately, despite these promising results, the research literature also provides a basis on which to question the effectiveness of CISD. First, a review of 67 studies concluded that debriefing does not mitigate the effects of traumatic stress.[18] Second, based on a meta-analytic review, other authors found that single-session debriefing was less effective than other forms of intervention and less effective than no intervention in reducing the effects of traumatic stress.[19] Finally, growing lists of studies suggest that individuals receiving CISD interventions may experience exacerbated traumatic reactions and more adverse outcomes.[20] These findings violate the widely accepted maxim that psychological interventions should in the first instance do no harm. The inconsistent findings as to the effectiveness of CISDs suggest the need for more research in this area, to identify whether some elements of CISDs are helpful and should be retained and whether some are harmful and should be removed from such programs.

Getting Back to Normal

Getting back to normal after an emergency is not as straightforward as a simple return to work. Depending on the circumstances, individuals may continue to experience stress reactions. They may also continue to live with the effects of the emergency (e.g., damaged housing, loss of income, transportation) long after its acute phase has passed. For example, Hurricane Juan in Nova Scotia passed in one night, but some individuals were without electricity for up to 14 days after the hurricane.

Given these potential reactions and experiences, it is unlikely that individuals will return to the workplace focused on the task at hand. Employers should display some tolerance for distractions and for employees' need to share their experiences. Adjusting to normal work may take some time (see **OH&S Notebook 11.8**).

critical incident stress debriefing (CISD)

a post-trauma intervention focused on providing victims with an opportunity to discuss their experiences and reactions to a traumatic event

OH&S Notebook 11.8

BUSINESS CONTINUITY PLANNING

Even during an emergency, critical services must be continued. Some employers may have to continue operations during an emergency, and all employers will eventually have to return to "normal" operations. Business continuity planning is a proactive approach to ensuring that critical services and products continue during an emergency. Developing a business continuity plan will help ensure that employers recover data, assets, and facilities and have the necessary resources (including human resources) to continue business.

Source: Adapted from: *Keeping Canadians Safe: A Guide to Business Continuity Planning*. Published by Public Safety Canada. Found at: http://www.ps-sp.gc.ca/prg/em/gds/bcp-en.asp#4. Reproduced with the permission of the Minister of Public Works and Government Services Canada, 2010.

Employers may inadvertently increase employee stress as a result of how they handle personnel decisions related to the emergency. In Halifax following Hurricane Juan, employers had to make several decisions that affected their employees. For instance, they had to make decisions about compensation for lost workdays following the storm and about employee attendance during the state of emergency. Similar decisions made after the February Blizzard (White Juan) elicited considerable anger from some employees. For an example, see the Weblinks section.

SUMMARY

The goals of an emergency plan are to reduce injuries and property damage and to restore the organization to its normal operations. Emergency preparedness consists of preparing an emergency response plan, designating and training those responsible for its implementation, and communicating it to employees. Developing an evacuation plan, establishing a fire prevention and suppression program, and controlling fire hazards are other elements of emergency preparedness.

Key Terms

critical incident stress
   debriefing (CISD) 295
emergency 283
fire 290
free-burning stage 291

incipient stage 290
reactive material 292
smouldering stage 291
uncontrolled fire stage 292

Weblinks

Canadian Red Cross
http://www.redcross.ca

Canadian Standards Association
http://www.csa.ca

CBC News, "Indepth: SARS—Severe Acute Respiratory Syndrome"
http://www.cbc.ca/news/background/sars

Emergency Management and Public Safety Institute
http://www.centennialcollege.ca/empsi

Government of Canada, "Public Safety Canada"
http://www.publicsafety.gc.ca/index-eng.aspx

Government of Nova Scotia, "Emergency Management Office"
http://emo.gov.ns.ca

Public Safety Canada, "Natural Hazards of Canada"
http://www.publicsafety.gc.ca/res/em/nh/index-eng.aspx

Simon Fraser University, "SFU Emergency and Continuity Planning"
http://www.sfu.ca/srs/emergency.html

St. John Ambulance
http://sjatraining.ca

University of Guelph, "Emergency Action Plan"
http://www.uoguelph.ca/police/campus-safety/emergency-action-plan

Required Professional Capabilities (RPCs)

The following RPCs, listed by their CCHRA number, are relevant to the material covered in this chapter. All RPCs can be found at http://www.chrp.ca/rpc/body-of-knowledge.

RPC:170 Develops, implements, and ensures the application of policies, regulations, and standards relating to occupational health and safety.

RPC:172 Ensures due diligence and liability requirements are met.

RPC:174 Develops and implements policies on the workplace environment.

RPC:175 Ensures adequate accommodation, modified work and graduated return to work programs are in place.

RPC:178 Provides information to employees and managers on available programs.

RPC:179 Ensures that mechanisms are in place for responding to crises in the workplace, including critical incident stress management.[*]

RPC:182 Responds to serious injury or fatality in the workplace.[*]

RPC:183 Analyzes risks to employee health & safety and develops preventive programs.[*]

RPC:185 Ensures that security programs and policies minimize risks while considering the obligation of the employer and the rights of employees, union, and third parties.

[*]Canadian Council of Human Resources Associations, Human Resources Professionals in Canada: Revised Body of Knowledge and Required Professional Capabilities (RPCs ®), 2007.

Discussion Questions

1. Who should be involved in developing emergency response plans?
2. What types of emergencies should organizations in your area be prepared for?
3. Decide what type of fire extinguisher would be most effective in the following fire situations:

   a. a hair dryer engulfed in smoke
   b. grease burning in a frying pan
   c. rags smoking in the garage
   d. a log that has rolled from the fireplace onto the living room floor
   e. a coffee machine whose wires are shooting flames

4. Though this chapter has focused on health and safety implications, there are also public relations issues in an emergency. What principles would be appropriate for an organization to adopt in dealing with the media and public during an emergency?

Using the Internet

1. What emergencies have occurred in your local area in the past five years? How effective was the emergency response? (*Hint:* Local EMO sites often have debriefing reports on past emergency responses.)
2. What plans are being made for the predicted flu pandemic in your area? (*Hint:* What information is available from government agencies; what firms are publishing pandemic plans?)

Exercises

1. Determine whether your workplace or school has an emergency response plan. Compare this plan with the one outlined in this chapter.
2. Prepare a fire prevention and suppression plan for your own home or apartment.
3. What does it cost to create and maintain a comprehensive emergency plan for a specific organization? Choose a specific organization and try to estimate these costs. Consider the costs (e.g., time) associated with developing a plan, training employees in the plan, drills or practice (e.g., evacuation drills), and maintaining the plan to ensure currency.

Case   BIOLOGICAL TERRORISM

In recent years, there have been heightened concerns about biological terrorism. Specifically, there is concern that it is possible to spread toxic organisms (e.g., anthrax) by mailing them. In the past three months there have been at least four incidents in which a firm or office building has been the target of such an attack (i.e., a suspicious envelope or parcel arrives in the mailroom with some indication that it contains a highly contagious toxin). Senior management in your firm is concerned. They have asked you to develop an emergency plan for dealing with such an occurrence. What do you need to consider and do to develop such a plan? Identify the elements of emergency preparedness and how each should be implemented.

NOTES

1. C.M. Pearson, J.A. Clair, S.K. Misra, and I.I. Mitroff, "Managing the Unthinkable," *Organizational Dynamics* 26 (1997): 51–64.

2. B.T. Blythe, *Blindsided: A Manager's Guide to Catastrophic Incidents in the Workplace* (New York: Portfolio, 2002).

3. Pearson et al., "Managing the Unthinkable."

4. C.M. Pearson and J.A. Clair, "Reframing Crisis Management," *Academy of Management Review* 23, no. 1 (1998): 59–76.

5. I.I. Mitroff, C.M. Pearson, and L.K. Harrigan, *The Essential Guide to Managing Corporate Crises* (New York: Oxford University Press, 1996).

6. Blythe, *Blindsided.*

7. Pearson and Clair, "Reframing Crisis Management."

8. M. Braverman, "Managing the Human Impact of Crisis," *Risk Management* 50, no. 5 (2003): 10–14.

9. E.K. Kelloway and J. Mullen, "The Stress (of an) Epidemic," manuscript submitted for publication, 2007.

10. N.R. Lockwood, "Crisis Management in Today's Business Environment: HR's Strategic Role," *HR Magazine* 50 (2005): 1–9.

11. F.H. Norris, C.M. Byrne, E. Diaz, and K. Kaniasty, "50,000 Disaster Victims Speak: An Empirical Review of the Empirical Literature, 1981–2001" (2001), http://www.dhss.mo.gov/SpecialNeedsToolkit/General/disaster-impact.pdf, May 29, 2010.

12. A.C.H. Schat and E.K. Kelloway, "Reducing the Adverse Consequences of Workplace Aggression and Violence: The Buffering Effects of Organizational Support," *Journal of Occupational Health Psychology* 8 (2003): 110–22.

13. A. Baum, R. Fleming, and L.M. Davidson, "Natural and Technological Catastrophe," *Environment and Behavior* 15 (1983): 333–54.

14. J.R. Freedy, M.E. Saladin, D.G. Kilpatrick, and H.S. Resnick, "Understanding Acute Psychological Distress Following Natural Disaster," *Journal of Traumatic Stress* 7, no. 2 (2004): 257–73.

15. K. Byron and S. Peterson, "The Impact of a Large-Scale Traumatic Event on Individual and Organizational Outcomes: Exploring Employee and Company Reactions to September 11," *Journal of Organizational Behavior* 23, no. 8 (2002): 895–910.

16. J. Mitchell and G. Bray, *Emergency Services Stress* (Englewood Cliffs: Prentice-Hall, 1990).

17. R. Leonard and L. Alison, "Critical Incident Stress Debriefing and Its Effects on Coping Strategies and Anger in a Sample of Australian Police Officers Involved in Shooting Incidents," *Work and Stress* 13 (1989): 144–61.

18. M. Arendt and A. Elklit, "Effectiveness of Psychological Debriefing," *Acta Psychiatry Scandanavia* 104 (2001): 423–37.

19. A.A.P. Van Emmerik, J.H. Kamphuis, A.M. Hulsbosch, and P.M.G. Emmelkamp, "Single Session Debriefing After Psychological Trauma: A Meta-Analysis," *The Lancet* 340 (2002): 768–71.

20. I.V.E. Carlier, R.D. Lamberts, A.J. Van Uchelin, and B.P.R. Gersons, "Disaster-Related Posttraumatic Stress in Police Officers: A Field Study of the Impact of Debriefing," *Stress Medicine* 14 (1998): 143–48; R.A. Mayou, A. Ehler, and M. Hobbs, "Psychological Debriefing for Road Accident Victims: Three-Year Follow Up of Randomized Control Trial," *British Journal of Psychiatry* 176 (2000): 589–93; R. Small, J. Lumley, L. Donohue, A. Potter, and U. Waldenstroem, "Randomized Controlled Trial of Midwife Led Debriefing to Reduce Maternal Depression After Operative Childbirth," *British Medical Journal* 321 (2001): 1043–47.

Incident Investigation

CHAPTER LEARNING OBJECTIVES

After reading this chapter, you should be able to:

- describe the intent and steps of an incident investigation
- gather information to analyze the human, situational, and environmental factors contributing to incidents
- outline the legal requirements of incident investigation results
- explain the concept of a walkthrough survey
- list the steps to conducting interviews concerning an incident
- conduct a re-enactment
- complete the various types of incident and injury reports

FLIGHT 491

Cougar Flight 491 was a Sikorsky S-92 helicopter that was transporting workers to an oil rig in the Hibernia oil field off the coast of Newfoundland. The helicopter ditched on March 12, 2009, resulting in the death of 17 people on board. Ostensibly, the "cause" of the crash was the failure of titanium studs that allowed oil to leak out of the gearbox. It only took 11 minutes from when the crew noted a loss of oil pressure to the helicopter ditching in the Atlantic Ocean.

Investigation of the incident took two years with a final report released in February 2011. Although this might seem like a lengthy interval, like most incident investigations the obvious "facts" (i.e.,

the failure of the studs in the gearbox) are only the beginning of the story. The Transportation Safety Board (TSB) went beyond the immediate "cause" to consider what might have been done to lessen the impact of the incident and what might mitigate the consequences. Thus, although the titanium studs pose a small risk of failure, the TSB recommended that helicopters should be designed to fly for at least 30 minutes after the loss of oil in the gearbox. Moreover, noting that all 18 people on board survived the helicopter going down (17 died after it went in the water), the TSB noted that better flotation and breathing equipment would have reduced the magnitude of the tragedy.

Source: R. Antle, "Lessons learned," *Atlantic Business*, Vol. 13, Issue 1, 2011. Found at: http://www.atlanticbusinessmagazine.ca/feature/lessons-learned/ (Accessed Mar. 4, 2013).

The investigation of incidents is a vital component of an organization's health and safety program. This chapter describes the rationale for incident investigations, the critical factors in the investigative process, the types of information to be collected, and the investigative methods and tools for conducting an investigation. The importance of reporting and keeping records is also discussed.

RATIONALE FOR INCIDENT INVESTIGATION

RAC program
a hazard recognition, assessment, and control program; a key element in most health and safety programs

The investigation of incidents is an important component in a hazard recognition, assessment, and control **(RAC) program**, which in turn is an integral part of a health and safety program. One study identifies the benefits of incident investigation as follows:[1]

1. *Determines direct causes.* An investigation uncovers the direct causes of an incident, thereby allowing for the subsequent exploration of corrective measures.
2. *Identifies contributing causes.* Some incidents may be the result of many factors. For example, the direct cause of an incident may be inadequate safeguards on equipment, but there may also be contributing factors, such as loose clothing on the employee and a lack of instruction in the proper procedures for equipment use.
3. *Prevents similar incidents.* Once the direct and contributing causes are identified, corrective measures such as training programs or equipment design improvements can be implemented to prevent similar incidents.
4. *Creates a permanent record.* The reports generated by an investigation can be used by HR and safety specialists to identify trends (e.g., sites of

frequent incidents, inefficient layouts and designs, unsafe acts, improper operating procedures). Reports can also be valuable in the event of litigation or compensation claims. Actions taken to improve safety records can be cost efficient in the sense that money and time is being allocated to sites or equipment that generate the most frequent or most severe incidents and injuries.

5. *Determines cost.* The delineation of the exact situation may help the organization determine the actual costs accruing from an incident. All factors, even a worker's lost time, count more than once if there were multiple activities by this worker directly related to the event.

6. *Promotes safety awareness among employees.* When a thorough investigation is conducted, employees realize that management is serious about safety and interested in their well-being. This should motivate employees to show greater concern for safe practices.

CRITICAL FACTORS IN THE INVESTIGATIVE PROCESS

Incident investigations are strongly influenced by timing, severity, and legal requirements.

Timing

Timing is a critical factor in incident investigations. Time affects several types of information. Delays in an investigation may lead to partial or complete memory loss by the witnesses, changes at the incident site, and removal of important evidence. Furthermore, those directly involved in the incident, be they witnesses or late arrivals, tend to discuss the incident, and details may become distorted in the retelling.

Of course, the investigation should start only after any injured people have received medical attention and the incident site has been secured to prevent access, further injuries, and attempts by helpful observers to "fix" the hazard.

Severity

Given that investigations are time consuming, companies tend to examine only those incidents that have the most serious consequences. Yet incidents that result in minor injuries often signal a hazard that may one day have more serious consequences.

One corporate director of health and safety recommends that the following types of incidents be investigated: those resulting in lost-time injuries beyond the day of the incident; those in which the injury was minor, but the employee was treated by a doctor and there was potential for a serious injury; close calls; incidents without injuries but property damage in excess of $1,000; and lost-time incidents resulting from aggravation of a previous injury.[2] Regardless of the system used to judge seriousness, organizations have a legal obligation to report injury-related incidents.

OH&S Today 12.1

What to Investigate

A wide variety of safety-related events may be subject to investigation. OH&S legislation may mandate post-incident investigations in some cases, depending on the nature and severity of the incident. For example, when a workplace death occurs, it is clear that external agencies such as the police will become involved and assume the primary investigative role. When injury-causing incidents are severe or constantly recurring, provincial or territorial and federal health and safety agencies (such as the Labour Program of Human Resources and Social Development Canada) may appoint an investigator to inspect the workplace and may require the submission of a formal report. In B.C., for example, employers are required to investigate (a) any incident that requires reporting to the board (e.g., incidents resulting in serious injury or death, incidents involving major structural collapses, incidents involving release of a hazardous substance), (b) incidents resulting in an employee requiring medical treatment,

and (c) incidents that could have resulted in serious injury but did not. Standards for determining which incidents need to be investigated may also be set by the employer (note that the employer's standards must meet or exceed those required by legislation—the employer *can* investigate incidents that are not speci-fied by legislation but *must* investigate any incident specified in legislation). The OH&S policy at Dalhousie University, for example, mandates the investigation of the following types of incidents:

1. All serious-injury incidents that result in hospitaliza-tion or absences for two or more days

2. All fires or explosions

3. All major spills or releases of chemicals

4. Any incident or series of incidents that the environ-mental health and safety committee wants to have investigated

Sources: Dalhousie University, Health and Safety Policy and Procedures. Found at: http://environmentalhealthandsafetyoffice.dal.ca/radiatio_1536.html (Accessed May 29, 2010); WorkSafeBC. Found at: http://www2.worksafebc.com/Publications/OHSRegulation/Workers CompensationAct.asp#SectionNumber:Part3Div10Sec173 (Accessed April 12, 2010); E.K. Kelloway, V. Stinson, and C. MacLean, "Can Eyewitness Research Improve Occupational Health and Safety? Towards a Research Agenda," *Law and Human Behavior*, Vol. 28 Pg. 115, 2004.

Legal Requirements

Depending on the seriousness of the incident, the presence of an injury, and the jurisdiction in which the incident happened, employers have reporting requirements to fulfill. Certain types of events—those in which an injury requires medical aid or results in lost time, for instance—must be reported to a Workers' Compensation Board, normally within three days. Forms are supplied by the board.

TYPES OF INFORMATION COLLECTED

Most incidents are the result of many contributing factors. The Three Mile Island disaster (a nuclear plant disaster near Harrisburg, Pennsylvania, on March 28, 1979) was preceded by multiple contributing factors ranging from inadequate emergency training, through equipment failing to shut down, to fail-safe systems that failed to consider the human equation. Although no lives were lost in that incident, public trust in the nuclear-power industry plummeted.

The area supervisor should conduct the investigation, assisted by the HR or safety specialist. When investigating an incident, the HR or safety specialist

OH&S Notebook 12.1

THE STEPS OF AN INCIDENT INVESTIGATION

To some extent, every incident investigator has his or her own "method" of conducting incident investigations. Legislative or policy requirements may mandate an investigation but often do not specify *how* the investigation is to be conducted. There are few "hard and fast" rules; that said, a general approach to incident investigation would be to:

a. *Secure the scene:* The initial response to an incident should be to secure the scene—ensure that injuries are treated, that individuals are evacuated if necessary, and that immediate steps are taken to control hazards. The investigator will also need to ensure that the scene of the incident, and any relevant evidence, is protected until the investigation is concluded. The incident should be reported as soon as possible.

b. *Gather evidence:* After the scene is secured, the investigation should commence immediately. The investigator will want to gather evidence—including witness reports, pictures, and physical evidence—before too much time has elapsed or the scene of the incident is disturbed.

c. *Analyze the information:* Information must be collected in order to identify the probable cause(s) of the incident. Rarely will an incident have just one cause, and it is important to consider the contributions of human, situational, administrative, and environmental factors to the incident.

d. *Report the results of the incident investigation:* Reports must be made to the relevant authorities. Internally, this may be to a JHSC or to a health and safety coordinator; externally, this may be to the Department of Labour or the Workers' Compensation Board.

e. *Make recommendations:* A primary reason for conducting an incident investigation is to prevent the recurrence of incidents. Every incident investigation should result in specific recommendations to ensure that similar incidents are not repeated.

f. *Follow up:* The process does not stop with making recommendations. The JHSC or its designate needs to follow up to ensure that the recommendations have been implemented and to assess whether they are achieving the desired effects.

should concentrate on three factors: human, situational, and environmental. These factors, while similar in name, are not the same as the sources of hazards described in Chapter 4 (see **OH&S Notebook 12.1**).

Human Factors

Studying the worker as a source of incidents does not mean that the investigator is looking for a scapegoat. As emphasized throughout this text, the intent is to collect facts, not assign blame. The following questions could be asked when investigating human factors:

• What was the worker doing at the time of the incident? Was he or she performing a regular task or a different task, doing maintenance work, or helping a coworker?

• Was the work being performed according to procedures? Were the tasks or procedures new?

- Was a supervisor present?

- What was the employment status of the worker—seasonal, part-time, or full-time?

- How much experience did the employee have with respect to this particular operation?

- What was the posture and location of the employee?

- Did some unsafe act contribute to the event?

Situational Factors

An analysis of the unsafe conditions that led to the incident is a critical step in an incident investigation. The equipment and tools must be examined. The following questions could be asked when investigating situational factors (see **OH&S Notebook 12.2**):

- Was the machine operating in a satisfactory manner?

- Were all the control and display positions working and ergonomically sound?

- Were the safety measures satisfactory and functioning?

- Does an analysis of failed materials or equipment indicate how the incident happened? For instance, if a shaft broke, causing a machine part to fly off, an engineer can examine the break and determine the mode of failure. A failure of metal through shear or bending will leave definite patterns at the failed ends. Once the mode is known, the cause is usually easily determined.

- What was the site or location of the incident?

OH&S Notebook 12.2
THE EYEWITNESS

Most incident investigations rely on eyewitness accounts and those of individuals involved in the incident. Yet there is good reason to suspect the accuracy of eyewitness statements. A review of the literature on eyewitness testimony indicated that "what we know about eyewitness memory comes from hundreds of studies ... Overall, this body of research tells us that eyewitness testimony is not like a videotape recorder; memory is fragile, malleable, and susceptible to forgetting, even in optimal conditions." The authors cite an example of an airplane crash that killed nine people. Dozens of people witnessed the crash and at least one insisted at the inquest that the plane had nosedived into the ground. Photographic evidence proved that, in fact, the plane had coasted down and skidded for nearly 300 metres.

Source: E.K. Kelloway, V. Stinson, and C. MacLean, "Can Eyewitness Research Improve Occupational Health and Safety? Towards a Research Agenda," *Law and Human Behavior*, Vol. 28, Pg. 115, 2004.

- What tools, equipment, or objects were involved in the incident?
- Was the correct equipment available and being used to do the job?
- What personal protective equipment (gloves, goggles, etc.) was being worn?
- Were guards in place?
- What time of day did the incident occur?
- What shift was being worked?

Environmental Factors

Environmental factors such as light and noise may increase the likelihood that an incident will occur. The setting sun may blind the driver of a delivery truck; the noise of a machine may mask the approach of a vehicle; the vibrations of a certain piece of equipment may dislodge another tool.

Who Investigates?

Numerous individuals may be involved in incident investigations, including the following:

- *The supervisor.* The supervisor possesses a detailed knowledge of the work and the working conditions and is therefore well positioned to conduct the investigation. In most companies, supervisors assume principal responsibility for the investigation.

- *Technical advisers and specialists.* It may be appropriate to bring in technical advisers or specialists when incidents are serious and involve highly technical processes. Bringing in outside expertise may also enhance the objectivity of the investigation.

- *Safety and health officer.* The department or company health and safety officer can offer guidance in coordinating an incident investigation. The health and safety representative may be more aware of, and familiar with, health and safety issues than is the supervisor.

- *Safety and health committee or representative.* Where there is an established health and safety committee, that committee must take part in the investigation.

- *A safety team.* In the event of a serious incident—especially when it is difficult to determine the cause of an incident—a team approach is highly recommended. The team would include the supervisor, the health and safety officer, members of the health and safety committee, and, possibly, outside experts.

INVESTIGATIVE METHODS

A variety of methods may be used in conducting the investigation (see **OH&S Notebook 12.3**).

OH&S Notebook 12.3

ANALYSIS OF AN INCIDENT

A carpenter is making some tool holders and needs to trim about 0.5 cm off the length of a piece of 4 × 4 wood. The 4 × 4 is 121 cm long. The carpenter spends 15 minutes adjusting the table saw to remove the correct width of material. In the process, the carpenter also removes the legally required saw guard because it tends to interfere with cutting. The supervisor had been after the company to purchase a new and proper guard for the saw. The usual answer has been: "Why buy a new guard when one came with the machine?" The carpenter decides not to replace the guard for this cut because the last time this operation was performed, the wood snagged on the guard support and allowed the blade to burn the cut surface. This necessitated extra sanding to remove the stain. However, this time, even though the carpenter uses the proper hand pusher and guides, the saw hits a knot, causing the work piece to jump up from the spinning blade. Luckily, the carpenter receives only minor lacerations.

The unsafe acts in this incident are (1) the carpenter removing the guard and leaving it off during the operation, (2) the supervisor allowing the saw to be used with the poor guard and not insisting on replacing the defective guard, (3) the carpenter continuing to use a piece of unsafe equipment, and (4) the company purchasing the saw without specifying the correct type of guard.

The unsafe conditions are (1) having the improper guard on the machine, (2) providing a machine without a proper guard, and perhaps (3) the supervisor being unaware of the use of the improper guard.

In most provinces and territories, a company official such as the plant manager may be found liable if an identified unsafe act or condition is ignored. The carpenter displayed voluntary risk in that the saw was used even though it was known to have a defective guard.

Identify the human, situational, and environmental factors that contributed to this incident.

Observations or Walkthroughs

walkthrough

inspection of the incident scene to get a picture of the total environment

At the beginning of an investigation, an overall picture of the total environment is achieved by means of a **walkthrough**. Observation of causal factors, physical conditions, and work habits will help the specialist identify potential causes of the incident. Because the manager may not be totally familiar with the details of the operation, the specialist should turn to the supervisor for any necessary information.

Interviews

The following are some basic rules for conducting an interview:

1. Interview witnesses on the spot as soon as possible after the event, while their memories are still fresh. Inform each witness of the purpose of the interview and of what you hope to accomplish.
2. Interview witnesses separately and in a neutral location, such as the cafeteria. Do not use your office, since it could have an authority stigma associated with it. The witness should be permitted to have a worker representative present if he or she desires. Make sure the representative listens and says little or nothing.
3. Put the witness at ease. If the person witnessed a serious injury, he or she may well be shaken or upset. If the person witnessed a death, counselling

may be necessary before any discussion can take place. Reassure the witness that you are simply trying to gather information, not to lay blame.

4. Let the individual recall the event in his or her own way. Do not try to bias the account with questions that are pointed or directed. "Will you please tell me in your own words what you saw or heard?" is much better than, "Can you think what prompted John to do what he did?"

5. Ask necessary questions at appropriate times, without interrupting the speaker's train of thought. The questions should serve to clarify a point or fill in gaps, not to support conclusions you may be forming. "Can you explain again how you knew the machine was turned off?" is preferable to, "You commented that the table saw was not running—did you see the worker turn it off?"

6. Give the witness feedback. "Based on what you said, this is my understanding of what you saw. If there is something I missed or haven't got right, please add to or clarify it." By the time you have finished, both you and the witness should be able to agree that the statement is a factual representation of what was said.

7. Make sure that critical information—either from the witnesses or from your own observations—is recorded in a timely fashion. The longer the delay, the more bias will affect the results. Supplement your written record with visuals (e.g., sketches, photographs, videos).

8. End the interview on a positive note by thanking the witness for his or her valuable time and assistance. Encourage the witness to come to you with any further information that may emerge (see **OH&S Notebook 12.4**).

OH&S Notebook 12.4

COGNITIVE INTERVIEWING

Cognitive interviewing is a technique that was developed for police officers conducting forensic investigations. A great deal of research suggests that cognitive interviews are effective in retrieving accurate eyewitness testimony. Cognitive interviews result in more information and a higher accuracy rate than do "regular" investigative interviews. Some preliminary evidence shows that the cognitive interview elicits more accurate statements from incident witnesses. A typical cognitive interview follows this sequence:

1. *Introduction:* Develop rapport, communicate needs, encourage active participation

2. *Open-ended narration:* Establish mental context, note mental images, develop plan for probing

3. *Probing:* Use richest images to probe, ask questions related to images

4. *Review:* Review information reported

5. *Close:* Finish official business and encourage future contact

Sources: C. MacLean, V. Stinson, & E.K. Kelloway, "Cognitive Interviewing of Incident Witnesses: An Initial Test," paper presented at the annual meeting of the Canadian Psychological Association, St. John's, 2004; R. P. Fisher, "Interviewing Victims and Witnesses of Crime," *Psychology, Public Policy, and Law,* Vol. 1, Pg. 732–64, 1995; R. P. Fisher, R. E. Geiselman, & M. Amador, "Field Test of the Cognitive Interview: Enhancing the Recollection of Actual Victims and Witnesses of Crime," *Journal of Applied Psychology,* Vol. 74, Pg. 722–27, 1995; R. P. Fisher, M. R. McCauley, & R. E. Geiselman, "Improving Eyewitness Testimony with the Cognitive Interview," in D.F. Ross, J.D. Read, and M.P. Toglia, eds., *Adult Eyewitness Testimony: Current Trends and Developments* (New York: Cambridge University Press, 1994), Pg. 245–72.

Re-enactments

Re-enactment is a powerful incident recall method that requires careful handling and planning. The most obvious problem is the danger that simulating an actual injury will produce another one.

Circumstances will dictate whether a re-enactment is essential to complete a thorough investigation. In one documented case, the safety professional was on-site when a worker was impaled between the couplers of two boxcars in a company's railyard. That person filmed the car separation and the removal of the body. Then, while all the witnesses were present and all of the details were fresh—horribly so—in their minds, he had each witness walk through what he or she saw. The local coroner complimented the safety officer on the thoroughness of the evidence, and a re-enactment was obviously unnecessary.

The following are some guidelines for conducting a re-enactment:

1. *A qualified observer is necessary.* If none are available, the in-house specialist will have to do the job. If it appears that evidence is being gathered for an inquest or court hearing, every possible explanation—even suicide—must be considered.
2. *Do not show—tell.* Have all the witnesses relate in their own words what they observed. You as the analyst have to know precisely what took place during the event. Their stories will provide that information. You cannot afford any surprises that might lead to additional injury. Filming can be very helpful, but if, and only if, the witness agrees.
3. *Shut down every energy source and lock them out.* Follow the lockout procedures discussed in Chapter 4. Have the professional who is conducting the re-enactment control the major key for the lockout.
4. *Carefully act out the events.* The witness will describe what happened at each step (just as he or she did when verbally describing the events), and then, with the specialist's approval, will act out that step. For obvious reasons, the re-enactment will stop before the point of incident.

INVESTIGATIVE TOOLS

The walkthrough, the interview, and the re-enactment can be supplemented by the following:

- *Photographs.* Incident photography is helpful and even necessary for efficient incident investigation. When pictures are being taken, make sure they show the whole area, as well as every angle and every nook and cranny. Colour is best, though black and white can be useful. One advantage of black-and-white photographs is that they can be scanned and included in the incident report. Investigators with limited photographic experience will find a Polaroid camera relatively easy to use. Photographs taken with this camera can be examined on the spot for focus and framing problems. Point-and-shoot cameras also require minimal operator skill. Digital video cameras are effective and preferred, since the film can be viewed immediately and the data can be entered into the computer.

- *Drawings*. After the interview, prepare a series of sketches or drawings of the incident scene. These can be complemented by "instant" photographs or video. A good CAD program such as Cadkey or Cadkey Lite will facilitate the drawing process. If you do not have access to CAD software and the training to use it, then a scale pencil sketch is fine. Make sure all parts of the drawing are well labelled.

- *Computers*. Incident recall involves gathering and recording large amounts of information. A computer with a user-friendly database is a necessity. Portable laptops can be taken directly to the scene of an incident. Any computer will facilitate the structured entry of data and facts into the safety files.

- *Other tools*. Depending on the circumstances of the event, other tools such as tape measures, clipboards, water-resistant pens, and flashlights will be of assistance to the investigator.

- *Record check*. Training records and maintenance or production schedules can offer the investigator some valuable insights. A careful review of training records can provide the answers to some questions: Was the worker properly instructed in the accepted and safe methods of doing the job or task? Was he or she aware of the rules of operation, and were they followed? Has the worker signed a training attendance sheet or examination form? Maintenance logs and records should provide information about potential hazards within the company and about what, if anything, was done to address them. Preventive maintenance data are particularly important, since they can be used to predict possible future failures in equipment.

INCIDENT/ACCIDENT REPORTS

Once all the information from the investigation has been gathered, incident/accident reports must be completed. These reports should provide some explanation of causal factors. Though the principal causes will be unsafe acts (e.g., not using a personal protective device) or unsafe conditions (e.g., a broken guard), there may be other explanatory factors. The factor most closely associated with the cause of an incident is referred to as the *agency*. The following are some examples of agents:

- animals (insects, dogs, raccoons, etc.)
- pressure vessels (boilers, piping)
- chemicals (solvents, explosives)
- materials-handling systems (conveyers, forklift trucks)
- dust, fumes, smoke, mists (silica, wood)
- electrical equipment (motors, fuses, wiring)
- elevating devices (elevators, vertical stop belts)
- tools (hammers, wrenches)
- lifting devices (hoists, cranes)

- machine tools (lathe, drill press)
- motive power sources (engines, vehicles)
- radiation (X-ray, ultraviolet)

The *agency* refers to the subgroup of the factors listed above. For example, a dog bite would be the agency part of the animal group.

Another consideration in reports is the *incident type,* which attempts to categorize the nature of the incident. Some examples:

- caught in or between (e.g., crushed between two moving machines)
- struck by (impact or blow to the body by an object)
- struck against (walking into a door)
- fall to the same level (tripping on a level walkway)
- fall to a lower level (falling off a ladder)
- fall to a higher level (tripping while walking up steps)
- abraded, scratched, or punctured (an injury such as hitting the face when falling)
- overexertion (sprains, strains, etc., caused by a greater-than-average effort)
- contact with an energy (mechanical, kinetic, electrical, chemical, thermal, gravity, or radiation)

Personal factors (e.g., lack of knowledge, fatigue, restricted vision) should also be included on the incident investigation form to assist in entry, recordkeeping, and analysis.

The actual report format will vary by company. (Samples of short and long reports are provided in Figures 12.1 and 12.2, respectively.) Organization and layout should be straightforward. Accuracy and thoroughness are also important. Where information is unknown or is not applicable, the respondent should indicate "information unknown" or "not applicable." Abbreviations such as "n/a" for "not applicable" should not be used (it can mean "not available" as well). Do not leave the space blank!

Reports that must be submitted to outside parties such as OH&S agencies or WCBs should include basic information about the company (i.e., type of industry, number of employees, etc.).

A description of any injury that was sustained should be included. A separate physician's report (see Figure 12.3) should also be provided, along with a witness report (see Figure 12.4).

Completed reports are submitted to the senior managers, the JHSC, others directly involved, and possibly the Ministry of Labour if the incident involved serious injury. It is then up to the senior manager directly responsible for the operation in question to implement the recommendations contained in the report.

FIGURE 12.1

Short Report

PE+E Supervisor's Accident/Incident Report

A. General Information

last name: _____ first name: _____ gender: [ ] male [ ] female

department: _____ job title: _____

type: [ ] full time   [ ] part time   [ ] casual

date of injury: _____ time of injury: _____ [ ] am [ ] pm

date reported: _____ time reported: _____ [ ] am [ ] pm

incident category: [ ] illness   [ ] injury   [ ] first aid   [ ] medical aid

B. Accident Investigation

Nature and extent of injury: [ ] left   [ ] right _____

What job was the employee performing: _____

Was this part of regular duties: [ ] yes   [ ] no _____

Length of time employee performing this type of work: _____

Exact location of accident: _____

Describe sequence of events leading to accident. Name tools, machines, materials used.
Provide sketch on reverse if necessary.
_____
_____

Describe any unsafe mechanical or physical condition involved in accident: _____

Describe any unsafe act involved in accident: _____
_____

Name and address of hospital or clinic: [ ] company doctor: _____
_____

Doctor's name: _____   Doctor's estimate of lost time: _____

Measures taken to prevent similar accidents: _____
_____
_____
_____

(*continued*)

FIGURE (12.1)

Short Report (*continued*)

C. Diagrams

Diagrams or photographs may be placed here:

Witness name: _____   Witness name: _____

Address: _____   Address: _____

Phone: Res: _____   Phone: Res: _____

       Bus: _____   Bus: _____

Supervisor's signature: _____   Date: _____

Employee's signature: _____   Date: _____

Please have this document processed and forwarded to   *Original to:*   Manager, Safety and Environment

                                                           Copies to: Vice President, Manufacturing,

                                                                      Manager, Human Resources

                                                                      Department

The information you provide on this document will enable PE+E to effectively manage claims. Thank you for taking as much time as possible.

FIGURE **12.2**

Long Report

Supervisor's Accident/Incident Report

To be completed by the supervisor with the employee immediately after an accident/incident
Please Print

last name   first name   gender
_____

street   apt   city   prov
_____

postal code   telephone   date of birth   marital status
_____

date of employment   department   job title
_____

[ ] full time   [ ] part time   [ ] casual   hrs/week
_____

years' experience   social insurance number
_____

accident/incident occurred: yyyy mm dd (   )   hhmm (   ) am/pm
_____

reported to employer: yyyy mm dd (   )   hhmm (   ) am/pm
_____

who was accident reported to
_____

location of accident (dept, machine, location of machine)
_____

supervisor's name
_____

witness name(s)
_____

Has this employee ever had a similar work-related injury or non-work-related injury? [ ] yes   [ ] no

If yes, explain:
_____

_____

List the employee's job description/task analysis at the time of the injury

(Include job title, duties, weights, sizes of equipment, tools, etc.)
_____

_____

_____

_____

_____

_____

What physical effort was involved? (List job function plus weights and sizes of materials used.)
_____

_____

_____

_____

_____

_____

_____

(continued)

FIGURE 12.2

Long Report (*continued*)

Investigation of accident/incident (*who, what, why, where, how*)

Who was involved?
_____

Where did the accident/incident occur?
_____

What happened to cause the accident/incident? (explain—facts only)
_____
_____
_____
_____

Why did the accident/incident occur? (be objective, do not lay blame)
_____
_____

How did the accident/incident occur? (based on facts only)
_____
_____

Injury

[ ] lost time   [ ] medical aid   [ ] first aid   [ ] information only or [ ] hazardous condition, no injury

treatment memorandum sent   [ ] yes   [ ] no   modified work form sent   [ ] yes   [ ] no

Causes

[ ] unsafe act   [ ] unsafe condition   [ ] information only or [ ] poor/damaged equipment

[ ] no/poor training   [ ] no/poor procedures   [ ] other

Explain
_____
_____
_____
_____
_____
_____
_____

FIGURE **12.2**

Long Report (*continued*)

Accident type

[ ] overexertion/strain   [ ] caught in/between   [ ] slip/fall   [ ] struck by/against   [ ] exposed to
[ ] motor vehicle   [ ] contact with/by   [ ] other
Explain:

Injury type

[ ] bruise   [ ] burn (heat)   [ ] burn (chemical)   [ ] cut   [ ] crush   [ ] strain
[ ] twist   [ ] lift   [ ] electric shock   [ ] inhalation   [ ] occupational illness
[ ] rash   [ ] other
Explain:

Part of body injured   *[ ] left   [ ] right*

[ ] head   [ ] face   [ ] eye   [ ] ear   [ ] neck   [ ] chest
[ ] lungs   [ ] abdomen   [ ] groin   [ ] back-upper   [ ] back-middle   [ ] back-lower
[ ] buttock   [ ] shoulder   [ ] arm   [ ] wrist   [ ] hand   [ ] finger: th 2 3 4 5
[ ] leg   [ ] knee   [ ] ankle   [ ] foot   [ ] toe: big 2 3 4 5   [ ] other
Explain:

Suggested corrective action

[ ] review procedures   [ ] protective equipment   [ ] repair equipment   [ ] develop procedure
[ ] re-instruction of staff
Explain:

(*continued*)

FIGURE **12.2**

Long Report (*continued*)

name & address of hospital or clinic

name of attending doctor   estimated time off work

name of family physician

address

date & hour last worked   Work hours: from   to

shift information: [ ] Day   [ ] Afternoon   [ ] Midnight

hours worked: from: to: days/week:

provide average gross earnings   [ ] hourly   [ ] daily

Additional information

Diagram of accident

Employee's signature   Date

Supervisor's signature   Date

MAKE COPIES AND SEND TO:

[ ] *Manager, Loss Control (original)*   [ ] *Human Resources*   [ ] *Department*

FIGURE  12.3

Physician's Report

INJURY/ILLNESS ASSESSMENT FORM
to accompany employee to physician

For use in on-duty instances of sickness or injury to determine the rehabilitation duties to which an employee can return in the workplace as presented in Bill 162 of the Workers' Compensation Act.

To be completed by an Employee's Supervisor (please print)

A. Personal Data   Date:_____

Employee's Name: _____   Signature: _____

Job Title: _____   SIN: _____

Date of illness or injury on duty: _____   Date of birth: _____

Date absence commenced: _____   Health No.: _____

Nature of injury: _____

Supervisor's Name: _____   Department: _____   Telephone: _____

To be completed by Physician (please print)

B. Assessment of fitness to work

1. [ ] Employee is fit to return to regular work.

2. [ ] Employee is fit to return to modified work—with restrictions as indicated in C & D (reverse).

   Indicate number of hours to be worked and on what basis?

   [_____] hours   [ ] daily   [ ] weekly

   Estimate date of return to modified work:_____

3. [ ] Not fit for work at this time.

   Employee to return for medical reassessment on (yyyy mm dd) _____

See reverse side for Physical Evaluation to be completed by the Physician

Please return this completed form to the Manager, Loss Control via the Employee

(continued)

FIGURE (12.3)

Physician's Report (*continued*)

To be completed by the treating Physician

C. Physical Evaluation

Step 1 *Location of problem*

a) head: include vision, hearing, speech
b) neck
c) upper back, chest or upper abdomen
d) lower back, lower abdomen or genitalia
e) shoulder or upper arm
f) elbow or lower arm
g) wrist or hand
h) hip or upper leg
i) knee or lower leg
j) ankle or foot
k) systemic or internal organ

Right   Left

Step 2 *Please indicate restrictions for modified work*

1. Walking: [ ] only short distances   [ ] other
2. Standing, not more than: [ ] 15 minutes [ ] 30 minutes [ ] other
3. Sitting, no more than: [ ] 30 minutes [ ] 60 minutes [ ] 2 hours [ ] other
4. Bending and twisting, explain:
5. Lifting, floor to waist, not more than: [ ] 7 kg   [ ] 14 kg   [ ] 25 kg   [ ] other
6. Lifting, waist to head, not more than: [ ] 7 kg   [ ] 14 kg   [ ] 25 kg   [ ] other
7. Carrying, not more than: [ ] 7 kg   [ ] 14 kg   [ ] 25 kg   [ ] other
8. Climbing stairs: [ ] no stair climbing   [ ] 2 or 3 steps only   [ ] only short flight
9. Climbing ladder: [ ] no climbing   [ ] 2 or 3 steps only   [ ] 4 or 6 steps only
10. Manual dexterity, not able to: [ ] type   [ ] sort   [ ] other
11. Pushing and pulling trolley, not more than: [ ] 16 kg   [ ] 25 kg   [ ] other
12. Can operate motorized equipment: [ ] any vehicle [ ] forklifts [ ] not recommended
13. Vision, potential safety hazard   [ ] yes   [ ] no   [ ] other
14. Other comments (explain)

D. Treatment

1. Is the employee's prescribed treatment likely to impair performance or safety?   [ ] yes   [ ] no
2. Is the employee referred to: [ ] physiotherapy   Date commenced:_____
                                     [ ] occupational therapy   Duration:_____

Physician's Name: _____   Telephone: _____

Address: _____

Date: _____   Signature: _____

FIGURE  **12.4**

Witness Report

Accident/Incident Witness Statement

Injured employee: _____   Date of injury: _____

Witness name: _____

Does the witness have knowledge of the accident or injury?   [ ] yes   [ ] no

Did the witness see the injury happen?   [ ] yes   [ ] no

If yes to either of the above, please explain below:

Knowledge of injury: Explain what you know about the injury/accident (e.g., what type of work was being done at the time of the injury/accident, what happened to cause the injury/accident, how seriously was the injured employee hurt). _____

_____

_____

_____

_____

What witness actually saw: Please identify what you saw before the injury/accident, during the injury/accident, and immediately after the injury/accident. _____

_____

_____

_____

_____

Give your **opinion** as to how this injury/accident could have been prevented. _____

_____

_____

_____

_____

Witness signature: _____   Date: _____

Incident Analysis

Once the data are collected, the next task is to analyze the information to identify the cause of the incident. A variety of analytic models and techniques are available for use in assessing the cause of an incident.

Domino Theory

domino theory
the theory that every incident results from a series of events

Every event—incident or disaster—comprises a series of happenings that result in some negative condition. The **domino theory**, developed by H.W. Heinrich, is based on a set of five dominos, labelled as follows:[3]

1. *Background:* a lack of control over the management function (planning, organizing, leading, controlling)
2. *Personal defects:* personal factors such as physical or mental problems, and job factors such as normal wear and tear of equipment3. *Unsafe acts and conditions:* (described earlier)
4. *Incident:* a series of undesired events with release of energies that can cause harm
5. *Injury:* the most undesired result (e.g., trauma or property damage)

Though there are other models, such as those dealing with the release of energy[4] and with the theory of multiple factors,[5] the domino model is the easiest to illustrate. The domino theory asserts that if any one of the domino categories does not happen, injury probably will not occur (see Figure 12.5). For example, if a worker is trying to make a production quota (background), is wearing loose clothing (personal defects or unsafe conditions), and is operating a machine at unsafe speeds (unsafe act), an incident or injury will be more likely to occur. However, if the worker is wearing well-fitting clothes or operating the machine at the proper speed (removal of domino number 2 or 3), the risk of an incident is greatly reduced.

The Swiss Cheese Model

J. Reason presented an updated version of the domino model that is often depicted as series of dominoes with holes in them.[6] In this view (often called the "Swiss cheese model"), an incident results when the holes line up (i.e., there are failures at multiple levels). Reason's model focuses on the series of events that must occur

OH&S Today 12.2

Hazardous Occurrence Investigation in the Canadian Forces

The Canadian Forces through the Director General Safety advocates the analysis of hazardous occurrences as a means of preventing their recurrence. The focus here is on identifying the root causes of incidents by assembling, categorizing, and analyzing all relevant data. In their view, the fact that an incident has occurred is evidence of a failure in one or more of five major categories: Materials, Task, Management, Personnel, or The Environment.

Source: Ministry of National Defence, "A DND/CF Hazardous Occurrences Investigator's Guide." Found at: http://www.vcds.forces.gc.ca/dsafeg-dsg/pd/sg-gsg/index-eng.asp (Accessed May 29, 2010).

FIGURE 12.5

Heinrich's Domino Model

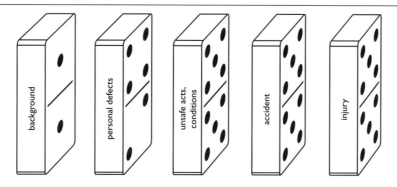

a) five factors in accident sequence

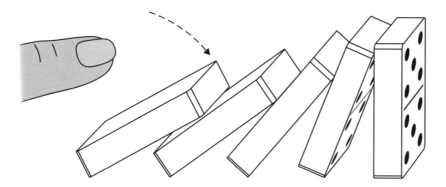

b) injury caused by action of preceding factors

c) removal of a factor may prevent the accident from occurring

for an incident to occur. His model emphasizes that unsafe acts cannot be viewed in isolation; they are a product of the organizational culture, the level of supervision, and a variety of other contextual factors. It follows that incident analysis focuses on identifying these factors to "plug the holes" in the Swiss cheese.

Reason's incident causation model specifies four levels of defence:

1. Organizational influences
2. Local working conditions
3. Unsafe acts
4. Defences, barriers, and safeguards

For example, an organization with a poor safety culture may not have a high incident rate if it has well-developed safe working procedures or safety-conscious supervisors. Similarly, committing an unsafe act may not result in an incident if appropriate safeguards are in place. It is only when organizational influences and local working conditions allow for an unsafe act and there are no safeguards against such an act that an incident results.

Bow-Tie Analysis

A more modern way of analyzing risks in the workforce is known as bow-tie analysis. It gets this name because the figure that results from the analysis resembles a bow-tie (see Figure 12.6). Essentially a bow-tie analysis combines a fault tree with an event tree. On the left of the diagram is a listing of potential hazards and the measures taken to control those hazards. On the right of the diagram are the measures taken to mitigate the consequences of an event and the resulting consequences. The "knot" in the bow-tie is the event or incident to be prevented. An overview of the bow-tie methodology can be found at http://www .bowtiepro.com/bowtie_uses.asp.

normal incidents

the theory that incidents are expected outcomes of interactive complexities

high-reliability organizations

organizations in hazardous industries that maintain a high safety record over time

Normal Incidents

The theory of **normal incidents**,[7] especially in **high-reliability organizations** (e.g., chemical plants, nuclear plants),[8] suggests that incidents result from the interactive complexities in the technological system. That is, no single event causes an incident,

FIGURE 12.6

Bow-Tie Analysis

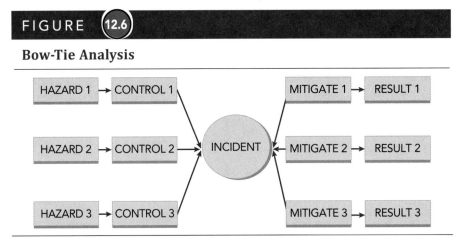

Source: Author has created a diagram based on material found on this website: http://www.bowtiepro. com/bowtie_uses.asp.

and the search for a single discrete cause, analogous to a single perpetrator, may well be fruitless in such an environment. The futility of the endeavour may be difficult to recognize, given the common tendency to make sense out of organizational events. As one researcher notes, "people who know the outcome of a complex prior history of tangled, indeterminate events remember that history as being much more determinant, leading 'inevitably' to the outcome they already knew."[9]

THE PSYCHOLOGY OF INCIDENTS: COGNITIVE FAILURES

In many incident investigations, focus is placed on human error. As a result, we often end up concluding that highly trained and experienced workers simply "made a mistake" in the routine performance of their duties. Psychologists refer to these slips or lapses as a "cognitive failure."[10] There seem to be at least three forms of cognitive failure; these relate to memory, focus, and physical skills. Forgetfulness is when you forget (even momentarily) things you ordinarily know (e.g., the name of your spouse or partner). Distractability is a failure in focus—finishing reading a page of text and realizing you have no idea what you just read is a common example of distractability. Finally, physical blunders include actions such as tripping over your own feet or bumping into things. Though much more research is required, we know that **cognitive failures** are often a sign of individuals under stress and that cognitive failures are related to the occurrence of both motor vehicle and work-related incidents.[11]

cognitive failure
a mistake or failure in the performance of an action that an individual is normally capable of performing

SUMMARY

Incident investigation is a very important part of an OH&S program. The reasons for conducting an investigation are primarily to identify direct and contributing causes and to ensure that the incident does not recur. Timing and severity are the important variables in investigations. The types of information collected can be grouped under human factors, situational factors, and environmental factors. The investigative methods include observations or walkthroughs, interviews, and re-enactments, all of which are complemented by investigative tools such as cameras and computers. Records also supply information that may be important in determining causes. The reporting and analysis of the information collected is the last step in incident investigation.

Key Terms

cognitive failure 325
domino theory 322
high-reliability organizations 324
normal incidents 324

RAC program 302
re-enactment 310
walkthrough 308

Weblinks

Canadian Centre for Occupational Health and Safety, "What Is an Incident and Why Should It Be Investigated?"
http://www.ccohs.ca/oshanswers/hsprograms/investig.html

Construction Safety Association of Ontario: Guide to Incident Investigation
http://www.csao.org/images/pfiles/26_DS029.pdf

Incident Investigation: A Four-Step Process
http://www.cos-mag.com/legal/legal-stories/4-steps-for-conducting-internal-
accident-investigation.html

Required Professional Capabilities (RPCs)

The following RPCs, listed by their CCHRA number, are relevant to the material covered in this chapter. All RPCs can be found at http://www.chrp.ca/rpc/body-of-knowledge.

RPC:170 Develops, implements, and ensures the application of policies, regulations, and standards relating to occupational health and safety.

RPC:171 Ensures compliance with legislated reporting requirements.

RPC:172 Ensures due diligence and liability requirements are met.[*]

RPC:178 Provides information to employees and managers on available programs.

RPC:179 Ensures that mechanisms are in place for responding to crises in the workplace, including critical incident stress management.

RPC:181 Responds to any refusals to perform work believed to be unsafe.[*]

RPC:182 Responds to serious injury or fatality in the workplace.

RPC:183 Analyzes risks to employee health & safety and develops preventive programs.[*]

RPC:184 Establishes an investigation process for incidents and accidents in the workplace.[*]

RPC:185 Ensures that security programs and policies minimize risks while considering the obligation of the employer and the rights of employees, union, and third parties.

RPC:187 Prepares Organizational Health & Safety files for investigation and/or for litigation.

Discussion Questions

1. What are the three factors that should be considered as potential contributors to any incident?
2. Describe the methods that can be used in incident investigation.
3. What tools can assist the incident investigator?
4. What steps should be taken to properly re-enact an incident?
5. Give an example of how human, environmental, and situational factors can combine to result in an incident.

[*]Canadian Council of Human Resources Associations, Human Resources Professionals in Canada: Revised Body of Knowledge and Required Professional Capabilities (RPCs ®), 2007.

6. Given our focus on analyzing and understanding incident causation, it is worth noting that some safety professionals now refuse to use the term "incident." They claim that doing so implies that incidents are random, unforeseeable events, whereas we know that most incidents result from a foreseeable series of events. What are the merits (pros and cons) of this position? Do "incidents happen," or are all incidents preventable?

7. Some safety professionals now talk about the notion of "system risk." In essence, they suggest that incidents or accidents do not result from single causes. Rather, they suggest that incidents are the result of multiple events working together. How might the factors identified in this chapter interact to result in an incident?

Using the Internet

1. Search news media and online reports to find accounts of workplace incidents. For at least one such report, try to identify the human, situational, and environmental factors contributing to the incident.

2. Take the incident investigation training for supervisors presented at http://employment.alberta.ca/whs/learning/Incident/Incident.htm.

Exercise

Many incident investigations, such as traffic and airline incident investigations, conclude that "human error" was the principal cause. We know that situational and environmental factors also play a role. Why do we emphasize the role of humans in incident causation? Does this result in an underemphasis of these other factors?

Case 1 INCIDENT INVESTIGATION

You are the president and largest shareholder of an original equipment manufacturer (OEM) that employs 300 workers. You do not have a safety specialist, but you do take a personal interest in incident prevention. Recently, you assigned general responsibility for safety to the day shift superintendents as a minor part of their regular duties.

The plant has never been thoroughly analyzed for hazards, and you are aware that the operation is not as safe as it could be. Many of the operations require considerable ongoing maintenance by the workers to prevent incidents. Since for several years the business has only been breaking even, you have delayed making any improvements to the plant and equipment. You and the superintendents have concentrated your efforts on preventing unsafe acts by the employees. An elaborate system of worker reminders, such as posters and instruction by supervisors, has been used to make the workforce safety conscious.

For the past few years, your performance with respect to medical aid and lost-time injuries has been average for your WCB rate group. Your company has escaped any lost-time injuries for the past two years, including the current year to date. The continuation of that record has become an important goal. Signs in the plant indicate the number of days that have passed without a lost-time injury.

Today, at 15:30 hours, a container of nearly red-hot, upper-control-arm forgings was overturned. The hot forgings fell on a worker who was helping the drop forge machine operator. The worker suffered third degree burns over 20% of his body. Though he is expected to recover, the worker will lose most of his right arm, right ear, and sight in his right eye. Describe the investigative methods and tools you would use to investigate this incident.

Case 2 OFFICE INCIDENT

Cathy Calvin is the newly appointed coordinator of health and safety for the local school board. She has just been told of an incident experienced by an employee in the administrative office. It seems that two employees were trying to move a full filing cabinet from one corner of the office to another. The cabinet tipped, crushing the foot of one of the employees. The office staff applied first aid and rushed the injured employee to the hospital. The employee will be off work for at least two weeks. Board policy requires a full investigation of any lost-time injury. As a relative newcomer to the health and safety role, Cathy has never conducted an incident investigation before. Can you help Cathy design an appropriate strategy for approaching the investigation?

NOTES

1. P. Laing, ed., *Incident Prevention Manual for Business and Industry: Administration and Programs*, 10th ed. (Washington: National Safety Council, 1992).
2. T. Ryan, "Incident Investigations: II Group Investigations," in F. Briggs, ed., *Guide to Health and Safety Management* (Toronto: Southam, 1991).
3. H.W. Heinrich, *Industrial Incident Prevention* (New York: McGraw-Hill, 1936).
4. W. Haddon, Jr., "The Changing Approach to Epidemiology, Prevention and Amelioration of Trauma: The Transition to Approaches Etiological Rather Than Descriptively Based," *American Journal of Public Health* 58 (1968): 8.
5. V.L. Gross, "System Safety in Rapid Rail Transit," *ASSE Journal*, August 1972.
6. J. Reason, *Human Error* (Cambridge: Cambridge University Press, 1990).
7. C. Perrow, *Normal Incidents: Living with High-Risk Technologies* (New York: Basic, 1984); idem, "Incidents in High-Risk Systems," *Technological Studies* 1 (1994): 1–20.

8. K. Roberts, "Some Characteristics of High-Reliability Organizations," *Organization Science* 2 (1989): 160–76; K.E. Weick, K.M. Sutcliffe, and D. Obstfeld, "Organizing for High Reliability: Processes of Collective Mindfulness," *Research in Organizational Behavior* 21 (1999): 81–123.

9. K. Weick, *Sensemaking in Organizations* (Thousand Oaks: Sage, 1995).

10. J.C. Wallace and S.J. Vodanovich, "Can Incidents and Industrial Mishaps Be Predicted? Further Investigation into the Relationships Between Cognitive Failure and Reports of Incidents," *Journal of Business and Psychology* 17 (2003): 503–14.

11. Ibid.

Disability Management and Return to Work

CHAPTER LEARNING OBJECTIVES

After reading this chapter, you should be able to:

- articulate the financial and legal motivations for disability management programs
- describe the goals and values of disability management programs
- discuss the important outcomes used to evaluate disability management efforts
- argue in favour of the systems approach to disability management
- discuss the best practices in disability management programming
- identify the stakeholders in disability management programs
- consider potential barriers to successful disability management

RETURN TO WORK: HIGH-PROFILE STYLE

Most Canadians know the basic facts about hockey hero Sidney Crosby's career. Hailing from Nova Scotia, it's largely agreed that Crosby is one of the best the game has ever seen. Memorable moments include his scoring the winning goal for Canada—in over-time—in the Gold Medal game at the 2010 Vancouver Olympics and leading the Pittsburgh Penguins to the 2009 Stanley Cup Championship. Unfortunately, most Canadians can also tell you a thing or two about Mr. Crosby's injury status. Two on-ice hits to the head in January 2011 radically changed his career. Long-lasting, concussion-like symptoms kept him largely out of the game for nearly two years—two prime playing years.

If you follow Crosby's high-profile case, you can easily see some of the elements we'll consider in this chapter on disability management and return to work. He sustained work-related injuries that resulted in a lost-time injury. During his initial recovery period, media reports detailed his efforts to regain his health and ease back to work. For example media stories reported that Crosby laced up for 'no contact' practice with the team. In late 2011, Crosby officially returned to the ice with the Penguins, however less than a month later his symptoms returned and he was off the ice once again for three additional months. In other words, his initial return to competitive play was not sustained. At the time of writing this chapter, it is January 2013 and Mr. Crosby is back in the NHL. Things look positive. Mr. Crosby reports that he feels in good health and good shape and holds a new contract with the Penguins that makes him one of the highest paid players in the NHL.

There are other stories of elite athletes who return to high-level competition following injury or illness. Hockey legend Mario Lemieux beat cancer to return to play in the NHL and win Olympic Gold for Canada in 2002. Italian race car driver Alex Zanardi, whose legs were severed in a horrific racing crash during the 2001 CART racing league's season, returned to pro-fessional racing less than two years after the accident in a race car adapted to use hand controls. Later, switching gears (pardon the pun), Mr. Zanardi turned to handcycling, winning the Gold Medal in the sport at the London 2012 Paralympic games.

In these stories we see evidence of determination and learn that it is possible to return in a meaningful way to one's work after experiencing serious injury or ill-ness. We can imagine that during these recoveries the athletes dug deep into their inner strength and used specific strategies to rebuild their physical strength to return, perhaps gradually, to competition. We also see with Mr. Zanardi's case that equipment can be adapted to facilitate that return. In this chapter we explore how disability management programs can help injured or ill workers return successfully to the workplace.

Sources: CTV News, "Sidney Crosby ready to put concussions behind him." Found at: http://www.ctvnews.ca/sports/sidney-crosby-ready-to-put-concussions-behind-him-1.1115158 (Accessed Jan. 23, 2013); Postmedia, News, "Sidney Crosby cleared for practice with the Penguins." Found at: http://www.canada.com/Sidney+Crosby+cleared+practice+with+Penguins/5413600/story.html (Accessed Jan. 23, 2013); The Canadian Press, "Sidney Crosby's contract: The breakdown." Found at: http://www.cbc.ca/sports/hockey/nhl/story/2012/07/01/sp-sidney-crosby-contract-penguins.html (Accessed Jan. 23, 2013); Vancouver Sun, "Sidney Crosby's Olympic OT goal saves Canada from a nervous breakdown." Found at: http://www.vancouversun.com/sports/Sidney+Crosby+Olympic+goal+saves+Canada+from+nervous+breakdown/2625243/story.html#ixzz2IpWHJELQhttp://www.vancouversun.com/sports/Sidney+Crosby+saves+Canada+from+nervous+breakdown/2625243/story.html; Vista Magazine Online, "Hockey Legend with a Higher Purpose: Mario Lemieux." Found at: http://issuu.com/chartsky/docs/vistamag58 (Accessed Jan. 23, 2013); The Independent, "Alex Zanardi: A Fierce Spirit Triumphs in Return to the Track." Found at: http://www.independent.co.uk/sport/%20motor-racing/alex-zanardi-a-fierce-spirit-triumphs-in-return-to-the-track-532558.html (Accessed Jan. 23, 2013); The Telegraph, "Paralympic handcyclist champion Alex Zanardi would not change his life for the world." Found at: http://www.telegraph.co.uk/sport/olympics/paralympic-sport/9766587/Paralympics-2012-Day-7-Paralympic-handcyclist-champion-Alex-Zanardi-would-not-change-his-life-for-the-world.html (Accessed Jan. 23, 2013).

Work-related injuries are prevalent and costly. Each year an estimated 270 million workplace accidents occur worldwide. The annual cost of these accidents is \$US1.25 trillion, which is about 4% of global GDP.[1] Canadian estimates suggest that occupational injury costs the Canadian economy \$9.7 billion per year in direct costs (e.g., compensation benefits). This number jumps to $19 billion per year when indirect costs are also included.[2] Some estimates suggest that the costs relating to workplace disability range from 8% to 15% of an organization's payroll.[3] To give a Canadian perspective, in 2011 Workers' Compensations Boards across Canada accepted 294,511 claims for lost-time injuries at Canadian workplaces.[4] In 2010, for every 100 employees who worked for employers covered under Workers' Compensation Boards, there were 1.76 compensated lost-time injuries. The rates of lost-time injury claims vary somewhat across jurisdictions. For instance, in Newfoundland and Labrador in 2011, for every 100 workers there were 1.99 compensated lost-time injuries. While in Manitoba, this value was reported to be 3.27.[5] Note that direct comparisons between the values reported across jurisdictions are complicated by several factors including different waiting periods before injuries are compensated.

Injured individuals experience social costs over and above the financial costs incurred by their employers, public and private insurers, and the health care system. There are emotional and health costs associated with not working, including higher rates of depression, social exclusion, and illness.[6] Anxiety and depression are prevalent among injured workers.[7]

There is growing concern that the various costs of workplace injury and illness will continue to increase. The prevalence of chronic disorders among the workforce, due in part to demographic factors such as labour shortages and an aging population, may result in even more lost work time.[8] Organizations act on these concerns by attempting (a) to reduce the direct costs (such as Workers' Compensation premiums) associated with disability and (b) to ensure that injured workers return to the workplace as quickly as possible. Ensuring a timely and safe return to work helps both the individual and the organization. The individual returns to his or her full income as quickly as possible; the organization minimizes costs associated with replacing employees and retains the valuable skills of current employees.

▶ OH&S Notebook 13.1

THE BUSINESS CASE FOR DISABILITY MANAGEMENT

Organizations have an obligation to facilitate timely and safe return to work for injured employees. However, an effective disability management and return-to-work program also makes good business sense. There are numerous employer benefits of effective disability management and return-to-work programs. These include:

- Minimizing the costs of disability
- A quicker return to previous productivity levels

- Reduced work delays
- Improved employee morale
- Retainment of skilled employees
- Improvement in the company's reputation and image
- Reduced training costs

Sources: New Brunswick WHSCC, "Workplace Disability Management: A Guide to Establishing a Program in your Workplace." Found at: http://www.employabilitypartnership.ca/Guide%20to%20Establish%20a%20Disability%20Management%20Program. pdf (Accessed Jan. 25, 3013); WSIB, "Return to Work and Disability Management: The Business Case." Presented at the Education Safety Association of Ontario Conference. May 2009. Found at: http://www.esao.on.ca/conferences/2009/conf_ notes/RTW%20Panel2.pdf (Accessed Jan. 22, 2013).

duty to accommodate

legislated responsibility of employers to accommodate workers who are attempting to return to work following an injury or illness via changes in job tasks and/or the work environment to enable workers with a temporary or permanent disability to perform work productively

undue hardship

aspect of human rights legislation that means that employers must accommodate the needs of a disabled worker unless the necessary modifications would lead to health and safety difficulties or present unsustainable economic or efficiency costs

Besides financial motives, there are legal ones. In Canada, legislation protects the rights of disabled workers, including those who lose work time due to an injury or work-related illness. Under Canadian human rights legislation, employers have a **duty to accommodate** individuals as they return to work.[9] That is, employers are held to a high standard in their obligation to accommodate workers who are attempting to return to work following an injury or illness, in that they are required to implement changes in job tasks and or the work environment to enable workers with a temporary or permanent disability to perform work productively.[10] For example, a worker who has sustained a back injury may return to work on light duties that do not involve heavy lifting. Organizations are expected to engage in reasonable accommodations up to the point of **undue hardship**. Undue hardship is evaluated in the context of the organization in question; there is no precise legal definition of the concept.[11] However, it is generally interpreted to mean that employers must accommodate the needs of a disabled worker unless the necessary accommodation would lead to health and safety difficulties or present unsustainable economic or efficiency costs. For instance, a company would not be expected to accommodate an injured worker if the cost of the specialized equipment the worker required would result in bankruptcy or if the employee wished to return to a given job before the employer felt certain that the worker could perform the job safely. The duty to accommodate and the concept of undue hardship are outlined in more detail in **OH&S Today 13.1**.

DISABILITY MANAGEMENT

disability management

proactive employer practices with the goals of preventing or reducing workplace disability, intervening early in the face of risk or injury, and providing coordinated management and rehabilitation functions to promote workers' recovery and safe and timely return to work

systems approach

an approach to disability management that emphasizes the work and organizational context

In light of financial and legislative realities, organizations develop disability management programs to prevent workplace injury and illness and to accommodate workers in a manner that facilitates early and safe return to work. **Disability management** encompasses a set of proactive employer practices whose goals are: to prevent or reduce workplace disability; to intervene early in the event of risk or injury; and to provide coordinated management and rehabilitation functions that promote workers' recovery and safe and timely return to work.[12] The goals of disability management programs include promotion of safe workplaces; coordinated programming in health, rehabilitation, and accommodation interventions; and representation of all stakeholders, including workers, unions, management, government, and insuring agencies.[13]

Disability management programs are most effective when developed and applied using a **systems approach**.[14] A systems approach to disability management emphasizes the work and organizational context—for instance, the type of work and the safety record of the organization—instead of focusing solely on individual employees. When disability management efforts are fully integrated into the workplace, the workplace culture reflects the overarching commitment to prevention and restoration. Senior managers and frontline employees alike appreciate the value of safety and support the goals of the disability management initiatives.

The research indicates that workplaces with a people-focused workplace culture, positive safety attitudes, and articulated policies on disability management tend to report shorter absences, lower disability costs, and less frequent absences arising from workplace injury.[15] The value of this type of support

OH&S Today (13.1

The Duty to Accommodate

Case law has increasingly placed the onus on employers to accommodate workers with disabilities. In the well-known case of *British Columbia (Public Service Employees Relations Commission) v. BCGSEU*, 3 S.C.R. 3, commonly referred to as the *Meiorin* decision, the Supreme Court of Canada established that employers have an obligation to accommodate individuals and to be proactive in removing discriminatory workplace practices. This groundbreaking case has led to changes in the expectations placed on organizations to accommodate for disabilities. The duty to accommodate appears to be defined by 10 general principles:

1. An employer has the obligation to accommodate employees who suffer from a disability to the point of undue hardship.

2. Employees must produce medical or psychological evidence that they are suffering from a disabling condition if they expect to be accommodated by their employer.

3. Disruptive behaviour associated with a disability or failure to perform assigned duties by an employee with a disability is not sufficient cause to terminate the employee, provided he or she makes known the disorder.

4. Failure of an employee to adhere to a medical regimen and therapy that may be prescribed to address the disability may be sufficient grounds for termination of the employee.

5. The risk associated with the position occupied by a person with a disability may mitigate the nature of the accommodation.

6. The severity and stability of the condition can be considered as part of an employee's return-to-work and accommodation.

7. The employee can make reasonable objections, including economic loss, to the accommodation that is offered by the employer; however, the employee must accept reasonable accommodation offered by the employer, even though that accommodation may not be perfect from the employee's perspective.

8. Accommodation cannot be made on the basis of a stereotype held by the employer about the employee with a disability. The employer must investigate to determine what the individual employee is capable of doing.

9. Large organizations, particularly government departments, will be held to a higher standard with respect to their duty to accommodate employees with disabilities and with respect to the point where undue hardship begins.

10. Arguments of undue hardship will be assessed to determine whether they represent *bona fide occupational requirements*, that is, they are essential to organizational function.

Source: *Psychological Disorders in the Canadian Forces: Legal and Social Issues - Contractors report*, National Defence Headquarters, National Defense 2004. Reproduced with the permission of the Minister of Public Works and Government Services Canada, 2013.

from the top makes sense; the most intense efforts of frontline supervisors to help injured employees return to work will be futile if organizational policy and practice do not support return-to-work practices, such as modified or light-duty work.

The systems approach to disability management, where organizations heavily influence treatment plans, and where the return-to-work process and organizational context are both taken into account, stands in contrast to earlier models of injury management and return to work. In the past, physicians were at the centre of a **full recovery model** of return to work. Under this model, injured workers were absent from the workplace under a system of physician-certified leave. The

full recovery model

a former approach to disability management that operated completely outside the workplace and was dictated by the physician's assessments of recovery

OH&S Notebook 13.2

REEMPLOYMENT OBLIGATIONS

Under Canadian human rights legislation, Canadian employers have a duty to accommodate, to the point of undue hardship, employees with disabilities. That said, Workers' Compensation Acts for various Canadian jurisdictions differ in their requirements pertaining to duty-to-accommodate and re-employment obligations. For example, in Manitoba, new legislation pertaining to re-employment went into effect in 2007. In that province, employers with 25 or more employees are required to re-employ injured workers who worked for them for at least 12 continuous months prior to the injury. Moreover, they must accommodate those employees to the point of undue hardship. Several other jurisdictions have exemption policies for small employees—for instance, New Brunswick exempts employers with

fewer than 10 employees. In some provinces, such as Alberta, the relevant acts are silent on the issue of re-employment obligations, though Canadian human rights legislation pertaining to the duty to accommodate workers with disabilities still applies.

The limits of re-employment also differ by jurisdiction. In Manitoba, for instance, the obligation to re-employ ends two years after the date of the injury, six months after the worker is medically able to perform his or her pre-injury job, or the normal retirement date of the worker, whichever comes first. Those working in the field of disability management should check the local requirements of their province or territory to ensure that they are upholding the relevant legislation.

Sources: Workers' Compensation Board of Manitoba, "Reemployment Obligations." Found at: http://www.wcb.mb.ca/sites/default/files/WCBReEmploymentBrochure.pdf.pdf (Accessed Jan. 22, 2013); Association of Workers' Compensation Boards of Canada, "Rehabilitation/Return to Work." Found at: http://www.awcbc.org/common/assets/benefits/rehab_return_to_work.pdf (Accessed Jan. 23, 2013).

full recovery model operated completely outside the employing organization. Only when the physician deemed that the worker had fully recovered and could resume his or her original job tasks was the individual cleared to return to work.[16] Waiting for a period of full recovery before returning to work lengthens the duration of disability absences and the associated costs. The systems approach has benefits for multiple stakeholders, including the employee (who can experience the emotional and financial benefits of earlier return to work) and the employer (who realizes savings in terms of disability costs).

The Goals of Disability Management Programs

The National Institute for Disability Management and Research (NIDMAR) is a Canadian organization. In collaboration with the International Labour Organization, it has developed a Code of Practice for Disability Management. That code lists the values for disability management, two of which are: safe and productive employment for individuals, including those with disabilities; and reduced *incidence* and *impact* of workplace injury and illness.[17] Clearly, rates of safety incidents and occupational illnesses can provide important information for those evaluating the effectiveness of disability management programs.

But such evaluations must also consider the impact of those injuries and illnesses that do occur. How is the impact of workplace injury and illness evaluated? There are four important financial and social indicators of the impact of workplace disability:

1. *Duration of the work disability.* The duration of the disability is the most commonly used outcome in research on return to work and disability management. It is often reported as the amount of time that a worker receives benefits.[18] Absence duration has both financial and social implications. Longer absences are more costly for the employer. They may also be associated with negative emotional experiences for the individual workers—for example, anxiety and depression are prevalent among injured workers who have not successfully returned to work.

2. *Associated costs.* Various associated costs of the disability are also used to evaluate the impact of workplace injury. These costs include wage replacement, health care costs, and intervention costs.[19] Reducing the duration of the disability can help decrease associated costs.

3. *Sustained return to work.* The extent to which workers are able to sustain their return to the workplace provides important information about disability management efforts. If employees are returning to work quickly following an injury, but not maintaining their participation in the workplace, there may be problems with the return-to-work planning. Recent studies have considered not simply the timing and sustainability of return to work, but also the work attitudes and quality of work experiences for those who are returning, noting that successful return to work also includes such things as high at-work and mental functioning, job satisfaction, and commitment to the organization. [20]

4. *Quality of life.* Quality-of-life indicators for injured or ill workers, including such things as their symptom severity and general health, are considered important outcomes in disability management and return-to-work programs.[21] Clearly, the programs are viewed as more successful when injured workers report that during their time in the disability management program they exhibit fewer symptoms and have begun to feel better.

Best Practices in Disability Management

It has long been established that the severity of a worker's injury or illness and the physical demands of that worker's job are important predictors of initial and sustained return to work.[22] For example, for a worker who has sustained a musculoskeletal injury, returning to a job that involves heavy physical labour or working in awkward positions may take longer, or require more substantial accommodations, than returning to a job that is more sedentary.[23] A more serious injury, such as losing a limb, will obviously require a longer recovery than a less serious injury, such as sustaining a deep cut that requires stitches.

However, the nature of the injury and the job are not the only important predictors of return to work and effective disability management. Research has identified several best practices that can reduce the incidence and impact of workplace disability. These are outlined below.

1. *People-focused climate.* As noted above, a disability management program has the potential to be most effective when it is embedded in an organizational system that values its human resources and is supportive of safety initiatives. In workplaces with a **positive safety climate** there is a well-communicated commitment to occupational health and safety that

positive safety climate
organizational context with a well-communicated commitment to occupational health and safety; employees generally share the perception that their safety is valued

is emphasized in company policy and practices, including training efforts around safety and disability. Managers and all employees generally share the perception that their safety is valued.

Part of the expression of a safety climate that is supportive of disability management initiatives is the involvement and empowerment of employees.[24] Employees should have a voice—perhaps through their union—in the development and delivery of disability management programs.[25] Furthermore, *all* employees should be educated on their company's safety values and disability management program, including their rights and responsibilities within that program. Injured workers need to feel that they are welcome to return to the workplace and that the organization values their contributions. Injured workers are empowered when they are given an active role in their rehabilitation and return-to-work plans, including any necessary workplace accommodation.[26]

2. *Prevention focus.* A common theme in disability management is "prevention first."[27] Prevention efforts that reduce the incidence of illness and injury result in cost savings for organizations.[28] A good starting point when developing a disability management program is to examine the organization's safety record. Are there particular jobs or worksites where injuries are prevalent? Are there injuries that employees report frequently? Aiming prevention efforts at injuries that are frequent or particularly costly will increase the company's return on investment. For example, if an analysis reveals that carpal tunnel syndrome is a common experience among press operators in a particular company, that organization might engage in directed prevention efforts, such as training on proper techniques to operate the press and the provision of personal protective equipment such as wrist braces.

Organizations can also use their benefits programs as a way to promote prevention. For instance, by regularly using such services as massage therapy, workers may avoid sustaining certain types of injuries or avoid some of the physical manifestations of stress. **Employee and Family Assistance Programs (EFAPs)**—services to help employees with problems that may interfere with productivity, such as alcohol and drug abuse, emotional or behavioural problems among family members, and financial or legal problems—may also serve a preventive function if employees are able to address personal concerns before these begin to cause problems at work.[29]

3. *Early intervention.* Organizations with progressive disability management programs continually assess risk for injury or illness in workplaces and take swift and early steps to eliminate or reduce these risks. They extend this model of early intervention to cases where an injury has occurred. A core aspect of disability management is for employers to make "early and considerate" contact with injured workers and to begin rehabilitation efforts as soon as possible.[30]

The exact timing of early contact from the employer depends on the worker's situation. However, within a week or two is a suggested guideline for the immediate supervisor to place a call to the employee.[31]

Employee and Family Assistance Programs (EFAPs)

programs designed to help employees and members of their families with problems that may interfere with worker productivity, including alcohol and other drug abuse, emotional or behavioural problems among family members, and financial or legal problems.

The goal of this contact is to express that the employer cares about the worker and his or her well-being. Experts advise against fault finding or discussing the causes of the injury because if the employee senses that the contact is motivated by the employer's concern about finances, it can undermine return-to-work efforts.

Early contact is associated with better return-to-work outcomes. Early referral to a disability management program can decrease the length of absences and result in net savings for companies.[32] One study showed that early contact with the worker was predictive of increased perceptions of fair treatment among injured workers, which in turn predicted higher commitment to their organizations and better mental health.[33] Ongoing contact for the duration of an injured worker's absence is also a useful technique for helping the worker feel involved in and remembered by the workplace.

4. *Work accommodation.* **Workplace accommodation** offers, also called offers of modified work arrangements, are strongly associated with reduced disability duration and reduced disability costs for permanently and

workplace accommodation modifications to the arrangement of work that promote early and safe return to work for injured, ill, or disabled workers

OH&S Today 13.2

Disability Management at Vancouver Coastal Health

Vancouver Coastal Health (VCH) was recognized as one of B.C.'s top employers in 2012. VCH delivers health care to more than 1 million people in the greater Vancouver area. Via its 13 hospitals and numerous other worksites, VCH provides a range of services including primary care, public health, and addictions treatment. VCH has more than 10,000 full-time employees. They offer a range of benefits and perks often seen in top employer award winners. For instance, they have tuition subsidies, parental leave salary top-ups, on-site amenities (including daycare at one location), and mentoring programs. In their strategic framework, they highlight a goal to develop the best workforce. They have as a noted objective to encourage a culture that promotes safety and respect.

VCH has also invested in an in-house approach to disability management. In 2008, VCH faced staffing shortages and escalating workers' compensation and long-term disability claims, particularly involving musculoskeletal problems and mental health concerns. They also had a poor record in return-to-work outcomes. Following an audit, VCH opted to move its disability management operations in house. Engaging with the union and focusing on early intervention, the first phase of the redesign also worked on gaining senior management buy-in. The changes saw the time-to-first contact when someone was off work cut in half and the time from the start of leave to return to work substantially improved. The cost of long-term disability claims also fell. However, despite the success, some cracks in the system became apparent. Running a successful disability management program was a lot of work and the program needed more staff and a better employee data base. A successful business case saw more resources invested into the program. The disability management program now reflects a more integrated approach that connects several programs targeted at employee wellness and return to work. This successful transition is saving the organization millions of dollars and it is part of what makes VCH a good place to work.

Sources: Vancouver Coastal Health. Found at: http://www.vch.ca/home/ (Accessed Jan. 25, 2013); Eluta, "Vancouver Coastal Health chosen as one of BC's top employers for 2012." Found at: http://www.eluta.ca/work-at-vancouver-coastal-health-authority (Accessed Jan. 25, 2013); L. Doyle, "How to fix a disability management program," *Benefits Canada*, Mar. 1, 2012. Found at: http://www.benefitscanada.com/benefits/health-benefits/how-to-fix-a-disability-management-program-25743 (Accessed Jan. 25, 2013).

temporarily disabled workers.[34] Estimates based on a comprehensive literature review suggest that injured workers who receive offers of work modifications return to work twice as often and that their absence durations are about half as long as for workers who are not given an accommodation offer.[35] What does modified work look like? Some common types of modified work arrangements include:[36]

light duty work

workplace accommodation where workers return to a job that is less demanding than their previous job

(a) **Light duty work**. When injured workers are offered light-duty accommodations, they return to work in a capacity that is less demanding than their regular job. This might involve adapting the tasks of the person's pre-injury job or placing the person in a different job in the organization. For example, a courier who has sustained a lower-back injury might return to her work but be assigned tasks that do not involve heavy lifting. Alternatively, a master mechanic with an upper-extremity musculoskeletal injury who can no longer sustain certain positions—such as reaching above his head for long periods of time—might return to modified work tasks that involve quick diagnostics of potential problems with vehicles, after which he passes the detailed repair off to another mechanic; or the modified task might involve more interfacing with clients of the service centre. These arrangements can be permanent or temporary, depending on the worker's condition and changing abilities.

gradual work exposure

a type of light-duty accommodation where job demands slowly increase until the workers are performing the full requirement of their pre-injury jobs

(b) **Gradual work exposure**. Gradual exposure is a form of light-duty work in which a person's hours and expected duties slowly increase until the worker is able to perform his or her pre-injury job without any problems. This type of modification is also referred to as *work hardening*.

work trials

a form of accommodation where workers return to work on a trial basis

(c) **Work trials**. Workers may return to work on a trial basis to evaluate whether they are able to withstand the demands of the workplace, given the current state of their recovery. The length of the trial may be at the discretion of the employer, the worker, or (possibly) the worker's physician.

supported and sheltered work

modified work arrangements designed to help those with permanent disabilities who have either not been successful in competitive work environments or require substantial support to return to work

(d) **Supported and sheltered work**. These types of modified work arrangements are designed to help those with permanent disabilities who have not succeeded in competitive work environments or who require substantial support to return to work. This type of accommodation may be offered in regular work environments (supported) or in special worksites offered via social services (sheltered). For example, an individual who sustained a traumatic head injury after a fall off a ladder while working in a large hardware store may require supervision from a job coach to return to supported work in a retail environment.

Work accommodations are among the most cost-saving strategies in disability management. Bringing employees back to work once they can perform at least some of their tasks can speed up recovery by giving an employee practical goals to achieve during rehabilitation. It can also serve a work-hardening function by gradually strengthening the employee's ability, thereby reducing the risk of reinjury. In many jurisdictions the early return to work via modified work is a formalized aspect of Workers' Compensation, and Workers' Compensation Boards may offer programs designed to promote early and safe return to work.[37]

5. *Return-to-work case management.* Case management refers to the coordination of health and social services so that those who are injured, disabled, or ill receive care that is appropriate, timely, and efficient. The goals of case management are to enhance the injured worker's quality of life and, if possible, reduce the costs associated with care. Case management should therefore begin early in the process to ensure that injured workers are receiving the most effective and cost-efficient services available.

6. *Return-to-work coordinator.* Return-to-work outcomes, such as duration of absence and disability costs, are improved when organizations have a **return-to-work coordinator** who is responsible for return-to-work case management.[38] The coordinator ensures that there is ongoing communication among the stakeholders, including the worker, the supervisor, and those providing treatment such as a physician or an occupational therapist.[39] The coordinator works with these stakeholders to plan the appropriate work modifications and to monitor over time the effectiveness of the accommodations.

   One function that the return-to-work coordinator might provide is to facilitate communication between the employer and the injured worker's health care providers. There is strong evidence that this type of contact reduces the duration of absences.[40] When the employer provides information about the job demands, and about the work modifications that are possible in a given case, health care providers such as physicians, occupational therapists, and physiotherapists can provide better advice to workers about return to work. They can also become partners in decision making.[41]

   What might such an exchange between an employer and a health care provider look like? It might be a simple exchange of printed information such as a letter, a job description, or a list of the accommodation options available under the disability management program. In some cases this type of information might be exchanged over the phone. It is also possible that a health care provider will visit the workplace to observe the work activity. Of course, in all cases the worker must consent to this communication, and it is ideal when the worker participates in the exchange.[42]

7. *Educate supervisors about disability management.* At times supervisors will be called upon to support the disability management, in its preventive and return-to-work senses. For example, it is often the supervisor who makes early contact with an injured employee. Supervisors can engage in various practices to show their support for returning employees. For instance, they can be inclusive of returning employees by doing such things as meeting them when they return to work, trying to make the first weeks back to work less stressful, and explaining any changes in work practices. Supervisors can also be generally supportive by being approachable and remaining positive throughout the return-to-work process. Supervisors should also be careful to avoid negative actions such as losing patience or excessively questioning the returning employee.[43] The supervisor will also have to work with the return-to-work coordinator to ensure that work modifications for a returning employee address the needs of both the returning worker and the supervisors and coworkers. Coworkers or supervisors may be suspicious or resentful of a work modification that increases coworkers' workloads or that threatens the group's

return-to-work coordinator person who is responsible for return-to-work case management

ability to meet production goals.[44] The company can begin by expanding the role of the supervisors to include assistance for employees with disabilities.

8. *Integrated claims management and monitoring systems.* When workers require a leave from work due to illness or injury, they submit compensation claims to a benefits program. The compensation provides workers with financial support during their absence. These benefits may be provided by different providers, depending on the situation. Depending on the type of job and industry, and various other eligibility criteria, injured or ill workers may apply for compensation through the public Workers' Compensation system or via a private insurer.[45] In an integrated claims management system these processes are facilitated within the disability management program, which ideally leads to a more timely resolution of the compensation claim, thus ameliorating a potentially adversarial aspect of workplace disability insurance claims. If claims are not processed in a timely and sensitive fashion, workers may become frustrated because they are without an income for a period of time. Furthermore, workers may begin to develop doubts about rehabilitation and return to work.[46]

Integrated systems also allow tracking of where an injured or ill employee is in the claims, recovery, and rehabilitation process.[47] The amalgamation and availability of this information aids in the planning of return-to-work efforts and outcomes. It may also help organizations monitor their safety and disability management performance. For example, potential risks may be uncovered if certain injuries are commonly occurring; or weaknesses in the return-to-work offerings may be identified if patterns about the success of return-to-work experiences emerge. For instance, examining amalgamated data may permit a return-to-work coordinator to detect which worksites appear to have a good record of sustained return to work and others where the record is not as strong. Particular interventions can be developed on the basis of this information.

Employee databases can be a vital tool in an integrated disability management program. In-house databases that log employee information such as sick time, injury dates, and contacts with health care providers can help to manage individual cases. They can also help track valuable statistics, like average days post-injury until first contact, or the average length of short-term leaves. In larger organizations, such databases might be Web-based and integrated across sites. For instance, the Provincial Health Services Authority in B.C. hosts a Web-based employee database called The Workplace Health Indicator Tracking and Evaluation (WHITE™) database.[48] This Web-based system allows centralized management and tracking of information for all the health authorities in the province. Features include modules to record incidents, claims, and leaves. One can see that these types of databases permit employers to track the effectiveness of their disability management efforts, including preventive measures, by identifying common injuries and illnesses among employees.

Another valuable resource in disability management programming are broad-based databases that provide resources to disability management specialists. For instance, the National Institute of Disability

OH&S Notebook 13.3

STIGMA AND RETURN TO WORK

As we've seen so far in this chapter, many factors influence successful return to work. Increasingly, the role of the social context of the workplace is being examined for its influence on return-to-work outcomes. Sometimes injured workers report feeling stigmatized during the return-to-work process. From a social psychological perspective, individuals are stigmatized if they are thought to possess attributes or characteristics that are devalued. Injured workers sometimes feel stigmatized in their interactions with workers' compensation systems, physicians, coworkers, and their employers, leading to feelings such as humiliation, anxiety, and depression.

Returning employees often worry about social aspects of their return. Some feel that important others, such as coworkers or supervisors, do not regard their injuries as authentic and possibly resent the job modifications necessary for timely return to work. Returning workers may be stigmatized if their injury prompts negative stereotypes, which are common in society. Injured workers sometimes report being treated as either malingerers or criminals. Feeling devalued at work can undermine the goals of timely and safe return to work. For example, some may return to work too early to show that they are committed and diligent workers.

What Can an Organization Do?

Organizations and individuals can work to reduce stigma for returning workers. In Canada, human rights legislation places considerable onus on employers to work proactively to eliminate sources of workplace discrimination. Therefore, employers must look for ways to manage the stigma and its negative outcomes. *Education* programs aimed at reducing the stigma associated with workplace injuries may help replace myths with accurate information. For instance, organizational health and safety committees might sponsor awareness programs about often misunderstood occupational injuries, such as those to soft tissues. Promoting *contact* between injured and noninjured workers—for instance, at work-related social events—can also help alleviate stigma. This will allow the coworkers to get to know the situation of the returning employee. Also, organizations can *diminish barriers* between injured and noninjured workers by emphasizing similarities such as the fact that they are all employees of a single organization. On-site disability case managers have important roles to play in implementing these types of strategies.

Organizations should also ensure that their safety values are not communicated in a way that devalues those who have experienced a near miss, a safety incident, or a lost-time injury. Rewarding individuals or groups that have good safety records, withholding rewards from employees who have a safety violation on their record, or publicly emphasizing the company's safety record—such as number of days without a lost-time injury—may add to the stigma experienced by a returning employee, especially if other employees feel they have been "robbed" of a valuable reward or that their organization's reputation has been somehow blemished by the injury. We in no way mean to imply that employee safety should not be actively promoted and valued by organizations—rather, with respect to the stigmatization of injured workers, organizations may be wise to emphasize the importance of employee well-being in general, instead of safety in the narrower sense of reducing lost-time injuries or costs.

Sources: J. Crocker, B. Major, & C. Steele, "Social Stigma," in D.T. Gilbert, S.T. Fiske, and G. Lindzey, eds., *Handbook of Social Psychology*, Vol. 2, 4th ed. (Boston: McGraw-Hill) Pg. 504–53, 1998; J. M. Eakin, "The Discourse of Abuse in Return to Work: A Hidden Epidemic of Suffering," in C.L. Peterson and C. Mayhew, eds., *Occupational Health and Safety: International Influences and the "New" Epidemics* (Amityville: Baywood) Pg. 159–74, 2005; K. Lippel, "Workers Describe the Effect of the Workers' Compensation Process on Their Health: A Québec Study," *International Journal of Law and Psychiatry*, Vol. 30, Pg. 427–43, 2007.

Management and Research (NIDMAR) provides free access to its REHADAT Canada database.[49] This database contains information on disability management practices, assistive devices, case studies, and current research. Clearly, such a tool could be useful to help create or improve disability management programming in an organization. It might also be helpful in addressing individual cases. For example, an occupational therapist engaged in treating a client or a disability case manager designing modified work spaces may search such a database for information on assistive devices.

It is standard practice in most countries that only those employees who are injured at work or who develop illnesses that can be definitively linked to the workplace are eligible for Workers' Compensation and other work-related rehabilitation services. Increasingly, employers are realizing that it makes financial sense to invest in the return-to-work efforts of employees who sustain non–work-related injuries or illnesses. Thus, disability management programs are providing services to support these individuals as well.

Stakeholders in Disability Management

It is evident from the discussion that there are several important stakeholder groups in disability management and return to work, each with its own roles and responsibilities. These stakeholders should be recognized and included when developing disability management programs and when executing return-to-work case management. Each of these stakeholders has been referenced at various points in this chapter; it would be useful now to bring them all together in a summary.

1. *Injured or ill workers.* Workers who have been injured or who have sustained an occupational illness are major stakeholders in disability management. Broadly speaking, workers should be empowered in disability management programs. They should have input into the development of related workplace policies and procedures, and they should be educated on their organization's disability management program.

    The injured or ill worker also has several responsibilities to uphold in the disability management process.[50] They must report their condition as soon as possible and take an active role in developing a return-to-work program. They need to comply with treatment recommendations, work to maintain and improve their health, and keep their employer up to date on their health status during the return-to-work process.

2. *Employers.* Employers need to foster a workplace that supports the goals of disability management. They should ensure that adequate resources are available to the program.[51]

    Supervisors of returning workers have particular responsibilities in return-to-work case management. They need to help identify options for work modifications and monitor the safety of returning employees. In doing so they should keep in close contact with the employees in question and their return-to-work case managers. They should also be available to coworkers who might have concerns about work modifications.[52]

    The disability management or return-to-work coordinator will work closely with returning employees and play a large role in return-to-work planning. That person will also assist the injured or ill employee in applying for financial benefits and seeking treatment. Besides working with the employees who are enrolled in the program, they will play a liaison role with other stakeholders and contribute to policy development and evaluation of the disability management program.[53]

3. *Unions.* Ideally, workplace unions will help develop the disability program, perhaps through a joint labour/management committee. Union officials need to support the program and promote disability management goals when negotiating collective agreements. They can also serve as advocates for employees with disabilities and communicate the benefits of disability management to their members.[54]

4. *Health care providers.* Working with injured, ill, or disabled workers and the employers, health care providers need to review the job requirements so as to suggest possible job modifications that would facilitate return to work.[55] With the employee's permission, it can be beneficial for the health care provider to have direct contact with the employer.[56]

5. *Insurance providers.* Public and private insurers provide benefits to workers who are on leave. They may also be involved in identifying and facilitating return-to-work options and return-to-work readiness among injured, ill, or disabled employees. The exact services they provide differ somewhat from provider to provider. As an example, the Workplace Safety and Insurance Board (WSIB) of Ontario, which is a public insurer, facilitates disability and return-to-work case management as part of its *Road to Zero* 2008–2012 strategic plan. Its service delivery model for return to work involves, among others, case managers, who focus on options for and barriers to return to work; nurse consultants, who can provide medical information and help interface with the health care system; and prevention specialists, who work with employers to improve their safety records and develop disability management plans.[57]

6. *Governments.* Governments can develop legislation that supports the values of disability management—for example, the availability of rehabilitation options and disability programs for employees, and return-to-work clauses in collective agreements.[58]

7. *Disability management contractors.* Some private firms provide disability management services to organizations on a contract basis. They offer services to organizations that help realize the goals of disability management. These services may include case management and rehabilitation. Private firms should stay in close contact with the employees who are using their services and with the employer to facilitate early and safe return to work.

Barriers to Return to Work

Early and safe return to work has many benefits to employees and employers. However, there are potential barriers that can interfere with the goal of returning injured, ill, or disabled workers to the workplace. Problems or delays can stem from several stakeholder groups and can ultimately pose barriers to return to work. A recent study illustrated that seemingly mundane factors such as health care providers being too busy to quickly file paper work, employers inaccurately reporting their ability or willingness to accommodate, an individual being referred

OH&S Today   13.3

Careers in Disability Management

Throughout this chapter we have referred to staff positions in disability management programs, such as return-to-work coordinator. What type of training prepares a person to work in disability management? Several institutions in Canada offer certificate or degree programs in Disability Management and Return to Work. For instance, Dalhousie University offers a diploma in disability management that is designed to supplement work experience in that field. McGill University offers a Master of Occupational Health Sciences for individuals with a background in disciplines related to occupational health and safety. Pacific Coast University, a new institution in B.C.,

specializes in workplace health sciences. The National Institute of Disability Management and Research (NIDMAR), headquartered in British Columbia, offers an online program to train return-to-work coordinators. Institutions offering similar programs include Grant MacEwan University in Edmonton, Mohawk College in Hamilton, and the University of Northern British Columbia in Prince George. Professionals with sufficient experience working in disability management and with the appropriate education can write national exams to earn the Certified Return to Work Coordinator (CRTWC) or Certified Disability Management Professional (CDMP).

Sources: Dalhousie University, Diploma Program in Disability Management. Found at: http://disabilitymanagement.distanceeducation.dal.ca (Accessed Jan. 24, 2013); McGill University, Master of Occupational Health Sciences. Found at: http://www.mcgill.ca/occh/programs/msc (Accessed Jan. 24, 2013); Pacific Coast University. Found at: http://www.pcu-whs.ca/ (Accessed Jan. 24. 2013); NIDMAR, *Expanding Your Horizons: A Career Guide in Disability Management.* Found at: http://www.nidmar.ca/career/career_horizons/horizons_contents.asp (Accessed Jan. 24, 2013).

to a retraining program that is not suitable, or injured workers not understanding formal letters issued by WCBs can interact to increase the length of absence from work.[59] Psychosocial factors, such as those we discussed in Chapter 7, can affect return to work. Low-quality jobs—for instance, those with high demands, job stress, or a lack of control—are associated with delayed return to work.[60]

Without proper assurances, employees may resist return-to-work opportunities out of fear. They may think that taking a modified job means they won't get their regular job back. They may also fear reinjury or exacerbation of their condition, or they may simply feel unable to return to work.

Disability-related absence is often described as having three stages: acute (1–30 days), subacute (31–90 days), and chronic (91 + days).[61] Long absences can be a barrier to successful return to work. Estimates from private insurers suggest that the average length of a chronic disability is nearly three years.[62] Certainly the amount of time someone is away from work on a disability leave reflects heavily the severity of the injury or illness. That said, to the extent that early and safe return is possible, facilitating early return is important. Statistics suggest that in the case of leaves lasting longer than six months, 95% of people do not return to their old job and as many as 85% do not return to the workforce at all.[63]

What happens when an employee's return to the original workplace is not possible? Labour Market Re-entry programs can help an individual who cannot return to the original workplace owing to the nature of the injury or the former employer's limited ability to accommodate. During a Labour Market Re-entry process, the injured, ill, or disabled worker's capabilities, experience, and training is reviewed. Additional skills training may be provided to help that worker find employment that provides earnings comparable to those in the previous job.

SUMMARY

Throughout this chapter we have explored the costs of workplace injury and the benefits that disability management programs bring to employees, employers, and society at large. In Canada, human rights legislation protects the rights of disabled workers and employers have the duty to accommodate—to the point of undue hardship—injured, ill, or disabled workers. In general, disability management programs that focus on prevention and early intervention when injuries or illness do occur are associated with improved outcomes, including earlier return to work and sustained return to work. These disability management programs are most effective when fully integrated into a workplace system that is supportive of safety and return to work. When the stakeholders in disability management, including employers, employees, unions, and health care providers, work together they can overcome the barriers to return to work and help employees achieve the psychosocial and financial benefits that come with full and active participation in the workforce.

Key Terms

disability management 334
duty to accommodate 334
employee and family assistance
    programs (EFAPs) 338
full recovery model 335
gradual work exposure 340
light duty work 340

positive safety climate 337
return-to-work coordinator 341
supported and sheltered work 340
systems approach 334
undue hardship 334
work trials 340
workplace accommodation 339

Weblinks

CHRC, "A Guide for Managing the Return to Work"
http://www.chrc-ccdp.ca/pdf/gmrw_ggrt_en.pdf

Firefighting in Canada, "Back to Normal: Why Fire Departments Need Back-Injury Programs"
http://www.firefightingincanada.com/content/view/1774/213

FIT For Work
http://www.fitforwork.com

Institute for Work and Health, "Return-to-Work Practices"
http://www.iwh.on.ca/return-to-work-practices

International Association of Professionals in Disability Management
http://www.cspdm.ca

Minerva: Safety Management Education, "Early and Safe Return to Work at Canadian Pacific Railway Company: A Case from a Best Practice Employer"
http://www.safetymanagementeducation.com/en/data/files/download/Documents/2007_cpr_case_study.pdf

National Institute of Disability Management and Research
http://www.nidmar.ca/index.asp

Vancouver Coastal Health
http://www.vch.ca

Work Able Centres Inc.
http://www.workablesolutions.ca

Required Professional Capabilities (RPCs)

The following RPCs, listed by their CCHRA number, are relevant to the material covered in this chapter. All RPCs can be found at http://www.chrp.ca/rpc/body-of-knowledge.

RPC:170 Develops, implements, and ensures the application of policies, regulations, and standards relating to occupational health and safety.[*]

RPC:171 Ensures compliance with legislated reporting requirements.

RPC:172 Ensures due diligence and liability requirements are met.

RPC:173 Ensures that policies for required medical testing fall within the limits of statute & contract.[*]

RPC:174 Develops and implements policies on the workplace environment.

RPC:175 Ensures adequate accommodation, modified work and graduated return to work programs are in place.[*]

RPC:176 Ensures that modifications to the work environment are consistent with worker limitations.[*]

RPC:177 Develops or provides for wellness and employee assistance programs to support organizational effectiveness.[*]

RPC:178 Provides information to employees and managers on available programs.[*]

RPC:179 Ensures that mechanisms are in place for responding to crises in the workplace, including critical incident stress management.

RPC:180 Establishes a joint Health & Safety Committee as required by law.

RPC:181 Responds to any refusals to perform work believed to be unsafe.

RPC:182 Responds to serious injury or fatality in the workplace.

RPC:183 Analyzes risks to employee health & safety and develops preventive programs.

RPC:184 Establishes an investigation process for incidents and accidents in the workplace.

RPC:185 Ensures that security programs and policies minimize risks while considering the obligation of the employer and the rights of employees, union, and third parties.

RPC:186 Establishes and implements strategies to minimize workers' compensation costs.[*]

RPC:187 Prepares Organizational Health & Safety files for investigation and/or for litigation.

---

[*]Canadian Council of Human Resources Associations, Human Resources Professionals in Canada: Revised Body of Knowledge and Required Professional Capabilities (RPCs ®), 2007.

Discussion Questions

1. What are some ways to empower employees when developing and implementing a disability management program?
2. How can organizations create a climate/culture that supports a safe working environment?
3. Can the organization really prevent stigma from occurring? If so, how? How can we reduce injured or ill employees' fears about stigma?
4. Do you think any of the disability management best practices are more important than others? For example, do you think an organization focused solely on prevention will be equipped to handle injuries and compensation when they do occur?
5. Can you think of any reasons why employees may be hesitant to use their disability management programs, particularly those offered in-house?

Using the Internet

1. Many organizations post their disability management policies online. Search out companies representing different sectors (e.g., manufacturing versus universities) and compare their programs.
2. Search for news articles related to compensation, injuries at work, and return to work claims. Determine what strategies were used by the employers.
3. Look up the WBC guidelines in your jurisdiction to seek its policies and practices in a return-to-work program. Compare them to those of another jurisdiction.
4. Compare Canadian Human Rights and Disability Management guidelines and practices in disability management and return to work to those of another country of your choosing.
5. Some organizations rely on external providers to provide their disability management services. Search out a company that specializes in providing external disability management services. What types of programs does it offer?

Exercises

1. Think of policies and practices that were in place in an organization where you have worked. What were the risks for injury? Could the organization do anything to prevent them? Were safeguards in place? Did the organization appear to support the overarching values of disability management?
2. Companies like OPG that use in-house disability management programs tend to employ nurses and other staff solely focused on health and safety and disability management. Other organizations contract out their disability management services. Contrast and compare the pros and cons of in-house and contracted disability management services.

3. What are the challenges faced by small organizations when facing accommodations, disability management, and return to work? How do these compare with the challenges faced by large organizations? Outline how an organization can play to its strengths when addressing disability management issues.

Case 1 — FORGOTTEN ORDERS: A CASE OF MEMORY IMPAIRMENT IN A RESTAURANT

Lan sustained a head injury following a slip-and-fall accident in her job as a waitress at a busy family restaurant. Lan has been off work on Workers' Compensation benefits for six weeks and is in the care of a physician and an occupational therapist. Since the fall, Lan has had some problems with her short-term memory. She loses track of tasks and has trouble focusing on what she's supposed to be doing. Otherwise she feels fine and would like to be working again. Lan, her boss, and her health care providers agree that unless her memory symptoms improve, Lan cannot perform her duties as a waitress. Lan's boss has suggested that she return to work in the kitchen, washing dishes. Lan is insulted by this suggestion. She has four years' experience as a successful waitress and is concerned that if she says yes, she'll never get her job back. Her physician and occupational therapist aren't particularly familiar with her workplace and aren't quite sure what to recommend. You are the Workers' Compensation case manager who has been assigned to Lan's case. What would you do to facilitate the interactions among Lan, her boss, and the health care providers? What suggestions might you have for a return-to-work plan for Lan?

Case 2 — OUT OF CONTACT AT WIDGIT

You are a certified return-to-work case manager at WidgIT, a company that manufactures computer parts. WidgIT has a disability management program with a successful track record of achieving its goals of early intervention and sustained return to work. In fact, the company has been nationally recognized for its disability management program. Tyler, one of WidgIT's employees, sustained injuries to his back and leg after being pinned between two pieces of equipment. You intervened right away and have helped Tyler get immediate and sustained medical treatment and helped him navigate the necessary documents to file for compensation. He's now been off work for five weeks. Tyler has been completely out of touch for three weeks, ever since you indicated that you'd like to have contact with his physician. You have tried reaching him by phone and email, but he does not return your calls or messages. You are now worried that Tyler has become suspicious and has disengaged in the process. What do you do?

NOTES

1. N. Buys and C. Randall, "Disability Management: A Global Response to Disability in the Workplace," in C.A. Marshall, E. Kendall, M.E. Banks, and R.M.S. Gover, eds., *Disabilities: Insights from Across Fields and Around the World* 3 (Santa Barbara: Praeger/ABC-CLIO, 2009), 129–43.

2. J. Gilks and R. Logan, "Occupational Injuries and Illnesses in Canada, 1996–2008: Injury Rates and the Cost to the Economy" (July 2010), Human Resources and Skills Development Canada, accessed January 28, 2013, http://publications.gc.ca/collections/collection_2011/rhdcc-hrsdc/HS21-4-2008-eng.pdf.

3. D.S. Salkever, J. Shinogle, and M. Purushothaman, "Employers' Disability Management Activities: Descriptors and an Exploratory Test of the Financial Incentives," *Journal of Occupational Rehabilitation* 10, no. 3 (2000): 199–214.

4. Association of Workers' Compensation Boards of Canada, Key Statistical Measures, https://aoc.awcbc.org/KsmReporting/ReportDataConfig, accessed January 23, 2013.

5. Ibid.

6. E.K. Kelloway, D.G. Gallagher, and J. Barling, "Work, Employment, and the Individual," in B.E. Kaufman, ed., *Theoretical Perspectives on Work and the Employment Relationship* (Champaign: Industrial Relations Research Association, 2004), 105–31; G. Murphy and J. Athanasou, "Unemployment and Mental Health," *Journal of Occupational and Organizational Psychology* 73 (1999): 83–99; E. Harris and M. Morrow, "Unemployment Is a Health Hazard: The Health Costs of Unemployment," *Economic and Labour Relations Review* 12 (2001): 18–31.

7. A. Stelmakowich, "Fractured Bond," *Occupational Health and Safety Canada* (September 2009).

8. World Economic Forum, *Working Towards Wellness: The Business Rationale* (Geneva: 2008).

9. Canadian Human Rights Commission, "CHRC's Guide for Managing Return to Work" (n.d.), http://www.chrc-ccdp.ca/publications/gmrw_ggrt/toc_tdm-en.asp, February 25, 2010.

10. National Institute of Disability Management and Research (NIDMAR), *Code of Practice for Disability Management* (Vancouver: 2000).

11. Canadian Human Rights Commission, "CHRC's Guide for Managing Return to Work" (n.d.), http://www.chrc-ccdp.ca/publications/gmrw_ggrt/toc_tdm-en.asp, February 25, 2010.

12. R.M. Williams and M.G. Westmorland, "Perspectives on Workplace Disability Management: A Review of the Literature," *Work* 19 (2002): 87–93; NIDMAR, *Code of Practice for Disability Management*.

13. NIDMAR, *Code of Practice for Disability Management*.

14. Buys and C. Randall, "Disability Management."

15. B.C. Amick, III, R.V. Habeck, A. Hunt, A.H. Fossel, A. Chapin, R.B. Keller, and J.N. Katz, "Measuring the Impact of Organizational Behaviors on Work Disability Prevention and Management," *Journal of Occupational Rehabilitation* 10, no. 1 (2000): 21–38.

16. Stelmakowich, "Fractured Bond."

17. NIDMAR, *Code of Practice for Disability Management*.

18. R.L. Franche, K. Cullen, J. Clarke, E. Irvin, S. Sinclair, J. Frank, and Institute for Work and Health Workplace-Based RTW Intervention Literature Review Research Team, "Workplace-Based Return-to-Work Interventions: A Systematic Review of Quantitative Literature," *Journal of Occupational Rehabilitation* 15, no. 4 (2005).

19. Ibid.

20. H.L. Hees, K. Nieuwenhuijsen, M.W.J. Koeter, U. Bültmann, and A.H. Schene, "Towards a New Definition of Return-to-Work Outcomes in Common Mental Disorders from a Multi-Stakeholder Perspective," *PLOS One* 7(2012): e39947; C.G. Hepburn, E.K. Kelloway, R.-L.

Franche, "Early Employer Response to Workplace Injury: What Injured Workers Perceive As Fair and Why These Perceptions Matter," *Journal of Occupational Health Psychology* 15(2010), 409–20.

21. R.L. Franche, K. Cullen, J. Clarke, E. Irvin, S. Sinclair, J. Frank, and Institute for Work and Health Workplace-Based RTW Intervention Literature Review Research Team, "Workplace-Based Return-to-Work Interventions: A Systematic Review of Quantitative Literature," *Journal of Occupational Rehabilitation* 15, no. 4 (2005).

22. N. Krause and T. Lund, "Returning to Work After Occupational Injury," in J. Barling and M. Frone, eds., *The Psychology of Workplace Safety* (Washington: APA, 2004).

23. N. Krause, L. Dasinger, and A. Weigand, "Does a Modified Work Facilitate Return to Work for Temporarily or Permanently Disabled Workers? Review of the Literature and Annotated Bibliography," unpublished report prepared for the Industrial Medical Council of the State of California and the California Commission on Health and Safety and Workers' Compensation, University of California, 1997.

24. Buys and Randall, "Disability Management; Williams and Westmorland, "Perspectives on Workplace Disability Management."

25. NIDMAR, *Code of Practice for Disability Management.*

26. Buys and Randall, "Disability Management."

27. NIDMAR, *Code of Practice for Disability Management.*

28. Buys and Randall, "Disability Management."

29. EAPA, *Standards of Practice.*

30. Institute for Work and Health (IWH), "Seven 'Principles' for Successful Return to Work" (Toronto: March 2007).

31. IWH, "Seven `Principles.'"

32. Franche et al., "Workplace-Based Return-to-Work Interventions."

33. C.G. Hepburn, E.K. Kelloway, and R.-L. Franche, "Early Employer Response to Workplace Injury: What Injured Workers Perceive As Fair and Why These Perceptions Matter," *Journal of Occupational Health Psychology* 15(2010), 409–20.

34. Franche et al., "Workplace-Based Return-to-Work Interventions"; N. Krause, L.K. Dasinger, and F. Neuhauser, "Modified Work and Return to Work: A Review of the Literature," *Journal of Occupational Rehabilitation* 8, no. 2 (1998); and C.G., Hepburn, R.-L. Franche, and L. Francis, "*Successful Return to Work: The Role of Fairness and Workplace-based Strategies*," *International Journal of Workplace Health Management* 3(2010): 7–24.

35. Ibid.

36. Ibid.

37. J.M. Eakin, "The Discourse of Abuse in Return to Work: A Hidden Epidemic of Suffering," in C.L. Peterson and C. Mayhew, eds., *Occupational Health and Safety: International Influences and the "New" Epidemics* (Amityville: Baywood, 2005), 159–74.

38. Buys and Randall, "Disability Management."

39. IWH, "Seven `Principles.'"

40. Franche et al., "Workplace-Based Return-to-Work Interventions."

41. IWH, "Seven `Principles.'"

42. Ibid.

43. F. Munir, J. Yarker, B. Hicks, and E. Donaldson-Fielder "Returning Employees Back to Work: Developing a Measure for Supervisors to Support Return to Work (SSRW)," *Journal of Occupational Rehabilitation* 22(2012): 196–208.

44. IWH, "Seven `Principles.'"

45. NIDMAR, *Code of Practice.*

46. Buys and Randall, "Disability Management."

47. NIDMAR, *Code of Practice*; Williams and Westmorland, "Perspectives on Workplace Disability Management."

48. Provincial Health Services Authority, WHITE™ database, accessed January 28, 2013, http://www.phsa.ca/HealthProfessionals/Occupational-Health-Safety/WHITE-Database.htm.

49. NIDMAR, REHADAT database, accessed January 28, 2013. http://www.nidmar.ca/rehadat/rehadat_database/rehadat_database.asp.

50. NIDMAR, *Code of Practice.*

51. Ibid.

52. Ibid.

53. Ibid.

54. Ibid.

55. Ibid.

56. IWH, "Seven `Principles.'"

57. WSIB Newsroom, "Service Delivery Model," http://www.wsib.on.ca/wsib/wsibsite.nsf/public/NSDM, April 3, 2010; WSIB Road to Zero, "Five Year Strategic Plan 2008–2012," http://www.wsib.on.ca/wsib/wsibobj.nsf/LookupFiles/DownloadableFile5YrPlan/$File/3255A_FiveYearPlan.pdf, April 3, 2010.

58. NIDMR, *Code of Practice.*

59. E. MacEachen, A. Kosny, S. Ferrier, and L. Chambers "The Toxic Dose of Systems Problems: Why Some Injured Workers Don't Return to Work as Expected," *Journal of Occupational Rehabilitation* 20(2010): 349–66.

60. N. Krause, L.K. Dasinger, L.J. Deegan, R.J. Brand, and L. Rudolph, "Psychosocial Job Factors and RTW After Low Back Injury: A Disability Phase-Specific Analysis," *American Journal of Industrial Medicine* 40 (2001): 374–92.

61. Krause and Lund, "Returning to Work After Occupational Injury."

62. Canada Life, "Disability Insurance," http://www.canadalife.com/003/Home/Products/DisabilityInsurance/index.htm, April 3, 2010; Great-West Life, "Disability Insurance," http://www.greatwestlife.com/001/Home/Individual_Products/Insurance/Disability_Insurance/index.htm, accessed January 28, 2013.

63. Stelmakowich, "Fractured Bond."

CHAPTER

14

Workplace Wellness: Work–Family and Health Promotion Programs

CHAPTER LEARNING OBJECTIVES

After reading this chapter, you should be able to:

- discuss the concept of healthy workplaces
- describe the goals of worksite health promotion and family-friendly programs
- discuss the various types of worksite health promotion and family-friendly programs
- comment on the effectiveness of various types of worksite health promotion and family-friendly programs
- identify variables critical to the success of worksite health promotion and family-friendly programs
- discuss the importance of systematic evaluation of worksite health promotion and family-friendly policies

SNOOZING ON THE JOB: NOT SUCH A BAD IDEA AFTER ALL?

You snooze, you lose. Not that long ago, suggesting that someone was asleep on the job was a severe criticism. It implied that a person was lazy or not respectful of company time. Recent research on sleep deprivation suggests that a nap at work might be just what the doctor—and HR manager—ordered.

Today's busy workplaces and lifestyles are prompting many people to sacrifice their sleep hours to meet all their work and family demands. This strategy is detrimental to one's health. Not getting enough sleep is associated with a number of health problems, including hypertension, heart disease, and depression. A study in *Archives of Internal Medicine* demonstrated that afternoon naps are associated with a decreased risk for coronary mortality. From a business perspective, estimates suggest that sleep deprivation is costing American employers $150 billion annually in reduced performance and safety incidents. A power nap might be the solution.

Sara Mednick's book *Take a Nap! Change Your Life* advocates naps at work. It prescribes a nap during a work shift as a potential remedy for the productivity and health and safety costs associated with a sleep-deprived workforce. Some employers are taking notice, providing nap rooms for sleep-starved employees. For example, The Huffington Post provides nap rooms to employees as do Google and Nike. The rooms at the Huffington Post have been dubbed NapQuest rooms and feature sleep pods that block light and sound. The afternoon power snooze might just be the coffee break of the future when it comes to revitalizing employees.

The "nap room" is a novel idea for employee health promotion. It can benefit both the employee and the employer in many ways. In this chapter we explore a variety of workplace wellness programs designed to improve employee health, well-being, and productivity.

Sources: CBC, "Siestas Have Heart-Healthy Effects, Study Suggests." Found at: http://www.cbc.ca/health/story/2007/02/12/siesta-heart.html (Accessed Mar. 8, 2013); CTV News, "A Nap a Day Keeps Lost Productivity at Bay." Found at: http://www.ctv.ca/servlet/ArticleNews/story/CTVNews/20070115/takeanap_070115/20070115 (Accessed Mar. 8, 2013); S. Mednick & M. Ehrman, *Take a Nap! Change YOUR Life* (New York: Workman Publishing) 2006; A. Naska, E. Oikonomou, A. Trichopoulou, T. Psaltopoulou, & D. Trichopoulos, "Siesta in Healthy Adults and Coronary Mortality in the General Population," *Archives of Internal Medicine*, Vol. 167, Pg. 296–301, 2007; *Huffington Post*, "How to Nap at Work." Found at: http://www.huffingtonpost.com/2012/01/26/how-to-nap-at work_n_1232352.html#slide=640048 (Accessed Mar. 8, 2013).

Given that people spend a substantial portion of their time at work, most would agree that active attempts should be made to ensure a healthy and safe work environment. Throughout the 1990s, the concept of wellness at work emerged as an occupational health concern, augmenting organizations' more traditional concerns about employee safety. This interest in workplace wellness continues to grow. Some estimate that health-related programs are found in as many as 90% of mid-sized companies in the United States.[1] A survey of more than 1,000 U.S. employers found that more than 90% of responding organizations offered their employees eight or more programs or policies to help support work and life balance.[2] The major motivators of this trend include a desire to reduce rising health care costs, improve productivity, and build a supportive organizational culture.

Workplace wellness initiatives are also present in Canadian companies. Estimates are that 64% of Canadian companies offer some form of wellness program.[3] For work–family balance in particular, results from a recent survey indicate that 67% of Canadian organizations attempt to address employee concerns about work–life balance.[4] Some have suggested that because Canada has a public health care system, Canadian companies assume less of the cost for illness and therefore have less of a financial impetus to develop employee health initiatives. However, the focus on health at work is now rapidly growing in Canada. For instance, in January 2013 the Canadian Standards Association released CSA-Z1003-13 a voluntary workplace standard for psychological health and safety in the workplace. This standard was developed in conjunction with the Mental Health Commission of Canada. The presence of a national standard on psychological health at work not only directs attention to the issue of psychological well-being at work, but also likely sets a new standard for organizations wanting to exercise due diligence in the provision of programs to promote psychologically healthy workplaces.

Many experts believe that health is more than just the absence of illness and that active attempts to improve health will result in individuals "feeling good" as opposed to "not feeling bad." This notion is sometimes referred to as "positive health." Indeed, the World Health Organization defines health not simply as the absence of illness or disease, but rather as an overall state of mental, physical, and social well-being.

It makes sense to focus on health at work. Employed adults spend a great deal of time in the workplace, so the worksite provides a convenient means of reaching many adults. Also, the health of employees affects their performance at work; therefore, companies should be interested in promoting worker health. In this chapter we consider two broad categories of initiatives that companies can take to promote well-being at work: family-friendly policies and health promotion programs (see Figure 14.1).

WORK–FAMILY CONFLICT: FAMILY-FRIENDLY POLICIES IN THE WORKPLACE

Most people in today's workforce are attempting to balance work with family demands.[5] We discussed **work–family conflict** in depth in Chapter 7, where we learned that demographic realities such as the large proportion of working parents and the prevalence of dual-income families means that employees need to constantly balance work and family commitments. In this chapter we explore programs that organizations can provide to help employees manage their work and family commitments.[6]

Work–family conflict is expensive for organizations. High work–family conflict is associated with reduced work performance and higher rates of absenteeism. Estimates suggest that the direct organizational costs of work–life conflict to Canadian organizations to be in the range of $3 billion to $5 billion annually.[7] When *indirect* costs are factored in, the figure is considerably higher—an estimated $6 billion to $10 billion per year.[8]

Work–family conflict is also associated with substantial health and well-being costs for individuals. A high degree of work–family conflict, be

work–family conflict
a type of inter-role conflict in which the role pressures experienced in the work and family domains are incompatible

FIGURE 14.1

Flow Chart of Workplace Well-Being Initiatives

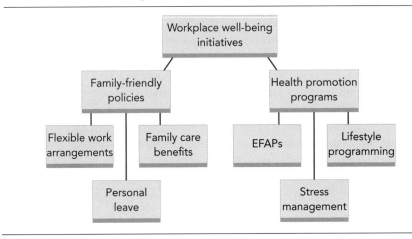

it work-to-family or family-to-work, contributes to perceived stress, poorer physical health, decreased family functioning, increased mental health concerns (depression, anxiety, psychological distress), and increased alcohol use.[9] So it is important that individuals and organizations attempt to reduce this type of inter-role conflict.[10] In the following sections we examine some of the family-friendly policies that organizations have implemented in an effort to reduce work–family conflict and thereby avoid the resulting negative outcomes. Such policies are assuming greater importance as companies recognize that a growing number of employees have both childcare and eldercare responsibilities in addition to work responsibilities. The existence of these policies can help organizations recruit and retain employees. Most family-friendly policies are attempts to help employees balance their work and family responsibilities. Given that this chapter focuses on workplace policies and programs, we will be emphasizing organizational rather than individual efforts to reduce work–family conflict. We will consider three broad categories of family-friendly programs: flexible work arrangements, work leave systems, and family-friendly employee benefits.

Drawing on the Preventive Stress Management framework introduced in Chapter 7, one could consider these programs as interventions designed to manage stressors related to work–family demands. Depending on the circumstances in which they are introduced, these programs can reflect primary, secondary, or tertiary interventions. For example, Ella uses a flexible work arrangement offered by her company as a primary intervention to help avoid her work demands becoming a stressor that disrupts her family life and vice versa. However, for Sylvia, who is experiencing high family stress because of a recent divorce, the flexible work arrangements offered by her workplace are helping her to manage her family stressors and avoid strain. In this case flexible work arrangements are being used as a secondary intervention.

OH&S Today 14.1

Recognizing Excellence: Healthy Workplace Awards

All across the country, organizations are getting excited about workplace wellness. More than ever, companies are making efforts to promote health and well-being among their employees. Many companies excel at these efforts and at winning awards that reflect their successes. Two popular healthy workplace award programs are Excellence Canada's Canada Awards for Excellence and the American Psychological Association's Psychologically Healthy Workplace Awards.

Excellence Canada, formerly known as the National Quality Institute (NQI), states that the mission of its awards program is to "inspire organizations by promoting excellence and showcasing their success as role models in an interdependent global economy that benefits all Canadians." These awards for quality and healthy workplaces have been presented annually since 1984. Past winners include Dofasco, 3M Canada, TELUS, and Solareh Inc.

The APA awards recognize employers who foster employee health and well-being in the areas of employee involvement, work–life balance, employee growth and development, health and safety, and employee recognition. Award competitions are held at the state, provincial, and territorial levels, with state and provincial winners having the opportunity to be nominated for the APA's overall awards. These awards are offered in several Canadian provinces. Canadian winners of the APA Psychologically Healthy Workplace Awards or Best Practice Honors include the Toronto Police Service (Ontario), Secunda Marine Services (Nova Scotia), and Advanced Solutions (British Columbia).

Sources: Excellence Canada, Canada Awards for Excellence (CAE) Overview. Found at: http://www.nqi.ca/en/awards/about-the-canada-awards-for-excellence/Overview%20and%20Benefits (Accessed Mar. 8, 2013); APA Center for Organizational Excellence, The Psychologically Healthy Workplace Program. Found at: http://www.phwa.org/awards/ (Accessed Mar. 8, 2013).

FAMILY-FRIENDLY POLICIES

Flexible Work Arrangements

Flexible work arrangements (FWAs) are modifications to the traditional work schedule. There are two basic versions of FWAs. First, some programs are designed to help mitigate work–family conflict by reducing the amount of *time* spent in the workplace. An example of this type of FWA is the **compressed workweek**. Under this option, employees can choose to work full-time hours in fewer days, for instance 40 hours in four days rather than five. The compressed work schedule can help employees reduce work–family conflict by allowing longer stretches of time at home, which also cuts down on commuting time.

Job sharing and job splitting programs also fall under this category of FWA. In **job sharing** programs, two employees share the responsibilities of a single position. In this case, the two employees have overlapping duties and must be sure to communicate with each other about all aspects of the work. In **job splitting**, two employees split job responsibilities so that each takes sole responsibility for various components of the job. Job sharing and job splitting arrangements typically benefit employees who want to work part-time hours. Job sharing and splitting options reduce the amount of time an employee must spend on work-related tasks and likely lead to a reduction in work role overload.

flexible work arrangements (FWAs)
family-friendly policies that involve modifications to the traditional work schedule

compressed workweek
flexible work arrangement in which employees work full-time hours in fewer days per week

job sharing
flexible work arrangement in which two employees share the responsibilities of a single position

job splitting
flexible work arrangement in which two employees divide the responsibilities of a single position

As such, these types of arrangements may reduce the incidence of work–family conflict.

The second large category consists of FWA programs designed to increase the amount of *control* that individuals have over their work schedule. A common example of this type of arrangement is **flextime**. In flextime schedules, employees are permitted variable start and finish times to their workday. For instance, one employee at a company offering flextime may choose to work from 7 a.m. to 3 p.m. Another employee may opt to start work at 10 a.m. and work until 6 p.m. In this case, during several hours of the day all employees are at work and group or team-related matters can be dealt with. This degree of control over start and finish times can help employees better manage work and family demands. For instance, Edward, a working father who worries about his children being home alone after school, prefers to start early and finish at 3 p.m. so that he can supervise his children after school or help them get to and from after-school activities.

Telecommuting is a second example of this category of FWA. Telecommuting programs (also known as telework or work-at-home programs) allow employees to complete their work assignments away from the office. The employee uses telecommunications technology such as the Internet and phone to keep in touch with the worksite. This option can help some employees better blend their work and family responsibilities. For instance, a person who works from home can delay the start of the workday until children leave for school and then immediately start working without losing time to things like commuting. Telework may also be helpful for individuals who have elders living with them, as they are able to be at home in case of emergency.

flextime

flexible work arrangement that permits employees to have variable start and finish times to their workday

telecommuting

flexible work arrangement in which an employee regularly makes use of telecommunications technology to complete work assignments away from the office, usually at home

Personal Leave Systems

Another broad category of family-friendly policies involves the provision of leave time to employees. Examples are maternity leave, parental leave, personal days, family leave, and sick leave. These leave programs are designed to help employees meet their family demands, thereby reducing the occurrence of family-to-work conflict. Consider an employee who has a chronically ill child. This individual may use family leave and personal days to accompany the child on doctor's visits and to care for the child. The existence of such a leave program should reduce the incidence of unexcused absenteeism and tardiness. Maternity leave programs allow new mothers to take paid time away from work shortly before and for some time after the birth of a child. Parental leave programs permit new mothers and fathers to take a leave from work responsibilities when a child is born or placed with them through an adoption. In Canada, the federal government provides a one-year maternity and parental leave program that permits an individual to collect a portion of his or her regular earnings through the Employment Insurance program. Some companies have chosen to provide additional parental benefits that top up the amount the parent earns while on leave. For instance, a company may continue to pay employees a top-up amount so that their total earnings while on leave equal 95% of their regular earnings. Employment Insurance pays an employee 55% of insurable earnings. In 2013 the maximum insurable earnings was $47,400, thus the maximum employment insurance payment was $501 per week.

Leave-related benefits aim to reduce the amount of work–family conflict experienced by employees. Consider the case of a new parent: Having to return to work shortly after the birth of a child will probably result in a high degree of work–family conflict. The new parent is adjusting to newly increased family demands, and these demands can often interfere with work performance. The availability of company-sponsored financial benefits for parental leave also reduces the considerable financial strain that would otherwise prompt an individual to return to work earlier than initially planned.

Family Care Benefits

The final category of family-friendly policies we discuss in this chapter is family care benefit programs. Daycare and eldercare benefits fall under this category. Employers can help employees who have children reduce their experience of work–family conflict by supporting daycare programs. This might involve an on-site daycare, which reduces the stress associated with dropping children off at various locations before getting in to work. Additionally, on-site daycares may reduce some of the stress associated with having children in nonparental care. When the daycare is at the work location, the working parent knows that he or she is nearby in case of an emergency. Additionally, the parent can drop in to see the child while at work. They may also have increased trust in the daycare provider, as it is a division of their own workplace. In some cases, employers who cannot provide on-site daycare can arrange to have daycare facilities near the worksite.

Another option under this category of family-friendly programs is subsidized dependant care. Here, organizations might provide employees with money to help cover the cost of eldercare or childcare, or to enroll elders or children in various programs. For instance, an employee who cares for an elderly parent might use this budget to enroll the parent in a seniors' program. As another example, an organization might sponsor summer camps for children of employees. In each case, we can see how these programs could reduce worries about responsibilities for dependant care.

FAMILY-FRIENDLY POLICIES: AN EVALUATION

Data from the United States suggest that family-friendly options are increasingly available to employees. The prevalence of telework increased throughout the 1990s, with estimates now suggesting that anywhere from 16 to 28 million American workers are currently engaged in this work arrangement.[11] It also appears that family-friendly policies are increasingly common in Canadian organizations. However, the available data are somewhat mixed regarding the availability of family-friendly work programs in Canadian organizations. A Conference Board of Canada survey suggested that as of 1999, 88% of Canadian employers offered flextime, 48% offered a compressed workweek, 52% provided job sharing options, 50% made provisions for telework, and 63% offered family responsibility leave. However, a 2003 analysis of Statistics Canada's Workplace Employee Survey of more than 20,000 employees from more than 6,000 employers differed in its conclusions. This report supported the claim that flextime is the most prevalent family-friendly work option, but also indicated that only about one-third of employees had access to it. Rates of telework and access to childcare services were even lower, at about 5%. The report identified organizational factors that appear to moderate the availability of family-friendly programs. Flextime and telework were more commonly reported by employees who worked in small organizations, whereas childcare and eldercare benefits seemed more prevalent in larger workplaces.[12] A survey of a large sample of Canadians working in mid-size to large organizations found that most organizations did not demonstrate best practices in the area of family-friendly programming.[13]

Little systematic research has been conducted on the effectiveness of the family-friendly policies described in this chapter. As such, the extent to which these programs actually reduce work–family conflict, and their impact on organizational functioning, are unknown. Certainly, anecdotal evidence attesting to their effectiveness in reducing work–family conflict is readily available. However, the available research provides mixed results as to their *actual* impact on work–family conflict.[14] Some studies suggest that family-friendly policies do indeed reduce work–family conflict.[15] Flextime has been associated with an increase in the degree to which people feel they are in control of their work and family lives.[16] Other studies report that family-friendly policies such as flextime and telework do *not* affect the occurrence of work–family conflict and may even increase it.[17] One interesting study found that the availability of family-friendly policies reduced the extent to which work interfered with family responsibilities but had no impact on family-to-work conflict.[18] However, other studies have found that telework in particular may reduce work interference with family but *increase* family-to-work conflict.[19] Contextual factors seem to play a role in the success of teleworking. People who spent more of their working hours engaged in telework reported reduced work-to-family interference but *increased* family-to-work interference. Furthermore, those who had higher degrees of autonomy and flexibility in their jobs reported a greater positive effect of telework on their experiences of work–family conflict.[20]

Researchers have also examined the impact of family-friendly policies on organizations. Again, there are mixed results for the effectiveness of family-friendly initiatives. One recent study found that telework was associated with increased commitment to the organization and reduced intentions to quit.[21] It appears that flexible work options, such as flextime and telecommuting, have a positive impact on job satisfaction and decrease absenteeism.[22] However, the impact of these policies on productivity is uncertain. Some studies report that flexible arrangements contribute to improved productivity; others report no significant effects.[23]

Additional research on the organizational and individual impacts of work–family policies is warranted. This research should specifically consider the type of work–family policy and the nature of the conflict (i.e., work-to-family versus family-to-work).[24] It should also ask questions about why companies choose to implement the policies they do.[25] Little research is available regarding the extent to which employers consider work–family policies to be strategic human resource initiatives, even though the existence of these programs may be important in terms of recruiting and retaining high-quality employees.[26]

Future studies should distinguish between the availability of family-friendly policies and the extent to which employees actually use them. Employer and employee surveys paint two different pictures regarding flexible work arrangements.[27] Some employers who have family-friendly options make those programs

OH&S Notebook 14.1

REDUCING WORK–LIFE CONFLICT: STRATEGIES FOR ORGANIZATIONS

A Health Canada–sponsored report on work–family conflict suggests that employers aiming to help employees create work–life balance should *reduce demands* placed on employees and *increase the control* that employees have over their work. Some of the specific recommendations include the following:

- Reduce employee workloads
- Recognize when work demands are unrealistic and acknowledge that such loads are not sustainable
- Track the costs of understaffing and unrealistic work demands
- Avoid reliance on overtime work; hire more people if the need arises
- Track the direct and indirect costs of role overload and work–life conflict (absenteeism,

overtime, employee assistance programs, turnover)

- Have policies about the use of office technology (e.g., change expectations about after-hours email)
- Offer "cafeteria-style" benefits programs so that employees can choose the services that benefit them
- Support child- and dependant-care needs (paid leave, care options)
- Offer flexible work options to help reduce role overload
- Reduce the incidence of nonsupportive management

Sources: L. Duxbury & C. Higgins, *Work–Life Conflict in Canada in the New Millennium: A Status Report, Final Report*, Oct. 2003. Found at: http://publications.gc.ca/collections/Collection/H72-21-186-2003E.pdf (Accessed Mar. 8, 2013); C. Higgins, L. Duxbury, and S. Lyons, *Reducing Work–Life Conflict: What Works? What Doesn't?* (2008). Found at: http://www.hc-sc.gc.ca/ewh-semt/alt_formats/hecs-sesc/pdf/pubs/occup-travail/balancing-equilibre/full_report-rapport_complet-eng.pdf (Accessed Mar. 9, 2013).

available only to a select group of employees—for instance, people in a particular job classification. Also, the data suggest that in some organizations, employees choose not to use family-friendly policies such as flextime because they fear that doing so will negatively affect their career progress. Clearly, the formal existence of a policy does not guarantee that employees will make use of it. In the real world, the culture of the organization shapes the extent to which employees are willing to use work–family policies.

One report indicated that the characteristics of work groups affected whether employees opted to use FWAs.[28] Individuals who worked in groups that were more supportive made greater use of these options. This study stressed the importance of organizational support for family-friendly initiatives. If employees fear that they will be looked down on or damage their career prospects, they may choose not to take advantage of available family-friendly programs.

HEALTH PROMOTION PROGRAMS

Wellness or health promotion programming is the active attempt to improve employee well-being through worksite interventions. The rationale for such programming is that many health-related concerns can be prevented through lifestyle changes such as diet, exercise, and smoking cessation. Given that employed adults spend many hours in the workplace and that the health of employees affects organizational and individual functioning, the workplace is a convenient and appropriate venue for reaching many adults. This is why more and more workplaces have launched health promotion programs.

Health promotion efforts combine diagnostic, educational, and behavioural change initiatives with the goal of helping people attain and maintain positive health. An emerging concept in health promotion—one of particular interest for worksites—is health and productivity management. Health and productivity management programs integrate health promotion activities in ways that simultaneously increase employee well-being and decrease the organization's health-related costs, such as absenteeism and reduced work performance.[29] It would be useful here to trace the development of employee assistance plans (EAPs)—now often called employee and family assistance programs (EFAPs)—before addressing health promotion programs (HPPs).

health promotion

a combination of diagnostic, educational, and behavioural modification activities designed to support the attainment and maintenance of positive health

Employee and Family Assistance Programs (EFAPs)

Employee and family assistance programs (EFAPs) provide counselling and assistance to members of an organization and in some cases to members of their families. Generally, these programs help individuals control personal concerns—such as alcoholism, drug use, and stress—that may affect their performance at work.[30] The roots of EFAPs date back to the nineteenth century and the social betterment movement. Initiatives included inexpensive housing, company-sponsored unions, sanitary working conditions, insurance, pension plans, banking, recreation, medical care, and education facilities. After the social betterment movement subsided in the 1920s and 1930s, personal counselling emerged. Management trained some shop workers to listen to workers' problems thus to reduce those problems' interference with productivity. For example, in 1917, Macy's Department Store established a program to assist employees who were dealing with personal problems. By 1920, one-third of the 431 largest companies in the United States had a full-time welfare secretary whose major role was as a counsellor.[31]

employee and family assistance programs (EFAPs)

programs designed to help employees and members of their families with problems that may interfere with worker productivity, including alcohol and other drug abuse, emotional or behavioural problems among family members, and financial or legal problems

In the 1940s arose the Occupational Alcohol Movement, generally acknowledged to be the direct predecessor of the EFAP.[32] Alcoholism was recognized as a serious impediment to productivity, and these programs sought to help workers troubled by this problem by offering alcohol-related and personal problem counselling. The 1970s were a period of rapid growth for EFAPs. In the 1980s EFAPs expanded to include stress management. Today, EFAPs address all types of problems that may interfere with worker productivity, including alcohol and other drug abuse, emotional or behavioural problems among family members, and financial or legal problems.[33]

Currently, it is difficult to distinguish between EFAPs and health promotion programs, and health promotion programs are now viewed as subsuming the earlier EFAPs. The primary objectives of EFAPs are to help employees and their immediate family members address personal concerns and to help organizations identify and address productivity concerns relating to their employees.[34] Typically, health promotion programs include interventions aimed at *stress management* and *lifestyle changes* (e.g., diet, smoking cessation, physical fitness). We next turn our attention to these two classes of health promotion initiatives.

OH&S Notebook 14.2

BUILDING A BUSINESS CASE FOR WELLNESS

Canadian organizations have endorsed the use of employee and family assistance programs (EFAPs), but have been somewhat slower to adopt broader-based wellness or health promotion programming. When suggesting the need for more comprehensive programming, HR professionals will have to develop the business case for health promotion planning. Potential benefits from such programs include the following:

- reduced absenteeism and associated costs
- reduced turnover and associated costs
- reduced insurance rates (e.g., from better disability management, reduced smoking)
- added inducement when recruiting new employees

- improved morale, job satisfaction, and reduced stress
- increased employee health while at work

Ill health while working has been associated with decreased productivity. For instance, conditions such as hypertension, migraines, and respiratory infections have been associated with three to four unproductive hours in an eight-hour shift. Indeed, the phenomenon of presenteeism—that is, working while ill—is very costly for organizations. Some estimates suggest that presenteeism may account for as much as 63% of an organization's medical costs.

Sources: Adapted from: J. Hummer, B. Sherman, & N. Quinn, "Present and Unaccounted For," *Occupational Health and Safety*, Vol. 71, No. 4, Pg. 40–44, 2002; P. Hemp, "Presenteeism: At Work—but Out of It," *Harvard Business Review*, Vol. 82, No. 10, Pg. 49–58, 2004.

Stress Management Programs

The goals of stress management programs are to educate workers about the causes and consequences of stress and to teach skills for managing physiological and psychological symptoms. Again, we can reflect back to the models of stress introduced in Chapter 7. Persistent exposure to stressors can contribute to the experience of stress. Likewise, prolonged or intense experiences of stress can contribute to symptoms of strain such as psychological concerns, physical health problems, or negative behaviours.

In terms of helping employees recognize the causes of stress, programs might draw attention to the pertinent workplace stressors such as workload and work pace, role stressors, and interpersonal relations. Programs that help people to reduce their exposure to these stressors would be primary interventions. Other programs offer secondary interventions and focus on helping employees manage stress that they are experiencing. Still other programs are tertiary in nature and help people who are experiencing the symptoms of strain. The most common stress management program is relaxation training. Cognitive-behavioural skills training and programs designed to increase social support are also fairly common.[35]

Cognitive-Behavioural Skills Training

Cognitive-behavioural programs are developed in terms of the cognitive model of stress, which posits that emotional responses to situations are largely determined by how they are thought about and interpreted. The training helps people to think about events in new ways and to be aware of how they are viewing stressful events; it also provides skills for coping with stress. The goal is to alter both cognition of stressful events and behaviour toward them. For example, participants in stress inoculation sessions might be trained in self-instruction, cognitive restructuring, problem solving, and relaxation. The training program itself might use techniques such as role playing and classroom instruction. In a recent review of stress management interventions, cognitive-behavioural interventions proved to be the most effective.[36]

Relaxation Training and Meditation

Relaxation training teaches things such as progressive muscle relaxation and breathing exercises. If you have ever taken a class in yoga, martial arts, or even aerobics, you have probably experienced something similar to this. Someone may ask you to lie down on the floor, close your eyes, and focus your mind on your body and your muscles. Then, they may ask you to relax every muscle in your body, slowly working from the bottom up or the top down. The purpose of this type of training is to provide people with skills to physically relax the body. Over time, individuals will learn to recognize the physical feelings associated with stress and to counteract these feelings by calling on the relaxation response. In doing so, they prevent stress leading to the type of strain reactions discussed earlier.

Relaxation training focuses on relaxing the physical body; meditation focuses on quieting the mind. There are many approaches to meditation, and you are probably familiar with at least some of them. Meditation helps individuals withdraw from a stressful situation and re-energize through mental exercise. The most widely used form of meditation in the workplace involves sitting quietly for 20 minutes, repeating a single word on each exhalation.[37] Meditation practice seems to lead to positive physical and psychological outcomes in the workplace.[38] Relaxation training is a commonly used workplace stress intervention that seems to be moderately effective in reducing employee stress.[39]

Increasing Social Support

A different strategy for reducing work-related stress is to provide a more supportive environment. One way of doing this is by training workers in how to seek social support and in how to create a more supportive workplace. For example, caregiver support programs are designed to help people deal with the stresses of providing care for others. The goal of such programs is typically to increase social support and participation in work-related decisions. Caregiver support programs are designed to teach employees the benefits of support systems, enhance their skills in mobilizing support, educate them about participatory problem-solving approaches, and show them how to build skills to implement these approaches in team meetings.

Effectiveness of Stress Management Training

Results are mixed regarding the effectiveness of stress management training programs. The lack of comprehensive, well-designed studies on workplace stress management interventions makes it difficult to assess the effectiveness of such programs.[40] Some programs appear to be effective at reducing the experience of job-related stress; others are not. As noted earlier, one large review study found that cognitive-behavioural interventions appear to be the most effective.[41] For example, in one study on stress management training, participants were exposed to a variety of stress management techniques, including cognitive restructuring, positive self-talk, deep muscle relaxation, autogenic instructions, and imagery exercises.[42] The training program included nine hours of instruction over six sessions. The researchers found that compared to a control group, those receiving training did not show a significant increase in learning or job satisfaction, or a significant decrease in blood pressure, somatic data, or anxiety. However, when a self-management module was included as part of the training, significant differences were found for all measures except job satisfaction. The self-management module included three hours of training in self-monitoring, specifying goals, evaluating behaviour against goals, and self-reinforcing. This study suggests that simply providing training is not enough to make a difference; participants must be provided with strategies to help them apply what they have learned. Interestingly, this is the same conclusion reached for safety programs in general—training alone is often insufficient to effect change.

Conversely, another study showed that stress management training was effective in reducing the interpersonal aspects of stress.[43] However, this program was custom designed with the needs of the users in mind and may have been more effective than "out of the can" stress management programs. Social support programs are also effective. Typically, such programs increase the amount of supportive feedback on the job, enhance perceptions about the ability to handle disagreements and work overload, and improve work team climate. Another study found that a high degree of participation in a program that targeted psychosocial stressors reduced the negative effects of a large personnel cutback in a health care setting.[44]

Worksite Health Promotion: A Focus on Lifestyle Changes

Worksite health promotion programming can be classified into three categories: screening, education, and behavioural change. Many types of programs are being delivered in each of these various categories. The most common are those designed to affect an employee's health practices or physical lifestyle (e.g., in terms of exercise, eating habits, sleep patterns, weight control, alcohol use, smoking cessation, substance abuse). These efforts are often referred to as "lifestyle programming." It is generally thought that a healthy lifestyle helps promote physical and mental health on the job. Employers are trying to capitalize on this connection. A recent survey of Canadian companies reported that 40% of Canadian employers offer lifestyle-focused programming for their employees.[45] Some programs include activities designed to improve psychological aspects of an individual's lifestyle (e.g., social relations, intellectual activity, occupational conditions), but these programs are still the exception rather than the rule.

On-site programs may include fitness facilities, nutritional assessment and counselling, weight control groups, and smoking cessation help. Typically, these opportunities are available on a voluntary basis. Some may be offered only to individuals at a certain level in the organization (e.g., membership in an off-site health club for managers). Though the organization may provide incentives for using such programs, it would have difficulty mandating that employees alter their lifestyle. Though it is possible to make safety training (even stress reduction training) mandatory, it would be difficult to insist that all employees quit smoking or have a perfect body mass index. Indeed, to the extent that addiction or obesity is considered a disability, doing so might violate human rights legislation. Instead of attempting to mandate such programs, organizations involved in worksite health promotion should develop cultures and environments that are highly supportive of healthful lifestyle practices.

Though health promotion programs are diverse, many are secondary-level interventions designed to help individuals who are feeling stress and who are at risk for illness. Worksite health promotion (WHP) programs typically include three steps:

Step 1: Physical or psychological assessment

Step 2: Counselling concerning the assessment findings and recommendations about personal health promotion

Step 3: Referral to in-house or community-based resources

If we focus on WHP programs that are more tertiary in nature—that is, those designed to help people who are currently experiencing symptoms or illness, such as alcohol and other substance abuse, hypertension, or psychological stress—the key components in such programs should include the following:

- The identification of currently symptomatic as well as high-risk individuals

- The appropriate referral or treatment of individuals

- Treatment directed at the symptom, delivered by the appropriate professionals

- Follow-up with the client to ensure the treatment was effective

- Evaluation of health improvement and cost efficacy

Components of an effective employer-sponsored health promotion effort include employee education for health promotion or disease prevention; management training to raise awareness and identification of occupational health issues; EFAP services; redesigned benefit programs to provide easy access to interventions; a comprehensive data collection plan for use in program decision making; the integration of corporate health-related services; and greater attention to organizational health. We next turn our attention to some specific categories of WHP programs. In particular, we look at efforts focused on changing some aspect of an employee's lifestyle (i.e., lifestyle programming).

Smoking Cessation

One of the most popular worksite health promotion interventions in recent years has been smoking cessation. As worksites have increasingly banned smoking, either voluntarily or because of legislation, more and more employers have seen the wisdom of helping employees quit smoking. Research has consistently documented that smokers are absent more than nonsmokers; this provides employers with an economic incentive for smoking cessation programs.[46] Some estimate the costs associated with smoking (i.e., those attributable to absenteeism, lost productivity, and increased insurance premiums) to be in the neighbourhood of $2,500 per year per employee.

Smoking cessation programs typically combine education, group support, counselling, and behavioural change techniques. The success rates of such programs have varied between 25% and 60%. Several studies support the effectiveness of various targeted worksite interventions for reducing smoking.[47] More recently, pharmaceutical aids such as nicotine gum, the nicotine patch, and other medications have enhanced success rates. It is important to note that these aids do not replace traditional approaches. Rather, the greatest success seems to come from a combination of psychoeducational and pharmaceutical approaches to smoking cessation. Note that organizational bans on smoking do not seem to be associated with reduced smoking behaviour among employees.[48]

Alcohol and Drug Testing Programs

Research suggests that alcohol and drug use have negative effects in the workplace. For example, there are studies linking the prevalence of heavy drinkers in a workplace to increased incidence of gender harassment and the frequency of heavy drinking to increased absenteeism.[49] Furthermore, to the extent that alcohol and drug use may decrease alertness and quick thinking, they may lead to performance concerns, particularly relating to safety. As described above, EFAPs, both historically and currently, are avenues for employees to seek guidance and explore means of treatment for alcohol and drug addictions.

Because of the potentially severe outcomes associated with alcohol and drug use, some employers have introduced direct alcohol and drug testing programs to screen employees for recent drug or alcohol consumption. These programs are controversial. Some argue in support of drug testing because there is support for the claim that workplace testing deters drug and alcohol use.[50] Others argue against the practice for a variety of reasons, including the fact that drug testing detects exposure to a drug but not necessarily current impairment. Besides this, the practice violates employee privacy.[51]

Canadian employers are subject to the Canadian Human Rights Commission's policy on alcohol and drug testing. Under that policy, such testing is considered a discriminatory practice. The policy statement indicates that while drug testing can assess exposure, it does not assess ability impairment at the time of the screening. There are some apparent exceptions relating to alcohol screening for individuals who are in safety-sensitive positions because alcohol detection is indicative of impairment at the time of the test. If such alcohol screens are in place, employers must accommodate the needs of those who test positive and are identified as being dependent on alcohol. As with other discriminatory practices, Canadian employers can justify drug and alcohol testing if they can demonstrate that it is a *bona fide* occupational requirement. In those cases testing may occur for reasonable cause (e.g., the employee is unfit for work) or following a significant safety incident in which the employee is implicated.[52] This policy is available online for download.

Hypertension Screening

hypertension
elevated blood pressure

Hypertension, or high blood pressure, has been called the "silent killer." Individuals can have hypertension for a long time without knowing it or without experiencing symptoms. Though it may seem relatively innocuous, hypertension is considered one of the major (and most easily controlled) risk factors in heart-related diseases. Workplace programs aimed at addressing hypertension vary widely but typically consist of four interrelated steps:

1. *Education.* Employees are alerted to the dangers of hypertension and the benefits associated with treatment.
2. *Screening.* Employees are screened using blood pressure clinics in which participants have their blood pressure read by a medical professional.
3. *Referral.* Employees with elevated readings are referred to medical treatment.
4. *Follow-up.* Referred employees are followed up to verify the outcome of treatment and to monitor progress.

Worksite hypertension programs typically result in approximately 25% of participants being identified as hypertensive—about the same prevalence as in the general population. Outcome studies suggest that programs are very effective in bringing hypertension under control through diet and medication. Moreover, some evidence shows that programs with more elements (e.g., those that include frequent monitoring and follow-up) are more effective than simple screening or educational programs.

Nutrition and Weight Control

Nutrition programs in the workplace typically take one of two forms. First, educational programs are aimed at providing instruction or information on the selection of foods, the basics of meal planning, and so on. Posters in the cafeteria promoting *Canada's Food Guide* are an example of educational programming. The second type of activity is to actually change the food available in the workplace. Providing healthy, low-fat alternatives in the cafeteria and changing the contents of vending machines in the workplace help employees maintain a healthy diet. There is empirical evidence for the effectiveness of some nutrition-focused worksite health promotion programs.[53]

Weight control programs are becoming increasingly popular and are often offered in conjunction with established weight loss programs (e.g., Weight Watchers, TOPS). Again, such programs rely on education, counselling, and group support. Several studies indicate that worksite weight loss programs can be effective; however, attrition rates tend to be high. In other words, those who stay with the program may lose weight, but there is a high dropout rate and, hence, a large number of people for whom the programs are not effective.

Physical Fitness Programs

Fitness programs can be implemented in three levels.[54] The most basic efforts—Level I programs—focus on awareness and typically comprise newsletters, health fairs, screening sessions (e.g., body mass index assessments), posters, and brochures. Level I programs are not aimed specifically at change, but rather at making individuals aware of the need for change and the resources available to support change.

Level II programs last eight to 12 weeks and attempt to achieve long-term effects by fostering specific health-related habits. Corporations that offer specific fitness courses (e.g., strength training or lower-back training) are engaged in Level II programming. Level III programs attempt to support individual change by creating a work environment that promotes a healthful lifestyle. Ensuring that cafeterias offer healthful foods, providing bike racks or locker facilities in the workplace, having on-site fitness facilities, and removing cigarette or candy machines from the workplace are all examples of Level III programs. All three levels of programming have proved effective in enhancing individual physical fitness.

Some studies report that workplace fitness programs are associated with decreased health care costs, decreased hospital admissions, and decreased absenteeism for those who take part.[55] Though little convincing evidence exists that such programs result in increased job performance, a substantial number of studies show increases in employee morale associated with the provision of fitness programming. Other studies present a different view, suggesting that there is little evidence supporting the effectiveness of workplace fitness interventions.[56] However, research does show that individually tailored programs— those designed with a particular employee's needs in mind—appear to be more successful than generic fitness programs.[57] Some evidence also suggests that programs that combine physical activity and nutrition interventions are most effective in reducing morbidity due to being overweight.[58]

OH&S Today 14.2

Healthy Organizations: Wellness and Work–Family Programming at a Canadian Company

Many Canadian companies have excellent and well-deserved reputations for the high level of wellness programming they endorse. Consider ArcelorMittal Dofasco Inc. as an example. This Hamilton-based company is one of the most profitable steelmakers in North America and was recognized by *The Globe and Mail* as one of Canada's 50 best places to work. Often claiming "Our Strength Is People" ArcelorMittal Dofasco Inc. has a longstanding emphasis on employee engagement and well-being. As part of its Healthy Lifestyles programs, ArcelorMittal Dofasco provides numerous family-friendly and health-focused options, including employee access to a multisport recreation and learning centre and several health promotion initiatives such as on-site, subsidized Weight Watchers meetings, smoking cessation programs, first aid training, a comprehensive employee assistance program, and health assessments. This company's high investment in employees has been a success. There is a high degree of program participation and attendance among employees. From a financial perspective there has been a marked reduction in lost-time injuries, Workers' Compensation premiums, and incidence of non–work-related injuries since the health programs were initiated.

Sources: ArcelorMittal. Found at: http://www.dofasco.ca (Accessed Mar. 8, 2013); Gordon DiGiacomo, Canadian Labour and Business Centre, *Case Study: Dofasco's Healthy Lifestyle Program*, March 2002. Found at: http://www.clbc.ca/files/casestudies/dofasco.pdf. (Accessed Mar. 8, 2013).

DEVELOPING A SUCCESSFUL WORKSITE HEALTH PROMOTION PROGRAM

A program is worthwhile only if it is achieving its goals. A worksite health promotion (WHP) program will succeed only if employees are making use of what it offers. Research on worksite health promotion efforts has provided some key evidence-based insights on the factors that contribute to successful program implementation. The following list of essential elements for an EFAP can easily be extended to WHP programs in general:[59]

1. *A clear, written policy regarding assistance.* The policy must balance worker privacy (e.g., if an employee voluntarily seeks help, it will be kept confidential) with the needs of the company (e.g., if a serious behaviour problem, such as the use of drugs on the job, is uncovered by a supervisor, disciplinary action will be taken). There is a need to avoid stigmatizing individuals and to ensure the confidentiality and safety of the program; otherwise, employees won't use it.

2. *Management support.* As with all important organizational initiatives, a lack of cooperation at any level can undermine the goals of the program.

3. *An on-site program coordinator.* This person coordinates and administrates the program, ensuring that those who seek help receive appropriate treatment. Thinking regarding whom this person should be varies. Some feel that anyone with a caring attitude can fill this position; others feel that it should be someone with formal training (e.g., a clinical psychologist, psychiatrist, or social worker). This decision may depend on the extent to which problems will be handled in-house as opposed to being referred to outside agencies.

4. *Supervisory training.* Supervisors are often in a position where they must make referrals to the coordinator. It is these individuals who see the employees on a day-to-day basis and to whom the employees may go if they are experiencing problems. Supervisors must be trained to recognize and act on problems that arise.

5. *Employee education about the benefits of the program.* Promoting the program will help ensure that it is used and that employees are receiving assistance with work-related stress issues and with health issues in general.

6. *Counselling.* Either in-house or external services may be available to employees. The advantage with external services is the reduced likelihood of conflicts of interest for the coordinator; the major drawback is that the referral agency may have little experience with work settings, so worker productivity is de-emphasized in favour of counselling and more expensive treatments.

7. *Union support.* Businesses that want to institute an EFAP are wise to consult with the relevant unions and get them involved. This will help build trust and cooperation and increase the likelihood that the program will succeed. EFAP coordinators often have to walk a careful line between union and management. For example, management may view the EFAP with suspicion, particularly when it comes to cost; unions may feel that EFAPs are the company's way of usurping union power.

ISSUES WITH EFAPS AND WHP PROGRAMS

The expanding definition of an EFAP, especially now that it has been usurped by the broader worksite health promotion (WHP) program, means that there may be some uncertainty concerning the policy's implementation. For example, how do you define "general mental health"? Where does an EFAP coordinator draw the line in intervening? Successful EFAPs must have clear guidelines that are understood by managers and employees at all levels.[60]

One shortcoming of EFAPs is that they provide limited feedback to management about the sources and effects of stress in the organization. Because employees are approaching and using the intervention system on an individual basis, and are guaranteed confidentiality, there is no effective way for the program to inform the organization if there is a stress "hot zone." Another shortcoming is the same complaint expressed about many secondary interventions: they focus on the characteristics of the employee and not on the working environment that may be the cause of the stress.[61]

The issue of confidentiality in EFAPs is very important. If a person's privacy is not respected, people will hesitate to seek help for fear there will be job-related repercussions. Thus, all records should be kept confidential and separated from an employee's personnel file. Many programs with high compliance rates owe their success to the steps taken to ensure confidentiality and job security.

UNINTENDED CONSEQUENCES OF WHP PROGRAMS

The goal of health promotion is to reduce costs to the organization in terms of health care, lost time, turnover, and so on. However, some unintended consequences of WHP programs need to be considered. First, the reduction of health care utilization by employees (offered through benefits plans) may lead to a higher unit cost for those employees who do use health and medical benefits. The individual cost of offering certain benefits decreases with a high enrolment rate because the risk to insurance companies of having to pay out on claims is reduced with a large subscription. Reduced enrolment in some aspects of a cafeteria-style benefits plan (in which employees have some options concerning the coverage they want in areas such as medical, dental, life insurance, etc.) may make it prohibitive for those employees who need access to those benefits. A second potential consequence is that participation in exercise or fitness programs may cause work disruptions, increase fatigue, lower performance, and increase accidents among those who are beginning such a program.

Also, health promotion can cause friction among workers. For example, smoking restrictions may produce conflict between smokers and nonsmokers, produce negative attitudes about smoking, and reduce productivity among smokers if they must leave the workstation to smoke. Finally, the diagnosis of previously unknown risk factors may contribute to absenteeism (e.g., doctor's appointments). For example, individuals who did not know they were hypertensive may exhibit increased absenteeism as a result of being informed of their condition.

OVERALL EVALUATION

How successful are worksite health promotion programs? Once again, we find "success" to be a difficult thing to assess. Some studies show that these programs can be effective. Estimates on a company's return on investment in health promotion programs vary. One review of health promotion studies found that, in terms of savings, health care costs of WHP programs netted the company $3.48 for every $1 they spent on the program. In the same review, costs savings from reduced absenteeism associated with participation in worksite health promotion programs ranged from $2.50 to $10.10 for every dollar the company invested in the programs.[62] In fact, a recent study evaluating a multifaceted worksite health promotion program's effect on absenteeism reported that program participants were absent an average of three fewer days per year than nonparticipants. The associated cost savings for the organization was $15.60 returned for every $1 initially invested in the program.[63] So, for every dollar spent on program expenses such as extra staff to run the program, advertisements for the program, or equipment and facilities to support the program, companies can experience substantial cost savings by way of such factors as reduced absenteeism, benefits costs, or health care costs.

However, not all studies support the success of WHP programs. In fact, some authors argue that there is simply not enough systematic research on the various categories of WHP programs to reach a definitive conclusion about their efficacy.[64] Some point out that the available studies that do show positive effects are plagued with methodological weaknesses.[65] For instance, it is not uncommon for studies in this area to lack the necessary control groups, randomization of participants, and well-defined outcome measures that are needed to reach strong conclusions about the program under investigation. Another problem common in this area of research is the use of cross-sectional rather than longitudinal designs. As such, researchers cannot assess the potential long-term benefits of WHP programs.

Overall, the jury is still out on the benefits of WHP programs. Some recent evidence suggests that comprehensive health programs are cost effective and yield positive cost and health-related benefits.[66] However, the links between health promotion efforts and performance improvement, absenteeism and turnover, and morale and attitude improvement are spurious in the research literature, which makes it difficult to reach firm conclusions on the success of such programs. The lack of evaluation studies relying on rigorous scientific methodology contributes to this problem. The available research does suggest that management support is vital if worksite health promotion initiatives are to succeed.[67]

Beyond the lack of solid research to demonstrate their effectiveness indisputably, two additional factors have been noted as limitations to worksite health promotion programs.[68] First, these initiatives have been criticized for focusing heavily on individual attitudes and behaviour and for often excluding organizational and management factors (e.g., job design) that also have a high degree of influence on employee health. Alternatively, a class of interventions called quality-of-work–life programs has objectives similar to worksite health promotion, but rather than presume the employee's lifestyle is responsible for health, well-being, and performance, they focus on what an employer can do to improve the employee's working conditions.

A second criticism of worksite health promotion programs is that they are often carried out in isolation from other human resource practices. Here, they have much in common with work–family policies that are often overlooked as strategic human resource functions.[69] The lack of integration with other human resource functions may be detrimental to the ultimate success of existing WHP programs. In reviewing key evidence-based elements for effective worksite health promotion programs, one study noted that health promotion programs are most likely to be effective when they are fully integrated into strategic human resource efforts.[70]

A recent report sponsored by Health Canada summarized the organizational factors that positively affect worker health.[71] The factors that contribute to a healthy work environment include leaders who value employees as key to organizational success, supervisors who support employees and wellness initiatives,

OH&S Notebook 14.3

USING EVALUATION TO BUILD A BUSINESS CASE FOR HEALTH PROMOTION AND FAMILY-FRIENDLY PROGRAMS

Given the large investment that organizations make in health promotion and family-friendly workplace policies, it is important to investigate the effectiveness of such initiatives. One way for HR managers to make a business case for continued or increased funding for workplace wellness and family-friendly programs is by demonstrating that they work. To that end, the outcomes associated with such programs should be subjected to careful study. Organizations can conduct evaluation studies to assess the success of their health-related initiatives. Some characteristics of thorough evaluation studies include the following:

1. *Pre-intervention and post-intervention assessments of relevant variables.* This approach allows the evaluator to use the pre-intervention measure as a baseline to assess the extent of improvement experienced by the program participants and the organization. Ideally, there should also be multiple post-intervention assessments to allow researchers to gain an understanding of the long-term effectiveness of the program.

2. *Consideration of the extent to which employees participate in the program.* Knowing whether employees take part will help the evaluator

understand the outcomes associated with the program. If there does not appear to be improvement in important variables, it will be valuable to know whether the lack of change is associated with low participation or whether employees are participating in a program that is not working.

3. *Reliable and valid measures of relevant individual and organizational outcome variables.* Depending on the exact nature of the program, employees in a health promotion program might fill out a questionnaire regarding their anxiety levels and degree of job satisfaction, or have their blood pressure monitored. The organization might monitor such factors as absenteeism rates, production rates, or incidence of lost-time injuries. If the program is effective, these variables would indicate as much.

4. *Some type of control group, if possible.* Comparing the outcomes of those employees who took part in the program with a comparable group who did not would provide valuable information regarding the effectiveness of the WHP initiative.

communication throughout the organization, a high degree of employee participation and control, and an organization that values work–family balance and employee health. These ingredients contribute to a holistic approach to workplace wellness that involves individuals and organizations in the creation of healthier employees and workplaces.

SUMMARY

A broad array of programs can be offered in organizations under the rubric of work–family and worksite health promotion programming. For the most part, the jury is still out on whether these programs offer significant benefits to organizational outcomes. However, some evidence shows that work–family programs have *some* positive impact on the experience of work–family conflict. Similarly, health promotion programming can succeed in changing individual behaviour to enhance health. One positive spinoff of the programs for organizations is the general increase in employee morale (e.g., satisfaction, commitment) that is associated with making health promotion and family-friendly programs available in the workplace.

Key Terms

compressed workweek 359
employee and family assistance
    programs (EFAPs) 364
flexible work arrangements (FWAs) 359
flextime 360
health promotion 364

hypertension 370
job sharing 359
job splitting 359
telecommuting 360
work–family conflict 357

Weblinks

APA Psychologically Healthy Workplace Program
http://www.phwa.org

Arcelor/Mittal Dofasco
http://www.dofasco.ca

Canadian Centre for Occupational Health and Safety, "Work–Life Balance"
http://www.ccohs.ca/oshanswers/psychosocial/worklife_balance.html

Canadian Human Rights Commission's Policy on Alcohol and Drug Testing
http://www.chrc-ccdp.ca/pdf/padt_pdda_eng.pdf

Centre for Families, Work, and Well-Being, University of Guelph
http://www.uoguelph.ca/cfww

CCOHS, "Active Living at Work"
http://www.ccohs.ca/oshanswers/psychosocial/active_living.html

CCOHS, "Healthy Eating at Work"
http://www.ccohs.ca/oshanswers/psychosocial/healthyeating.html

CCOHS, "Substance Abuse in the Workplace"
http://www.ccohs.ca/oshanswers/psychosocial/substance.html

Health Canada, "Healthy Workplaces"
http://www.hc-sc.gc.ca/hcs-sss/hhr-rhs/strateg/p3/index-eng.php

National Quality Institute
http://www.nqi.ca

Public Health Agency of Canada, "Business Case for Active Living at Work"
http://www.phac-aspc.gc.ca/pau-uap/fitness/work/index.html

Required Professional Capabilities (RPCs)

The following RPCs, listed by their CCHRA number, are relevant to the material covered in this chapter. All RPCs can be found at http://www.chrp.ca/rpc/body-of-knowledge.

RPC:170 Develops, implements, and ensures the application of policies, regulations, and standards relating to occupational health and safety[*]

RPC:174 Develops and implements policies on the workplace environment[*]

RPC:177 Develops or provides for wellness and employee assistance programs to support organizational effectiveness[*]

RPC:178 Provides information to employees and managers on available programs[*]

RPC:179 Ensures that mechanisms are in place for responding to crises in the workplace, including critical incident stress management[*]

RPC:183 Analyzes risks to employee health & safety and develops preventive programs[*]

RPC:186 Establishes and implements strategies to minimize workers' compensation costs[*]

Discussion Questions

1. EFAPs often have two routes of entry. An individual can voluntarily contact the EFAP for assistance with a problem, or a supervisor can refer the individual. In the latter case, a supervisor who notes a decline in performance can insist that an individual seek assistance or be disciplined (including dismissal). Is this degree of coercion justified? Is it likely to facilitate a change in behaviour?

2. The logic of health promotion programs in the workplace is based on the observation that the workplace provides a convenient way to reach large segments of the population. Yet many individuals wonder whether organizations have the right to get involved in employees' lifestyle choices. What do you think? Should organizations be involved in these programs?

3. What benefits would you expect to see from implementing a physical fitness program (e.g., paid memberships in the local health club) in your workplace?

---

[*]Canadian Council of Human Resources Associations, Human Resources Professionals in Canada: Revised Body of Knowledge and Required Professional Capabilities (RPCs ®), 2007.

4. Is stress management training an effective approach to dealing with work-place stress? Why or why not?

5. Generate some strategies that a dual-income couple might use to help them manage work and family demands more effectively. How might their employers help them enact some of these strategies?

Using the Internet

1. Visit the websites of a number of companies representing a variety of job sectors (e.g., manufacturing, high tech, communications, medical). Search the Web pages to find information on the types of health promotion programs (e.g., smoking cessation, fitness) and family-friendly policies (e.g., flextime, telecommuting) they offer.

   a. Identify the proportion of the companies that offer health promotion programs or family-friendly policies.

   b. Which health promotion programs and family-friendly policies appear to be most commonly available?

   c. What are some of the company characteristics that appear to be related to the programs they offer? For instance, are companies in a particular sector or of a particular size more likely to offer health promotion and family-friendly programs?

   d. Discuss with your classmates the extent to which the availability of health promotion and family-friendly programs is important to them when they are looking for a job. Which programs appear to be the most desirable to job seekers?

2. Health promotion programs are more likely to succeed if they are based on a thorough needs assessment (i.e., assessments of the needs of the organization and its employees). Design a needs assessment instrument for measuring the need for health promotion programming in your current or a former workplace. If your work experience does not provide a suitable example for this Internet exercise, interview someone about his or her workplace and develop a needs assessment instrument for that work environment. The Internet will be very helpful in this task. Search the Web using keywords such as "wellness" and "health promotion." This search will help you identify many components of such a needs assessment instrument.

3. Search the Internet to learn details about government-sponsored mandatory parental or maternal leave benefits in different countries (e.g., Canada, the United States, the United Kingdom). Compare the policies in each country. Also, search the websites of various organizations that have operations in each of the countries you chose to determine whether they provide additional parental leave benefits to their employees. Afterwards, discuss the following issues in class:

   a. What impact would the policies in each of these countries and companies have on a new parent's experience of work–family conflict? Would these policies help a working parent balance work and family roles?

    b. What are the advantages and disadvantages of these programs for the person taking the leave?

    c. What are the advantages and disadvantages of these programs for the organizations that have employees taking leave?

    d. What are the advantages and disadvantages of these programs for families?

4. Each year, *Report on Business* magazine releases a ranking of the Top 50 Employers in Canada. Access a "50 Best Employers" list from a recent year, and search the websites of five of these top employers. Assess the extent to which they offer work/family-friendly and worksite health promotion programs. Describe some of the programs they offer.

Exercises

1. With a small group of classmates, discuss the following scenario: Imagine your current work hours are Monday to Friday, 9 to 5. At present, the start time of 9 a.m. is strictly enforced. However, the company is considering implementing a new flextime approach to work scheduling. Under this program, employees will be able to start their eight-hour workday any time between 7 a.m. and 11 a.m. However, each employee must work a continuous shift (i.e., there is no flexibility midday).

   Each person in the group should reflect on how such a change would benefit or disadvantage him or her, given current circumstances. Additionally, discuss how the move to flextime might affect the following individuals or groups:

   a. A working parent who has small school-aged children

   b. Someone who is not a morning person

   c. A person who commutes a long distance to work

   d. An individual who has substantial eldercare responsibilities

   e. Coworkers of individuals who opt to use the flextime arrangement

   f. The organization implementing the change

   What other types of flexible scheduling might help some of these people manage their multiple responsibilities to work and family?

2. In this chapter we have discussed the importance of evaluating health promotion programs. For any program, a number of outcome variables might offer insight into the success or failure of the program. One approach would apply the four types of strain introduced in Chapter 7 (organizational, psychological, physical, behavioural). With your classmates, brainstorm some of the pertinent outcome variables relating to each of these broad categories; then incorporate those variables into each of the following types of health promotion programs. The group should also consider how they might measure each of these variables.

   a. smoking cessation

   b. on-site physical fitness centre

   c. lunchtime Weight Watchers program

   d. off-site, call-in EFAP

   e. subsidized yoga classes

Case 1 MANDATORY AEROBICS

As a new manager, Jean McDonald is eager to improve morale and productivity in the work group. Believing that people will work better if they feel better, Jean has scheduled a group aerobics class in which all group members must participate. Several group members object to enforced exercise and have approached you (as Jean's immediate supervisor) with their concerns. What do you tell the employees? What do you tell Jean?

Case 2 EVALUATING THE BENEFITS OF WHPS

Quan Dar is the human resource manager of a mid-sized insurance firm. A faltering economy has resulted in the need to re-examine all current expenditures and to find areas in which to cut costs. Senior management is questioning the amount of money the firm spends on health promotion programs. Currently, the firm offers weight loss clinics, subsidized smoking cessation products, an on-site fitness program, regular stress prevention training programs, and an employee assistance program. Quan feels that these programs have value and add significant worth to the firm. However, senior management demands evidence. Quan has approached you for advice—how can he demonstrate the value of these programs to the firm?

Case 3 JOB SHARING IN A TELECOMMUNICATIONS FIRM

Sherry and Marco are highly skilled marketing managers at a large telecommunications firm. In their time with the company, Marco and Sherry have worked very long hours. Indeed, they have worked well as a team to design several large-scale, successful advertising campaigns for new products and services. However, both are now parents of young children, and they are feeling the pressure of competing work and family demands. Of late, both have expressed concerns about their ability to keep up with the fast pace of their home and work responsibilities and have mentioned the possibility of either cutting back their time at work or leaving their jobs altogether. As the director of human resources, you don't want to lose such valuable talent in the marketing department. You begin to think that Sherry and Marco might be ideal candidates for the company's new job-sharing program. How might you facilitate a job-sharing arrangement for Sherry and Marco? What types of working arrangement might you suggest to them?

NOTES

1. S.G. Aldana, "Financial Impact of Health Promotion Programs: A Comprehensive Review of the Literature," *American Journal of Health Promotion* 15 (2001): 281–88; J.E. Riedel, C. Baase, P. Hymel, M. Lynch, M. McCabe, W.R. Mercer, and K. Peterson, "The Effect of Disease Prevention and Health Promotion on Workplace Productivity: A Literature Review," *American Journal of Health Promotion* 1 (2001): 167–90.

2. J.T. Bond, E. Galinsky, S.S. Kim, and E. Brownfield, *2005 National Survey of Employers, Families and Work Institute* (2005), http://familiesandwork.org/site/research/reports/2005nse.pdf, April 27, 2010.

3. G.S. Lowe, *Healthy Workplaces and Productivity: A Discussion Paper* (Ottawa: Minister of Public Works and Government Services, 2003).

4. Towers Watson, "Pathway to Health and Productivity: 2011/2012 Staying@work™ Survey Report, North America" 2012, http://www.towerswatson.com/assets/pdf/6031/Towers-Watson-Staying-at-Work-Report.pdf, February 8, 2013.

5. L. Duxbury and C. Higgins, "Work–Life Conflict in Canada in the New Millennium: A Status Report (Final Report)," Public Health Agency of Canada (2003), http://www.phac-aspc.gc.ca/ publicat/work-travail/index-eng.php, February 16, 2007; C. Higgins, L. Duxbury, and S. Lyons, "Reducing Work–Life Conflict: What Works? What Doesn't?" (2008), http://www.phac-aspc.gc.ca/publicat/work-travail/index.html, April 21, 2010.

6. E.K. Kelloway and L. Francis, "Stress and Strain in Nova Scotia Organizations: Results of a Recent Province-Wide Study," paper presented at the Nova Scotia Psychologically Healthy Workplace Conference, Halifax, February 2006.

7. Duxbury and Higgins, "Work–Life Conflict in Canada."

8. C. Higgins, L. Duxbury, and K. Johnson, "Exploring the Link Between Work–Life Conflict and Demands on Canada's Health Care System," Public Health Agency of Canada (2004), http://www.phac-aspc.gc.ca/publicat/work-travail/report3/pdfs/fvwklfrprt_e.pdf, April 27, 2010.

9. G.A. Adams, L.A. King, and D.W. King, "Relationships of Job and Family Involvement, Family Social Support, and Work–Family Conflict with Job and Life Satisfaction," *Journal of Applied Psychology* 81 (1996): 411–20; Duxbury and Higgins, "Work–Life Conflict in Canada"; M.R. Frone, "Work–Family Balance," in J.C. Quick and L.E. Tetrick, eds., *Handbook of Occupational Health Psychology* (Washington: APA, 2003), 143–62.

10. K. Bachman, *Work–Life Balance: Are Employers Listening?* (Ottawa: Conference Board of Canada, 2000).

11. T.D. Golden, J. Veiga, and Z. Simsek, "Telecommuting's Differential Impact on Work–Family Conflict: Is There No Place Like Home?" *Journal of Applied Psychology* 91 (2006): 1340–50; NIOSH, "The Changing Organization of Work and the Safety and Health of Working People," DHHS (NIOSH) Publication no. 2002–16.

12. D. Comfort, K. Johnson, and D. Wallace, "Part-Time Work and Family-Friendly Practices in Canadian Workplaces," Statistics Canada, Human Resources Development Canada (2003), http://www.statcan.ca/english/freepub/71-584-MIE/71-584-MIE2003006.pdf, April 27, 2010.

13. Higgins et al., "Reducing Work–Life Conflict."

14. Frone, "Work–Family Balance."

15. C.A. Thompson, L.L. Beauvais, and K.S. Lyness, "When Work–Family Benefits Are Not Enough: The Influence of Work–Family Culture on Benefit Utilization, Organizational Attachment, and Work–Family Conflict," *Journal of Vocational Behavior* 54 (1999): 392–415.

16. L.T. Thomas and D.C. Ganster, "Impact of Family-Supportive Work Variables on Work–Family Conflict and Strain: A Control Perspective," *Journal of Applied Psychology* 80 (1995): 6–15.

17. S.J. Goff, M.K. Mount, and R.L. Jamieson, "Employer Supported Childcare, Work/Family Conflict, and Absenteeism: A Field Study," *Personnel Psychology* 43 (1990): 793–809; L.M. LaPierre and T.D. Allen, "Work-Supportive Family, Family-Supportive Supervision, Use of Organizational Benefits, and Problem-Focused Coping: Implications for Work–Family Conflict and Employee Well-Being," *Journal of Occupational Health Psychology* 11 (2006): 169–81.

18. T.A. Judge, J.W. Boudreau, and R.D. Retz, "Job and Life Attitudes of Male Executives," *Journal of Applied Psychology* 79 (1994): 767–82.

19. T.D. Golden, J. Veiga, and Z. Simsek, "Telecommuting's Differential Impact on Work–Family Conflict: Is There No Place Like Home?" *Journal of Applied Psychology* 91 (2006): 1340–50; LaPierre and Allen, "Work-Supportive Family."

20. Golden et al., "Telecommuting's Differential Impact."

21. T.D. Golden, "Avoiding Depletion in Virtual Work: Telework and the Intervening Impact of Work Exhaustion on Commitment and Turnover Intentions," *Journal of Vocational Behavior* 69 (2006): 176–87.

22. B.B. Baltes, T.E. Briggs, J.W. Huff, J.A. Wright, and G.A. Neiman, "Flexible and Compressed Workweek Schedules: A Meta-Analysis of Their Effects on Work-Related Criteria," *Journal of Applied Psychology* 84 (1999): 496–513; D. Comfort, K. Johnson, and D. Wallace, "Part-Time Work and Family-Friendly Practices in Canadian Workplaces," Statistics Canada, Human Resources Development Canada (2003), http://www.statcan.ca/english/freepub/71-584-MIE/71-584-MIE2003006.pdf, February 18, 2007.

23. Baltes et al., "Flexible and Compressed Workweek Schedules"; D.A. Ralston, "The Benefits of Flextime: Real or Imagined?" *Journal of Organizational Behavior* 10 (1989): 369–73.

24. Frone, "Work–Family Balance."

25. NIOSH, "The Changing Organization of Work and the Safety and Health of Working People" (2002), DHHS (NIOSH) Publication no. 2002–16.

26. E.E. Kossek, "Workplace Policies and Practices to Support Work and Family: Gaps in Implementation and Linkages to Individuals and Organizational Effectiveness," paper presented at Workforce/Workplace Mismatch: Work, Family, Health and Well-Being, Washington, June 2003.

27. K.L. Johnson, D.S. Lero, and J.A. Rooney, *Work–Life Compendium 2001: 150 Canadian Statistics on Work, Family, and Well-Being* (Guelph: Centre for Families, Work, and Well-Being, 2001).

28. M. Blair-Loy and A.S. Wharton, "Employees' Use of Work–Family Policies and the Workplace Social Context," *Social Forces* 80 (2002): 813–45.

29. L.S. Chapman and S. Sullivan, "Health and Productivity Management: An Emerging Paradigm for the Workplace," *The Art of Health Promotion* 7 (July–August 2003): 1–9.

30. Employee Assistance Professional Association (EAPA), *Standards of Practice and Professional Guidelines for Employee Assistance Programs* (London: 1994).

31. P.R. Popple, "Social Work in Business and Industry," *Social Services Review* 6 (1981): 257–69.

32. M.T. Matteson and J.M. Ivancevich, "Health Promotion at Work," in C.L. Cooper and I.T. Robertson, eds., *International Review of Industrial and Organizational Psychology, 1988* (Chichester: Wiley, 1988), 279–306.

33. C.L. Cooper, P. Dewe, and M. O'Driscoll, "Employee Assistance Programs," in J.C. Quick and L.E. Tetrick, eds., *Handbook of Occupational Health Psychology,* (Washington: APA, 2003), 289–304.

34. Ibid.; EAPA, *Standards of Practice.*

35. L.R. Murphy, J.J. Hurrell, Jr., S.L. Sauter, and G.P. Keita, "Introduction," in Murphy, Hurrell, Sauter, and Keita, eds., *Job Stress Interventions* (Washington: APA, 1995), xi–xiii; K.M.

Richardson and H.R. Rothstien, "Effects of Occupational Stress Management Training Intervention Programs: A Meta-Analysis," *Journal of Occupational Health Psychology* 13 (2008): 69–93.

36. Ibid.

37. R.E. Quillian-Wolever and M.E. Wolever, "Stress Management at Work," in J.C. Quick and L.E. Tetrick, eds., *Handbook of Occupational Health Psychology* (Washington: APA, 2003), 355–75.

38. L.R. Murphy, "Stress Management in Work Settings: A Critical Review of the Health Effects," *American Journal of Health Promotion* 11 (1996): 112–35.

39. Richardson and Rothstien, "Effects of Occupational Stress Management Training Intervention Programs."

40. D.T. Kenny and C. Cooper, "Introduction: Occupational Stress and Its Management," *International Journal of Stress Management* 10 (2003): 275–79.

41. Richardson and Rothstien, "Effects of Occupational Stress Management Training Intervention Programs."

42. J.A. Thomason and S.B. Pond, "Effects of Instruction on Stress Management Skills and Self-Management Skills Among Blue-Collar Employees," in Murphy, Hurrell, Sauter, and Keita, eds., *Job Stress Interventions* (Washington: APA, 1995), 7–20.

43. J.B. Keyes, "Stress Inoculation Training for Staff Working with Persons with Mental Retardation: A Model Program," in Murphy, Hurrell, Sauter, and Keita, eds., *Job Stress Interventions* (Washington: APA, 1995), 46–56.

44. I.L. Petterson and B.B. Arnetz, "Psychosocial Stressors and Well-Being in Health Care Workers: The Impact of an Intervention Program," *Social Science and Medicine* 47 (1998): 1763–72.

45. Towers Watson, "Pathway to Health and Productivity: 2011/2012 Staying@work™ Survey Report, North America" 2012, http://www.towerswatson.com/assets/pdf/6031/Towers-Watson-Staying-at-Work-Report.pdf, February 8, 2013.

46. J.E. Henningfield, L.M. Ramstrom, C. Husten, G. Giovino, J. Barling, C. Weber, E.K. Kelloway, V.J. Strecher, and M.J. Jarvis, "Smoking and the Workplace: Realities and Solutions," *Journal of Smoking-Related Diseases* 5 (1994): 261–70.

47. H. Moshammer and M. Neuberger, "Long-Term Success of Short Smoking Cessation Seminars Supported by Occupational Health Care," *Addictive Behaviors* 32 (2007): 1486–93; I. Nerín, A. Crucelaegui, A. Más, J.A. Villalba, D. Guillén, and A. Gracia, "Results of a Comprehensive Workplace Program for the Prevention and Treatment of Smoking Addiction," *Archivos de Bronconeumologia* 41 (2005): 197–201.

48. J. Goldgruber and D. Ahrens, "Effectiveness of Workplace Health Promotion and Primary Prevention Interventions: A Review," *Journal of Public Health* 18 (2010): 75–88.

49. S.B. Bacharach, P.A. Bamberger, and M. Biron, "Alcohol Consumption and Workplace Absenteeism: The Moderating Effect of Social Support," *Journal of Applied Psychology* 95 (2010): 334–48; S.B. Bacharach, P.A. Bamberger, and V.M. McKinney, "Harassing Under the Influence: The Prevalence of Male Heavy Drinking, the Embeddedness of Permissive Workplace Drinking Norms, and the Gender Harassment of Female Coworkers," *Journal of Occupational Health Psychology* 12 (2007): 232–50.

50. C.S. Carpenter, "Workplace Drug Testing and Worker Drug Use," *Health Services Research* 42 (2007): 795–810; M.T. French, M.C. Roebuck, and P.K. Alexandre, "To Test or Not to Test: Do Workplace Drug Testing Programs Discourage Employee Drug Use?" *Social Science Research* 33 (2004): 45–63.

51. D.R. Comer, "A Case Against Workplace Drug Testing," *Organization Science* 5 (1994): 259–67; H.M. Trice and P.D. Steele, "Impairment Testing: Issues and Convergence with Employee Assistance Programs," *Journal of Drug Issues* 25 (1995): 471–503.

52. Canadian Human Rights Commission, "Canadian Human Rights Commission's Policy on Alcohol and Drug Testing" (2009), http://www.chrc-ccdp.ca/pdf/padt_pdda_eng.pdf, April 22, 2010.

53. S.A.A. Beresford, B. Thompson, Z. Feng, C. Christianson, D. McLerran, and D.L. Patrick, "Seattle 5 a Day Worksite Program to Increase Fruit and Vegetable Consumption," *Preventive Medicine* 32 (2001): 230–38; Goldgruber and Ahrens, "Effectiveness of Workplace Health Promotion"; M. Kramish Campbell, I. Tessaro, B. DeVellis, S. Benedict, K. Kelsey, L. Belton, and A. Sanhueza, "Effects of a Tailored Health Promotion Program for Female Blue-Collar Workers: Health Works for Women," *Preventive Medicine* 34 (2002): 313–23.

54. D.L. Gebhardt and C.E. Crump, "Employee Fitness and Wellness Programs in the Workplace," *American Psychologist* 45 (1990): 262–72.

55. S.G. Aldana, R.M. Merrill, K. Price, A. Hardy, and R. Hager, "Financial Impact of a Comprehensive Multisite Workplace Health Promotion Program," *Preventive Medicine* 40 (2005): 131–37; Gebhardt and Crump, "Employee Fitness and Wellness Programs."

56. R.K. Dishman, B. Oldenburg, H. O'Neal, and R.J. Shephard, "Worksite Physical Activity Interventions," *American Journal of Preventive Medicine* 15 (1994): 344–61; A.L. Marshall, "Challenges and Opportunities for Promoting Physical Activity in the Workplace," *Journal of Science and Medicine in Sport* 7 (2004): 60–66.

57. Dishman et al., "Worksite Physical Activity Interventions"; K.I. Proper, V.H. Hildebrandt, A.J. Van der Beek, J.W.R. Twisk, and W. Van Mechelen, "Effect of Individual Counseling on Physical Activity Fitness and Health: A Randomized Controlled Trial in a Workplace Setting," *American Journal of Preventive Medicine* 24 (2003): 218–26.

58. Goldgruber and Ahrens, "Effectiveness of Workplace Health Promotion."

59. J.S. Mio and C.K. Goishi, "The Employee Assistance Program: Raising Productivity by Lifting Constraints," in P. Whitney and R.B. Ochsman, eds., *Psychology and Productivity* (New York: Plenum, 1988), 105–25.

60. Cooper et al., "Employee Assistance Programs."

61. Murphy et al., "Introduction."

62. Aldana et al., "Financial Impact of Health Promotion Programs."

63. S.G. Aldana, R.M. Merrill, K. Price, A. Hardy, and R. Hager, "Financial Impact of a Comprehensive Multisite Workplace Health Promotion Program," *Preventive Medicine* 40 (2005): 131–37.

64. K. DeRango and L. Franzini, "Economic Evaluation of Workplace Health Interventions: Theory and Literature Review," in J.C. Quick and L.E. Tetrick, eds., *Handbook of Occupational Health Psychology* (Washington: APA, 2003), 417–30.

65. Ibid.

66. K.R. Pelletier, "A Review and Analysis of the Clinical and Cost-Effectiveness Studies of Comprehensive Health Promotion and Disease Management Programs at the Worksite: Update VI 2000–2004," *Journal of Occupational and Environmental Medicine* 47 (2005): 1051–58.

67. Idem, "A Review and Analysis of the Clinical and Cost-Effectiveness Studies of Comprehensive Health Promotion and Disease Management Programs at the Worksite: 1998–2000 Update," *American Journal of Health Promotion* 16 (2001): 107–16.

68. Lowe, *Healthy Workplaces and Productivity.*

69. Ibid.

70. J.B. Bennett, R.F. Cook, and K. Pelletier, "Toward an Integrated Framework for Comprehensive Organizational Wellness: Concepts, Practices and Research in Workplace Health Promotion," in J.C. Quick and L.E. Tetrick, eds., *Handbook of Occupational Health Psychology* (Washington: APA, 2003), 69–95.

71. Lowe, *Healthy Workplaces and Productivity.*

INDEX

A

ABC model of behaviour, 256
ability, in safety performance, 254*f*
abrasives, 90
absence, disability-related, 346
absenteeism, 168, 240
accident, 83
accident investigation. *See* incident investigation
accident proneness, 8
accident reports, 311–312
accident/incident witness statement, 321*f*–322*f*
accountability, 252, 269
acids, 151, 156
act, 26
Act to Amend the Ontario Occupational Health and Safety Act, 34
active transactional leadership, 265
activity sampling, 86
acute stressors, 170, 294
acute toxicity, 152
addiction, 54
administrative control. *See also* engineering control; hazard control
    awards, 104
    cold control, 131
    defined, 102
    exposure controls, 161–162
    heat control, 129
    housekeeping, 104–105
    incentives, 104
    medical surveillance, 162
    personal protective equipment, 161
    preventive maintenance, 105–108
    safety awareness, 103
    special events, 103
    struck-by-object injuries, 106
    visible reminders, 103
Advanced Solutions, 359
aerosols, 148
agents, 160
aggression, 196. *See also* workplace aggression
AIDS (acquired immunodeficiency syndrome), 156
alcohol and drug testing programs, 369
alcoholism, 364
alcohols, 157*t*
aldehydes, 157*t*
aliphatic hydrocarbons, 157*t*
alkalines, 151, 156
alveoli, 150
ambient, 118

American Conference of Governmental Industrial Hygienists (ACGIH), 26, 40
American National Standards Institute (ANSI), 26, 267
American Psychological Association (APA), 359
ammonia, 153, 154
amotivation, 260
anesthetics, 154
antecedents, 256
anthrax, 282
apprenticeship, 232
ArcelorMittal Dofasco Inc., 371
Archives of Internal Medicine, 356
aromatic hydrocarbons, 157*t*
artistic occupations, 94
asbestos, 5, 15, 146, 152, 155
asbestosis, 15
asphyxiants, 154
assault cycle, 202–203
assessments (Worker's Compensation), 65–67
assumption of risk, 7
asthma, 148
attention, 237
attenuation, 122
audiometer, 122
audio-visual methods, 232
auditory system, 120*f*
audits, 86, 110
authority, and workplace aggression, 202
auto-ignition temperature, 155
automobile instrument panels, 97–98
autonomous motivation, 260
awards, 104
awkward working positions, 95

B

back injuries, 91
bacterial biological agents, 159*t*
barriers, 96, 101
bases, 156
Bata Industries, 46
behaviour modelling, 232
behaviour modification, 256
behaviour sampling, 86
behavioural interventions, 253, 256
behavioural involvement, 185
behavioural programming, 256
behavioural strain, 177
behaviour-based safety program. *See also* safety behaviours
behaviour-based safety programs, 255, 257
behaviourism, 256
behaviourist theory, 236

benzene, 152, 155
Berdahl, Jennifer, 211
Bethlehem Steel Company, 100
Bill C-45, 47
billboards, 103
biohazard, 144, 156
biological agents, 144, 156. *See also* chemical agents
    agent groups, 159*t*
    bacterial, 159*t*
    chlamydiae, 159*t*
    classification of, 158
    control of exposures, 157–162
    fungal, 159*t*
    rickettsia, 159*t*
    viruses, 159*t*
Biosafety Level 1 (BSL 1), 158
Biosafety Level 2 (BSL 2), 158
Biosafety Level 3 (BSL 3), 158
Biosafety Level 4 (BSL 4), 158
black legged ticks, 144
blisters, 151
body as a machine system, 127*f*
body thermal balance, 127–128
boiling point, 153
Bornstein, Stephen, 148
Borrelia burgdorferi, 144
bow-tie analysis, 324
British Columbia (Public Service Employees Relations Commission) v. BCGSEU, 335
British Columbia Workers' Compensation Act, 57
British Petroleum, 282
British Standards Institute, 267
brown lung, 7
buffers, 174
bulletin boards, 103
bullying, 197
burns, 151
burnt out, 175
business continuity planning, 296
byssinosis (brown lung), 7

C

CAD-7, 68
Canada Awards for Excellence, 359
Canada Labour Code, 211
Canada Labour (Safety) Code, 7, 105
Canada Labour (Standards) Code, 7
Canada's Food Guide, 370
Canadian Centre for Emergency Preparedness, 287
Canadian Centre for Occupational Health and Safety (CCOHS), 12, 88, 118, 122, 135, 144, 188, 262